THINKING THINGS THROUGH

MAYLON H. HEPP

PROFESSOR OF PHILOSOPHY

DENISON UNIVERSITY

Thinking Things Through

AN INTRODUCTION TO LOGIC

42914

NEW YORK

CHARLES SCRIBNER'S SONS

TO C. J. DUCASSE

PREFACE

With the exception of two or three footnotes later on, the four paragraphs immediately following this one are the only part of the book that is not addressed directly to the beginning student of logic. Such readers should not feel detained by the present account, but should read the acknowledgements which follow and then move on to the remarks "To the Student" and Chapter 1, "What Logic Is All About." In taking up a new textbook, teachers are first of all interested in its general approach and in the ways in which it differs from other current texts in the field. The next four paragraphs seek to answer these questions.

The present writer conceives of elementary general logic as the study of the principles and problems of thinking things through. The three typical questions of "What does it mean?", "What follows from this?", and "What are the facts?" are viewed as generating the three logical disciplines of semantics, syntactics, and empirics, dealt with in the three successive Parts of this book. Part I deals with such traditional problems as language functions, definition, and ambiguity, but also with the less traditional but increasingly pertinent topic of elementary propaganda analysis.

In Part II, formal logic is treated in a way which seeks to do justice both to traditional and to contemporary modes of analysis. A statemental approach is taken, and an argument is conceived as an expression, in statements, of a line of reasoning. Arguments are analyzed both in terms of traditional maxims for the various specific forms, and also by means of more general principles which illustrate the power of contemporary modes of analysis. The latter analysis is conducted in terms of an elementary validity test (the contraform), which provides a unified approach to both truth-functional (molecular) and class arguments (including the traditional syllogism). This test draws on certain features of truth-table analysis (which, as it stands, is suitable only for truth-functional arguments) and the Ladd-Franklin antilogism analysis (which, as it stands, applies only to categorical syllogisms). Truth-functional arguments are considered first, and a reinterpreted form of truth matrix called a "consistency table" is introduced and correlated with a Boolean-type notation (zeroforms) which is carried through both truth-functional and class-relation analyses. More stress than usual is placed throughout on the fundamental logical relation of contradiction. The student is introduced to the more elementary forms of contemporary logical symbolism, and an effort is made to help him see the advantages which such a notation has in achieving a general mode of analysis which can be used on arguments of many different forms. The categorical syllogism is dealt with in terms of both the traditional maxims and the more general contraform principles. Special attention is given to the problems raised by the particularized syllogism, and this form is treated both by specific maxims and by the more general contraform test.

Part III deals with problems traditionally associated with "inductive logic" and "scientific method." Empirics is viewed as the study of the principles and problems of determining both singular and general facts. The central importance of the concept of probability is stressed throughout Part III, without introducing the complications of the formal calculus of probability. Four basic forms of argument by which we seek to determine what is probably the case are distinguished: analogy, diagnosis, induction, and deductions of probability. The treatment of diagnosis and induction in Chapters 27 and 29 reflects the author's conviction that the beginning student learns much more about the principles of empirical inquiry from an extended and detailed analysis of examples of such inquiry occurring at the level of enlightened common sense, than from either a discussion of general principles considered by themselves or an analysis of examples from sciences with which he is not thoroughly familiar. In the treatment of causal generalizations, much less emphasis than usual is placed on Mill's Methods and the customary criticisms of them.

The organization of the text makes possible a number of types of emphasis or balance among the three areas of logic, and between the traditional and contemporary approaches to formal logic. To permit greater freedom in these respects, the book purposely contains somewhat

more material than will normally be covered in a typical three-hour
semester course.

It is not too much to hope that a teacher, as well as his students, will
learn something from the textbooks used in his course. What he learns
may range all the way from certain vivid examples which become so
familiar that he forgets that he did not make them up in the first place, to
effective ways of presenting a difficult topic or even to a general conception of the field. In my own case, I am aware of my indebtedness at many
points to the two textbooks that I have principally used over the past ten
years or so: Frye and Levi's *Rational Belief* (New York, Harcourt, Brace
and Company, 1941) and, more recently, Max Black's *Critical Thinking*
(New York, Prentice-Hall, Inc., 1946, 1952). The discerning reader will,
I suspect, find that I have been influenced by these texts, particularly the
latter, in ways more subtle and pervasive than those I have been able to
acknowledge specifically.

I am also indebted to friends and former and present colleagues for encouragement and constructive criticisms. I should like especially to thank
the following, without implicating them in any way in the inadequacies
which may still remain: C. J. Ducasse of Brown, Douglas V. Steere of
Haverford, and my Denison colleagues, Harold H. Titus, Francis C. Bay-
ley, and Cleveland J. Bradner, Jr. The latter two have generously given
me the benefit of their experience in using preliminary editions of this text
in the classroom for several semesters. The reactions and suggestions of
my students have also helped me greatly in preparing the present edition.
To the administration and trustees of Denison University go my thanks
for the sabbatical leave during which I worked out the first draft of Part
III. Thanks too to the members of the New Mexico Philosophical Society,
who let me try out on them a version of the chapter on the particularized
syllogism during their annual meeting in Socorro. In many ways this
book has been a family project. Special thanks are due my wife, Anne
Woodbury Hepp, for her encouragement and constructive criticisms, and
for her help with typing, indexing, and proofreading. Thanks also to our
three children, Barbara, Susanna, and David, whose contributions ranged
from keeping out of the way at crucial times, to more specialized tasks.
One of the pleasantest aspects of writing this book has been the cor-

respondence with my editor and publisher, Mr. Charles Scribner, Jr. His editorial wisdom and detailed knowledge of contemporary logic have helped make this a much better book than it would otherwise have been.

Permission to quote from various sources is gratefully acknowledged; sources of quotations are fully indicated at the appropriate points in the text.

M. H. H.

Cherry Ridge,
Granville, Ohio

CONTENTS

CONTENTS

CONTENTS   *xiii*

PART III

EMPIRICS: THE LOGIC OF FACTUAL INQUIRY

TO THE STUDENT

As a student, particularly one beginning a new subject, the first thing you want a textbook to do for you is to give you some idea of what the subject is all about. Chapter 1 is written with your question in mind. As you start using this book, watch for the various ways in which it is designed to make your task easier and more profitable, and get in the habit of making the most of them. Every chapter begins with a short "Preview" which gives you a bird's-eye view of what the chapter will contain. Section headings help you see the general structure of the chapter. When a new term is introduced, or a familiar term is used in what may to you be a new sense, you will find the word printed in SMALL CAPITALS at the point at which its use is first explained. If in reading along you find that you have forgotten the meaning of a term, the index at the end of the book will help you locate the defining entry.

At the end of a chapter (and occasionally in the middle too), you will find a list of statements headed "Some Reminders." This is the best name I could think of for them, since it states their purpose and scope clearly. They *remind* you of *some* important points that have come out in the preceding discussion. When the material of the chapter has been fairly simple, these reminders are purposely quite sketchy; in more difficult cases, they are sometimes quite detailed and explicit. They are for use *after* you have read the chapter; they will help you recall key points and may sometimes indicate things you might have failed to notice sufficiently the first time through. If you find you don't understand a given Reminder, this will indicate that some section of the chapter will need further study. You will find, I think, that most of the Reminders have been worded in such a way that they are practically useless as a substitute for studying the chapter itself.

Don't skim over the concrete examples and illustrations used in the course of the discussion. They are naturally easier reading than the more general statements of logical principles, but they have an important role to fill; they help you understand these general principles better, by show-ing how the principles apply in everyday cases and how they work out in practice. The Applications at the end of a chapter or group of sections will give you a chance to apply the logical principles you have learned to concrete materials. Occasionally these Applications have a somewhat different role; they raise related issues for you to think through.

You are probably as revolted as I am by titles such as "Fun With Inte-gral Calculators" or "Logic for Laughs." Thinking things through is mostly hard work; that's why we do so little of it. But don't overlook the possibility of really getting excited about logic and of discovering that rigorous thinking can be a stimulating and satisfying form of human activity. You need only watch a philosopher or a theoretical scientist at work to see that there must be something in thinking for its own sake, quite apart from its obvious importance in solving our practical problems and in helping us act somewhat less foolishly.

THINKING THINGS THROUGH

CHAPTER 1

WHAT LOGIC IS ALL ABOUT

PREVIEW

In this introductory chapter we shall remind ourselves of three different types of question that face us when we try to think things through. These questions give rise to the three fields of logic: semantics, syntactics, and empirics. Logic is the attempt to think systematically about the principles and problems involved in handling these questions successfully.

1.1. HAVE YOU EVER STOPPED TO THINK?

Did you ever enroll in a course late, say, after the first week or so of the term? You missed those first sessions in which one hopes to get some sense of what the course will deal with. You lost out on those elementary but altogether crucial explanations of certain basic ideas in the field. Your classmates who had been there from the first had already caught on to some of the strange terminology characteristic of this new subject matter. But as you came into class, a week or so late, the instructor seemed to be talking about like this:

> Now, in the fourth place, morthroplats must be carefully distinguished from brictoplats. The former all possess grandopores and hence are tryphoglyptera. Brictoplats, however, have no grandopores. Thus they cannot possibly be tryphoglyptera, for as we learned at our last meeting, all tryphoglyptera have grandopores. Now are there any questions?

You have plenty of questions, so many in fact that it is a little hard to tell where to begin. Certainly the first thing you would like to know is: What does all this *mean?* The instructor's sentences seem to be put together correctly from the grammatical point of view, but their significance quite escapes you. Presumably, they make sense, but not to you. What

3

does "brictoplat" mean, anyway? And what does it mean to say that they have no grandopores? What does "grandopore" mean? And "tryphoglyptera"? Your first and most urgent questions, then, are about MEANINGS.

But there are two other quite different types of question that you might also ask. In fact, if you are really going to think things through, you must ask them. How about the instructor's line of REASONING here? From certain assertions he seems to be inferring certain others. Which assertions are being used as evidence for further assertions? What does he conclude? Does this conclusion really follow, so that if one accepts his data, one must logically accept what he derives from them? A second group of questions, then, has to do with the rigor and correctness of the reasoning involved.

There remains a third type of question that is equally important. How about his data? How about the evidence itself upon which his conclusions were based? Does he have his FACTS straight? Even granting that *if* we accept his premises, we must logically accept his conclusion too, what grounds are there for the premises themselves? Is it really true, for example, that no brictoplats have grandopores? What are the facts?

Whether you have ever actually entered a course late or not, the general situation we have been discussing is by no means new to you. We are continually finding ourselves in situations in which the only appropriate response is to "stop and think." These three types of question persistently confront us as we try to think things through. In our day-to-day thinking, we regularly have to face questions of meaning, questions of logical "following" or validity, and questions of fact. Three KEY QUESTIONS, then, whenever we try to think things through, are these:

---

1. **WHAT?**
   (Questions about meaning)
2. **SO WHAT?**
   (Questions about what follows logically
   from given information)
3. **WHAT'S WHAT?**
   (Questions about the facts)

But, you may say, what of it? Don't I already know how to think? Of course you do. But although every one of us is continually having to deal with questions of these three kinds, few of us have ever given ourselves the benefit of a systematic attack upon them. As "practical" people, we treat each case as it comes along, without paying very much attention to the general principles which the separate cases exhibit. By this casual method, most of us eventually succeed in developing patterns of thinking that get us by. But we might reasonably wish for more than this.

1.2. ROOM FOR IMPROVEMENT

Most of us will admit that there is room for improvement in our thinking. For example, when our emotions are deeply stirred or our prejudices are aroused, we all find it difficult to think clearly and to the point. We might reasonably wish for a better understanding of the principles that determine "what follows from what." Such understanding should make it easier for us to think things through even when we are stirred up.

Again, we might reasonably wish for a keener awareness of the persuasive techniques or propaganda devices to which we are continually exposed. Such awareness might make us less gullible than we sometimes are. It should make it easier for us to respond to appeals in terms of their worth, rather than in terms of their emotional impact.

Or again, we might reasonably wish for a better grasp of the logical principles involved in factual inquiry, not merely in the sciences, but perhaps more particularly at the level of everyday experience. Such a grasp might help us to make our attack on our own everyday problems more systematic and skillful, and to see the sense in which even our personal problems may be approached in a "scientific" spirit.

These are some of the areas in which most of us feel that our thinking could stand improvement. Logic is concerned to help us with these problems through a systematic study of the principles of thinking things through.

1.3. TWO WAYS TO BUILD A BRIDGE

If you plan to build many bridges in your lifetime, you might of course just start out and build them, hoping either to learn fast enough or to run fast enough to escape being crushed by one of your mistakes. As an intelligent person, however, you would probably choose a different approach.

You would, before you built bridges, study engineering and learn the basic principles that are involved in making bridges that will stand up. Probably no amount of "practical experience" in just going ahead and building bridges could ever compensate for the lack of a knowledge of the basic principles of engineering relevant to bridge-building.

This is not to overlook the fact that, in the first instance, man's knowledge of principle had to be gained this hard way. He had to keep trying, and then had to reflect on his failures and his successes. What was it about this bridge that made it fall down, while this other stood up? But in bridge-building, at least, it is no longer necessary to proceed in this dangerous and laborious fashion. The basic principles of engineering applicable to bridge-building are today well-known and well established. It is sensible to learn them before trying to build many bridges.

But just knowing the principles will not be enough, will it? To be effective, to get any bridges built, these principles must be applied. Not only will your understanding of the principles be deepened as you get experience in applying them to actual bridges. Your skill in applying them will also increase with practice.

So it is with thinking. The basic principles involved in thinking things through are well established. There is no need of working out these principles for ourselves the hard way. This part of the job has already been done for us. But here again, as in bridge-building, it is one thing to know the principles, and another to be able to apply them. Throughout our present study, we shall therefore be seeking two things: (1) an understanding of logical principles, and (2) practical skill in using these principles for the treatment of concrete situations.

1.4. THE THREE AREAS OF LOGIC

When we stop dealing with problems of thinking simply as isolated, individual cases, and turn to an investigation of the general principles of sound thinking, we find that we are faced with three intimately related areas of inquiry. These three areas are, in fact, blocked out by the three types of question we asked ourselves about the lecture on brictoplats. Together, these three areas constitute the field of logic. LOGIC is the study of the principles and problems of thinking things through.

SEMANTICS, THE LOGIC OF MEANING

The study of the principles and problems of meaning has in our day come to be called SEMANTICS. To this area we shall first turn our attention. We shall want to remind ourselves of the different functions which signs, particularly words, perform in thinking and communication. We shall want to examine some typical failures and distortions of the sign-process, and see if we can discover ways of detecting and curing them. We shall try to become more aware of how continuously we are responding to signs, especially linguistic signs presented to us by other human beings. We shall need to realize that it is naive to suppose that language is used solely to inform. We must understand better the way language can be used persuasively by others to mold our feelings and attitudes and to stimulate us to action. We shall discover how even an elementary grasp of the principles of propaganda analysis will help us to weigh more intelligently the many appeals to which we are subjected, and enable us to respond to them less emotively and more reasonably.

SYNTACTICS, THE LOGIC OF VALID REASONING

From the study of semantics we shall turn to the area of the second type of question: "So what?" Not that we shall then be "through" with semantical problems, and thus free to turn to problems of another type. Rather, we shall find that semantical problems, problems of meaning, will continue to crop up in these other areas, and will have to be dealt with as they emerge. But it is not enough merely to know what we mean. We also want to know what inferences we are warranted in drawing from certain given information. We want to know what follows logically from the data in our possession. If all tryphoglyptera have grandopores, but no brictoplats do, what further is implied about brictoplats?

The study of the principles and problems which confront us as we attempt to draw out the implications of given statements is called SYNTACTICS. This use of the term for an area of logic is based on an analogy with grammar. Just as grammatical syntax is concerned with the rules of correct grammatical form, so logical syntax is concerned with the rules of correct logical form. Because the investigation of logical forms is central to syntactics, this area of logic is traditionally called FORMAL LOGIC. As we shall see more clearly later, questions of what follows logically from given information turn out to be questions which are decidable in terms of the form of the statements involved and the form of the argument into which they enter. In a relatively simple case like the above question about brictoplats, you can probably already sense the logical form clearly enough to recognize that the question can be given a precise and definite answer on the basis of the supplied information. You don't even need to know what brictoplats, tryphoglyptera, and grandopores are. The fact that you don't, in this sense, even need to know what you're talking about in order to see what is implied, is itself of considerable interest. We shall examine this strange state of affairs more fully in Chapter 7. For the present, we may merely note that these questions of logical form are so central that the application of the term *logic* has sometimes been confined to this area alone.

The problem of syntactics might be thought of as that of determining the principles of *straight* thinking. Given certain data or premises, what do they strictly imply? But thinking "straight" in this sense is only one element in thinking soundly. If you were to argue that all dogs purr, and were to defend this conclusion on the grounds that all dogs are birds, and that all birds purr, you would be thinking "straight" enough. The grounds upon which you base your conclusion really do guarantee it. You would have argued from these grounds straight to their logically warranted conclusion. The unsatisfactory nature of the argument consists not in a lack of straightness or formal correctness in your thinking, but rather in the factual unsoundness of the grounds on which you based your conclusion. We usually want not merely straightness but truth. Walking straight north for one mile will always bring you home *if* you start in the right place. Similarly, thinking straight from certain premises will always bring you to a true conclusion *if* you start with true premises.

EMPIRICS, THE LOGIC OF FACTUAL INQUIRY

How do we get at the truth? How do we discover the facts? How do we find out "what's what"? The usual answer, "by turning to experience," indicates the direction of our remaining investigation, and the general subject matter of the third area of logic. What are the logical principles involved in getting at the facts? Or, a little more elegantly, what are the principles of empirical inquiry? (EMPIRICAL is an adjective derived from the Greek word for "experience.") We may call this third area EMPIRICS, or the logic of factual inquiry.

Since the most developed patterns of factual inquiry are to be found in our sciences, this third logical discipline is often spoken of as the study of "scientific method." This is a convenient label, but we need to remind ourselves that the search for what's what is by no means confined to those areas we call "sciences." It also occurs insistently at the common-sense level of everyday experience.

• SOME REMINDERS

1. Three types of question continually confront us in our thinking: "What?" (the question of meaning), "So what?" (the question of what logically follows from given data), and "What's what?" (the question of what the facts are).

2. The systematic exploration of the principles involved in answering these three types of question is *logic,* which comprises the three logical disciplines of semantics, syntactics, and empirics.

3. Our main aim in studying logic is to improve our ability to think things through. This requires (a) a knowledge of logical principles, (b) practice in applying these principles to concrete cases, with the purpose of making this application of sound principles more and more habitual.

APPLICATIONS

1. Study the "lecture" on brictoplats, and the three types of question raised about it. Can these questions be answered in *any* order, or does the answer to one or more of them have to be settled before it is possible to answer the others? Be specific, and give your reasons.

2. The question was asked: "If all tryphoglyptera have grandopores, but no brictoplats do, what further is implied about brictoplats?" Can you answer this question? Can you *prove* that this answer necessarily follows if you accept the given information? What would "proof" mean in this connection?

3. The "lecture" was wholly fictitious, but you probably felt that its subject matter was *like* the subject matter in some particular field. Which one? Now try to analyze clearly just what it was that made you feel this way. What clues were you using? What were the grounds for your inference or your hunch?

4. Analyze the analogy between bridge-building and thinking. What have these two activities in common? How and where do they differ? At what points does the analogy break down?

5. Illustrate a semantical problem, a syntactical problem, and an empirical problem by drawing on your personal experiences of the past week.

PART I

SEMANTICS

THE LOGIC

OF MEANING

CHAPTER 2

SIGNS, MEANINGS, AND LANGUAGE

PREVIEW

In this area of our work, we shall be concerned with problems of meaning. *Signs* are the vehicles by which meanings are conveyed. Problems of meaning are thus intimately related to problems of using and interpreting signs. We shall first have a look at the nature of signs in general, and shall then focus our attention on the intricate system of artificial signs that we call *language* and upon the basic ways in which language functions.

2.1. SOME SUBSTITUTES FOR SHOVING

If you are faced with the problem of arranging the furniture in your room, one way to tackle it is to shove the furniture around, this way and that, until you finally get each piece in a place where it will fit and where it will prove more or less convenient and esthetically satisfying. For a small project like arranging the furniture in a dormitory room, this direct muscular activity of pushing and shoving may be the simplest approach. If you try a desk between two cots, and find that there isn't space enough for it, you can push it across to the opposite wall, or perhaps swing the cots around to make room for it.

But there are other ways of attacking such a problem, ways which are often much more efficient and effective than dealing directly with the objects themselves. You might, for example, draw a simple floor plan of the room, roughly to scale, and then cut out pieces of paper to represent the different items of furniture to be rearranged. By shifting these pieces of paper rather than the furniture itself, you might be able to explore many more possibilities in much less time with considerably less effort. Or you might at least take a yardstick and measure the desk, before shoving it

13

across the room, in order to make sure it would fit in the space available. Or you might just sit down and contemplate the room and the furniture, imagining different arrangements, and then finally choose one to try out.

The thing to note about these other ways of tackling the job, whatever their merits in the simple case we are considering, is that they proceed indirectly. Instead of moving the furniture, we move bits of paper, or we compare two measurements on a yardstick, or we juggle "thoughts" or "images." All these substitute for the actual furniture; they *stand for* it, or represent it. They are *signs* of it.

2.2. WHAT IS A SIGN?

A SIGN is anything which represents something else. The distinctive thing about a sign is that we respond not merely *to* it, but *through* it to something else. The something else is, as we commonly say, what the sign "means." [1] As human beings, concerned with thinking things through, our attention naturally centers upon verbal or linguistic signs (words and sentences). Yet we need to remind ourselves of the wide variety of nonverbal objects that may function as signs. A dark cloud, a red traffic light, smoke, a shrug of the shoulders, a high fever, the sound of a door opening —the list of possible signs seems endless, for virtually anything may function as a sign in appropriate circumstances. In the next section we shall want to examine these circumstances more fully. For the moment, let us emphasize the fact that an object is a sign by virtue of its *representative* function.

This representative function may be fulfilled in a number of different ways. Let us note two of the most important. [2] Some signs represent by serving *as substitutes for* something else. The signs that we considered in Section 2.1 above are all of this kind. The floor plan, the bits of paper, a certain number of inches on the yardstick, and so on, all functioned as signs by *standing for,* by serving as substitutes for. A convenient name for a sign which performs its representative function in this particular way is SYMBOL. The mark which in everyday English we call a "multiplication

[1] "Means" and "meaning" are ambiguous and troublesome words. We shall later want to distinguish various types and dimensions of meaning. At present, however, we purposely use this catch-all word from everyday language.
[2] The need for distinguishing these two representative functions was first brought to my attention by C. J. Ducasse. See, for example, his *Nature, Mind, and Death,* La Salle, The Open Court Publishing Company, 1951, pp. 361–370.

sign" functions as a sign by symbolizing or standing for a certain arithmetical operation.[3]

Some signs perform their representative function in a quite different way. Instead of standing for, they *serve notice of.* They represent, not by symbolizing, but by *announcing.* An obvious example of a verbal sign which functions in this way is a "For Sale" sign posted on a piece of property. But some of the most important cases are not verbal signs at all. The signs to which we refer in everyday English by the phrase, "a sign of . . .", are usually of this type. Smoke is said to be a sign of fire, not because it stands for fire, but because it announces the presence of fire. Similarly, an abnormal yellowing of a patient's skin functions as a sign by announcing to the informed physician the probable presence of a liver or gall bladder disorder. The jaundiced skin is not a *symbol* of the disorder, but rather a *symptom* of it. In fact, this common medical term is so useful in reminding us of a particular way in which a sign may function, that we may conveniently extend its application to any sign which functions in this way. By a SYMPTOM, then, we shall mean a sign which functions by announcing or serving notice of something else.

It is interesting to note that a given sign may function both as a symbol and as a symptom. Thus, for example, a cross on top of a steeple is at once a symbol of the Christian faith and a symptom of the presence of a house of Christian worship.

2.3. THREE ELEMENTS IN EVERY SIGN-SITUATION

We have said that almost anything can function as a sign in appropriate circumstances. But what circumstances are appropriate? What conditions must be present in any situation in which a given object actually functions as a sign?

In the first place, of course, there must be the object which is functioning as a sign. In a language system, this object is a sound or group of sounds, or a set of written marks. But we have already noted that many other kinds of object may serve as signs.

In the second place, if a given object is to be a sign, it must, as we

[3] A multiplication sign is a *symbol* both in the functional sense just defined and also in the familiar but narrower sense of a special compact nonverbal mark. Compare the chemical symbol "H_2O" and the logical symbols like "$\supset$" and "$\vee$" introduced in Part II of this book.

saw in the preceding section, somehow serve as a representative of something else. This something else, which we commonly call the *meaning* of the sign, is the second element of a sign-situation. This meaning may be another particular object (for example, the Empire State Building), or a particular person (for example, your roommate), or a class of objects (for example, cats), or a quality (for example, red), or a set of characteristics (for example, being a plane figure bounded by three straight lines), or a relation (for example, inside of), or such things as feelings (for example, displeasure) and attitudes (for example, believing).

No object, however, can actually function as a sign unless there is also *someone* for whom the sign has this representative role. No object is intrinsically a sign. It becomes a sign if, and in so far as, it represents something to some organism or person. A third element, then, in every sign-situation is the INTERPRETER for whom the sign has meaning. Smoke, for example, does not indicate the presence of fire, and hence is not a sign of fire, except to an interpreter who has learned through experience or hearsay of the intimate natural connection between the two. A skin rash of such-and-such a kind is not a sign of such-and-such a disease except to a person trained or informed to recognize the relation. The word "cat" does not mean a particular kind of furry-purry animal except to a person who has learned to associate this verbal sign with this kind of animal. The statement, "It is a hot day," does not call attention to a particular state of the weather except to a person who understands at least this much English.

The four examples just mentioned will repay further attention. The first two differ significantly from the latter two in an important respect. Do you see what it is?

2.4. NATURAL AND ARTIFICIAL SIGNS

Smoke serves as a sign of fire to an informed interpreter because of a natural connection between smoke and fire that man has discovered but did not invent. Smoke and fire are intimately associated whether man knows it or not, but once man has learned of this connection, smoke can serve him as a symptom of the presence of fire. Similarly, physicians did not set up the relation between a particular type of rash and a certain disease. Rather, they discovered that these two were as a matter of fact regularly associated, so that one of them could be used as a sign of the other. In these two examples, then, the success with which the one object serves as a sign of the other rests, not upon some human convention or resolution, but upon a natural connection which holds whether man has discovered it or not. (This is not, however, to say that smoke and rash could *function as signs* apart from interpreters, and you will need to guard yourself against such a confusion.) Signs of this kind are called NATURAL SIGNS because they are related to their meanings by a natural connection which man may discover but did not invent. Can you think of some other examples of natural signs?

Our other two examples, the word "cat" and the statement, "It is a hot day," are quite clearly of a different kind from the two cases just considered. "Cat" serves as a sign of such-and-such a kind of animal to interpreters who understand English, not because of any natural connection between the word "cat" and this type of beast, but because of a human custom or convention shared by those who speak English. The ability of the statement, "It is a hot day," to call an interpreter's attention to a particular state of the weather similarly depends upon a human convention rather than upon a natural connection. Such signs are called ARTIFICIAL SIGNS, not because the *signs* are "man-made," but rather because the *connection* between the sign and what it means was created by man rather than discovered in nature.[4]

2.5. WORDS AND LANGUAGE

If you were asked to name the most remarkable works of man, what things would occur to you? Chances are that you would make quite a list before thinking of human language. For in spite of its undoubted place among the greatest of human achievements, language is so central and indispensable a part of our lives that we take it for granted. It is only when the "right" word eludes us, or we fail to understand what another person means, that we are forced to pay attention to language and to consider its role in our lives. We typically pay attention to words in much the manner in which we pay attention to our health; we tend to ignore them

---

[4] The need for the warning contained in this sentence is vividly illustrated by considering the case of an involuntary belch. The belch is, of course, in one sense "man-made," but this does not make the belch an artificial sign. Rather, it is to the informed interpreter a natural sign of gastric perturbation. It is instructive to contrast the involuntary belch with the ceremonial belch induced, we are told, at polite Chinese dinner parties as a sign of appreciation and as a formal compliment to one's cook or hostess. Such a belch is a genuine artificial sign, quite as much as the words, "Thank you for a delightful meal."

until they fail us. When we are fully in command of language, and words flow freely, they have an almost transparent character. We are unaware of them, quite as we are unaware of a clear window as we contemplate the landscape beyond. When language is functioning effectively, our attention is not upon words but upon what they mean. We see through them, as it were, to what lies beyond them.

Words are the most important, but not the only, artificial signs. They differ from various other artificial signs in being LINGUISTIC SIGNS, that is, they form part of a language system shared by a linguistic community. A language consists not merely of words, but also of certain conventional rules governing the way in which words may be combined into larger units. The most important of these larger units is, of course, the sentence. Sentences, as we know, are of various types. One type of sentence, the *statement,* is of particular concern to us because of its crucial role in thinking and knowledge. Among all the works of man, statements have a remarkable and unique characteristic which sets them apart: they are capable of being true or false. So basic is this characteristic that "statement" may be defined in terms of it. A STATEMENT is a complex verbal sign which is either true or false.[5]

2.6. ARE SOME WORDS NATURAL SIGNS? A NOTE ON ONOMATOPOEIA

In the preceding section, we described words as a particular type of artificial sign. The occurrence in a language of so-called *onomatopoetic* words raises the interesting question of whether some words are not, after all, natural signs rather than artificial ones. Let us explore this matter briefly.

An ONOMATOPOETIC WORD is one which more or less imitates or reproduces some nonverbal sound. Examples of such words are "drip," "purr," and "whippoorwill." "Drip" suggests the sound made by a drop of liquid when it hits something; "purr" sounds somewhat like the noise made by a contented cat; "whippoorwill" is a rough imitation of the whistle of a bird that we call by that name. These examples give us, perhaps, a fairly good cross section of the type of word with which we are here concerned. The first is a word associated with an inanimate object, a drop of liquid. The second names an activity of an animal, but does not name the animal it-

---

[5] For a further discussion of statements, see Section 4.7.

self. The third names the organism which produces the sound which the name resembles.

Now the question is this: Since these words, and others like them, imitate sounds which themselves may serve as natural signs, must not these words also be regarded as natural signs? If so, we shall have to reject the view that all words are artificial signs. Let us first examine a little more closely the three natural sounds from which these words are derived. In what sense can these sounds themselves serve as natural signs? It is interesting to note that these actual sounds (as distinguished from the words which roughly copy them) function as *symptoms* rather than as *symbols*. To the informed interpreter, the dripping sound announces that a liquid is falling and hitting something; more specifically, it may inform a housewife that a faucet has not been turned off tight, or that a washer is probably worn out. Similarly, the purring sound informs an experienced interpreter of the presence of a cat, or perhaps that a cat already known to be present is contented. So too, the call of a whippoorwill at dusk notifies the listener of the presence of the bird. These natural sounds, then, in so far as they function as signs, are symptoms rather than symbols. We need not insist that this is always and inevitably the case, only that it is typical of such natural signs.

When we turn from the natural sounds themselves to the words which more or less imitate them, we make an equally interesting discovery. Such words, we find, function typically not as symptoms but as symbols. That is, they *stand for* rather than *announce the presence or imminence of.* The word "drip," whether as a noun or verb, names a type of occurrence or event. The word "purr" names a feline activity. The word "whippoorwill" names the bird which produces a somewhat similar sound. All three words, and others like them, typically function as symbols, not symptoms.

This difference is not, of course, enough to establish that these words are artificial rather than natural signs. But it does show that there is a fundamental distinction between the way in which such onomatopoetic words are signs and the way in which the original nonverbal sounds are signs.

As we carry the investigation further, we become increasingly aware of the extent to which a conventional, that is artificial, factor enters into the formation and use of onomatopoetic words. This point is perhaps most readily seen if we consider a hypothetical Frenchman who knows no English. We may assume that he recognizes, as well as we do, the sound of a leaky faucet. We may say that he understands what the sound means. But will he, without further linguistic instruction, be able to understand the English word "drip"? Not likely. Once he has been taught the word, he will, like us, presumably recognize some resemblance between its sound and the natural sound of which it is a name. But there seems to be a rather clear conventional factor here which should not be overlooked. The presence of an artificial or conventional element in onomatopoetic words is even more apparent in the case of the English word "purr." When we explain to our French friend that "purr" is the sound made by a contented cat, he is quite likely to think that we have had no experience with cats, and simply don't know what we are talking about. He may deny that this is what cats say at all, and insist that when they are happy they say *"ronron"*—or at least that *French* cats do. Such a reply would be linguistically naive, but at least it would give us a deeper insight into the extent to which even onomatopoetic words are conventional and artificial signs, rather than natural ones. Our present purpose has been adequately served once we become aware of this conventional aspect of such words. As for the suggestion that the word "whippoorwill" is really a natural sign, one might urge with equal cogency that the bird's call of "Whip poor Will!" shows that he has not only an English vocabulary of three words, but also a rudimentary knowledge of English sentence structure.

• SOME REMINDERS

1. A sign is anything which represents something else. We respond *through* the sign *to* something else which the sign "means."

2. Virtually any object may function as a sign in appropriate circumstances. The general nature of these circumstances is analyzed in the text.

3. In terms of the specific nature of their representative function, symbols may be distinguished from symptoms.

4. The distinction between natural signs and artificial signs rests upon the nature of the *connection* between the sign and its "meaning."

5. Words are a special and highly developed type of artificial sign. Even onomatopoetic words involve a conventional or artificial factor.

6. Certain complex groups of words have the unique characteristic of being either true or false.

APPLICATIONS

1. Analyze four or five situations from your own recent experience in which you were responding to a natural sign. In each case, point out (a) the situation or context in which the sign functioned, (b) the sign, (c) its "meaning" in the context, (d) your response.
2. Analyze in the same way four or five situations from your recent experience in which you were responding to an artificial sign.
3. Name some examples of artificial signs which are *not* words or groups of words.
4. Prof. F. H. Parker has raised the interesting question of whether all signs really do require interpreters in order to be signs. If they do, then he urges that an undeciphered ancient "language" such as Cretan should not really be called a language, since any language—properly so called—is a system of verbal *signs*. And how could Cretan be a system of *signs* if signs must have interpreters but nobody can interpret Cretan? How would *you* deal with this problem?
5. Examine four or five onomatopoetic words in the light of the analysis set forth in Section 2.6. To what extent do they confirm the argument of that section? To what extent do they undermine it?

2.7. BASIC USES OF LANGUAGE

What are the uses of language? What is language good for? Among the almost endless variety of uses we might mention, five are more primary than others. It is these five basic uses that are of particular importance in thinking, in communication, and in living together. We may conveniently label them (1) the cognitive, (2) the expressive, (3) the evocative, (4) the directive, and (5) the ceremonial. We shall want to see both how these uses differ, and also how they are frequently combined in a single instance of language.

The most obvious use of language is to formulate and convey information about what is the case or is believed to be the case. We call this the COGNITIVE USE of language, not to imply that we always know what we are talking about, but because of its central role in setting forth *knowledge*. This use of language is seen in its purest form in a telephone directory, and in its most highly developed form in a scientific report. The technical language of a science is the result of a long process of refinement, of increasing precision, and of progressive elimination of noncognitive aspects of language. At the level of ordinary English, we are most likely using language in a primarily cognitive way when, for example, we call a particular animal a "cow," or report that we have been studying all morning, or announce that we didn't sleep a wink all night.

But we also use language for emotive purposes, either to *express* our own feelings or to *evoke* a feeling response from others. Our announcement, for example, that we had a sleepless night may be intended, not so much to convey information as to make people feel sorry for us. In such a case, our intent will have been EVOCATIVE rather than cognitive; we will have been using language to arouse a feeling of sympathy in our hearers. But language may be used not merely to *elicit* emotion but also to *express* our own emotion; this is language in its EXPRESSIVE USE.[6] This use is seen in its most rudimentary form in ejaculations such as "Ouch!" and in its highest form in lyric poetry.

While the evocative use of language is aimed at getting someone to feel somehow, the DIRECTIVE USE is concerned with getting someone to do something or to refrain from doing it. It deals not with emotions, but with action or restraint of action. This use occurs in a simple form in such a sign as "KEEP OUT. THIS MEANS YOU," and in its most developed form in the directives sent out by Washington bureaucrats to their subordinates. The arousal of feeling and the inciting to action often occur almost simultaneously, but this must not lead us to identify these two uses of language. We may appreciate their distinctness but possible concurrence by considering three simple examples. A poem about the beauties of nature may evoke feeling in the hearer without leading him to do anything about it; in fact, this mood of feeling-without-action is characteristic of esthetic contemplation. On the other hand, a simple request like "Please pass the butter" will normally lead to overt activity on the part of the hearer (he will pass the butter) without evoking any particular feeling from him. A successful pep-talk to the team between halves, however, is incitive in both these ways. It evokes feeling—the "fighting spirit"—and stimulates action.

When a friend greets us with a "Good morning," we are not expected to reply, "Yes, it is a good morning, isn't it?" or "I disagree with you; I don't see what's good about it." Our friend's remark was not intended to convey information about the weather or the state of the world; it was

---

[6] Note that when "expressive" is thus employed as the name of a use of language, it is being taken in a more restricted sense than in everyday English. In common speech we talk of "expressing" *cognitive* material as well as feelings; we speak of expressing our "thoughts" and "ideas," or say that a true statement expresses a fact.

not primarily or obviously cognitive.[7] His remark is not meant to be examined from the point of view of whether it is true or false; it is not a statement. Nor do such conventional polite forms of discourse seem particularly intended to elicit action, although we do find that they normally lead to some conventional reply no more to be taken literally than the original remark. Here we have a simple but typical case of the CEREMONIAL USE of language.

Similarly, the question, "How are you?", need not be a request for information about the state of our health, nor need our reply, "Fine!", have anything whatever to do with how we really feel. Does this mean that our friend is being hypocritical in asking the question when he does not expect an informative answer, or that we are lying when we reply "Fine" but really have a rather bad headache? If you think about these questions, you will discover how little we ordinarily expect such remarks to be taken cognitively.

Again, it would be a mistake to regard such ceremonial remarks as particularly expressive of the real feelings of the speaker. Every chairman, upon introducing the speaker of the evening, is as a matter of routine expected to say how pleased and honored he is to do the job. The speaker himself is expected to say how delighted he is to appear before so alert and distinguished an audience. Why? Because it is the thing to do. But why this convention?

The purpose of such ceremonial language may escape us as long as we confine our attention to isolated cases. But when we consider the over all role of such utterances in communal living, we see that they do perform a useful function. Even when they become so automatic as to lose any literal significance, they still serve to grease the machinery of social interchange, and to keep the channels of communication open. When they are not purely automatic, they usually are both mildly expressive and mildly evocative. They may express at least a modicum of good will, and may evoke at least a mildly pleasant feeling in both the speaker and the hearer.

Nothing that we have said implies that such ceremonial forms may not also on occasion be genuinely informative, nor that they may not sometimes express how we actually feel. Sometimes when we say, "I've had a wonderful time," we really mean it. And sometimes when, in answer to the

---

[7] It may none the less have an incidental cognitive effect in that it informs us that he is willing to communicate or is at least trying to be civil.

question, "How are you," we reply, "I'm fine," we really are fine. The point is that such ceremonial utterances have a function quite apart from their possible expressive, cognitive, evocative, or directive uses. The underlying purpose of such conventional ceremony is to make it easier for us to get along together, and to signalize our social togetherness. Much "small talk" and social conversation is primarily ceremonial.

Here, then, are five basic uses of language. We have already noted certain possible relations among them. We may observe further that since the expressive and evocative uses both have to do with emotions and feelings, it is sometimes convenient to refer to these two together as the EMOTIVE uses of language. Similarly, although all language used in communication tends to call forth some response in the hearer, this aspect is so striking in the case of the evocative and directive uses that they may be grouped together as INCITIVE uses of language.

2.8. GRAMMATICAL FORMS AND LANGUAGE USES

Certain types of sentence seem particularly appropriate for the several uses of language. A declarative sentence, for example, seems a normal vehicle for cognitive utterance, where our aim is to state a fact or to formulate or convey knowledge. Imperative sentences (commands) are particularly suited for setting forth directives. Interrogative sentences (questions), when they call for an answer, similarly serve a directive function. Exclamations are commonly expressive. But here again we must not think that things are simpler than they really are. A command, as every parent knows, may be much less effective in eliciting desired action than a more oblique approach. A blunt "Sukey, open the window!" is much less likely to get the desired result than the declarative sentence, "Sukey, if you open the window, I think you'll be more comfortable." Think of some other examples that will make it clear that, in spite of what we said above, the grammatical form of a sentence is not a reliable indication of the use to which it is being put or the effect it will have.

2.9. LANGUAGE AND COMMUNICATION

We have now come far enough in our analysis to see clearly that a mere list of language uses is only a starting place. Such a list helps us avoid the common but naive assumption that language is primarily cognitive; it reminds us of other equally important uses of language. But to understand the role of verbal signs in human life, we need more than this. We need to consider the uses of language in relation to the process of *communication,* and this requires that we pay attention both to the *intent* of the speaker or writer and to the *effect* upon the hearer or reader. (For brevity, we may say "speaker" when we mean speaker or writer, and "hearer" when we mean hearer or reader.)

Sometimes, let us admit, we talk "just to hear ourselves talk," but this is an exceptional case. Even when we are only "talking to ourselves," we are probably using language not idly, but to help us clarify our thoughts or formulate our beliefs. At times we not merely talk to ourselves, but also write to ourselves with more than idle intent. I know a very efficient but busy man who is continually writing notes to himself. This is not a game; he has found it a useful way to keep track of things and to get them done. These communications addressed to himself enable him to concentrate on the task at hand, without being distracted by all the other things he has to do later. The only flaw in the system is that he sometimes forgets to read his own notes at the proper time. In a less extreme form, most of us keep in touch with our future selves by jotting down assignments, appointments, and shopping lists. Or we write notes to ourselves about what the lecturer has said, so that we may inform ourselves of essential facts just before the next test. In such cases, we are using language for communication, but communication within its smallest circle, the self to itself.

For just as it takes two to make a quarrel, so it takes two to communicate, even though the "two" may be oneself at different moments or in different moods. Once we move out of this narrowest circle, the problems of communication multiply, and the difficulties of using language adequately and effectively increase. When we are communicating with ourselves, we give ourselves the benefit of the doubt; others may not do so. It becomes more important than ever to pay attention to both aspects of the communicative process: the *intent* with which the speaker uses language, and the *effect* of this language upon the hearer.[8]

From the point of view of the producer, that is the speaker or writer,

---

[8] When the effect is itself verbal and is directed back to the original speaker or writer, we call it a REPLY (literally, a "folding back"). In such cases we have not merely communication, but CONVERSATION (in the case of speech) or CORRESPONDENCE (in the case of writing).

the primary consideration in communication is *effectiveness*. An instance of language use is EFFECTIVE if it achieves the intent of the producer.[9] An utterance may have an effect quite different from what the producer intended. For example, a command with a directive intent may, because of its bluntness or for some other reason, elicit not the desired activity, but rather an emotive response (anger) and inactivity (refusal to carry out the request). Or again, an utterance made with purely cognitive intent ("I hear they have a thermonuclear bomb big enough to blow up the whole state of Rhode Island") may have an unexpectedly evocative effect ("Oh, don't say such dreadful things! They frighten me so!"). Even an intentionally evocative utterance may misfire by evoking a feeling other than the one intended ("I love you, Mabel." "Don't be a fool, George."). An expressive utterance ("I'm so happy!") will normally have a cognitive effect, in that it informs the hearer about one's feelings. It may also have an evocative effect upon the hearer, whether this was intended by the speaker or not. It is even worth noticing that an expressive utterance may not have had any particular intent; it may be more like an involuntary cry of pain or shout of joy.

The producer's main concern as a communicator is in the effectiveness of his language use. At times, the hearer shares this concern, as in the case of a friendly exchange of views or a scientific discussion. At times, however, the situation is quite different. The hearer may, in fact, be concerned to *prevent* the effectiveness of the speaker's language, or at least to suspend its effectiveness until the response can be deliberate and reflective rather than unthinking and spontaneous. In analyzing propaganda, for example, part of our problem as hearers is to determine the speaker's intent, if possible, but then to decide on perhaps quite independent grounds what our response should be. Nor dare we assume that the speaker's

[9] When an instance of the evocative use of language is effective, it leads to a feeling response on the part of the hearer. Some writers call this response the "evocative *meaning*" of the sign which caused it. But this appears to involve a confusion between the sign-meaning relationship and the cause-effect relationship. The sign-meaning relationship is always, in the broad sense, representational; the sign *represents* its meaning. (See Section 2.6 above.) The feeling evoked in the hearer is, however, not represented by the sign, but is rather elicited or *caused* by it. The evoked feeling is not the sign's *meaning*, but rather its *effect*. A parallel criticism applies to calling the response to an effective directive sign the "directive *meaning*" of the sign.

Similar objections do *not* however hold for the terms "cognitive meaning" (as applied to the information which the sign is intended to convey) nor to the term "expressive meaning" (as applied to the feelings of the speaker which the sign sets forth); in both these cases the relationship is genuinely representational, and hence is an instance of a sign-meaning relationship.

intent will always be what it appears to be. The cleverest propagandist may be precisely the one who is able to hide his real intent from us, and yet elicit from us the response he wanted all along. Thus, from the hearer's point of view, the effectiveness of the utterance is in certain cases by no means the sole consideration. To the speaker, that response will seem "appropriate" which makes his utterance effective. From the hearer's point of view, however, the "appropriateness" of his response cannot be measured in such simple terms.

2.10. SOME PRACTICAL VALUES OF THIS ANALYSIS

What are some of the practical values of such distinctions and observations? When we don't stop to think about it, we sometimes naively suppose that all language is primarily cognitive in intent. To act upon this assumption is to expose ourselves to confusion. Sometimes the result of such confusion is only humorous, as when we take cognitively a remark that had only a ceremonial intent. At other times the result of such confusion may be more serious, as when we accept a purposely biased and evocative utterance as if it were merely cognitive in intent.

We are all exposed to a continual barrage of words hurled at us day and night by commentators, advertisers, politicians, and just plain "thinkers." If we are to respond not blindly but intelligently to this deluge of words, we must be much more aware than we usually are of the diversity of ways in which language acts upon us. Such distinctions and observations as we have been making should be particularly helpful as background for our study of appeals.

• SOME REMINDERS

7. Five basic uses of language are the cognitive, the expressive, the evocative, the directive, and the ceremonial.

8. Certain grammatical forms seem particularly appropriate to the various uses of language. But in general the grammatical form of a sentence is not a reliable indication of the use to which it is being put nor of the effect it will have.

9. When language functions in a process of communication, we need to take into account not only the speaker's intent, but also the hearer's interpretation and response.

APPLICATIONS

1. Identify the use or uses of language in each of the following examples:
   a. Take one tablet with water every three hours.
   b. Have you read any good books lately?
   c. I see by the paper that the President is going to address Congress to-morrow.
   d. I'm so tired I could drop in my tracks.
   e. The line forms on the right.
   f. It's lovely seeing you again. I do hope you've had a wonderful vacation.
   g. The crazy fool! If I get my hands on him I'll wring his neck!
   h. Let the line AB be constructed perpendicular to the line CD.
   i. Darling, you're the most wonderful girl in the world.
   j. The Lord is in his holy temple; let all the earth keep silence before him.
2. On the basis of the discussion in Section 2.8, distinguish between grammatical form and the presumably intended language use in each of the following:
   a. This trunk is too heavy for me to lift alone.
   b. God loveth a cheerful giver.
   c. Look, Ma, no hands!
   d. If you aren't more careful, Billy, you'll break your neck.
   e. Let me out of here!
3. Even noncognitive uses of language often convey certain cognitive information indirectly. For example, the directive, "Please hand me that book," suggests that the speaker doesn't have it already, and that the hearer is in a position to give it to him. In each of the following, indicate the cognitive information that is indirectly conveyed or suggested by the utterance.
   a. Why didn't you stop when the light turned red?
   b. How much you've grown since I last saw you!
   c. Sit down!
   d. Which type of inlay shall I use, gold or porcelain?
   e. Give the Ambassador my regards.
4. Collect and analyze some interesting illustrations of basic uses of language, selecting your material from a variety of sources. Try to find samples of each of the following types:
   a. Clear cases of each of the basic uses;
   b. Cases in which the grammatical form does not give an accurate clue to the language use actually involved;
   c. Cases in which the response of the hearer suggests that he has misapprehended the intent of the speaker or is purposely making it ineffective.

CHAPTER 3

THE ANALYSIS OF APPEALS

PREVIEW

A given utterance may, as we have seen, combine several of the basic uses of language. We shall here consider one of the commonest and most important of such combinations: the cognitive-evocative-directive utterance of the type that may be called an "appeal." This chapter deals with elementary "propaganda analysis," although for reasons we shall examine, this name is likely to be misleading in certain of its applications. When you have studied this chapter and put it to work, you will still not be an expert. But you should by that time be more aware of how appeals achieve their impact upon you, more reflective in your consideration of them, and better equipped to react to them on their merits.

3.1. APPEALS AND INTERESTS

An APPEAL is an attempt, through the use of words or other signs, to get someone to take toward some issue the stand desired by the producer of the signs. A student trying to talk a pretty girl into going out with him, a professor trying to interest a class in the carbon cycle, a mother trying to persuade her small daughter that eating her supper will help make her cheeks rosy, a saint pleading with his hearers to turn from the vanities of this world, an advertiser urging you to use his brand of soap—all these are making appeals. Even so simple a case as "Ouch! Get off my foot!" or "For Pete's sake, watch where you're going!" is an appeal, although it will be more profitable to direct our attention in this chapter to somewhat more complex examples.

When we say, as we did above, that the appealer is trying to get someone to take a desired stand on some issue, "taking a stand" includes having

29

certain feelings or attitudes toward or against it, or taking or refraining from certain action with respect to it. The stand need not even be the one which the appealer himself takes toward the issue; perhaps it is only one he wants someone else to take. In many cases, of course, the stand is one to which the appealer is himself deeply committed, and one which he sincerely believes others too should take, not merely for his good, but for their own.

To be effective, an appeal must be "appealing." That is, it must touch some interest of ours, tie up with some belief or inclination or desire of ours. It must not be diametrically opposed to our fundamental outlook. To be effective, it must at least give the appearance of compatibility with our interests, and seem to afford some means of furthering or preserving them. For example, it will be difficult to interest a completely bald man in the purchase of a bottle of hair oil, unless the appeal arouses in him the hope that the oil will not only make hair lie down but grow, or unless he can be persuaded that it is, let us say, a good sunburn preventive. Or again, a student may rebel at a foreign language requirement until he is shown how a foreign language will contribute to his professional plans or his ability to get more out of his travels. People differ markedly in their specific interests and attitudes. Yet any appeal which is to be effective on a broad scale must somehow get beneath this surface variety to certain widely held interests.

In analyzing a particular appeal, we need to ask a number of questions. This chapter tries to help us see what some of these are, and to draw them together into a general pattern of analysis. At present, the question which concerns us is: What basic interests are being appealed to? Any attempted list of things that people are interested in is bound to be incomplete and to a certain extent arbitrary. Many alternative classifications are possible, none of them entirely adequate. This need not bother us unduly, for we now want merely to remind ourselves of the variety of interests to which an appeal may be directed. Advertising men have a very personal and practical interest in this question. Let us consider a check-list proposed by a leading New York advertising agency: [1]

People Want to GAIN . . .

(1) Health (2) Time (3) Money (4) Popularity (5) Improved Appearance (6) Security in Old Age (7) Praise from Others (8) Comfort

[1] Copyright 1949, Schwab and Beatty, Inc., 488 Madison Avenue, New York. Used by permission.

(9) Leisure (10) Pride of Accomplishment (11) Advancement; Business, Social (12) Increased Enjoyment (13) Self-Confidence (14) Personal Prestige.

They Want to BE . . .

(1) Good Parents (2) Sociable, Hospitable (3) Up-to-Date (4) Creative (5) Proud of Their Possessions (6) Influential Over Others (7) Gregarious (8) Efficient (9) "First" in Things (10) Recognized as Authorities.

They Want to DO . . .

(1) Express Their Personalities (2) Resist Domination by Others (3) Satisfy Their Curiosity (4) Emulate the Admirable (5) Appreciate Beauty (6) Acquire or Collect Things (7) Win Others' Affection (8) Improve Themselves Generally.

They Want to SAVE . . .

(1) Time (2) Money (3) Work (4) Discomfort (5) Worry (6) Doubts (7) Risks (8) Personal Embarrassment.

Are there other items that you believe should be added to this list? Have you some other classification to propose? Has the advertiser's concern with selling goods and services blinded him to areas of human interest that you believe important? Or has he done a pretty good job? Perhaps the best way to judge the adequacy of this check-list will be to use it as you get to work in analyzing concrete appeals.

3.2. TWO TYPES OF APPEAL

It is convenient to distinguish two extreme types of appeal, while recognizing that pure examples of the types seldom if ever occur in real life. Most appeals blend the two in varying proportions. At one extreme we may picture an appeal which is purely rational. It scrupulously avoids any attempt to stir the hearer's emotions. It limits itself to setting forth evidence which establishes the conclusion at issue, and it relies upon this appeal to *reasons* in getting the hearer to take the desired stand. We may approximate such purely rational appeals in certain scientific discussions, but we should not exaggerate their commonness. In many cases, such a purely rational appeal would prove ineffective through lack of motivating power, but that is not our present point. For convenience, we shall say that such an appeal is a case of CONVINCING, and that the appealer is trying to CONVINCE the hearer to take the desired stand. At the other extreme we may picture an appeal which is purely nonrational. It brings forth no evidence, it cites no reasons. It storms and growls or soothes and purrs. It appeals to our prejudices, stirs our emotions, and seeks to sweep us into taking the desired stand. Here again we may suppose that we are dealing with an extreme which is only approximated in real life, but the contrast with the previous type of case is an illuminating one. Such a nonrational appeal we shall, for convenience, call a case of PERSUADING rather than convincing.[2]

The appeals to which we are subjected in everyday life fall somewhere along the line between these two hypothetical extremes. In other words, they combine persuading and convincing in varying proportions. For a simple example of a case in which the rational, convincing aspect looms fairly large, we may imagine a physician talking to his patient:

> These tests that we have made show the source of your difficulties very clearly. The trouble, I am sorry to say, is a little more complicated than we at first supposed. I know that you are interested in regaining your health as soon as possible, and I want to do everything I can to help you. I count on you to do your part. The first thing we are going to have to do is to put you on a very strict diet. Now, nobody likes to diet—I hate it myself—but it is going to be essential to adhere to this diet very conscientiously. I believe that if you do so, there is some chance that the condition will correct itself, and there will be no need to operate.

This example illustrates an appeal in which the rational, convincing aspect is quite prominent. The physician appeals to evidence and gives reasons. He is, to a considerable extent, trying to convince rather than merely to persuade. But he knows human nature well enough not to let it go at that. Before going further, you may find it useful to analyze the above example more fully. What is the issue on which the physician is trying to get the patient to take a stand? What evidence does the physician adduce, what reasons does he present? To what feelings and attitudes of the patient does he appeal? How does he do it? Supposing you yourself were the patient, do you think the appeal would be effective? Or should the doctor have scared you more? Or should he have gone into more detail about the way in which diet might help to clear up the trouble? Such questions illustrate the type of thinking we need to do as we begin to size up an appeal.

[2] This terminology follows that proposed by L. S. Stebbing in her highly readable and instructive little book in the Pelican series, *Thinking to Some Purpose*, Harmondsworth, Middlesex, Penguin Books, Ltd., 1939, p. 63.

3.3. A CASE OF PERSUASION

Let us now consider an excerpt from a political speech. Your own preference and attitudes may get too much in the way if I tell you who is speaking, so we shall leave him unnamed. You should also note that we are not being fair in selecting just one short passage for analysis; perhaps what we shall find to be true of this passage does not apply to the speech taken as a whole.

> It happens [says the candidate for public office] that all of my mother's and three-fourths of my father's ancestors came to this country before the American Revolution. I love the Americanism I was taught to respect in the public schools of Iowa. That Americanism was betrayed after World War I by forces which found their origin in monopoly capitalism, yellow journalism, and racial bigotry. Today there is a greater menace than ever before—a menace more serious than has ever confronted the human race.

What is the point of such remarks? What uses of language are involved? What is the intent of the speaker? When you examine this passage in the light of these questions, what do you discover? You will admit that the passage has a certain cognitive effect; it is not *simply* expressive and evocative. We are, for example, informed about the speaker's ancestry, about his schooling, and less clearly about where he stands on certain obscurely identified issues. But none of this is really central, is it? To suppose that the *intent* of the words is primarily cognitive would be to miss the point. We need to consider the passage in the context of a political campaign and the candidate's desire to have us vote for him. In this context the evocative and directive intent becomes clearer. Without an awareness of this intent, we could scarcely understand the passage more than superficially or react to it intelligently. We get closer to the heart of the matter when we begin to think something like this: He wants my vote. He wants me to feel favorably disposed toward him and to believe that he is the man for the job. He wants me to adopt certain attitudes toward past and present events. He is trying to make me afraid of something (I don't know what it is yet) and to get me to take a hostile attitude toward it.

We must note that it is presumably *not* part of his intent that I should consciously make this analysis. I might be more likely to vote for him if I didn't analyze at all, but merely let his reference to his ancestry and to his love of Americanism move me, and his warning of a menace arouse fear in me, and his tone of competent confidence make me look to him as the man to protect this Americanism and avert this menace.

Should I, then, on the strength of this analysis, vote *against* him? Certainly not. I have only begun to think. To turn against him on this analysis alone would be as unreasonable as to side with him simply because I had failed to analyze at all. There is nothing in itself illegitimate or improper in his attempt to make me like him and to feel strongly enough about it so that I will vote for him and his program.

What, then, is the point of the analysis? Simply that it shows me that the passage in question is almost one hundred per cent *persuasion;* it doesn't really present a single *reason* why I should vote for him or accept his views on national issues; it has given me no rational grounds, no *evidence* that he knows what he's talking about or is the man for the job. I may like his speech and his sentiments, I may be glad that he went to school in Iowa (because, let us say, my parents were from Iowa too, and I spent many happy summers there as a boy, visiting in my grandmother's home, eating her good home-made bread, and so on). I may be glad to learn that he attended public school at least part of the time (for it is nice to be educated, and nice to mix with the common people instead of going off to some snobbish private school). I am thankful that he believes in Americanism (because I do too, although he has not given any content to that nebulous word, and we may not mean the same thing by it after all). I may also be grateful that he is going to point out a menace which I might have overlooked. But if I am to vote intelligently, if I am to act responsibly as a citizen in a democracy, I must have more than feelings to go on.

We noted at the outset that the passage does, to be sure, have certain cognitive effects. We know too that language in its cognitive aspects is well fitted to present evidence or reasons in support of a position. The interesting point here, however, is that the cognitive content of the quoted passage is not only meager, but has little or no bearing on our problem of whether the speaker is the man to vote for. It does not speak to the issue, but rather diverts our attention from it. Why, we may ask, would an appealer set forth irrelevant information? He might of course just be confused; perhaps more likely he is trying to confuse us. He may give his appeal the appearance of being rational by "citing facts" (such as that he went to school in Iowa), although the facts are logically irrelevant and constitute a *diversion* of our attention from the real issue. So too, a public figure called upon to explain his use of certain funds may call attention to the simple cloth coat his wife wears, and point out what a wonderful woman she is. When this technique was used during a recent political campaign, the overwhelmingly favorable response it brought from listeners indicated that the speaker knew what he was doing, even though the audience may not have. This irrelevant material no doubt had an emotive as well as cognitive role, but our present interest is in its cognitive aspects: the cognitive material was logically irrelevant to the purported topic of discussion. A convenient and familiar name for the use of cognitive material to distract attention from the main issue is SIDE-TRACKING.

In analyzing concrete written materials, it saves time and makes the analysis more vivid if we adopt certain easily remembered symbols which may be placed over an underlined word or phrase on which we wish to comment, or in the margin beside it. The symbol "Y" is a good one for Side-Tracking, since it may remind us of a railroad switch.

The presence of Side-Tracking is on the whole fairly easy to detect if we keep our wits about us. In evaluating the cognitive aspects of an appeal, there is however another less readily detectable possibility for which we need to watch. Perhaps we are being given "nothing but the facts," and perhaps the facts are all relevant to the point at issue. Yet we may have been given only one side of the picture; the facts reported may have been carefully selected to give the impression that all the evidence supports the appealer's position. Perhaps there are even weightier facts on the other side, but these have been passed over in silence to create the appearance of a "clear-cut case." This use of relevant but incomplete cognitive material to buttress one side of a case is called CARD-STACKING. A convenient symbol, which may be thought of as three cards leaning to "support" an argument, is " / / / ." We need to be on guard against this use of cognitive material, not only in analyzing the appeals of others, but also in our personal thinking. We all tend, often quite unconsciously, to notice and report those things which are favorable to our case, and to overlook or forget facts that go against it.

3.4. NEUTRAL AND EMOTIVELY TONED WORDS

Through usage and association, many words acquire what we may call an EMOTIVE TONE which is additional to their purely cognitive meaning. In everyday speech, "cancer" and "malignancy" have the same cognitive meaning, but some people carefully avoid use of the first word, or utter it only in a whisper. For them, "cancer" has an emotive force which "malignancy" either does not have, or has to a lesser degree. Yet both words refer to the same condition. Many times it is possible to find, for the same cognitive meaning, a word which carries a positive or favorable "tone," one which is relatively neutral emotively, and another which carries a negative or unfavorable tone. The word "statesman," for example, has for most people a favorable tone; "office-holder" seems quite neutral; "politician" is likely to be somewhat negative and unfavorable.

Adopting the widely used terminology proposed by the Institute for Propaganda Analysis, we may call the word "statesman" a VIRTUE WORD; that is, it has a positive or favorable emotive tone. Similarly, "politician" in some uses is a BAD NAME; that is, it carries a negative or unfavorable toning. In analyzing written materials, it is convenient to mark Virtue Words with the symbol " * ," and Bad Names with the symbol " ! ." [3]

The emotive impact of a persuasive appeal is often heightened by using words which have the desired emotive tone. Thus, in the speech quoted above, "yellow" as applied to journalism, "monopoly" as applied to capitalism, and "bigotry" as applied to racial attitude are all Bad Names. They not only serve to express the speaker's own attitudes, but tend to evoke similar attitudes in the hearer.

On the other hand, when our concern is to convince rather than to persuade (as in presenting the evidence for a scientific hypothesis), it may be important to avoid all words that have a strong emotive tone, and to select only those that are as nearly neutral as possible. In this way, the

[3] In *The Fine Art of Propaganda* by Alfred McClung Lee and Elizabeth Briant Lee, New York, Harcourt, Brace and the Institute for Propaganda Analysis, 1939, the following propaganda techniques were distinguished: Name-Calling (Bad Names), Glittering Generalities (Virtue Words), Transfer, Testimonial, Plain Folks, Band Wagon, and Card-Stacking. We shall use these terms with one or two additions. For somewhat revised accounts by two writers who played important roles in the work of the Institute, see Clyde R. Miller: *The Process of Persuasion*, New York, Crown Publishers, Inc., 1946, and Alfred McClung Lee: *How to Understand Propaganda*, New York, Rinehart & Company, Inc., 1952.

cognitive function of our words will have full play, without the distraction or distortion which might result had emotively toned words been used instead.

For these very reasons, the term *persuasion,* which we are using in this chapter, is probably preferable in elementary analytical work to the popular term *propaganda.* Social scientists and experts in public opinion have trained themselves to use the word "propaganda" in a neutral sense for any persuasive appeal (sometimes for any appeal whatever, whether primarily persuasive or convincing), but for most people the word has a definitely unfavorable or negative tone. In everyday speech, we commonly use the word only for certain persuasive appeals and not for others. If the appeal is directed *toward us,* we tend to call it "propaganda" only if we believe it to be counter to our own interests, values, and attitudes. We are not likely to call it "propaganda" if it merely serves to strengthen beliefs we already have, values we already cherish, or actions we already have some inclination to undertake. In such cases as these, we tend to call the appeal not "propaganda" but rather "just plain common sense" or "the simple truth." For such reasons it was preferable to name a certain government agency during World War II the "Office of War Information" rather than, let us say, "Office of Domestic Propaganda." When the appeal is directed not toward us, but toward our opponents or enemies, we do not feel quite the same reticence about the term "propaganda." Yet even in such cases we may find it comforting to refer to our own persuasive efforts as purely "informative."

For elementary analytical purposes, when we do not have time to train ourselves out of the emotive overtones which words like "propaganda" carry for many of us, it is better to adopt such relatively neutral terms as "appeal" and "persuasion" in place of "propaganda," and to refer to the person who is trying to get someone to take a stand as "the appealer" instead of as "the propagandist." Our terminology also avoids the need for taking sides on a verbal dispute now raging among social scientists over whether "propaganda" is to be used to name any appeal, or only those that seek to persuade rather than to convince. Our terminology also avoids offending the sensibilities of advertisers, who do not in general like people to call their work "propaganda," in spite of the fact that every advertiser knows that his task is to persuade as well as to convince.

When we are attempting to judge the emotive tone of a word, it is of course necessary to remember that the same word may have a favorable tone for one person or group and an unfavorable tone for another. The word "Communist" presumably has a quite different emotive tone for a member of the Communist Party and for a member of a House Committee on Un-American Activities. A member of the Ku Klux Klan and a southern Negro both know the cognitive meaning of "white supremacy," but the words will have an opposite emotive tone for each. At the height of a political campaign, the word "Democrat" may carry either favorable or unfavorable toning, depending upon one's own political alignment. At such a time, it may even be wiser for a Republican speaker to refer to the United States as "our great republic" instead of as "our great democracy," although he intends to make no cognitive distinction between the two names.

Just as a given word may have different emotive toning for different people, so a word which has a definitely emotive impact upon one person may be quite neutral for another. What is more, we need to remember that even the most neutrally toned language, such as that of a scientific report, may under certain circumstances be strongly evocative for a given reader. A scientist may become very excited by news of some important discovery in his field. Many Britons were deeply moved when the British conquest of Mount Everest was announced in the context of the coronation of Elizabeth II. Every parent of young children was affected more than cognitively by the announcement in April 1955 that a successful vaccine for polio had been produced. Emotively toned words often heighten the impact of an utterance, but we must not suppose that they are present in every case of an evocative response to language.

We can sometimes learn a good deal about the use of emotively toned words and their effect in suggesting attitudes by comparing two rival accounts of the same event. In his fictionalized *Adventures in Friendship*, Ray Stannard Baker ("David Grayson") gives an amusing but instructive account of a political meeting as reported by two opposing newspapers in his county:

> I take both of our weekly county newspapers [he writes]. This is necessary. I add the news of both together, divide by two to strike a fair average, and then ask Horace, or Charles Baxter, or the Scotch Preacher what really happened. The Republican county newspaper said of the meeting:
> "The Honourable Arthur Caldwell, member of Congress, who is seek-

ing a reëlection, was accorded a most enthusiastic reception by a large and sympathetic audience of the citizens of Blandford township on Tuesday evening."

Strangely enough the Democratic paper, observing exactly the same historic events, took this jaundiced view of the matter:

"Arty Caldwell, Republican boss of the Sixth District, who is out mending his political fences, spellbound a handful of his henchmen at the School House near Blandford Crossing on Tuesday evening." [4]

The opposed emotive tonings of the two reports may, when they are thus presented side by side, seem too obvious for further comment. It will be good preliminary practice, however, to go through these two accounts, considering the emotive tone of each word or phrase. If a word seems emotively toned, underline it. If it is being used as a Virtue Word, label it with a " *." If it is a Bad Name, mark it with " !."

This passage from Grayson may serve a further useful purpose at this stage of our inquiry. It reminds us that an appeal need not come clearly labeled as such. Offhand, it might seem absurd to look for an appeal in a column of news. Yet it is clear that each county editor is not merely reporting the news, but is at the same time making an implicit appeal. He is reporting what happened in a way calculated to influence our attitude toward it. He is trying to get us to react in a certain way desired by him. In the papers quoted, the emotive toning is not particularly subtle, yet if we were to read only *one* of the accounts, particularly the one which coincided with our own feelings toward Mr. Caldwell, we might mistakenly think we were reading "straight news." Our habitual unawareness of the extent to which news reports are "slanted" stems in part from our tendency to confine our reading to newspapers and our listening to commentators who confirm our own attitudes and prejudices.

3.5. SPECIFIC TECHNIQUES

Thus far we have raised questions concerning the issue, the desired stand, the interests appealed to, and the type of appeal. We turn now to consider specific techniques, largely persuasive in nature, which the appealer may use in his attempt to "put it across." [5]

[4] David Grayson: *Adventures in Friendship,* Garden City, N. Y., Doubleday, Page & Co., 1910, pp. 207 f.

[5] The techniques we shall now discuss are primarily emotive. We have already noted the cognitive techniques of Side-Tracking and Card-Stacking.

TRANSFER (→)

In order to get us to react favorably to his appeal, the appealer may try to tie it up with something toward which we already have favorable reactions. On the other hand, if his intent is to turn us against something, he may seek to associate it with something else toward which he believes we already have antagonistic feelings. He seeks to *transfer* to something new a feeling which we already have toward something else. An advertiser may hope that the pleasant reaction we have to the picture of the pretty girl in his advertisement will spread to the can of motor oil he is trying to sell us. A political speaker may seek to associate himself and his party with the Founding Fathers. An insurance company may hope that the confidence we all feel in the stability of the Rock of Gibraltar will by association be transferred to their organization. The lecturer may hope that the pleasure we feel toward his opening joke will spread to what he says later. In identifying a case of Transfer in the analysis of written material we may conveniently label it with an arrow.

TESTIMONIAL (")

One of the commonest techniques, with which advertising has made us all familiar, is the testimonial. The appealer tries to get us to favor something by quoting the approval of someone toward whom we have favorable feelings. The person quoted need not necessarily know what he is talking about, nor be in a position to judge of the issue to which he testifies. Sometimes, to be sure, he may be an expert on the matter, and may be able to present an opinion which carries evidential weight. Quite as often, however, the testifier may be chosen simply because he is well-known or well liked. At times, the Testimonial technique is combined with the Plain Folks technique (see below), and the person is quoted, not because he is known, but because he is just a "nice, ordinary fellow" like the rest of us. We feel he will look at things our way. The testimonial need not, of course, be positive; our disapproval of something may be aroused by quoting the disapproval of someone whom we like or respect. Or, to take another case, we may illogically be turned against something merely by learning that it is favored by someone whom we dislike.

Testimonial may be viewed as a special type of Transfer, but it is so important a variety that it is convenient to give it a name of its own. In practice, if we are in doubt whether to call a given instance Transfer or Testimonial, we may decide the point by noting whether the individual is actually being quoted (Testimonial) or is simply lending his prestige in some other way (Transfer). Quotation marks are an obvious and easily remembered symbol for Testimonial.

PLAIN FOLKS (=)

When a Presidential candidate poses in a farmyard in shirtsleeves and suspenders, or when a college professor goes out of his way to use what he takes to be the collegiate slang of the moment, or when an association of railroads runs an ad picturing a sweet old lady asking the brakeman, "Well, son, how's our railroad this morning?", we are dealing with cases of the Plain Folks technique. Its intent is to associate the appealer or his organization with "the rest of us" and to suggest that, in spite of possible appearances to the contrary, he is really "one of us." The equal-sign is an easily remembered symbol for this technique, since it reminds us of the feeling of equality which the technique seeks to arouse.

SNOB APPEAL (+)

But sometimes we don't want to feel like everybody else. After all, aren't we just a little better than other people? Don't we have loftier ideals, and don't we prefer the "finer things"? Many appeals cater to this feeling of smugness or superiority that we all have at times. Our colloquial term for this approach is "snob appeal." If an instance of the Plain Folks technique is symbolized by an equal-sign, a plus-sign would seem an appropriate label for a case of Snob Appeal.

BAND WAGON (#)

Since we don't like to be left out, the appealer can sometimes persuade us to do something simply because "everybody else" is doing it. This is of course scarcely a *reason* for doing anything, yet the call to "get on the band wagon" is often an effective one. At times the Band Wagon technique may be combined with Plain Folks or Snob Appeal, so that it says in effect, "Come on, be like the rest of *us* (the plain folks or the snobs, as the case may be). All of *us* do it this way; so should you." A musical sharp is a convenient label for this technique.

When we consider these special techniques as a whole, we realize the extent to which they are persuasive and emotive rather than convincing and rational. The fact that an appeal is tied in with something else toward which I have pleasant feelings throws no direct light on the value of the appeal itself. So too, the fact that some well-known individual approves of something is not by itself a reason for me to approve of it; it merely sets a problem for investigation: Does he know what he is talking about? Is he in a position to know? Does the fact that he is famous or popular make his opinion in this matter any more important than the next person's? Again, the appealer's ability to impress me with the feeling that he is a "regular fellow" or to arouse my snobbish feelings does not in itself offer reasonable grounds for accepting his appeal. Nor does the mere fact that "everybody else" is doing something, approving something, or hating something. To the extent that I respond to these appeal techniques spontaneously and automatically, without inquiring whether there are any good reasons for responding, I am being unreasonable.

3.6. A PATTERN OF ANALYSIS

The various aspects of appeal analysis which we have discussed fit together into a general pattern. The order of the steps below is not intended to be rigid, but it does indicate a normal progression of analysis. In many cases, we can at first deal with a given step in only a preliminary way, because a fuller insight into what is going on may require that other stages of the analysis be carried through. Thus, for example, our understanding of the real issue may become clear only after we have had a chance to reflect upon the impact the persuasive techniques have had upon us, and to take into account their possibly distorting effect.

    A. THE ISSUE
        1. What is the issue?
        2. Who is making the appeal?
        3. To whom is it directed?
        4. What stand does the appealer want us (that is, those to whom it is directed) to take?

    B. THE GENERAL APPROACH
        1. To what basic interests of ours (that is, those to whom it is directed) is he appealing?
        2. How does he do it?

        a. By supplying information? (Cognitive Aspects)
          i. Is the information relevant? Irrelevant, a case of Side-Tracking (Y)?
          ii. Is the information adequate? Inadequate? If it is inadequate:
            (a) Does inadequacy seem to stem from speaker's ignorance of certain facts?
            (b) Or does it seem to involve deliberate Card-Stacking (///)?
        b. By using toned language? (Emotive Aspects)
          i. What instances of Virtue Words (*)?
          ii. What instances of Bad Names (!)?

C. THE SPECIFIC TECHNIQUES
    1. Transfer ($\rightarrow$)
    2. Testimonial (")
    3. Plain Folks ($=$)
    4. Snob Appeal ($+$)
    5. Band Wagon ($\#$)

The application of this pattern of analysis to a given appeal should give us a fairly clear idea of what is going on and of how the effect is being achieved. This largely semantical analysis of the way in which signs are being used is an important first step toward reacting intelligently and responsibly to an appeal. That it is not in itself all-sufficient should be apparent. Some further essential steps which take us beyond semantics will be pointed out in Section 3.8 below.

3.7. ADVERTISING, A GOOD PLACE TO BEGIN

After you gain a little experience in applying the pattern of analysis outlined above, you will certainly want to try it out on materials dealing with some of the crucial issues of our day in the areas of politics, foreign policy, social philosophy, and the like. To begin with, however, you will find that you can learn most about the structure of appeals in the shortest time by turning to the rich and omnipresent field of American advertising. It provides a readily available and beautifully equipped laboratory for the analysis of appeals. Many factors make it a good place at which to begin. For one thing, analysis is simplified by the fact that we are seldom in doubt about the advertiser's interests and motives, although in other areas these are among the most difficult things to determine. The advertiser wants (1) to sell goods or services, or (2) to make us favorably disposed toward his company or type of business, or (3) to get support for some economic policy, governmental philosophy, or other cause in which he believes. The majority of advertisements are of the first type, although many companies spend a sizable proportion of their advertising budgets on "public relations" advertising of the second type, while labor unions, trade organizations, some professional groups, and a number of large corporations use advertising of the third type as well.

There are other factors that make advertising good subject matter for elementary analysis. One of the most practical considerations is its accessibility; it is all around us. Pick up any newspaper, turn on any radio or TV set, and you will find all the specimens you can handle. Again, the quality is good. Millions of dollars are put into getting the best talent available, the most persuasive approaches possible. Controls are fairly easy to apply; that is, the advertiser can find out whether his ad is doing a good job or not. If it isn't, that approach will be speedily abandoned, and a new one tried. This means that you, the analyst of appeals, are always assured of excellent materials on which to try your powers of analysis. Again, the materials are on the whole simple and the techniques fairly obvious. Finally, you probably already enjoy reading ads, and don't have to drum up any artificial interest to get on with the job. All these factors make the analysis of advertising appeals a good place to begin.

3.8. RESPONDING INTELLIGENTLY TO AN APPEAL

After you have submitted an appeal to the type of analysis set forth in this chapter, you still aren't through. Such analysis will increase your understanding of what is going on, but it is not self-sufficient. One of the chief values of the analysis is that it helps you to be more reflective and deliberative in your response to appeals. By helping you to understand how an appeal achieves its effect upon you, it makes it easier for you to distinguish between impact and merit. If analysis shows an appeal to be primarily emotive, it may put you on your guard and remind you that you had better consider whether there are any good *reasons* for accepting the appeal. As we have seen, the fact that an appeal depends upon persuasion is not in itself a ground for rejecting it. It rather indicates the need for caution and for a consideration of possible grounds and evidence. Again, an analysis may show that an appeal is primarily cognitive in approach, yet this in itself is not all we need to know. A bundle of lies or misinformation or a gross case of Card-Stacking may be presented in neutral language. In such a case, the very absence of emotive toning might arouse misplaced confidence in the appeal. All this reminds us that semantical analysis is not the whole story. No amount of insight into the way in which signs are being used can offset ignorance of the factual situation to which the signs may be claimed to refer. We need to investigate "the facts of the case."

But even when semantical analysis and factual inquiry have done their work, we still need something more. We need, as we say, to "know our own minds" and then to "make them up." Knowing the nature of the appeal and of the facts, we need to weigh the issue in the light of the needs, interests, and values around which our lives are centered. It is only when we have measured an appeal against the question, "What do we *really* want?", that we have an adequate basis for decision and action. To be in a position to react intelligently to an appeal is not easy. It requires not only semantical analysis, but factual inquiry, moral deliberation, and decision. It is the function of this chapter to help us take the first step in this process.

• SOME REMINDERS

1. To be effective, an appeal must be tied up with the interests of those toward whom it is directed.
2. Most appeals combine cognitive and emotive factors; we may distinguish between those aspects of an appeal which seek to *convince* and those which attempt to *persuade*.
3. To a given interpreter, a word may have positive (favorable) emotive tone, negative (unfavorable) emotive tone, or it may be relatively neutral. (Compare Virtue Words and Bad Names.)
4. Cognitive material presented to support an appeal may be open to criticism because of the presence of Side-Tracking or Card-Stacking.
5. Primarily emotive techniques which the appealer may use include Transfer, Testimonial, Plain Folks, Snob Appeal, and Band Wagon.
6. A pattern of analysis is set up for dealing with the mainly semantical aspects of an appeal.
7. An intelligent response to an appeal requires more than an understanding of semantical matters.

APPLICATIONS

1. Rewrite each of the following neutral statements first in positively (favorably) toned language, then in negatively (unfavorably) toned language.
   a. Mary spent seventy-five dollars for cosmetics last month.
   b. Mr. Jones is no longer employed by the First National Bank.
   c. Some people do not attend church regularly.
   d. The Senator stated that the Communists do not always do what they have said they would.
   e. The summer temperature in this city is often over 100 degrees.
   f. After using this preparation for three days, all his hair fell out.
   g. Professor Smith assigned his students 1000 pages of outside reading for next week.
   h. When her husband suggested that she sing something for us, she sang eight songs.
   i. I have spent an hour trying to understand this paragraph, but thus far I have not been able to do so.
   j. He wins every game of cards he plays.
2. Identify the appeal technique or techniques used in each of the following:
   a. The crass materialism of these Mammon-worshiping profiteers is wrecking the confidence of the American public in our cherished system of free enterprise.
   b. Be kind to your lungs! Join the millions of other smokers who are shifting to Nosmo, the smokeless cigarette.
   c. What if he did embezzle those funds? He used every cent of them to provide week ends in the country for slum children and their mothers.
   d. "I walk ten miles every day, rain or shine, so my shoes have to be right. That's why I always buy Hoofers, the shoes with the built-in spring," says genial Art Orton, veteran postman.
   e. FROM EVERY SINK-SIDE LET FREEDOM RING!
      Free yourself from Dishpan Drudgery!
      Let ISO-SOLVE solve *your* dishwashing problem!
      Once our valiant forefathers fought to free their loved ones from the yoke of a foreign despot. Today, American science frees you from Dishpan Drudgery.
      Out of the test tube comes a new miracle chemical, BIKININ, amazing product extracted by a secret process from the bladders of Bikini's famous radioactive fish.
      Let isotopes work for you. Simply sprinkle one teaspoonful of ISO-SOLVE over your dirty dishes. Then forget them. No washing or wiping. No harsh caustics. No germ-laden water. Yes, you don't even use water. Think of the savings on water bills alone!
      Lovely Wanda Martinson, glamorous TV star, says, "Now that I am rid of cracked, bleeding dishpan hands, I am more irresistible than ever."
      Make for yourself the discovery that millions of intelligent women are making. Try ISO-SOLVE on your dinner dishes—tonight!

f. LIBERTY OR DEATH?

A termite is at work undermining the very foundations of our fair college. This noble institution of higher learning was founded by God-fearing, freedom-loving men and women who sought to build here a bulwark of democratic liberty. But in our day the freedom they so dearly bought is crumbling under the harsh hand of regimentation. No longer are students free to leave class whenever they please; they must wait until the bell rings. The Student Director, one of the most popular men on the campus, has rightly said, "Fellow students, our present strait-jacket regulations, imposed by a power-mad administration, make a hollow mockery of the Liberty Bell." Let us all get together and insist upon our democratic right to be free.

g. "It's tough! The Army Officer Candidate School at Fort Riley, Kans., famed old Cavalry post, hallowed by the memories of Custer, Sheridan, and Patton, is a school where the men are separated from the boys!" (Recruiting Publicity Bureau, U. S. Army)

h. "If we pursue the lines of our own genius and resources, we can meet this—the greatest menace of a century. And being in the right the Almighty is on our side." (Herbert Hoover, radio address, Feb. 9, 1951)

i. "While in those countries which have entered the North Atlantic alliance a mad armament race is taking place and an unbridled war propaganda is being broadcast, and while the war psychosis is being incited more and more, the Soviet Union is the scene of peaceful, creative work. All the forces of our country are directed to the fostering of our national economy and to improve the standard of living and the welfare of the Soviet people." (Andrei Y. Vishinsky in U. N. General Assembly, Sept. 20, 1950)

j. "*Collectivism*—In the beginning, a dream   a figment of the imagination in the minds of people who do not know that large scale experiments in Collectivism have always failed.

"—a pig-in-a-poke swap of the free market system—which has done more to overcome poverty and establish well-being than any other system known to man—for an illusory security with no record of accomplishment and innumerable records of tragic failure.

"In the end, it offers regimentation for initiative, dependence for self-reliance, ration cards and quotas for abundance; red tape, controls, oppressive taxation, deceit, inflation, lower standards of living for all and, finally—slavery." (Editorial in *Christian Economics*, Sept. 26, 1950)

3. Write an advertisement for Toofyglint toothpaste, using as many of the appeal techniques as you can. Label each.

4. Write a considered presentation of the strongest reasons you can give for abolishing the grading system in your college. Use cognitive language and keep it as neutral in tone as possible.

5. Rewrite the above neutral account in persuasive language, using as many of the appeal techniques as you can. Label each.

6. Select carefully three or more advertisements from recent magazines or newspapers. Pick those which show a variety of appeal techniques or which

are outstanding examples of such techniques. Take time to get examples that are worth analyzing carefully.

a. Mount the advertisements, one to a page (folding them if necessary) on standard 8½ by 11 paper.

b. Indicate the source of the advertisement fully (periodical or newspaper, date, page).

c. Apply, in so far as you are able, the Pattern of Analysis set forth in Section 3.6. Underline and label techniques *on the body of the advertisement itself*. Add additional pages for your comments and further analysis.

7. Select with care a current or recent newspaper or magazine column of opinion, a political speech, or an editorial which is arguing for some program or point of view on a controversial matter. Follow the directions given under a, b, and c in Application 6 above.

CHAPTER 4

NAMES AS COGNITIVE SIGNS

PREVIEW

In this chapter we shall consider words in so far as they may function cognitively as names. We shall distinguish between two modes or "dimensions" of the cognitive meaning of names, and shall consider some of the reasons why it is important not to confuse the two. We shall also note certain parallels between names and the more complex cognitive signs called *statements*.

4.1. NAMES AND THEIR "MEANINGS"

We have seen that all signs "represent" in some sense or other, and that *symbols* represent by standing for. Among the most important symbols are words or phrases of the type called *names*. A NAME is a word (or group of words) which stands for one thing or kind of thing, where "thing" is interpreted broadly to include not only material objects, but anything whatever that can be referred to. Thus a word may be the name of a material object, of a concept or "idea," of a characteristic, quality, or property, of a relation, and so on. A *name* in this sense need not be what is called in grammar a "noun." The verbal symbol, "to the left of," is not a noun, yet it names a certain spatial relation. Note also that the term "name" as we are using it applies not merely to *proper names* like "Chicago," but also to *common* (or general) *names* like "city." [1]

A word which functions cognitively as a name may, of course, have

---

[1] "Proper" comes from a French word meaning "one's own." A strictly proper name applies to a single individual, while a "common" (or general) name applies to any individual of a certain *kind*. Names like "John" are not proper names in this strictest sense, for there are many individuals named "John." Such a name may, however, function as a proper name in a limited context (for example, a particular family) or if it is made more definite (for example, "John the Baptist," or "John R. Applequist, Jr.").

other functions as well. Thus, for example, the name of a loved one may affect us evocatively as well as cognitively. In the preceding chapter, we were concerned particularly with the noncognitive functions of words and other signs; here we shall confine our attention to words in their cognitive role of naming something.

4.2. NAMES AND TWO "DIMENSIONS" OF COGNITIVE MEANING

At first we are tempted to think of the name-meaning relation as a simple one which might be adequately pictured in some such way as this:

$$\text{NAME} \xrightarrow{\text{stands for}} \text{THING NAMED}$$

We might, of course, recognize that the diagram was oversimplified in that it left out of account the context in which the name functions and the role of the interpreter. But even if we should agree to simplify the matter in this way, the diagram still proves inadequate. For as we shall see in a moment, a name may "point" in one or both of two "directions"; its cognitive meaning may lie in one or both of two "dimensions." To speak less figuratively, we need to recognize two different modes of cognitive meaning which a name may have. To put it still another way, a name may function cognitively either by *signifying* or by *applying to,* or both. Thus in terms of our diagram, we need to split the arrow down the middle and point its halves in two different directions:

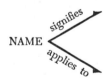

Let us begin with a simple example. What is the cognitive meaning of the word "eraser"? This name functions cognitively in calling our attention to a type of thing or to an instance of that type. If I were to ask you what "eraser" means, you might properly reply, " 'Eraser' means a kind of thing intended for rubbing out stuff." This account would probably be quite satisfactory for ordinary everyday purposes. You have told me what it is that makes a thing called an "eraser" different from other things. You have called attention to the function which such a thing must be capable of performing. You have indicated the basic properties or characteristics which anything must have in order to be what we call an "eraser."

The dimension of cognitive meaning which you have indicated in this way may be called the SIGNIFICATION of the word "eraser." When the occasion requires us to speak precisely, we shall say that "eraser" SIGNIFIES a kind of thing intended for rubbing out stuff. What we have here called *signification* is often referred to by logicians as "connotation." But this special semantical sense of the term is so different from the ordinary sense that its use is likely to be quite confusing. In everyday English, the "connotation" of a word commonly means not what the word signifies but, quite the contrary, what it merely suggests or intimates.

The first dimension of cognitive meaning which a name may have is thus what we shall call its *signification*. In order to get at the second dimension, let us begin again with the word "eraser" and my question, "What does 'eraser' mean?" You might have replied in quite a different way. You might, for example, have reached down into your desk drawer, picked up an eraser, held it up and said, "This is what 'eraser' means," or more idiomatically, "*This* is an eraser." In other words, instead of calling attention to the characteristics which make anything an eraser, you might have called my attention to one or more *cases or instances* to which the word "eraser" APPLIES. Now of course the reason the name *applies* to these cases is simply that these instances possess the basic characteristics which the name *signifies*. In calling my attention to such instances, you have been indicating the second dimension in which "eraser" has cognitive meaning, the dimension of APPLICATION. A particular instance to which the name applies, for example *this* eraser now before me, may be called an APPLICATE of the word "eraser." All the applicates of a name constitute its application.[2] Logicians sometimes use "denotation" or "extension" as synonyms for "application."

If this distinction between signification and application seems purely academic to you, wait until we have had a chance to see something of its practical bearing. But first let us make sure we understand the distinction. The signification of a name is a set of characteristics. Although we commonly call attention to such a set by *using* words, we are not talking *about* the words. The application of a name is all those particular items or cases

---

[2] Sometimes we need to distinguish the present or *actual* application (all cases now existing) from the *total* application (all cases whether past, present, or future).

which possess this set of characteristics. If a given item has these characteristics, then the name applies to it. Otherwise, it does not apply. These
then are the two modes or dimensions of cognitive meaning which a name
may have:

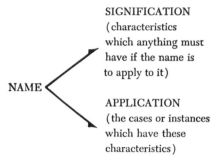

NAME

SIGNIFICATION
(characteristics
which anything must
have if the name is
to apply to it)

APPLICATION
(the cases or instances
which have these
characteristics)

Where you will have to turn to find an instance to which a name applies will of course depend upon what kind of name it is. An instance to
which "eraser" applies may be found in a desk drawer, but you will have
to look elsewhere for an applicate of "year" or "uncle of." For "year" is
not the name of a physical object, but of a certain span of time, and
"uncle of" is the name of a certain relationship in which a male human
being may stand to some other person. Our common tendency to think
of cases or instances as being limited to material objects is likely to confuse us when we look for the applicates of certain names, for many names
are not the names of material objects at all. Yet some names do not have
instances to which they apply. Once we understand this latter point, we
shall see one reason why we need to distinguish between signification and
application.

4.3. SOME NAMES HAVE NO APPLICATION

It sounds paradoxical to say that some names do not apply to anything.
One reason such an assertion troubles us is that we confuse it with the
statement that some names do not mean anything. This latter statement
is not only false but absurd, that is to say, self-inconsistent. For a name
is a kind of sign, and nothing can be a sign unless it does have meaning.
Now that we have begun to unravel the ambiguities of the word "meaning," however, we can understand that a sign might have meaning of one

kind without necessarily having meaning of some other kind. Specifically, we are in a position to see that a name may have cognitive meaning in the dimension of signification without having cognitive meaning in the dimension of application.[3] Hence there is no inconsistency in saying that some names do not apply to anything; such names are cognitive signs by virtue of their signification, not their application.

Let us consider a trivial example, the word "mermaid." Suppose I ask you what "mermaid" means. And suppose you reply, "It means a beautiful creature, woman from the waist up, fish from the waist down." What dimension of cognitive meaning is involved? You have undertaken to tell me what characteristics anything must have if the name "mermaid" is to apply to it, and hence you have been giving me the word's *signification.* Suppose I were to continue, "Well, this sounds interesting. Show me one. Not a picture, you understand, for a picture is only another kind of sign. I want to see the real thing." Of course I am doomed to disappointment and you to frustration. The name "mermaid" has no application; there just aren't any mermaids.[4]

This simple example helps us see that a name may have a perfectly clear cognitive meaning in the dimension of signification and yet not apply to anything. We all know what "mermaid" signifies, but we also know on empirical grounds that there isn't anything which is an instance of this signification, and presumably there never can be. Do you see how use of the ambiguous and undifferentiated word "meaning" obscures this whole issue? And do you see how the distinction between significative meaning and applicative meaning helps us to think clearly about it?

4.4. SIGNIFICATION DOES NOT GUARANTEE APPLICATION

Moving closer to the practical importance of this distinction, let us consider a more serious example. Suppose you agree with the widely held

[3] It is interesting to consider whether the converse of this ever holds. In other words, may a name have cognitive meaning in the dimension of *application* without having cognitive meaning in the dimension of signification? Some writers have urged that a proper name comes close to fitting this description.
[4] Encouraged by the comments at the end of the preceding section, one might urge that there *are* mermaids but that, unlike women and fish, they exist only in the "realm of the imagination." For some purposes, this manner of speaking is harmless enough, but it is likely to be confusing. In any case, this does not seem to be what we are ordinarily asking when we ask "Are there any mermaids?" We ordinarily think of mermaids *as if* they were flesh-and-blood creatures existing in space and time. Only we know that there are none such.

view that any teacher who is a member of the Communist Party is unfit to teach in an American college or university. Acceptance of this principle might reasonably lead you to urge the dismissal of "all members of the faculty who are also members of the Communist Party." This example, like that of "mermaid," may have evocative as well as cognitive impact, but let us confine our attention to its cognitive aspects. Here the name with which we are dealing is not a single word, but a descriptive phrase, "members of the faculty who are also members of the Communist Party." This phrase can function as a name just as a single word, let us say "faccomms," might. The descriptive phrase is certainly not cognitively meaningless. We all have a pretty good idea of what it means to be a member of the faculty of our college, and also what it means to be a member of the Communist Party. We also know what it means to say that a person is a member of both groups. This is all in the dimension of *signification*. But does it follow from the fact that the descriptive phrase has a reasonably clear signification that there *are* any members of the faculty who are also members of the Communist Party? In other words, that the phrase has any application? Of course not. Whether it does apply or not cannot be inferred from the signification of the phrase. It can be determined only by turning to experience, that is, by investigating the actual world to see whether it does contain any individuals manifesting this compound set of characteristics, that of being both members of the faculty and members of the Communist Party.

4.5. BUT SIGNIFICATION SOMETIMES GUARANTEES NONAPPLICATION

In the above example, it is clear that, however unlikely it may be that the phrase has application, there is no logical contradiction involved in supposing that it does. You might be interested to discover an example in which analysis of the signification of a sign shows us, on logical grounds, that there cannot possibly be any application. Such an example would be different from that of "mermaid"; there the lack of application rests not so much on logical grounds as on what we might call biological grounds. But consider the name, "members of the faculty who are not members of the faculty." At first we are tempted to say that the phrase is cognitively meaningless, but it would be more accurate to say that it is LOGICALLY

ABSURD. This is just another way to say that it attempts to combine two cognitive meanings that are logically inconsistent. It is not merely that there don't *happen to be* any members of the faculty who are not members of the faculty; the phrase can have no application because it involves a contradiction.

Another somewhat more subtle example is provided by the name "round-square." Here again we should not dismiss the name as cognitively meaningless; it is not too difficult to state precisely what we mean by it. This meaning, of course, is in the dimension of signification. "Round-square" means a geometrical plane figure which combines the essential characteristics of both a circle and a square. More specifically, "round-square" means a closed plane curve having four right angles and four equal straight sides, all the points on which are equidistant from a point within. What is more, I think I could recognize a round-square if I saw one. All I would have to do would be to test it to see whether it did as a matter of fact manifest these essential characteristics which anything must have in order to be named a "round-square." But I need not waste my time testing suspected instances of round-squares, any more than I need to take a poll of members of the faculty to see whether some of them are perhaps *not* members of the faculty. Why not? Because the signification of "round-square" is self-inconsistent; the properties signified by "round-square" are logically incompatible. Thus we can know in advance, on purely logical grounds, that there cannot be anything which manifests this signification.

4.6. RECOGNIZING APPLICATES vs. FORMULATING SIGNIFICATIONS

In such cases as "mermaid" and "round-square," even though it is impossible to indicate any application, it is not too difficult to express in words the precise signification of the name. You must not think, however, that this is in general the case. The problem of giving an accurate formulation of the signification of a name is often very difficult. It is not at all unusual to be able to recognize applicates of a name without being able to give an exact account of its signification. You can probably recognize a turnip when you see one, but you would probably find it very difficult to give a satisfactory account of the signification of "turnip." Precisely what characteristics must a thing have in order to be a turnip? In practice, we are often able to get by with a quite sketchy and personalized account. For some purposes, for example scientific work, this may not be enough.

Ability to state significations precisely comes only with considerable experience and practice, and then only in certain areas where we are particularly interested or where we have found precision essential. A child, because of both inexperience and inadequate verbal skill, usually finds it much easier to identify applicates than to formulate significations. In large areas, we all remain like children in this respect.

4.7. STATEMENTS, SIGNIFICATION, AND APPLICATION

Among cognitive verbal signs, some have the unusual characteristic of being either true or false. We called attention briefly to such signs in Section 2.5, and noted that such signs are named STATEMENTS. Although it would seem strange to think of a statement as the *name* of something, an interesting parallel exists between statements and names. We shall first clarify the meaning of the term *statement* and shall then consider the parallel with names.

A statement, we have said, is a cognitive verbal sign which is either true or false. Other types of sign, even of cognitive verbal signs, do not have this unusual characteristic. "House" is a cognitive verbal sign, and so is "into the house," but neither of these are either true or false, and hence are not statements. Statements are sentences, yet not all sentences are statements. "Please hand me the book" is a sentence, but it is not the special kind of sentence which is true or false. Similarly, the sentence, "How are you?", is not a statement, for a question is neither true nor false.[5]

In general, declarative sentences are statements, but even here we must note some important exceptions. (1) An *ambiguous* declarative sentence cannot function as a statement until the ambiguity has been removed, either by discovering the intended meaning or by distinguishing various possible meanings. In the latter case we end up, not with a single statement, but with two or more. Such problems of ambiguity are dealt with in the next chapter. (2) Many declarative sentences in poetry, for

[5] This is of course quite different from saying that a question is not cognitive. Most questions have a cognitive effect, informing the hearer that the speaker wishes information. Questions are also directive in effect, in so far as they elicit an answer. The verbal answer to a question, although not the question itself, is typically a statement.

example those which express metaphors, are not intended statementally, and to take them as if they were leads to ludicrous results. To urge, for example, that Alfred Noyes' sentence, "The road was a ribbon of moonlight," is false, would be to misunderstand what he was doing when he wrote the words. (3) Similarly, certain ceremonial sentences are not intended statementally, and it is inappropriate to raise the question of their truth or falsity. Such polite remarks as "It's the loveliest wedding I've ever seen" or "I do hope you all come to see us real soon" are probably not intended statementally nor reacted to as if they were. (4) So-called *stipulated definitions,* when viewed merely as decrees or resolves, are neither true nor false, any more than a wish or a command could be. This latter point will be clarified in Section 6.8.

We have already noted that some names, for example "cat," have both signification and application, but that certain other names, for example "mermaid," have signification but no application. This difference is also to be found among statements. Every statement, like every common or general name, has signification. Some statements, like many names, also have application. Let us see that this is so.

Every statement "proposes" or sets forth something, just as every common name signifies some set of characteristics. When we explain to someone just what a given name signifies, we normally *use* words to do so, although as we noted earlier we are not *talking about* the words. Similarly, when we call attention to what a statement *proposes* we have to use words to do so. But here again we are not talking about the words, but rather about what they signify. Thus, what the statement, "Jupiter is the largest planet," sets forth or proposes is simply that Jupiter is the largest planet. This is what the statement *signifies;* this is what we "grasp" when we "understand the statement's meaning." What a statement signifies or proposes is called a PROPOSITION. Do not get the idea that this name stands for something mysterious. A *proposition* is simply what you are understanding when you "grasp the meaning of" a statement, no matter whether the statement happens to be true or happens to be false. Against this background, "proposition" is very simply defined. "Proposition" means the signification of a statement.[6]

[6] The word "proposition" is unfortunately not used in the same sense by all logicians, nor even in a single sense by a single logician. Some even use it as a synonym for "statement," but we shall carefully avoid such usage. A "proposition" in our sense is not something verbal; a "statement" is.

So much, then, for the signification of statements. How about their application? In the case of simple names, we found that some have application and some do not. We have said that we would find a parallel situation with respect to statements. The question about the application of statements is intimately tied up with the question about their unique characteristic, that of being either true or false. *True* statements are precisely those that have application; false statements are those that do not. But what is meant by the *application* of a statement? It will be helpful here to drop back into everyday language. We don't ordinarily speak of "the application of a statement." What do we say? Something like this: "True statements express *facts;* false statements do not." We use the word "fact" in more than one sense, but the sense here involved is that which we find in statements of the form: "It is *a fact that* so-and-so is such-and-such." For example, "It is a fact that Columbus is the capital of Ohio." A synonym for "fact" in this sense might be "state of affairs" or "what is the case." Using "fact" in the sense explained, we may now say that the application of a (true) statement is a fact.[7] False statements have no application.

• SOME REMINDERS

1. A name is a verbal symbol which stands for one thing or kind of thing.
2. Signification and application are the two modes or dimensions of cognitive meaning which a name may have.
3. Since names are signs, all names must have some meaning, but some names do not apply to anything.
4. An analysis of the signification of a name may reveal that, on logical grounds, the name cannot have any application.
5. In other cases, however, the question of whether a name applies to anything or not can be answered only by factual inquiry.
6. Recognizing applicates is often easier than formulating significations.
7. Statements are cognitive verbal signs which are either true or false.
8. All statements have signification; true statements also have application.

---

[7] Various common meanings of the word "fact" are discussed in Chapter 23.

APPLICATIONS

1. Give the signification of the following words:
   a. book
   b. college
   c. store
   d. college bookstore
2. Explain how you would go about indicating the application of each of the above words.
3. Indicate which of the following words or phrases have application and which have not. In cases where they have no application, indicate whether this can be known by logical analysis of the signification or only by factual inquiry.
   a. the chaplain of our college
   b. the Buckeye State
   c. above
   d. four-legged bipeds
   e. Esperanto
   f. 529 A.D.
   g. Utopia
   h. left handed screwdrivers
   i. minotaurs
   j. democracy
   k. five-and-a-half ounces
   l. purple
   m. later than
   n. love
   o. rocket to the moon
   p. dinosaur
4. Find the signification of any unfamiliar words, then restate the question in simpler language.
   a. Have you ever seen the gyre of a tyre?
   b. Is the United States a gynecocracy?
   c. Does the Dean of Men approve of dudeens?
   d. Will a galloglass hold a gallon?
   e. Did you ever see anyone with a mazarine mazard?
5. Which of the following sentences are probably intended as statements?
   a. Please shut the door.
   b. Washington is south of Baltimore.
   c. If the shoe fits, put it on.
   d. Fire!
   e. Are both your parents still living?
   f. If last month was February, next month will be April.
   g. How are the mighty fallen!
   h. Life, like a dome of many-colored glass,
      Stains the white radiance of eternity.
   i. A square never has more than four interior angles.
   j. O that I had wings like a dove!
6. Which of the following statements have signification? Which have application?
   a. Some calendar years are longer than others.
   b. Portland is the capital of Maine.
   c. A straight line is the shortest distance between two points.
   d. Dinosaurs are now extinct.
   e. Some birds cannot fly.

f. The sun is nearer the earth in the daytime than at night.
g. Longfellow wrote "The Charge of the Light Brigade."
h. All men are mortal.
i. Marriage is illegal in some states.
j. Gold was invented by the ancient Greeks.

CHAPTER 5

AMBIGUITY AND WHAT TO DO ABOUT IT

PREVIEW

Sometimes we fail to understand what another person is saying, not because his remarks are meaningless to us, but because they mean too many different things, and we are puzzled about just which meaning he intends. And sometimes when we think we are arguing with someone over a matter of fact, we are really disagreeing not because of a different view of the facts, but because we are unwittingly using words in different ways. This chapter deals with these problems.

5.1. ONE WORD, MANY MEANINGS

In the preceding chapter, we saw that a word may have cognitive meaning in more than one dimension. We must now take account of another important fact about words: even within a single one of these dimensions a given word may have many meanings. Consider a word like "fine" in the dimension of signification. Think of the variety of meanings it has in such examples as "a *fine* day," "to pay a *fine*," "in *fine*," "a *fine* thread," "a lover of the *fine* arts," "a *fine* lady upon a white horse."

This characteristic of having more than one cognitive "value" or meaning within a given dimension may be called AMBIVALENCE. Most cognitive words are in this sense ambivalent. Notable exceptions include certain precisely defined technical terms that are not permitted to have variant significations, and logically proper names or completely definite descriptions which have a unique applicate.

As the above example, "fine," illustrates, the ambivalence of a word does not necessarily lead to semantical confusion. Even the slight amount of context provided in our example by using the word in short phrases

61

was probably enough to indicate to you the specific sense intended in each case. Sometimes, however, even considerable context is not enough to reveal the intended signification clearly. This is particularly true of abstract names like "democracy." Such a word, as we say, "means so many different things to so many different people" that we are often at a loss to know how to interpret it in a given case.

In this chapter we shall examine two specific types of semantical problem which stem from the ambivalence of words. One of these is the problem of personal ambiguity, the other that of interpersonal ambiguity. Certain other difficulties arising from ambivalence will be deferred until Section 31.2, where we shall summarize common semantical pitfalls in thinking.

5.2. PERSONAL AMBIGUITY

A word is PERSONALLY AMBIGUOUS or *ambiguous for a given interpreter* if in the context, or because of lack of adequate context, it suggests to him more than one signification or more than one application, *and* if he is in doubt as to which is intended. Ambiguity of this type always involves an interpreter's confusion, doubt, or hesitation when he is confronted with the sign.

We may note three typical situations in which a person may find an expression to be ambiguous. In the first place, he may be in doubt about which of two or more things is an applicate of a word or descriptive phrase clearly intended to apply to only one of them. For example, if I have two friends named Joe, and you tell me, "Joe wants you to phone him," I may be puzzled about which one of the two men is meant. Or, to take another example, if I ask you to get "the book on my desk" and you find several there, you will be uncertain about which book I had in mind.

In a second type of situation, the interpreter may find himself in doubt about whether something is in fact an applicate of a particular word or phrase, because he finds that some of the characteristics of the given thing are unusual. He does not know whether the intended signification of the expression really covers the case or not. For example, suppose I am trying to find my way to a friend's summer cabin in the mountains. He has told me to follow out a certain road and then to take "the first road to the left." I keep looking for it. Pretty soon I come to a rather faint and

AMBIGUITY AND WHAT TO DO ABOUT IT

overgrown track going off to the left. Is this what he meant? Or is this an old trail so faint that he didn't even count it?

Such instances of ambiguity may raise important practical difficulties, and are avoidable only if we are fortunate enough to get more specific, definite, and complete descriptions; for example, "Joe Naef," "the Leibniz volume on my desk," "the first graded road to the left, but don't count that overgrown logging trail."

A third type of situation arises when the interpreter's doubt is specifically about which of two or more possible significations is intended by the speaker. Suppose someone asks you, "Is the United States a Christian nation?" If this comes as a bolt from the blue and without any particular context, you will quite likely not know just how to answer. Your hesitation may not proceed at all from ignorance of the religious life and atmosphere of our country. It will probably stem instead from your puzzlement as to what your friend meant by "a Christian nation." Probably various possible significations are dimly present in your mind, but you are puzzled about just what set of characteristics a nation would need to have to lead your friend to call it "a Christian nation." Of course it is quite possible that your friend has only the fuzziest idea himself as to what he might mean by this.

The remedy for such a situation is well known but often difficult to apply: define your terms. The kind of definition usually asked for here is a statement of the *signification* of a particular word. (We shall later discuss various other ways in which one may define a word.) It is very helpful when we can get such a significative definition, but we saw earlier that a person may be able to recognize cases of the application of a name with a high degree of reliability and yet be quite unable to formulate an adequate statement of its signification. We ourselves want to develop this skill in clarifying the signification of our own terms. When, however, the problem is one of determining another person's significations, a more practical approach is often to get him to indicate additional instances to which he will apply the term. If we are skilled enough ourselves in examination of these instances, they may help us to clarify the signification sufficiently for the purpose at hand. Or again, we may ask him questions which will help him to explain his meaning more clearly. Did he mean to ask, for example, whether the United States has a state church which is Christian? Does he want to know whether all or most American citizens are Christians? Does he want to find out whether the government or a considerable portion of the population evaluates its policies and makes its decisions in the light of Christian ethical principles? And so on.

When it is not possible to conduct such a semantical investigation in an atmosphere of good will, we often have to guess and hope for the best, and in these matters, frequently the best is none too good.

The cases of ambiguity we have considered thus far have had to do with hesitation or doubt or confusion on the part of an interpreter of the sign. We next want to examine a closely related kind of case which is the source of some of the most heated and unrewarding arguments in which human beings get involved. What makes them heated and unrewarding is usually that one or both of the disputants is unaware of the semantical nature of the problem, and is trying to seek a solution which is altogether inappropriate to the kind of problem involved. And of course until we recognize the kind of problem we are facing, we are not very likely to be able to solve it.

5.3. INTERPERSONAL AMBIGUITY AND VERBAL DISPUTES

Suppose you and I are arguing over whether mathematics is a science or not. Let's suppose we both think we understand the question. I do not feel in doubt about what it means, and neither do you. Thus whatever is going on here, it is not a case of the kind we were considering when I was in doubt as to the first road or you were in doubt about what your friend meant by asking whether the United States is a Christian nation. We both think we understand the question. But we give opposite answers to it. Let us say that I insist that of course mathematics is a science. You, with equal vigor, maintain that it is obviously not.[1]

The troublesome thing about this kind of argument is that it appears to have the same general form as a dispute about objective fact. It looks similar to disputes over questions like: "Is a turtle a reptile?" "Was Aaron Burr ever President of the United States?" So our argument continues, getting hotter and hotter. Each of us thinks the other must be stupid not to know the facts, or bullheaded not to admit them. And yet we are not really disagreeing about the facts at all. What is going on then? Well,

[1] It is interesting to note that, even if you and I should have quite different meanings in mind, we might never discover this fact if our differing meanings led both of us to answer questions in the same way.

we happen to have different meanings in mind. It probably doesn't even occur to us that there might be any question about what is meant when we ask "Is mathematics a science?" It occurs to neither of us that the other has quite a different sense of "science" in mind from one's self. You, let us say, are a pre-med major. When you think of science, you think of things like biology and chemistry, perhaps physics. You recognize that all these sciences are characterized by a search for laws and generalizations about certain aspects of the world of nature. You know that they all make extensive use of experimentation, and that this experimentation consists in testing hypotheses against observable natural fact under controlled conditions. You are quite right in recognizing that mathematics is not thus characterized. Its procedures and intent are quite different. So you argue that, of course, mathematics is not a science.

But I, let us suppose, because of my interest in formal logic and logical systems, quite naturally have a somewhat different but equally legitimate meaning of "science" in mind. I am thinking of a science as any organized body of tested or validated knowledge. Hence I quite correctly insist that mathematics is a science. We are not really disagreeing about the facts at all. Our apparent disagreement about the facts is only apparent. It arises because we have quite different meanings in mind. In one of these meanings, the answer to our question is quite clearly "yes." In the other, it is equally clearly "no." Until we discover that this, rather than a factual disagreement, is the source of our dispute, we will be looking for the wrong kind of solution, a kind which cannot possibly be supplied.

Arguments of this kind are called VERBAL DISPUTES. Their troublesome peculiarity is that, to the disputants themselves, such arguments do not appear to be about verbal matters at all. If we want to bring out their close relation to the problem of ambiguity discussed above, we might call them cases of *interpersonal ambiguity*. We should have to contrast this type of ambiguity with the individual or personal ambiguity already defined. Here the different possible senses are not battling within the mind of a single interpreter, leading him to be in doubt. Rather, the confusion arises because each of the two parties to the dispute has a different meaning in mind from the other, but is not aware that he has. We may say that a word is INTERPERSONALLY AMBIGUOUS when, in a given context, it is being used in different senses by different people, without their being aware of that fact.

The psychological "feel" of interpersonal ambiguity is quite different from that of personal ambiguity. In the latter case, the interpreter is puzzled about which of two meanings was intended; he is in a state of doubt. In interpersonal ambiguity however, each disputant is quite unaware that a question of meaning is involved. He believes that he is arguing a point of nonverbal fact, and is likely to be provoked at his opponent for making such "obviously false" statements.

How can we handle cases of interpersonal ambiguity? First of all we have to become much more clearly aware than most of us are of the prevalence of this kind of dispute. We have to develop the habit of asking ourselves in a given case: Are we really in disagreement about the facts, or are we arguing because we have different meanings in mind? In the second place, it will be helpful to have in mind a standard pattern of analysis, a systematic mode of attack. I do not mean that you will trot this out to impress or overwhelm your opponent. But if you have it in mind yourself, it will help you remember what is needed. One of the most useful of such forms of analysis is that developed by James MacKaye.[2]

5.4. MACKAYE'S METHOD

First, MacKaye suggests, it is helpful to state the core of the dispute in the form of a question. We have already done this in the example we have been considering. The second step is to determine and indicate the precise location of the difficulty within the question. In our example it was the word "science." [3]

The next step, which we shall in practice treat as the third step (although it is really MacKaye's fourth), is to set forth the two or more meanings which "*are* sufficient to resolve the dispute, and the failure to distinguish which has caused it" (*op. cit.*, p. 126). This is usually the most difficult part of the analysis. But once it is accomplished, the rest is easy. The fourth step MacKaye calls "multiplied questions and answers."

[2] James MacKaye: *The Logic of Language,* Hanover, N. H., Dartmouth College Publications, 1939, Chapter V.
[3] In his own account of the method, MacKaye then introduces as the next step the statement of the insufficient meaning, a vague or loose meaning of the ambiguous word to which probably both antagonists would agree, but which fails to get at the point at issue. MacKaye is probably right in supposing that there is usually some such loose or general meaning in the background. But as MacKaye himself admits, it is often very hard to decide what this inadequate meaning may be. In practice, this step may usually be omitted without harm.

Here we ask the original question again, or rather we ask it in as many sufficient senses as we have had to distinguish. Is mathematics a science in sense 1? Is mathematics a science in sense 2? Frequently these different senses can be more meaningfully labeled by using appropriate adjectives instead of numbers. In our example, we might at this stage have identified the first sense as "*natural* science." We will of course find that the answers to these multiplied questions are in one case "yes" and in the other case "no." Otherwise the dispute never would have arisen.

It is very important to see that once the multiplied questions have been asked, we are at the end of the *verbal* aspects of the analysis. The answers to these multiplied questions cannot themselves be determined by semantical analysis or by stipulation. They are matters of nonverbal fact. The interesting thing is that when we and our opponents *now* face these nonverbal matters of fact, we usually find that we had been in agreement about *them* all along. But our agreement about these nonverbal truths was concealed by our verbal entanglement.

If it should happen, as it occasionally does, that a factual basis for dispute remains after we have cleared up the interpersonal ambiguity, we can then turn together to determine the facts. But the matter of the truth or falsity of an answer can be tackled only after we know what the question means. Hence the solution of the verbal dispute is logically prior to the solution of any remaining nonverbal issues.

Let us apply this standard form of analysis to a couple more examples. First let's take a very simple and trivial case. Two small boys are arguing. One says: "My dad's bigger than your dad." And the other says, "No he isn't." Let's suppose that this is purely a case of interpersonal ambiguity.

1. *Ambiguous question:* Is my dad bigger than your dad?
2. *Ambiguous word or phrase:* "bigger"
3. *Differentiated meanings:*
   "bigger"$_1$: larger up and down, taller
   "bigger"$_2$: larger around, fatter
4. *Multiplied questions and answers:*
   Is my dad bigger$_1$ than your dad? Yes
   Is my dad bigger$_2$ than your dad? No

As our final illustration, let us take a more significant example. Let's suppose that two people are arguing over the question, "Is Communism a religion?" And let us suppose further that they are really in fundamental agreement about the nonverbal facts. They are, of course, not aware of this agreement at the time, because an interpersonal ambiguity stands in their way. One speaker is arguing that Communism is obviously not a religion. The other is arguing that it clearly is. Analysis of the meanings which each of them has in mind might reveal something like this:

1. *Ambiguous question:* Is Communism a religion?
2. *Ambiguous word:* "religion"
3. *Differentiated meanings:*
   "religion"$_1$: a system of faith and practice centering around belief in and ultimate devotion to a supreme supernatural Being.
   "religion"$_2$: a system of faith and practice centering around belief in and ultimate devotion to something conceived as greater and more enduring than the individual.
4. *Multiplied questions and answers:*
   Is Communism a religion$_1$?: No
   Is Communism a religion$_2$?: Yes

5.5. ON CONSULTING A DICTIONARY

Perhaps you are puzzled or disturbed by the fact that we have not as yet said anything about consulting a dictionary. Isn't a dictionary an authoritative source of information on the meanings of words? If a word is ambiguous to you, why not look it up in the dictionary? Or if you are involved in a verbal dispute, why not turn to the dictionary as an arbiter of the dispute? Certainly, in so far as this approach will really work, we should be encouraged to use it. But quite apart from the fact that a dictionary may not be handy, there are other reasons why this type of authoritative appeal often fails to meet the issue.

Perhaps the traditional advice that we consult a dictionary when we "don't know what a word means" itself involves an ambiguity. Sometimes we don't know what a word means, in the sense that it either means nothing to us or has only a very fuzzy meaning. In such a case, a dictionary may be of great help, and may solve our problem speedily and completely. For a dictionary is a conveniently arranged report on the conventional meanings of words. By consulting it, we may discover what the puzzling word meant. But this sense of "not knowing what a word means" is not the one directly involved in our discussion in this chapter. The other sense of "not knowing what a word means" is the relevant one in a case of personal ambiguity: we know that the word in question commonly means two or more different things, but we are puzzled about *which* of these it means in the present case. In this situation, consulting the dictionary may do no more than tell us what we already knew before we consulted it. Here we are likely to make better progress by studying, not the dictionary, but the context in which the puzzling word occurs. If the producer of the word is available, a few well-placed questions are likely to clear up the difficulty.

How about cases of interpersonal ambiguity? Will a dictionary help us here? Possibly, but probably not. Our first need, of course, is to suspect that our dispute may have a verbal basis; this calls not for a dictionary, but for a suspicious frame of mind. Once we begin to inquire into the possibly verbal nature of our dispute, how much will it help to consult a dictionary? At times it may help considerably. If we can get certain recognized senses before us, we may get an insight into our particular difficulty. Or again, if you can show me that I have been using a word in an unrecorded sense, I may be traditionalist enough to back down and accept your meaning of the word to the exclusion of my own. But this may not work at all if I am stubborn, or if we are both excited by the argument. Appeals to the dictionary are often closely tied up with questions about "the correct meaning" of a word, but such questions may be quite irrelevant to our dispute. Our practical problem is to discover the semantical nature of our dispute, to clarify our divergent meanings enough so that we can understand each other, and then to move on to the remaining factual issues, if any. The meanings that we encounter in an actual verbal dispute are often much more specific and personal than the generalized meanings that will be given in a dictionary. We can determine these specific disputed meanings only in use, only in the concrete context of the actual argument. The fact that one of us might be able to show that his meaning was closer to a "standard" dictionary meaning than that of his opponent might make him feel good, but it would have little or nothing to do with the case.

• SOME REMINDERS

1. Confusion or puzzlement over the intended cognitive meaning of a word is a common obstacle to thinking and communication.
2. Whether a given word is ambiguous in a particular situation will depend upon a number of factors, including the context or lack of context, and the interpreter and his background.
3. The general remedy for ambiguity consists in definition of terms. But in practice, demand for a formal definition is frequently less helpful than more informal procedures, such as asking appropriate questions.
4. "Verbal disputes" involve a kind of interpersonal ambiguity.
5. MacKaye's Method gives a convenient form of attack upon ambiguities and verbal disputes.
6. Actual verbal disputes can seldom be settled merely by appealing to the dictionary. Concrete meanings have to be determined within the context in which they are being used.

APPLICATIONS

1. Distinguish between personal ambiguity and interpersonal ambiguity.
2. Distinguish three types of situation in which an interpreter may find an expression personally ambiguous. Give some concrete examples of each type.
3. Distinguish between a verbal issue and a nonverbal one. Give some examples of each.
4. Imagine two people arguing over each of the following questions. In each case, one of the disputants claims that the answer is "yes," while the other claims it is "no." Assuming that the basis of their disagreement is verbal, apply MacKaye's method to resolve the difficulty.
   a. Is capital punishment a form of murder?
   b. Can a parent be a consistent pacifist and still spank his children?
   c. Can a person get down off an elephant?
   d. Is the pen mightier than the sword?
   e. Do carrots taste better than spinach?
   f. Was Thoreau a free man even while in jail?
   g. Is the Bible mistaken in referring to a whale as a big fish?
   h. Are all men brothers?
   i. Can a person have a heart of gold?
   j. Does an education cost more than it's worth?
5. Report on one or more disputes from your own experience in which MacKaye's method would have been helpful.

CHAPTER 6

DEFINING YOUR TERMS

PREVIEW

You have no doubt noticed that in expressing the signification of certain names and in differentiating various meanings of ambiguous words, we were actually setting forth definitions of them. In this chapter we shall remind ourselves of the central use or basic purpose of definitions, and shall then consider various methods by which this purpose may be achieved. We shall distinguish between definitions which record established usage and those which create a new usage, and we shall consider the question of whether a definition is the kind of thing that can be true or false. Finally, we shall want to distinguish cognitive definitions from various other things with which they might be confused.

6.1. DEFINING "DEFINITION"

A DEFINITION is an explanation of the cognitive meaning of a word. It will be seen that the preceding sentence is itself a definition in the sense defined. We have by means of that sentence explained the cognitive meaning of "definition." It should be noted that our definition was given in terms of use or purpose; it tells us how a definition functions or what it is good for. The *method* we used in giving this definition was that of indicating the signification of the word; the particular kind of "cognitive meaning" which the definition explained was the *signification* of the word.[1] When in our second sentence, however, we pointed out that the first sentence was itself a definition, we were using a second method of defining; we were calling attention to a particular case or instance, to a particular applicate of the name "definition." This, too, was a way of explaining the

[1] Richard Robinson has done much to clarify thinking about definitions by his insistence that we distinguish clearly between the *purpose* of definition and the *methods* by which defining may be accomplished. See his excellent book, *Definition*, Oxford, Clarendon Press, 1950, especially Chapters 2–5.

71

cognitive meaning of the word, but in this latter case the method we used was to point to a particular instance to which the word applied. The particular kind of "cognitive meaning" which this second method explained was the *application* of the word. Thus far, then, we have defined "definition" in terms of the function which definitions have, and we have illustrated two basic methods by which this function may be carried out.

Perhaps this definition of "definition" bothers you in two quite different ways. On the one hand, it may seem too broad, in that you may be accustomed to confining the application of the word to cases which proceed by giving the *signification*. This is, to be sure, what we often have in mind, but once we consider the *purpose* of defining, we become aware of the fact that this purpose may be achieved in more than one way. You should note that we have here many of the materials for a verbal dispute. *Ambiguous question:* "Can you define a word by indicating an applicate?" *Ambiguous word:* "define." *Distinguished meanings:* (1) Define: to explain the cognitive meaning of a word. (2) Define: to give the signification of a word. *Multiplied questions and answers:* (1) Can you define (Sense 1) a word by indicating an applicate? Yes. (2) Can you define (Sense 2) a word by indicating an applicate? No. We have sought to forestall such a verbal dispute by indicating at the outset that we were concerned with giving a definition in terms of use or purpose.

On the other hand, you may feel that our definition of "definition" is too narrow. For you are probably used to speaking of giving definitions of *things* as well as of words. Here again there is ample precedent for your usage, although it may be confusing if it is not explained carefully. In any case, the question of defining *things* lies outside our present concern. This concern is semantical, that is, has to do with questions relating to signs and their meanings.

Let us now consider the more important ways in which the purpose of defining may be carried out.

6.2. DEFINING BY GIVING A SYNONYM

If we and our hearer have enough familiarity with the language, it is sometimes a simple matter to explain the cognitive meaning of a word by mentioning another word which has the same cognitive meaning. Thus if we are asked what the noun "feline" means, perhaps all that will be necessary will be to say that "feline" means the same as "cat." Such a definition is called a SYNONYMOUS DEFINITION, because it defines one word by giving a synonym of it. Note that, to express this form of definition clearly in writing, we place the synonym in quotes as well as the word being defined. The quotes show that we are talking about the *words* "feline" and "cat." What we are saying about them is that they have the same meaning.

It might at first seem that such a method of defining the word "feline" does not really fit our definition of "definition" at all. For we had agreed that a definition explains the cognitive meaning of a word, whereas here we seem merely to have given another *word*. Brief reflection will show, however, that this objection is unfounded. We have indeed mentioned another word, "cat," but our point in mentioning it was to inform someone that "feline" has the same *meaning* as this word. What made the definition successful was our hearer's prior knowledge of what "cat" means.

6.3. TWO WAYS OF DEFINING IN THE DIMENSION OF APPLICATION

Definitions which deal with the level of application are probably more primitive than those which deal with the level of signification. The former, or APPLICATIVE DEFINITIONS, are the kind we usually use with small children. If my young son asks me: "Daddy, what is a zinnia?" he is really requesting a definition. He wants to know what the word "zinnia" means. I might of course *begin* at the level of signification, and tell him that "zinnia" signifies a kind of flower. But if he is not completely satisfied and asks "What kind of flower?" we shall not get much further along this line. The account would soon either become too technical for him, or would reach the limit of my knowledge. For although I am reasonably sure that I can recognize a zinnia whenever I see one, I am quite unable to say just what characteristics a flower must have in order to be called a "zinnia." My son and I can both get along better at the applicative level. So I take him out into the garden and, pointing, say: "Here, David, these are all zinnias. Do you see?" I have helped him understand the meaning of the word by presenting particular concrete cases to which it applies. An applicative definition of this type may be called a PRESENTATIONAL DEFINITION. We explain the meaning of a word by presenting or pointing to one or more actual cases to which it applies.

Consider carefully both the strengths and the weaknesses of this presentational type of definition. Its strong points are that it is very vivid and concrete, and that it does not require much background, either in information or in grasp of the language. In its simplest form it might consist solely of a gesture of pointing combined with an utterance of the sound "zinnia." Its most obvious weakness is that it can be used only when actual instances to which the word applies are at hand. It has another less obvious but equally serious weakness. In spite of its great concreteness, it is quite unprecise. It does not adequately inform the questioner as to just what it is about these cases that entitles us to apply the word to them. Just what is it about these objects in the back yard that identifies them as zinnias? Is it that they have stems and leaves? Is it that they are orange and red? Is it that they are on the south side of the house? Is it that there are bees sitting on them? If these questions seem silly, it is only because you already know too much.

A closely related form of applicative definition is one which does not actually point to cases or *present* them, but which calls attention to them verbally, by *citing* them, even though they are not present at the time. We can explain the application of the word "cat" even when no cats are around, provided that our questioner already happens to be acquainted with one or more individuals who are cats. "You know Pandora, don't you? Well, she's a cat. And so are Chichibu and Tiny. So were Cherry and Meunière." Such an applicative definition proceeds by mentioning or *citing* one or more instances to which the word applies. We may call this way of explaining the applicative meaning of a word a CITATIONAL DEFINITION.

What are the strengths and weaknesses of a citational definition? Does it have any advantages over a presentational definition? Its most obvious advantage is that it can be used even when applicates are not present. But it does require more background, doesn't it? The questioner must already be acquainted with some applicates of the word, and he is still left in the dark as to just what it is about these cases that leads us to apply this word to them.

6.4. NEED FOR DEFINING IN THE DIMENSION OF SIGNIFICATION

As our linguistic skill, our background knowledge, and our demands for precision increase, we find it more and more important to make use of significative definitions. Dictionary definitions and definitions of terms in a science are very largely of this sort. We get to the place where we want, not merely to be acquainted with certain applicates of a word, but also to know precisely what it is that a thing must have in order for this particular word to apply to it. We want to be informed about the essential characteristics which constitute the word's signification.

We have already seen that a person may be able to use a word with a high degree of reliability at the level of application, without being able to give an adequate account of its signification. And yet for any advanced cognitive purposes, such definitions are essential. A botanist must not merely be able to recognize a zinnia when he sees one. He must also know just what it takes to be a zinnia.

6.5. GIVING A SIGNIFICATIVE DEFINITION BY GENUS AND DIFFERENCE

It might seem that any adequate significative definition would require an almost endless list of distinguishing characteristics. It is true that in beginning to open up a new field and to clarify the basic terms to be used within it, our initial significative definitions are likely to be rather cumbersome. But as our knowledge of the relations within the field and our terminology become more developed, very precise significative definitions can often be quite compactly given. This fact was recognized and explained over 2000 years ago by the Greek logician, Aristotle. We are still indebted to him for his account of significative definition.

For convenience, we may call a definition of this compact Aristotelian type a CLASS DIFFERENCE DEFINITION. The traditional name is definition *per genus et differentiam*. This means simply that we give the signification of the word in question by means of a general class and a differentiating characteristic. You are no doubt familiar, at least in a rough way, with the words "genus" and "species" as used in biology. The genus is the more *general* class which includes various more *specific* classes or species. The species are the subclasses of the general class. In biology, the levels of generality to which these two words, "genus" and "species," apply have in the course of time become quite rigidly fixed.

But in logic these terms are used in a purely relative way. Any class which comprises several subclasses is called a GENUS (plural: "genera") in relation to these subclasses. Any class which falls within a larger class is called a SPECIES of that class. Thus, college freshmen, sophomores, juniors, and seniors are four species of college student. The class of college students is a genus with respect to these four subclasses. On the other hand, the class of college students is itself a species of the more general class of students. The class of students is a genus with respect to this species. What does all this have to do with significative definitions?

A significative definition of the class-difference type treats the word to be defined as the name of a *species*. The species whose name we are defining is pinned down by doing two things:

1. By mentioning a more general class of which it is a sub-class—in other words by indicating a genus of it, and
2. By specifying some distinguishing characteristic of this species which makes it different from any other species of this general class.[2]

In picking a genus to be used in defining the name of a species falling under it, it is important to choose a genus that is not too much more general than the species whose name we are defining. The technical name of the kind of genus we want is PROXIMATE GENUS. "Proximate" means close to. Your proximate neighbors are those who live next door to you, as contrasted with other members of your neighborhood who live farther away.

Thus if I were trying to define "robin," I should have a poor definition from this point of view if I said: " 'Robin' means red-breasted organism." For although a robin is indeed an organism, the genus *organism* is of a high level of generality. The species *robin*, however, is quite specific. A better definition would be: " 'Robin' means red-breasted bird." This might do for a child who had never encountered red-breasted birds other than robins, but it is still too general for advanced purposes. A better definition would be: " 'Robin' means red-breasted thrush." *Thrush* is quite a proximate genus of *robin*. The unfortunate thing is that bluebirds are also thrushes, and also have red breasts. We really need to get down to the genus: brownish-gray thrush. Given this genus, mention of the differentiating characteristic of red-breastedness will give us, I believe, a precise definition.

---

[2] More precisely, we must distinguish this species from other *co-ordinate* species of this general class. CO-ORDINATE SPECIES are those at the same level of generality or specificity. Thus dog, cat, horse, and human being are co-ordinate species of animal. Mammal, horse, and collie, although they are all logical species (subclasses) of animal are not *co-ordinate* species. Horse is more specific than mammal, and collie is more specific than horse.

Just how proximate our selected genus must be depends in practice upon two considerations. (1) The most important one is that it must be proximate enough so that mention of it, together with mention of some differentiating characteristic, will uniquely specify the class (species) whose name we are defining. Our problem in defining "robin" will illustrate this point. We may also recall Aristotle's definition of "man" as the rational animal. His choice of *animal* is proximate enough, because he holds that man is the *only* rational animal. If frogs, say, were also rational, a more proximate genus, such as that of *mammal,* would have to be selected in defining the word "man." On the other hand, the genus *being* would not have been proximate enough for Aristotle's purpose. For he held that there are rational beings other than man, namely certain celestial intelligences, although these are not animals.

(2) The other practical consideration that must be kept in mind in deciding how proximate our genus should be is of quite a different sort. Unfortunately, it sometimes even comes into conflict with the first consideration, and we have to compromise in the light of the given situation. This second consideration is the knowledge and experience of our hearers. If for example we tell a small child that "robin" means such and such a kind of thrush, he may not understand what "thrush" means. In such a case, even at the cost of precision, we should have to use a more general and less proximate genus, such as *bird.* In practice, this second consideration often looms large, for a definition, no matter how precise, is no good if it fails in its essential purpose, which is to explain the meaning of the word to someone.

6.6. DISTINGUISHING DEFINITIONS FROM STATEMENTS ABOUT NONSEMANTICAL FACTS

In common practice, definitions of words are frequently given in a form which makes it difficult to distinguish them from nonsemantical statements. Thus, instead of saying that "clown" means funny man in the circus, we should commonly say: "A clown is a funny man in the circus." This latter definitional sentence is in form indistinguishable from the kind of sentence we use to express nonsemantical facts, for example: "A raincoat is a useful garment to have in April." This latter sentence does not explain what the word "raincoat" means. Rather, it is a statement about a particular kind of wearing apparel. In other words, a sentence having the general form of these last two examples may be intended in either of two quite different ways: (1) as a definition of what a particular word means, or (2) as a statement about some nonsemantical matter. This latter type of sentence is not a definition in our sense.

John Stuart Mill, the nineteenth-century British philosopher, made a practical suggestion that is of some help.[3] Suppose you encounter a sentence of the form: "A robin is a red-breasted thrush." Try putting quotes around "robin," drop the articles, and substitute the word "means" for "is." Thus: " 'Robin' means red-breasted thrush." Does the revised sentence fit in with the context? Does it seem an acceptable account of the intent of the original? If so, the original sentence was probably intended as a definition. On the other hand, if these substitutions do not seem to fit the context, the statement was presumably not a definitional or semantical one, but an assertion about a purported nonverbal fact.

• SOME REMINDERS

1. A definition is an explanation of the cognitive meaning of a word.
2. Different methods of offering such an explanation give rise to different types of definition. The following types are distinguished:
   a. synonymous
   b. applicative
      (1) presentational
      (2) citational
   c. significative
3. A compact but very precise form of significative definition is the *class-difference definition,* traditionally called definition *per genus et differentiam.* It treats the word being defined as the name of a species, and "pins down" this species by doing two things.
4. Each of these types of definition has certain strengths and weaknesses. These should be kept in mind in deciding which type to use in a given situation.
5. A practical device is explained which often helps to decide, in a given case, whether a sentence is intended as a definition.

---

[3] See John Stuart Mill: *A System of Logic,* Eighth Edition, New York, Harper and Brothers, 1881, p. 112.

APPLICATIONS

1. In general, no formal rules for good definitions can be given, since the adequacy of a definition will depend on the context in which it is used, including the background of the interpreter. Imagine circumstances in which each of the following attempts at definition would be ineffective, and explain why and how the definition might be improved.
   a. "Radar" means "radio detection and ranging."
   b. Utopia is nowhere.
   c. "Dog" means a kind of animal.
   d. "Green" means the color lying between yellow and blue on a color-wheel.
   e. Green is the color of the dress Barbara had on yesterday.
   f. "Green" means what you see when your retina is being stimulated by light-waves of a certain length.
   g. A *phot* is one lumen of light flux incident upon a surface one centimeter square.
   h. "Democracy" means what we have and the Russians don't.
   i. Love is the feeling you have when you really love somebody.
   j. A hole is to dig. (Title of a book of children's definitions.)
2. Give class-difference definitions of each of the following words:
   a. freshman   f. family
   b. planet   g. honesty
   c. refrigerator h. hat
   d. wheelbarrow   i. butter
   e. kitten   j. insurance policy
3. Using John Stuart Mill's practical test, decide which of the following sentences could reasonably be intended as definitions:
   a. This paper is white.
   b. "Paper" is a five-letter word.
   c. A shoat is a young hog.
   d. A standard piece of typing paper is $8\frac{1}{2}$ x 11.
   e. A triangle is a three-sided plane figure.
   f. She is the most beautiful girl in the world.
   g. A woman is an adult human female.
   h. Granville is in Ohio.
   i. The Lone Star State is Texas.
   j. God is love.

6.7. BUT WHOSE MEANING? CONVENTIONAL vs. STIPULATED DEFINITIONS

In an earlier discussion (Section 2.4) we noted that verbal signs are *artificial* in the sense that the connection between them and their meanings is created by man rather than discovered by him in nature. This does not mean that, for a given user, these connections are altogether *arbitrary*.

We are all born into some linguistic community whose language we are expected to acquire. Our effectiveness in communicating with our fellows depends upon our "learning the language." This involves not merely learning to make certain sounds and scratches, but to associate these sounds and scratches with meanings. These associations are indeed artificial, in the sense explained, but it is not in most cases for the individual to say what they shall be. To a great extent, he "inherits" these connections along with the sounds and scratches themselves. The words he is taught by the community already have certain customary or established meanings. To communicate with others in their language, he must learn what these are. Their language must become his. There is thus an important sense in which the usages or conventions of an established language confront the learner with something of the same impersonal objectivity he discovers in nonsemantical facts.

If a definition explains the cognitive meaning of a word, we may well ask, "Whose meaning?" The answer is usually "Our meaning," that is to say, the meaning that the word customarily or conventionally has in the linguistic community of which we are members. (In speaking of *the* customary or conventional meaning of a word, we are of course simplifying, for a great many words have more than one such meaning.) Most of the definitions we offer, then, and most of the definitions that are offered to us by others, are in effect reports of established or customary usage. A definition which thus explains the established or customary meaning which a word has in some linguistic community is called a CONVENTIONAL DEFINITION.

For most words that we use, fairly well established conventional meanings or ranges of meaning exist. When I say, "There is a book on the table," I am using words in a conventional sense which is known to everyone who understands everyday English. When, on the other hand, I describe a particular plant as having subterete scapes, with leaves coriacious, ovate to orbicular, often subcordate, the situation is different. For although I am still using words in a conventional sense, the convention is one shared not by all who speak English, but only by the linguistic community of botanists and others who have been initiated into the conventions of this specialized community.

But some definitions are not of this conventional sort. Instead of informing us about how a word has been used, they decree how a word shall be used. Rather than report a customary usage, they stipulate a new one. Such a STIPULATED DEFINITION creates by means of a resolve a connection between a verbal sign and a meaning. I may, for example, *stipulate* that the word "thrimb" is to mean a blue circle less than three inches in diameter. By a decree or resolution, I have created a relation between the word "thrimb" and a set of characteristics (its signification). You now understand what I mean by "thrimb." If you and I and others should happen to have frequent occasion to deal with blue circles, and if the fact that they were less than three inches in diameter had some important practical or theoretical bearing, we should quite likely need a word to apply to them. If my proposed name caught on, we should soon have a linguistic community using this word "thrimb" with this meaning. Thus among us a *verbal convention* would have been established. A relation between word and meaning which was originally created by stipulation would have become customary in our linguistic community.

Reflection on this example suggests that stipulation is prior to convention. All words which now have a conventional meaning must presumably have acquired that meaning originally by at least implicit stipulation. This introduction of new words, or of new meanings for old words, is a continuing process in any living language. "Radar" and "curium," for example, are words which have been recently introduced into English by stipulation.

6.8. CAN A DEFINITION BE TRUE OR FALSE?

We have many times found it important to stress the fact that the relation between a word and its meaning is an artificial one. We have said that the relation rests upon stipulation or convention. A definition, as we have seen, explains the (cognitive) meaning of a word. It either calls attention to some conventional relation between a word and its meaning (in other words, to a verbal habit of some linguistic community), or it creates by decree a new and as yet nonconventional relation between a word and a meaning. The artificial nature of the relation to which any definition points gives rise to the question: Can a definition be true or false? Is a definition the kind of thing to which the words "true" and "false" in their usual senses apply? Or to put the same question another way, can a definition be a *statement?*

An examination of this question should do two rather different things for us. (1) It should make us aware that although the word-meaning relation is an artificial one, there are none the less facts about words as well as facts about nonverbal things. (2) On the other hand, it should help us understand more clearly the type of situation in which there is no point in disputing about the "correct" meaning of a word.

Let us get the lay of the land by a survey of the various possible relations between a word and its meaning. By an "old word," in this connection, we shall mean a word already in use within a linguistic community. By an "old meaning" we shall understand a group of characteristics (signification) or a class of things (application) already discriminated within the experience of such a community. By a "new word" we shall understand any word which is not an old one in the sense defined, and similarly for "new meaning." We may distinguish four types of situation:

1. CONVENTIONAL USAGE: An old word used with its old meaning.
2. REDEFINING: An old word given a new meaning (or an old word given a *different* old meaning).
3. RENAMING: A new word for an old meaning (or a different old word for an old meaning).
4. COINING A WORD AND NAMING: A new word with a new meaning.

In any one of these situations, a definition might be called for. In the first case, a conventional definition would be needed; in the others, a stipulated one. In which of these situations, if any, would it make sense to raise the question of whether the given definition is true? In the first case our definition would involve an attempt to report an already existing usage for an already existing word. Here, obviously, it would be meaningful to ask whether the definition is true. Our definition would either correctly report the semantical fact of usage or it would not. Note carefully that the *artificial* nature of the relation between the established word and its conventional meaning does not affect the issue.

In the second case, we use an old word with a new meaning. Our definition, or rather redefinition, should aim at making clear what new meaning is being proposed for the old word. The Communists, for example, have undertaken just such a redefinition of the word "democracy." The question whether such a definition is true is an ambiguous one. If we are merely asking whether this is the way the word has been used in America and western Europe for the last century or so, the question makes sense. The answer is no, and the definition is false. But when we recognize that this redefinition is intended to link the old word (and we might add, its favorable *evocative* tone) with a new cognitive meaning, we see that the redefinition is in the nature of a decree rather than of a report of established usage. The Communists are saying, in effect, "Let 'democracy' mean thus and so" or "As far as we are concerned, 'democracy' shall be used to mean so-and-so." A stipulation is no more the kind of thing that can be true or false than a wish or a command is. "Would that I were a senior." "Turn in your papers when you leave." Such sentences are neither true nor false; in other words, they are not *statements*. Neither is a stipulation that "democracy" shall be used with a new range of meanings. The stipulated meaning may, to be sure, confuse those of us who use the word in a different meaning. In fact, it is probably not unfair to suggest that this confusion is counted upon by those who make this particular stipulation. For in the case of a word like "democracy," the *cognitive* meaning is by no means the only thing involved. The word "democracy" has for us definite evocative force. It would be to the advantage of the Communists to be able to transfer these favorable evocative overtones to the quite different cognitive meaning which they have in mind when they use the word "democracy." But consideration of these evocative factors raises some new problems, which we shall postpone until the following section, where we shall consider so-called "persuasive definitions."

The stipulation may succeed in establishing a new convention among Communists, as it appears to have done. Then, of course, it will make sense to ask, "Is this what 'democracy' conventionally means to Communists?" It is also reasonable to ask, "Is this what 'democracy' conventionally means to non-Communistic western Europeans and Americans?" These are of course quite different questions from the question of whether the *stipulation* is true or false.

When a person proposes a redefinition of a word we might also raise the questions: Does he really intend to stick to it? Is he as a matter of fact going to use the word in this announced way? These also are questions of a factual nature, and our answers again will be either true or false. But we must not confuse such questions with the quite different one of whether the redefinition itself is true or false. In so far as the redefinition is simply a stipulation, it is neither true nor false.

For another example of an old word with new meanings, we may turn to the sciences. When a scientist finds it necessary to name a newly discriminated set of characteristics, he will perhaps most often coin a new word. (This would be an example of our fourth type of situation: new word with new meaning.) But there have been some interesting cases in which, instead of coining a new word, an old word has been redefined.

Precisely this procedure has been followed in physics in the use of such words as "red," "blue," and "green." At the level of common-sense experience, these words are names of certain visual experiences or sensible qualities. When the physicist uses these words, he applies them to something radically different, namely, to light waves of certain lengths. Now that this originally stipulated physical meaning has become adopted by other physicists, it forms a part of the conventional language of physicists. Difficulties henceforth arise only when we get confused about contexts, or when we shift from the common-sense meaning to the physical meaning, without being aware of what is going on. In order to see the kind of confusion that can result from such unawareness, consider the question: "Is grass green even when no one is looking at it?" Analyze the ambiguity by means of MacKaye's Method, and show that it stems from confusing two languages, that of common sense and that of physics.

In the third type of situation (renaming), our definition explains that a new term is to be attached to an old, already discriminated meaning. This again is, in the first instance, a matter of stipulation. Such a definition, viewed as a stipulation, is obviously neither true nor false. We may, as in the above case, raise such *other* questions as: Has someone actually proposed that this new word be used for this old meaning? Is he going to abide by this proposal? Are other people adopting it? Is this word becoming conventional in certain circles? Such questions are about factual matters. Hence their answers are either true or false.

When a new set of characteristics is discriminated, or a new type of thing is discovered or invented, a name is needed. Sometimes an old word is, as we have seen, redefined to signify this new meaning. At other times—and this is our fourth situation—a new word is coined. Here the stipulative nature of the definition which explains the meaning of this new word is even more obvious than in the preceding two types of situation. Similar considerations apply.

6.9. PERSUASIVE "DEFINITIONS"

Thus far we have been considering definitions as cases of the cognitive use of language. Their function is to explain. The definitions we have ex-

amined have been intended either as explanations of how a word is customarily used (conventional definitions) or as explanations of how it is
proposed to use a word (stipulated definitions).

But sometimes we encounter a sentence which, although it has the
form of a cognitive definition, has quite a different intent. Its aim is not
to convey information, but rather to evoke feeling or influence attitudes.
Its appeal is emotional rather than rational. To distinguish this type of
"definition" clearly from cognitive definitions, we may call it a PERSUASIVE
DEFINITION.[4]

An extreme example of such a persuasive definition is Jack London's
"definition" of *scab:* "A scab is a two-legged animal with a cork-screw soul,
a waterlogged brain, a combination backbone of jelly and glue. Where
others have hearts, he carries a tumor of rotten principles." If you are in
doubt about how such a persuasive definition differs from a cognitive
definition, contrast it with the following cognitive definition of the same
word from Webster: "*scab:* a workman who works for lower wages than,
or under conditions contrary to, those prescribed by the trade union; also,
one who takes the place of a workman on strike."

Such an extreme case as London's is not difficult to detect. Its purpose
is obviously not primarily cognitive, and its choice of language reveals
its persuasive intent. Subtler cases are both more frequent and more
troublesome. As Stevenson points out (*op. cit.,* p. 210), the person giving a
persuasive definition of a word may appear to be attempting only to
introduce greater precision in the use of a word that is customarily used
rather loosely. Let us work up an example of our own.

The dictionary defines "patriotism" as devotion to one's country. This
definition, we may assume, has a wholly cognitive intent. In spite of the
fact that the word "patriotism" has evocative associations for all of us,
this definition does not seek to capitalize upon them for persuasive purposes. But note that it is after all rather vague. One might continue by
seeking to elucidate this cognitive meaning through a fuller definition of
the word. On the other hand, this vagueness of the original definition
might be exploited for persuasive purposes. Under the guise of offering a

---

[4] This use of the adjective "persuasive" conforms to that in Chapter 3, where we
adopted Stebbing's distinction between "persuading" and "convincing." The term
"persuasive definition" was used by C. L. Stevenson in an article in *Mind* for July
1938. See also Chapter IX of his book, *Ethics and Language,* New Haven, Yale University Press, 1944. Our analysis follows the general lines of his treatment.

fuller cognitive definition, one might seek to transfer the emotive tone attaching to the word "patriotism" to a particular position or set of values which one wanted to promote. Stevenson notes that a person giving a persuasive definition often appeals to the "true" or the "real" meaning of the word. In fact, the presence of these adjectives is often a practical guide to the fact that a persuasive definition is being offered (*op. cit.*, p. 213).

Let us continue with our example of "patriotism." The emotions aroused by the word have for the past several centuries been associated with the interests of nation-states. In the interests of world government, one might persuasively define "patriotism" in some such way as this: " 'Patriotism,' in its deeper sense, means loyalty to the fatherland of all mankind—the world." We may contrast this with another persuasive definition, reflecting a very different scale of values, offered in the interests of totalitarian nationalism: "Real patriotism," a totalitarian orator might persuasively urge, "is a loyalty to the state so deep that both the personal interests of the individual and the alien interests of the outside world are recognized as evils which must be rooted out in order that the supreme interests of the nation may prevail."

We are not saying that the use of persuasive definitions is always illegitimate. We are however reminding ourselves once again that the cognitive function is by no means the sole function of language. When our own aim is cognitive, we must recognize persuasive definitions for what they are. We must not let their form deceive us into accepting them as cognitive in function and intent. We need to be on the lookout for persuasive definitions, and to develop practical skill in detecting and evaluating them. Here are some practical suggestions:

FOR DETECTING PERSUASIVE DEFINITIONS

1. When the word being defined is one that has strong emotional associations, watch out. This is the kind of word most susceptible to persuasive definition.
2. When the definer urges that he is setting forth the "true" or the "real" definition of a word, or is explaining the word in its "deeper sense," watch out. He may be entering upon a persuasive definition.
3. If the language used in defining the word is itself emotively toned and evocative in effect (i.e. if it stirs your feelings) watch out. The definition is likely a persuasive one.

FOR ANALYZING PERSUASIVE DEFINITIONS

1. When you detect what appears to be a persuasive definition, ask yourself: what is the cognitive core of this definition? Try to state this cognitive core in neutral language.
2. How does this cognitive core compare with perhaps more usual cognitive uses of the word? What characteristics usually included in the signification of the word have been left out? What ones are being stressed? What unusual characteristics are being introduced?
3. Ask yourself: what is the specific intent of this persuasion? What values are being upheld? What attitudes are being advocated? What do I think of them, on independent grounds (i.e. quite apart from the persuasive appeal that is here being made)?

• SOME REMINDERS

6. The question of whether a definition is the sort of thing that can be true or false Is ambiguous. The answer will depend upon (a) the kind of situation in which the definition is being offered and (b) the interpretation we are making of it.
7. An account of a customary meaning of an established word will be true or false, depending upon whether the account does or does not accurately tell how the word is as a matter of fact customarily used.
8. A statement which announces that someone intends to use a word in such and such a meaning is true or false, depending upon whether it does or does not accurately state his intention.
9. At times we have cases like those mentioned in (7) and (8) in mind when we ask whether a definition is the kind of thing that can be true or false.
10. On the other hand, a stipulated definition, viewed merely as a resolve or a suggestion that such and such a word be used to mean thus and so, can be neither true nor false, any more than a wish or a command can be.
11. Some sentences having the form of a cognitive definition are not actually intended to convey information so much as to arouse feelings and shape attitudes.
12. Such persuasive "definitions" are often deceptive, because they may appear to be merely introducing greater precision in the cognitive use of a word.
13. Practical suggestions are given both for detecting and for analyzing persuasive definitions.

APPLICATIONS

1. Offer persuasive definitions of each of the following words, from the points of view indicated:
   a. "Christianity"
      1. from the point of view of one who wanted to stress and defend the institutional aspects of Christianity.
      2. from the point of view of one who wanted to stress and emphasize the element of immediate personal religious experience.
      3. from the point of view of one who felt that modern man no longer needs religion.
      4. from the point of view of one who wished to stress the "social gospel" and the reform of society.
   b. "Wall Street"
      1. from the point of view of a speaker who wished to influence his hearers to take a favorable attitude toward it.
      2. from the point of view of a speaker who wished to influence his hearers to take a hostile attitude toward it.
   c. "marriage"
      1. from the point of view of a cynical old bachelor.
      2. from the point of view of a happily married person.
      3. from the point of view of a romantic adolescent.
   d. "science"
      1. from the point of view of one who believed that the world's troubles would all be solved if men would face them scientifically.
      2. from the point of view of one who believed that the world's troubles can be solved only through moral and religious insight, inaccessible to the scientific approach.
2. Find some persuasive definitions and analyze them in accordance with the suggestions given in Section 6.9.

PART II

SYNTACTICS

THE LOGIC OF

VALID REASONING

CHAPTER 7

THE NATURE OF SYNTACTICS

PREVIEW

This chapter introduces you to the second area of logical concern, that of syntactics or formal logic. We shall consider the types of question dealt with by syntactics, and shall get acquainted with some of the basic concepts needed for dealing with these questions.

7.1. SYNTACTICS AND TWO COMMON-SENSE QUESTIONS

"SO WHAT?"

All of us have been irritated on occasion by the skeptical "So what?" of a friend. His question sometimes suggests that he thinks *we* don't know what we're talking about. Perhaps more often, however, it is simply a blunt way of letting us know that *he* doesn't see what we are driving at. He may be in complete agreement with us as to the facts of the case, but he wants to know what we think follows from them. Formal logic or SYNTACTICS [1] studies such questions as: Given a body of information, then what? Given a set of premises, what conclusions are we warranted in drawing from them—not in some loose casual way, but in a "strictly logical" manner?

[1] "Syntactics" is a contemporary logical term borrowed from linguistics. In the field of language study, *syntactics* deals with the rules of correct linguistic form, the principles in accordance with which words may be correctly put together to form larger verbal structures, namely, sentences. By analogy, logical syntactics deals with the rules of correct logical form, the principles in accordance with which statements may be correctly put together to form larger logical structures, namely, conclusive arguments.

In the present book, we are not concerned with what has come to be called *pure syntactics*, a discipline which deals with abstract and uninterpreted structures. Our concern is more practical, since we want to discover the rules which determine the validity of actual arguments. We shall deal not with uninterpreted marks, but with signs which have meaning in concrete arguments. Part II, in other words, purposely retains a strong semantical slant.

Certain statements follow logically from certain others. From the statements, "If it rains before evening, we'll have supper at home" and "It rains before evening," a further statement follows logically: "We'll have supper at home." We answer the question "So what?" by indicating a conclusion which we believe is guaranteed by the given statements.

"HOW COME?"

But often our problem is just the reverse. Instead of being asked to show what certain premises entail, we are challenged to support the conclusion we have announced. We are continually being put on the spot to justify the beliefs we hold, to give grounds to support the assertions we make.

> "Well, I guess we'll have supper at home after all."
> "How come?"
> "Well, it's raining, isn't it? And didn't we agree that if it rained before evening we'd have supper at home?"

We answer the question "How come?" by bringing forth evidence which we believe justifies our conclusion. Syntactics is concerned, then, not only with the question of what given information strictly implies, but also with the related question of what evidence is needed to guarantee or validate a given conclusion.

7.2. SYNTACTICS AND EMPIRICS

In many cases, our answers fall short of that conclusiveness which is the concern of syntactics. Often we can do no more than point to evidence which makes our conclusion more or less probable. And often this is all that is expected of us.

> "I believe it will rain before evening."
> "How come?"
> "I was just listening to the weather forecast on the radio."

We all know from experience that weather forecasts are sometimes mistaken, but we also know that they are more likely right than not, and that they are in any case more reliable than our own private hunches. It is therefore reasonable to accept a weather forecast, even though the forecast is only probably correct. Yet a person might, without contradicting himself, agree that the official forecast predicted rain, and yet hold that it was not really going to rain after all. In an argument of the conclusive type, however, one can never accept the premises without being logically committed to the conclusion which strictly follows from them.

Arguments which seek to establish probabilities are a very common and important type in human thinking, especially in the realm of factual inquiry. The analysis of such arguments does not form part of the task of syntactics, but will concern us in Part III where we shall study *empirics*, the logic of factual inquiry. Syntactics or formal logic, our present concern, deals with arguments in which we seek to bring forth reasons that "clinch" the argument, reasons that are conclusive, so that if one accepts the reasons, he cannot with consistency reject the conclusion. Such arguments are often described as involving a NECESSARY INFERENCE, in contrast to the *probable inferences* involved in most factual inquiry.[2]

An argument which claims to involve a necessary inference is called a DEDUCTIVE ARGUMENT, and the type of reasoning involved is called DEDUCTION.

> "Just look at that beautiful insect!"
> "Well, it's beautiful all right, but it really can't be an insect, you know."
> "How come?"
> "Because all insects have only six legs, and that thing has eight."

If our hearer agrees with us that all insects have only six legs, and if he also agrees that the animal before us does *not* have only six legs, then he must, to be logically consistent, also agree that the animal is not an insect. The reasons are sufficient to dictate, to guarantee, the conclusion. The conclusion, in the strictest sense, "follows from" the reasons given. The line of reasoning here is a conclusive one; the argument is a "clincher."

In this area of our work, then, we shall be concerned with arguments of this latter type, and with arguments which may appear to be of this conclusive type, but are really not so. We want to discover what determines whether an argument is conclusive or not. We want to find out how

---

[2] The term *probable inference* as applied to such arguments is perhaps not altogether clear. It does not of course mean that an inference is only *probably* involved in passing from the premises to the conclusion. It rather means that the structure of the argument is such that the evidence creates a *probability* in favor of the conclusion, but does not guarantee it.

we can tell what strictly follows from given information, and how we can avoid logical blunders in thinking things through.

7.3. SOME BASIC TERMS

In these opening paragraphs we have been speaking informally, for the most part using familiar words taken from everyday speech. We have spoken of "reasons" and "evidence" in relation to certain "beliefs" or "conclusions" for which they provide "grounds," and which they "dictate" or "guarantee." This everyday language helps us get started, but before we go further, we should get familiar with the more precise terminology which logicians use in talking about these matters.

One such mildly technical term we have already used, namely, ARGU-MENT. In ordinary speech, this word perhaps most often means a dispute or controversy. In syntactics, however, it means simply *the verbal or symbolic expression of a line of reasoning.* Any line of reasoning proceeds *from* something (reasons or grounds) *to* something else. In syntactics, we regularly call statements expressing these reasons the PREMISES of the argument. A statement which is held to follow from these premises is called a CONCLUSION.

Logicians do not ordinarily use the excellent slang word, "clincher," for an argument in which the conclusion follows rigorously from the premises; they have a slang or jargon of their own, and call such an argument valid. The word "valid," of course, is common enough in every-day speech, but it is crucial to see that it is here being used in a special restricted sense. In formal logic we never call an argument valid unless the given premises are such that if you accept them, you are logically committed to accepting the conclusion, too.

In the light of this preliminary discussion, we may now give a more precise definition of what is meant by a VALID ARGUMENT. This definition may be stated in either of two equivalent ways. First, to say that an argument is valid means that the premises are by themselves sufficient to dictate or guarantee the conclusion. Second, to say that an argument is valid means that its premises and conclusion are structurally related in such a way that *if* the premises are all true, then the conclusion *must* also be true.

This "must" indicates a logical necessity; to accept the premises of a valid argument while rejecting the conclusion would be to contradict oneself. As we shall see more fully in Chapter 8, an argument is valid, not because of its specific content or subject matter, but because of the way the argument hangs together. It is valid, not because of what it is "about," but because of its logical pattern, structure, or *form*. It is in this sense that validity is said to be a *formal* matter.

The conclusion of a valid argument may also be called valid. But note that this label applies to the conclusion, not as an isolated statement, but because it is related to the premises in a certain way. To speak of a valid conclusion is thus just a shorthand way of speaking of the conclusion of a valid argument. The fact that a conclusion is valid does not in itself throw any light on whether the conclusion is factually true or not. This may at first seem rather puzzling, so we had better explore more fully the relation between validity and truth.

7.4. VALIDITY AND TRUTH

As normal human beings, we are usually concerned in our thinking with something more than the question of formal correctness or validity. We want, if possible, to arrive at the truth. Validity is quite different from truth, and it is essential not to confuse the two.

Validity is a matter of how statements in an argument are related to each other; it is a matter of how they hang together. Truth is a matter of how statements are related to something other than themselves, something that we commonly mean when we speak of "the facts."

The problem of "determining the facts" will occupy us in the third area of our work, for the principles of factual inquiry are the concern of empirics. At present it will be sufficient if we see clearly that the question of the validity of an argument and the question of the factual truth of a statement are two quite different questions. The most vivid way of discovering this is to consider a number of simple arguments, each of which is valid. We shall not at present undertake to *prove* that these arguments are valid. Instead we shall try to pick examples that are simple enough so that we can with fair assurance "sense" or "feel" their validity on the basis of our present logical habits. We shall also select statements the truth or falsity of which are readily known.

Here are four arguments, each consisting of two premises and a conclusion which validly follows from them. The long line which separates the premises from the conclusion performs a function somewhat similar to the line we draw under a column of figures to be added. As we use it here, to separate the premises of an argument from its conclusion, the line may always be read as "therefore."

1.	All cats are mammals.	(True)
	All mammals are vertebrates.	(True)
	All cats are vertebrates.	(True)
2.	All cats are birds.	(False)
	All birds are vertebrates.	(True)
	All cats are vertebrates.	(True)
3.	All cats are vegetables.	(False)
	All vegetables are vertebrates.	(False)
	All cats are vertebrates.	(True)
4.	All cats are vegetables.	(False)
	All vegetables are planets.	(False)
	All cats are planets.	(False)

Examine each of these four examples. Recall what we mean by "valid." Can you see that each of these four arguments is valid? Could you, in any one of these cases, accept the premises and escape the conclusion?

Once you have seen that each of these four arguments is valid, consider the factual truth or falsity of the statements that make them up. There is nothing particularly puzzling about the first and the fourth cases. In the first, we begin with true premises and argue validly to a true conclusion. In the fourth, we begin with false premises and argue validly to a false conclusion. It does not seem very surprising that "thinking straight" from *false* premises should lead to a false conclusion.

Example 2, however, is more puzzling. Here, although one of our premises is false, we are able to draw a valid conclusion which happens to be true. This, however, can only be attributed to luck, or more precisely to the fact that I carefully constructed the argument to illustrate the point that a true conclusion may *happen* to follow validly from premises, one of which is false. If this is unsettling, Example 3 is even more so. For here *both* premises are false, yet the conclusion (which follows validly) happens to be true.

In the light of these four examples, it might at first seem as if there were no good reason for worrying about validity, since it appears that almost anything can happen. But this would be to overlook one very important case which can never happen. It can never be that from true premises, a false conclusion validly follows. The great practical importance of validity lies in the fact that *if* we begin with true premises and argue validly, we are bound to end up with a true conclusion.

But what of those frequent cases in which we are not sure whether our premises are true or false? Even here valid argument may serve an important function by helping us discover that something is wrong with our premises. For whenever a valid argument leads us to a conclusion which we know to be false, we can be sure that at least one of our premises is false.

7.5. ARGUMENTS THAT ARE NOT VALID

In this section, we shall consider three different ways in which an argument can be not valid. The first two ways are properly considered defects, although the first of the two is often easily remedied. The third way is not properly considered a defect at all.

AN ARGUMENT MAY BE MERELY INCOMPLETELY EXPRESSED

In everyday discourse we seldom express our reasoning completely. We assume a great deal of common information, and leave it to our hearer to supply premises which we do not take time to state. For example, in Case 1 above, if we were backing up our conclusion that all cats are vertebrates, we might merely say something like, "Why, of course cats are vertebrates, because *all* mammals are." In this form, the argument would not be valid, because the single premise, "All mammals are vertebrates," is not sufficient to guarantee the conclusion, "All cats are vertebrates." But in offering this condensed or incomplete argument, we should normally assume that our hearer shared with us the additional information that all cats are mammals. Once this additional assumption is explicitly introduced into the argument, the argument becomes valid. A practical difficulty which we often face in evaluating the reasoning of another person is in knowing just what he is assuming, in addition to what he explicitly states.

Some arguments, then, are defective simply because they are incomplete. They become valid once the unexpressed assumptions are brought into the open and incorporated into the premises. Such arguments are traditionally called ENTHYMEMES, from a Greek word indicating that part of the argument is "held in the mind" rather than being explicitly asserted.

With respect to validity, such arguments are clearly not valid as they stand. It seems a little strong to call them "invalid," however, for this name seems more appropriately reserved for the type which we shall next discuss. Enthymemes which become valid once the intended assumptions are made explicit may perhaps better be referred to as PREVALID, for this term suggests that they are on the way to being valid.[3]

AN ARGUMENT MAY CONTAIN A LOGICAL BLUNDER

Many arguments are not valid for a quite different reason. They commit some error in argumentation. In the late summer and early fall of 1950, anyone advocating a cessation of hostilities in Korea was likely to be accused of Communist sympathies. A movie studio even temporarily suspended production of a film dealing with the career of Hiawatha (who "smoked the calumet, the Peace Pipe, as a signal to the nations") on the grounds that the film might be labeled "Communistic." The general pattern of reasoning behind such cases seemed to be:

> All Communist sympathizers are advocating peace.
> He is advocating peace.
> _____
> He is a Communist sympathizer.

When our emotions are stirred and we feel deeply about the issues involved, we are likely to swallow and to commit logical blunders like this. In a different and less controversial setting, the same blunder would be detected by a six-year-old, if we were to hold up an apple and argue:

[3] As a purely formal exercise, virtually any enthymeme can be made valid by introducing an assumption, no matter how absurd factually, which will satisfy the formal requirements. Consider: "Of course she's over ten feet tall; she's a human being, isn't she?" The argument becomes valid if we supply the assumption, "All human beings are over ten feet tall." In everyday life, our rejection of this enthymeme would hinge, not on the question of validity, but on the factual question of the falsity of the supplied assumption.

When we are trying to supply not whatever may be formally required, but rather the assumption that is actually being made by the speaker, the situation may be different. For we may find that when he brings the assumption out into the open, we are willing to grant it, but that his argument still fails to make its point because it contains a formal fallacy.

All oranges are fruit.
This is a fruit.
———————————————
This is an orange.

There is, of course, a difference in the two cases, but it is not a difference of logical form. Both arguments are equally fallacious. The difference between them is that even the six-year-old can tell by looking that an apple is not an orange, whereas even a mature adult may have difficulty in determining whether a peace advocate does or does not have Communist sympathies.

An argument, then, may fail to be valid, not because it is incompletely expressed, but because it contains a FORMAL FALLACY, a defect in its logical structure, so that the argument does not hang together. Such an argument is called INVALID.

AN ARGUMENT MAY AIM, NOT AT CONCLUSIVENESS, BUT AT PROBABILITY

Still other arguments are not valid for a quite different reason. They make no claim to conclusiveness, but are concerned with establishing a probability in favor of some conclusion. Such arguments, as we saw earlier, are said to set forth a *probable inference* rather than a necessary one. Arguments of this type will, as we have noted, be examined more fully in Part III.

For the present, let us simply consider one more example of probable inference. An inspector for the Department of Agriculture certifies a carload of butter to be in good condition, not because he has conclusive evidence that each and every pound of butter in the car is in good condition, but because a reasonably wide sampling of the carload reveals that all the butter sampled is in good condition. His evidence does not dictate or guarantee the conclusion, "All the butter in this car is in good condition." It does, however, establish a reasonable probability in favor of that conclusion. In many cases, this is all we can or should ask for.

It should be apparent that arguments of this third type are not properly regarded as defective simply because they are not conclusive. Although they are not valid, arguments of this type often succeed in doing precisely what they set out to do, namely, to establish a probability in favor of some assertion. Here again, the term *invalid* seems somewhat strong and misleading as applied to arguments of this type, for the term suggests a defect. Such arguments may perhaps be better referred to by the more neutral term, NONVALID.[4]

• SOME REMINDERS

1. Two types of practical problem with which formal logic helps us are (1) determining what conclusions are warranted on the basis of certain information and (2) determining what evidence will adequately ground or justify a particular conclusion.
2. An argument is the verbal or symbolic expression of a line of reasoning, and consists of premises and conclusion.
3. A valid argument is such that the given premises are by themselves sufficient to guarantee or dictate the conclusion.
4. If the premises of a valid argument are all true, the conclusion is necessarily true too.
5. The question of the validity of an argument must be clearly distinguished from the question of the truth or falsity of the statements that make it up.
6. Some arguments are not valid, but this is not always to be considered a defect.
7. Arguments that are not valid may be either prevalid, invalid, or nonvalid.

APPLICATIONS

1. In each case, try to decide whether the argument in question is best regarded as valid, invalid, prevalid, or nonvalid. Give your reasons for classifying it as you do, and be prepared to consider the reasons of others who propose to classify it differently.
   a. It is unlikely that she is as young as she claims. Just look at all those gray hairs!
   b. It can't really be a peach, because all peaches are fuzzy.
   c. Some books must be novels, since all novels are books.
   d. This stone can't be a rolling one, for it has moss on it.
   e. I've told you at least ten times that it's dangerous to do that; you should know better by this time.
   f. It is clear that all squares are quadrilaterals, because some quadrilaterals are squares.
   g. I expect he is absent-minded too, because *all* the professors I have ever met have been absent-minded.

[4] Here again, the distinction between "invalid" and "nonvalid" is not a purely formal one, since it involves judging the aim or intent of the argument in question. If in doubt, label an inconclusive argument "invalid."

h. Since today is Monday, tomorrow must be Tuesday.
i. If you succeed, you must have tried, because if you really try, you'll always succeed.
j. I doubt that I can jump across this creek, because I've never jumped that far before.

CHAPTER 8

ANALYZING AN ARGUMENT

PREVIEW

This chapter will help you understand more clearly the meaning of the word "formal" as applied to this area of logic. We shall see that the validity of an argument depends upon its logical form. We shall also consider in a preliminary way how we may analyze an argument to determine whether it makes its point or not.

8.1. LOGICAL FORM, THE LOCUS OF VALIDITY

The validity of an argument turns out to depend, not on *what* we are talking about, but rather upon the manner in which we talk about it. More precisely, validity stems not from the content of our argument, but rather from how the argument hangs together, that is, from its pattern or form. The present area of our work is traditionally called "formal logic" because it is concerned with the *forms* of statements and arguments, and with the rules of patterning which determine validity.

In the preceding chapter we set forth four arguments having to do with cats. We claimed that all four arguments were valid, and since the arguments were not complicated, you were probably able to see this even though you had not yet made any systematic study of the principles of validity. What you really were basing your judgment of validity on was, whether you realized it or not, the form which the arguments took.

Let us look again at Example 1. We find that certain words in the argument have to do primarily with CONTENT; they tell us what the argument is about. Other words seem to serve a rather different function; they show the pattern or FORM of the argument.

Let's begin by putting parentheses around the content-words:

102

> All (cats) are (mammals).
> All (mammals) are (vertebrates).
> _____
> All (cats) are (vertebrates).

We might at first suppose that we could indicate the form of this argument adequately by simply dropping out the content-words, leaving a kind of skeleton:

> All ( ) are ( ).
> All ( ) are ( ).
> _____
> All ( ) are ( ).

But it is clear that we have really thrown out too much. Although the particular content-words are not important in indicating form, their *positions* are important. To preserve the form of the original argument requires that the *same* content be supplied after "All" in one premise and in the conclusion, that another content be supplied both after "are" in one premise and after "are" in the conclusion, and that still other content be supplied for both the remaining gaps.

We may preserve this important formal element of position, while abstracting from any *particular* content, by inserting letters in the proper places:

> All a are b.
> All b are c.
> _____
> All a are c.

The resulting diagram or pattern we may call an ARGUMENT-FORM. In this form, "a" should be thought of, not as an abbreviation for "cats," but merely as a convenient way of indicating that *whatever* content we supply in the one gap labeled "a" must also be supplied in the other gap labeled "a." Similar considerations apply, of course, to the "b" and the "c."

A letter or other symbol used in this way is called a VARIABLE. An argument-form yields a specific argument when content-words are substituted for the variables in the argument-form. The above argument-form is called a VALID ARGUMENT-FORM, because a valid argument results when content-words are thus substituted.

Just as the above diagram is not itself an argument, but merely an empty argument-form, so the expression "All a are b" is not a statement, but rather what we may call a STATEMENT-FORM. That it is not a statement will become clear if you recall that statements are either true or false, and then ask yourself whether "All a are b" is true or not. This statement-form yields statements when we substitute appropriate content-words for the variables.

Letters which serve as variables should be clearly distinguished from letters serving simply as shorthand or ABBREVIATION SYMBOLS for words or statements. When I initial a note "MHH," these three letters stand, not for any three names one may wish to substitute, but rather for my own. They serve as abbreviations, not as variables. Similarly, if we symbolize the statement "All cats are vertebrates" by the expression "All c is v," the letters "c" and "v" are not variables, but abbreviation symbols. The expression is thus not a statement-form, but rather a concrete *statement* written in a shorthand manner.

Remember that lecture on brictoplats? You can now see why you were able to tell what logically followed from the lecturer's "information" about brictoplats, even though you didn't know what "brictoplats," "tryphoglyptera," and "grandopores" meant. You *did* understand the form-words, "all," "no," and so on, and although the content-words were nonsensical, you were able to recognize the pattern of their recurrence. Thus you were able to grasp the *form* involved, even though you did not understand the content. And it is the form, not the content, that determines validity.

• SOME REMINDERS

1. The validity of an argument depends upon its form.
2. In a given argument, some words express form, while others give content.
3. The form of an argument is indicated in part by the form-words, and in part by the *position* or pattern of recurrence of the content-words.
4. The form of an argument may be represented by abstracting from the specific content through the use of variables in place of the given content-words.
5. The form of a statement may also be represented by this means.
6. A statement-form is not itself a statement, for it is neither true nor false.
7. Variables must be distinguished from abbreviations.

APPLICATIONS

1. Go back over the examples of arguments used in earlier parts of the text, and diagram their forms as best you can. Distinguish between form-words and content-words. Note any similarities of form between arguments having different content.
2. In each of the following prevalid arguments, distinguish between premises and conclusion. Make any needed assumptions explicit. (Write them out, but put square brackets [ ] around them to show they were not actually expressed in the original.) Where assumptions are needed, try to select those which, along with the given premises, will "clinch" the argument.
    a. He must have run a long way—just see how he's panting.
    b. Plato's dialogs are worth a lifetime of study, because they take us from the level of flux and change to the level of eternal realities.
    c. If those aren't false eyelashes she's wearing, I'll eat my shirt.
    d. No wonder I feel happy today. A bright October day always lifts my spirits.
    e. Boys are bound to get into a fight now and then, so don't blame George too much.

8.2. GETTING THE DRIFT OF AN ARGUMENT

In analyzing an actual argument presented in everyday discourse, the first thing to do (once any basic semantical difficulties have been cleared up) is to find out what the conclusion or "point" of the argument is. What is the argument driving at?

It would be naive to suppose that the conclusion is necessarily the last remark made. Frequently enough, we state our conclusion first, and then give the supporting evidence:

> He must be crazy. He was actually talking to the fish in the aquarium. Nobody in his right mind would do a thing like that.

Or again, we may set forth part of the evidence, then state our conclusion, and then round out our argument by giving the rest of the evidence:

> He was actually talking to the fish in the aquarium. He must be crazy. Nobody in his right mind would do a thing like that.

Sometimes we feel that the conclusion is so obvious that we do not even bother to state it. We give our premises, and leave it to our hearer to "draw his own conclusions":

Yes, he was actually talking to the fish in the aquarium.
Surely nobody in his right mind would do a thing like that.

For the purpose of formal analysis, we regularly state the conclusion last, separating it from the premises by a line, as in some earlier examples. But how, when an argument is stated informally, can we tell which of the statements are intended as premises, and which as conclusion? In actual conversation, the context, or emphasis of the voice, or various gestures help. But perhaps even more important are the various linking words we use in order to indicate to our hearer the drift of the argument. You will find it helpful to keep a list of words commonly used to introduce premises, and another list of words used to indicate conclusions. In the above examples, the word "must" in the conclusion helps to show that we regard the statement in which it appears as a logical consequence of the other statements. Here are some other examples to help you get started. You must be on your guard, however, for some of these words have other normal uses, too.

PREMISE INDICATORS	CONCLUSION INDICATORS
"since . . ."	"thus . . ."
"because . . ."	"hence . . ."
"for . . ."	"therefore . . ."
"inasmuch as . . ."	"consequently . . ."
"granted that . . ."	"so, you see . . ."
	"it follows that . . ."

8.3. GETTING ASSUMPTIONS INTO THE OPEN

When you are dealing with real flesh-and-blood arguments (in contrast to the neatly arranged skeletons found in logic texts), you will find that a good deal is taken for granted. We saw, in discussing arguments that are not valid, that many of them fail to be valid simply because they are not fully expressed. Certain assumptions are being made, and once these are brought out into the open, we may find that the argument, when so supplemented, becomes valid.

At other times, we may find that the assumptions needed to validate an argument are (on factual, not formal grounds) so extreme, or so obviously false, that no one would fall for the argument once these assumptions were clearly stated. So in either case, it is important to get the assumptions out into the open, to state them explicitly, so we can see what they are and see how they fit into the argument.

In formal analysis, it is helpful to place these supplied assumptions in square brackets, so that we can more easily remember what was actually stated and what we are taking to be unexpressed but intended assumptions.

Often, of course, the assumptions that the speaker intends us to supply are obvious. In the example of the man who talked to the fish, it seems pretty clear that we are intended to treat the expressions: "not in one's right mind" and "crazy" as—for the purpose of the argument—synonymous.

At other times it is not at all clear what assumptions are being drawn upon, and we must either use our ingenuity, or, when possible, question the speaker further. Unexpressed assumptions are conducive to muddy and to crooked thinking. We must do our best to force assumptions into the open.

8.4. HOW CAN WE TELL WHETHER THE ARGUMENT MAKES ITS POINT?

Once we have clearly distinguished between premises and conclusion of an argument, and have made its unexpressed assumptions explicit, it remains to find out whether the argument really makes its point. Are the grounds offered sufficient to guarantee the conclusion? Is the argument valid? How can we tell? We may distinguish three approaches to the problem.

THE COMMON-SENSE APPROACH

Up to this point, we have chosen rather simple examples, and have for the most part been trusting our logical "feelings" in deciding whether the arguments are valid or not. Often this approach gets us by; we all have logical habits that are fairly reliable in the simpler cases.

This approach is the most concrete. It sticks close to the given subject matter, and does not require any special training. But it soon reaches its limits. When the material becomes complex, or when the subject matter is emotionally charged, our "feelings" of what logically follows are less dependable. The common-sense approach to decisions about validity is "blind" in the sense that it proceeds largely in terms of uncriticized habits and unexamined feelings. In trusting our "common sense," we do not get very far toward drawing out the formal elements which actually determine validity and invalidity. We need a more general approach, one which will deal with arguments not merely in terms of their concrete content and how it makes us feel, but one that will go further toward getting at the logical patterns involved.

THE LEVEL OF MAXIMS

We have already had a little practice in abstracting the logical form of an argument from the specific subject matter. Once we clearly discern the form of an argument, the possibility of a more powerful approach than that of common sense suggests itself. Perhaps we could classify arguments according to their forms, and then discover special rules of validity for the various types. It is an exciting experience to discover what makes a particular form of argument valid, and then to formulate a rule or maxim that will guide one when an argument of this particular form crops up again. Later on, you will have a chance to make such a discovery for yourself. It should not detract too much from the sense of personal adventure to learn that you will probably be traveling a path that has been progressively explored for the past 2000 years. To reach this level of maxims marks a great advance. For at this level we grasp specific rules or maxims which determine validity for a certain special *type* of argument. Here we no longer need to treat each case as unique, nor to proceed in terms of uncriticized habits or intuitions. At this level we are in possession of specific rules which show us the formal similarity between many cases of a given type.

By a MAXIM (in this sense) we mean a formal rule covering some special type of logical situation. An example of such a maxim, which we shall later study, is the traditional rule for valid procedure in the second premise of a simple conditional argument: "Assert the antecedent or contradict the consequent." This maxim specifies valid procedure for *every* simple conditional argument, no matter what its content. Another example would be one of the traditional rules for the syllogism, such as: "There must be at least one affirmative premise."

The level of maxims is in practice a very useful one at which to work. It is more powerful and comprehensive than the common-sense level. It has attained general rules which apply to many cases of a particular type (for example, simple conditional arguments). Yet in spite of this additional power and generality, the level of maxims is still specific enough (that is, of a low enough level of generality) so that it indicates rather concretely the exact point of difficulty in an argument. The maxims for simple conditional arguments, for example, help us to pin down the precise area of the difficulty and to point out the specific fallacy committed (for example, the fallacy of asserting the consequent).

TOWARD A MORE GENERAL VALIDITY TEST— THE LEVEL OF PRINCIPLE

In spite of the usefulness of the level of maxims, students of logic have for a long time hoped for a still higher level of generality in their analyses. It has been an ideal of long standing to arrive at a more powerful analysis that would cover not merely a given *type* of argument, but many different types (for example, conditional arguments, alternative arguments, disjunctive arguments, dilemmas, syllogisms, and mixtures of these)—all under a single principle or set of principles. The practical aim would be a general validity test. A person in possession of such a test for validity could get along without the body of specific traditional maxims for this and that type of argument. This would not mean that the traditional maxims no longer held, but rather that he had reached a level of analysis that included them under a more general principle.

The attainment of this level of PRINCIPLE has been only recently possible, for it had to await the development of more powerful symbolic and analytical techniques than traditional logic possessed.[1] Many aspects of this level of principle lie clearly beyond the elementary work with which we are concerned. In the present book we shall develop a set of three principles which cover the traditionally distinguished types of argument normally studied in elementary logic, and many others too. While these CONTRAFORM PRINCIPLES do not achieve complete generality, they give us a unified approach to testing many of the arguments we encounter in everyday life.

[1] By TRADITIONAL LOGIC we mean the type of analysis initiated by Aristotle and developed and elaborated by medieval and modern logicians. It proceeds at the level of maxims, and treats the syllogism (see Chap. 19) as the central form of argument. By CONTEMPORARY LOGIC we mean the more powerful and general modes of analysis that have been developed over the past century.

• SOME REMINDERS

1. The first step in analyzing an argument is to distinguish between premises and conclusion.
2. Assumptions being drawn upon in an argument should be brought out into the open.
3. Analysis of an argument may be undertaken in terms of common sense, or in terms of special formal rules covering a given type of argument, or in terms of a general validity test. Each of these approaches has its advantages and disadvantages.

APPLICATIONS

1. If the argument is invalid, explain at the common-sense level why it fails to make its point. If it is prevalid, supply the additional assumption or assumptions needed for validity.
   a. He must be guilty, for no one else was in a position to commit the crime.
   b. If he really believes that, he is a dangerous man. But since he does not believe it, he is not a dangerous man.
   c. All horses have hooves, so we may be sure that all horses eat grass.
   d. She must be an actress, for only women are actresses, and she is certainly a woman.
   e. If the shoe fits, you will put it on. Since you have put it on, it must fit.
   f. Some sophomores appear friendly toward freshmen, but some people who appear friendly toward freshmen are only pretending. So we may be sure that some sophomores are only pretending.
   g. If you climb that rickety ladder, you'll kill yourself, because if you climb it, it is sure to break.
   h. Either A or B. If A, then C. Therefore either C or D.
   i. If A then B. Not A. Therefore not B.
   j. If A then B. Therefore B.
2. Distinguish three different approaches to the question of whether an argument makes its point, and explain the relative advantages and disadvantages of each.

CHAPTER 9

SOME BASIC TYPES OF STATEMENT

PREVIEW

We have seen that an argument consists of statements related to each other in such a way that one or more statements serve as premises for another statement which is held to follow from them. We have seen that both arguments and statements have form. We need now to explore the forms of certain statements more closely so that we can handle them when they appear in the arguments we wish to analyze.

9.1. THREE TYPES OF STATEMENT

Suppose there is a movie in town this evening that you want very much to see. Everything would be fine, let us say, except that you have a logic test tomorrow morning. You feel that unless you spend the evening on logic, you will not do well on the test. You weigh two possibilities in your mind:

going to the   doing well
movies this   on the test
evening   tomorrow

The more you think about it, the clearer it becomes that you cannot have it both ways. To realize one possibility involves giving up the other. You might state your predicament in various ways, but it is still the same predicament:

If I go to the movies this evening, then I'll not do well on
the test tomorrow.   (1)
Either I don't go to the movies this evening, or I'll not do well
on the test tomorrow.   (2)
I cannot both go to the movies this evening and do well on
the test tomorrow.   (3)

111

Note carefully that none of these ways of putting it rules out the dread possibility that you might stay home from the movies and still not do well on the test tomorrow. Statement 1 does not imply that if you do *not* go to the movies this evening, then you *will* do well on the test tomorrow. Statement 2 likewise leaves open the possibility that you don't go to the movies *and* don't do well on the test. Statement 3 similarly merely says that you cannot do *both* of two things; it does not rule out the possibility that you will not do *either*.

Let us examine the structure of these three statements. Each of these statements is compound in that it consists of two STATEMENTAL ELEMENTS (elements which are themselves statements), joined together by form-words called LOGICAL CONNECTIVES. More specifically, these form-words are STATEMENTAL CONNECTIVES, for they join together statemental elements.

In Statement 1 the elements are "I go to the movies this evening" and "I'll not do well on the test tomorrow." They are joined in a definite order by the connective, "IF . . . THEN." Such a statement is called a CONDITIONAL STATEMENT. The statemental element introduced by the "if" is called the ANTECEDENT, and the element introduced by the "then" is called the CONSEQUENT. In everyday English, we often omit the "then." In formal analysis, however, we usually state it, because it is a useful indicator of form. We shall see later that there are a number of different ways in which conditionals are expressed in colloquial English. Rather than set up separate forms for all these different modes of expression, we simplify our analyses by adopting the statement-form, "If A then B," as the STANDARD FORM of conditional statement. This notion of a standard form is a useful one on which we shall draw later.

"If . . . then" is a DIRECTIONAL CONNECTIVE, which is to say that interchanging the elements gives us a statement which is *not* logically equivalent to the original. Thus the statement, "If it's a sparrow, then it hatched out of an egg" is not logically equivalent to the statement, "If it hatched out of an egg, then it's a sparrow."

Statement 2 is called an ALTERNATIVE STATEMENT, and consists of two statemental elements joined by the connective, "EITHER . . . OR." This is a nondirectional or SYMMETRICAL connective; interchanging the elements does not alter the sense of the original. Try it out and see. The elements of an alternative statement are called ALTERNANTS.

Statement 3 is called a DISJUNCTIVE STATEMENT.[1] We could bring out its form more clearly, although less colloquially, by rewriting it: "Not both do I go to the movies this evening and do I do well on the test tomorrow." This latter way of writing it is, in fact, adopted as the STANDARD FORM OF DISJUNCTIVE STATEMENT for the purposes of formal analysis. The connective here is "NOT BOTH . . . AND." Is it directional or symmetrical? The elements of a disjunctive statement are called DISJUNCTS.

We may note in passing that there is a fourth basic type of compound statement, the CONJUNCTIVE STATEMENT, not illustrated by our examples. It consists of two statemental elements joined by the symmetrical connective, "BOTH . . . AND." Its elements are called CONJUNCTS. For the present, we shall focus our attention on the three types of statement illustrated above.

9.2. MOLECULAR AND ATOMIC STATEMENTS

Now let us have a closer look at the *elements* which enter into these three statements. I have urged that these elements are themselves statements. Do you see that they are? For example, the antecedent of our original conditional Statement 1 is, "I go to the movies this evening."

By a convenient analogy with physics, we may think of such an element as a logical atom, and of the compound statements into which it enters, as logical molecules. In terms of this analogy, statements which (like conditional, alternative, disjunctive, and conjunctive statements) consist of other statements joined together by statemental connectives, are called MOLECULAR STATEMENTS. Simple statements, the components of which are not themselves statements, are called ATOMIC STATEMENTS.

Just as physical atoms may be analyzed into subatomic components (electrons and so on) which are not themselves atoms, so atomic statements may, as we shall later see, be analyzed into their subatomic components which are not themselves statements.

Let us list the atomic elements of our three original statements, rewording the disjunctive elements slightly for the sake of uniformity, but without changing their logical import:

[1] Usage has not yet become standardized on this point. Some writers use the term "disjunctive" for what we have just called "alternative." Be sure you understand clearly how the terms are used in this book.

(1a)	I go to the movies this evening.	(1b)	I'll not do well on the test tomorrow.
(2a)	I don't go to the movies this evening.	(2b)	I'll not do well on the test tomorrow.
(3a)	I go to the movies this evening.	(3b)	I'll do well on the test tomorrow.

9.3. SYMBOLIZING ATOMIC STATEMENTS AND THEIR CONTRADICTORIES

As we look over this numbered set of atomic elements, we note that some of them are positively expressed, while others contain negative words like "don't" and "not." In the first column, for example, (1a) and (3a) are the same positive element, "I go to the movies this evening." The remaining element (2a) is like the other two in all respects except this crucial one: it contains the negative "don't." As we all know, a negative used in this way gives the statement in which it occurs the precisely opposite sense from an otherwise similar statement in which it does not occur. "I love you" and "I don't love you" are poles apart. Two statements related in this way are contradictory, and each is called the CONTRADICTORY of the other. Of any two contradictory statements, one must be true and the other must be false (even if we don't happen to know which is which).

For convenience, we shall adopt the convention of symbolizing positively expressed atomic statements by capital letters. Let us symbolize (1a) and (3a) by "M." We choose this letter to remind us of "movies," but remember that the letter stands for the *whole* atomic statement, "I go to the movies this evening." A letter used in this way is simply an *abbreviation.* You should contrast this use of letters with their use as *variables* standing for *any* element of a particular kind. Both uses of letters are important in formal logic, but they are not the same (see Section 8.1).

We symbolize the contradictory of a positively expressed atomic statement by adding a PRIME to the symbol for that statement. Thus, since (2a) is the contradictory of our statement, "M," we symbolize (2a) thus:

$$M' \text{ (Read: "Not-M" or "M prime")}$$

A positive statement like "I go to the movies this evening" is clearly atomic; its elements are not themselves statements. But how about the

contradictory negative statement, "I don't go to the movies this evening"?
For the purposes of the present book, it is simplest to treat this too as
atomic, and we shall do so. We can distinguish these two statements adequately for our purposes by calling attention to the fact that one is positive
while the other is negative.[2]

Two practical hints will help you handle the symbolizing of contradictories more readily:

First, it is simplest to symbolize a negatively expressed statement such
as (2a) with a primed letter, and a positively expressed statement such
as (1a) with an unprimed letter. This makes it easier to translate the
symbols back into English. We therefore adopt this as standard procedure.[3]

Second, if we have a statement symbolized by a primed letter and
want to symbolize its contradictory, we simply drop the prime. This follows our usual practice in ordinary English, where we similarly avoid
double negatives. "I don't want to go home" is contradicted by "I don't
not want to go home" (which is cumbersome because of the double nega-

[2] The differing approach common in more advanced symbolic work is sufficiently interesting to deserve comment, even though we shall not follow it here. It results
in the view that the contradictory of a positive atomic statement is not itself atomic,
but rather molecular. How is this possible?
From this more advanced point of view, it is convenient to place a word like "not"
in the list of statemental connectives (or operators), along with such words as "if . . .
then," "either . . . or," and "both . . . and." It is then held that any statement
containing a statemental connective or operator is by that very fact molecular, not
atomic. It is true that "not" is in one respect quite different from the other connectives mentioned. A connective like "if . . . then," for example, requires two
statemental elements in order to construct a molecular statement. Thus with the two
elements "I go to the movies this evening" and "I'll not do well on the test tomorrow"
we can construct a conditional statement by means of the "if . . . then" connective.
The word "not," however, can be used to construct a new statement out of a single
element. For example, the statement "I do not go to the movies this evening" may be
viewed as a complex (molecular) statement constructed from the positive statemental
element "I do go to the movies this evening," by means of the connective or operator
"not." This interpretation is perhaps easier to grasp if we remove the "not" from its
place within the originally positive element, and place it at the beginning: "Not (I
go to the movies this evening)."
Let us then recognize the usefulness and legitimacy of this approach for more advanced work. But let us agree, for our own elementary purposes, to treat both "I go
to the movies this evening" and "I do not go to the movies this evening," as atomic,
the one positively expressed, the other negatively.
[3] In practice, when you expect to compare your work with that of others, it is advisable to agree to symbolize a statement as positive unless it contains some obvious
negative word such as "no" or "not." This approach tends to avoid unrewarding
controversy over whether a word like "fail" or "hate" is really negative or positive.

tive) or more simply by "I want to go home." Similarly, "M′ " is awkwardly contradicted by "M″ " and more simply by "M." We adopt the simpler form as standard.

Start again by looking at (3b): "I'll do well on the test tomorrow." We shall symbolize this by "T." Now look at (1b) and (2b). Do you see that they are identical, and are the contradictory of "T"? How do you symbolize this contradictory?

9.4. ATOMIC STATEMENTS, SINGULAR AND GENERAL

Atomic statements like "I'll do well on the test tomorrow," "Thomas Jefferson lived at Monticello," and "This hat is too small," are called SINGULAR STATEMENTS, because the subject of such statements designates a single specific individual person or thing.

We may contrast such statements with other nonmolecular statements which are not about a single individual, but are rather about some or all individuals of a given type. For example, "Some freshmen do not register for logic," "Most logic books contain exercises," and "All frogs are vertebrates." Many of the statements used as illustrations in the two preceding chapters were of this kind. Such statements are called GENERAL STATE-MENTS, whether they refer to all or some of a given class, and whether they are positively or negatively expressed. We shall consider general statements to be atomic, for their elements are quite clearly not themselves statements.[4]

At present, we shall treat atomic statements, whether singular or general, as UNANALYZED units. This means that we shall not yet break them down into their component parts, but shall merely note whether the given statement is positive or negative. Positive atomic statements are for the present to be symbolized by capital letters, and negative atomic statements by primed capitals.

---

[4] Some writers, however, limit the term "atomic" to singular nonmolecular statements, and regard general statements as a third type, to be distinguished both from molecular and from atomic statements. When they do so, they usually have in mind a different analysis of general statements from that used in this book. This alternative analysis is discussed briefly in Section 16.8.

- **SOME REMINDERS**

1. A molecular statement has elements which are themselves statements.
2. In a molecular statement, the elements are joined by form-words of a type called "logical connectives," or more specifically, "statemental connectives."
3. At present, four types of molecular statement are distinguished: conditional, alternative, disjunctive, and conjunctive.
4. Some logical connectives are directional; others are symmetrical.
5. An atomic statement is symbolized by a capital letter if the statement is positively expressed, or by a primed capital letter if the statement is negatively expressed.
6. Such capital letters serve merely as *abbreviations* for the statements, and should be distinguished from capital letters used as *variables* in a statement-form.
7. A simple device for symbolizing contradictory pairs of atomic statements is explained, and a convention is adopted for getting rid of double negatives.
8. For the present, atomic statements are treated as unanalyzed units.

9.5. THE USEFULNESS OF SYMBOLS

Perhaps you are by this time asking yourself, "Why bother with symbols? Why not just use ordinary English?" I think you will need no convincing of the usefulness of logical symbols by the time we are through, but at present the question reasonably occurs to you. Until you know what logical symbols mean, it is perhaps natural to be frightened by the sight of a page filled with them. Wouldn't you feel the same way about the notation, "$2 + 2 = 4$," if you had always written out your sums in English words, "Two plus two equals four"?

Not long ago I came across a publisher's blurb for a logic text, quoting a reviewer as saying that "not a modern symbol is used nor a mathematical formula introduced from end to end." This was clearly thought of by the publisher, at least, as a commendation. But we may suspect that the publisher was also, through unfamiliarity, frightened by the look of logical symbols. Yet we may be sure that his wristwatch contained twelve symbols which no longer frightened him and which he found much more convenient for reading the time than the English words, however familiar, of "one," "two," "three," and so on.

To urge that we "stick to everyday English" for the purposes of logical analysis is a suggestion having, I believe, precisely the same weight as the parallel suggestion that we balance our checkbooks by writing:

> Two hundred twenty-nine dollars and thirty-four cents minus fourteen dollars and seventy-eight cents leaves a balance of two hundred fourteen dollars and fifty-six cents,

instead of writing:

$$\begin{array}{r} \$229.34 \\ -14.78 \\ \hline \$214.56 \end{array}$$

The main virtues of arithmetical symbols are that they are compact, clear, precise, and easy to handle. As you will see for yourself before long, the virtues of logical symbols are the same. Modern logical symbols are beautifully designed for the job of making an analysis of logical forms easy.

Perhaps you are willing to admit all this, but are concerned about the time it is going to take you to become familiar with the symbols. How long do you think it would take you to learn the symbols involved in the expression, "$(2 + 10) \div 3 = 4$," if you had never seen them before, but knew the corresponding English words and their meanings? I think this will give you a fairly accurate estimate of how long it will take you to learn the seven unfamiliar symbols to be used in this text. These symbols will all be introduced in their proper place, and will be easier to remember in context. But perhaps you'd like to have a quick look at them now.

You are already familiar with capital and lower-case letters, so we won't count them as new. We shall use capital letters primarily as abbreviations for statements, and lower-case or small letters as abbreviations for the names of classes. We have already had examples of both these uses. You already know that "$=$" means "equals," and that "0" means "zero," so we shan't count those either.

Here are the seven new symbols and their meanings in everyday English. There is no need to memorize them all now, but there is no harm in doing so if you wish:

SYMBOL	MEANING
$\supset$	if . . . then
$\lor$	either . . . or
$'$	not
$/$	not both . . . and
$\neq$	is not equal to
$<$	is included in
$\not<$	is excluded from

The first four symbols will be used at once. The fifth will not be used until Chapter 13, and the last two symbols not until Chapter 17.

9.6. SYMBOLIZING MOLECULAR STATEMENTS

SYMBOLIZING A CONDITIONAL STATEMENT

We shall now proceed to introduce the standard symbols for state-mental connectives. The symbol for the conditional connective is a HORSE-SHOE, "$\supset$." Note that it "walks" from the antecedent to the consequent, and reminds us that we are dealing with a directional connective. Our original conditional statement, "If I go to the movies this evening, then I'll not do well on the test tomorrow," is thus symbolized:

$$M \supset T' \quad (\text{Read: "If M then not-T."}) \text{ [5]}$$

In ordinary English, we permit ourselves to speak very loosely. Thus, sometimes when we say "If . . . then . . ." we mean this and nothing more, while at other times we may mean "If and only if . . . then . . ." This ambiguity of colloquial speech is absent from the symbol "$\supset$." It invariably means simply "if . . . then." We shall always interpret an English "If . . . then" as "$\supset$," unless we have clear evidence that the more complex "If and only if . . . then" is intended. A statement of this latter form is called a biconditional statement. We shall later consider how it is to be symbolized.

You will need to be on your guard in identifying a given statement as conditional. On the one hand, a sentence may contain "if . . . then" and still not be a conditional statement in our defined sense. On the other,

[5] The symbol "$\supset$" is often read "implies" or "materially implies." These readings, however, have given rise to various controversial questions which are best avoided in an elementary text.

a statement may be conditional even though it does not contain these words. Let us consider each of these points in turn.

It will be easier to understand the first point if you recall that a conditional statement, in the sense in which we have been using the term, is a particular kind of molecular statement. Ordinarily, when we refer to a statement as *conditional,* this is what we mean. When clarity requires it, we may call this type of statement a MOLECULAR CONDITIONAL. Its elements must themselves be statements.

But consider the following:

> If anyone wants to be a concert violinist,
> then he will need to practice.

Here the antecedent introduced by "if" is not a statement at all, but rather a statement-form containing the variable "anyone." (See Section 8.1.) The presence of the variable would perhaps have been more obvious if the whole statement had been expressed:

> Whoever x may be, if x wants to be a concert
> violinist, then x will need to practice.

Although the words "if . . . then" appear, this is clearly not a molecular conditional, for its elements are not themselves statements. Actually the statement in question is a form of general statement (see Section 9.4). In traditional logic it would normally be expressed: "All who want to be concert violinists will need to practice."

Since general statements are frequently expressed in "if . . . then" form, it is convenient to have a way of referring compactly to statements of this type. We shall agree to call such statements GENERAL CONDITIONALS. We must, however, avoid confusing them with molecular conditionals. Do not make the mistake, for example, of trying to symbolize the general conditional statement given above by means of "W ⊃ N," for this expression represents a *molecular* conditional. Remember also that, as noted earlier, the term "conditional statement," when used without qualification, always means a statement of the molecular type.

Sometimes it is difficult to be sure whether a given statement is intended as a molecular conditional or as a general conditional. How are we to take a statement like "If you want to understand, you will need to pay attention"? If we interpret the "you" generally, it functions as a variable like "anyone," and the statement is general rather than molecular. On this interpretation it would be a mistake to symbolize the statement by

"W ⊃ P," for (since we are trying to symbolize a specific statement and not just a statement-form) these capital letters should be abbreviations for genuine statemental elements.

On the other hand, if we interpret the "you" as a definite pronoun, it functions not as a variable but as a CONSTANT, just as if I had called you, the present reader, by name. On this interpretation, the statement can of course be symbolized simply, "W ⊃ P," for these capital letters now correctly symbolize elements which are themselves statements. In the examples and applications in the present part of our work, we shall interpret such words as "you" and "he" as substitutes for proper names, and shall treat the resulting statements as molecular conditionals.

So much for the first point mentioned above: a statement may contain "if . . . then" and still not be a molecular conditional. Now for the second point.

In analyzing and symbolizing statements originally expressed in normal English, we need to recognize that a statement may have a conditional import even though the words "if . . . then" do not occur. Syntactical analysis adopts "If A then B" as the *standard form* for conditional statements, and "A ⊃ B" as the standard symbolization. Let us consider some of the most frequent variant forms and see how they may be re-expressed or *reduced* to standard form. Consider the following three statements:

> We can now analyze many everyday statements, provided that we remember that a statement may have a conditional function without the words "if . . . then" appearing.   **(1)**
> Unless we recognize this fact, our analyses become needlessly complicated.   **(2)**
> The logical form of such statements becomes clear only if we restate them in standard form.   **(3)**

These three statements themselves provide illustrations of the variant forms. Statement 1 is the easiest to handle. Do you see that "provided that" is just another way of saying "if"? In Statement 2, the key word, "unless," is slightly more troublesome. It has the same force as "if *not*." The third statement is, for beginners, the most troublesome of all. Here the key words are "only if," and we are tempted to interpret them as meaning simply "if." This analysis is, however, quite mistaken, for it turns out that "only if" always introduces the *consequent*. As you think this over, make sure you are keeping these distinct: "if," "only if," and "if and only if." Consider the statement, "I'll go only if you agree to pay my way."

Sticking to what is actually expressed, we must restate this in standard form as follows: "If I go, then you will have agreed to pay my way." Note that if we take the original statement strictly, it does *not* say that if you agree to pay my way, then I'll go. I might, in complete consistency with the strict interpretation of the original, refuse to go even after you had agreed to pay my way. If you disagree with this interpretation, it is probably because you are taking the "only if" to mean not merely what it says, but rather to mean "*if* and only if."

We may apply these remarks by restating the three numbered statements in standard form:

> If we remember that a statement may have a conditional function without the words "if . . . then" appearing, then we can now analyze many everyday statements.   **(1a)**
> If we do not recognize this fact, then our analyses become needlessly complicated.   **(2a)**
> If the logical form of such statements becomes clear, then we shall have restated them in standard form.   **(3a)**

Statement 3a is a good illustration of the fact that the reduction cannot be purely mechanical, but must take into account the meaning of the original, and must choose a tense-sequence which preserves the intended meaning.

In formal analysis, always stick to the strict or minimum interpretation of a statement unless you have clear evidence that a richer interpretation was intended. For example, do not treat "only if" as meaning "if and only if" unless you can give evidence to support the fuller interpretation. Why is this good advice? There are, to be sure, areas of life in which a person should be willing to stick out his neck, but syntactics is not one of these. In formal analysis we never want to run the risk of reading more into a statement than was intended. The great sin of formal logic is invalidity, and we stand in peril whenever we go beyond the evidence.

SYMBOLIZING A BICONDITIONAL STATEMENT

As its name suggests, a BICONDITIONAL STATEMENT requires *two* conditional statements to give its full meaning. In English, a biconditional statement is normally expressed by means of the complex connective, "If and only if . . . then." As this English form clearly shows, the biconditional combines the meanings of an "if . . . then" statement and an "only if" statement. Now that we know how to handle the "only if" (it always introduces the *consequent*), we can go ahead and symbolize a biconditional statement by writing down separately the symbols for each of its two parts:

If and only if A, then B.
$$\begin{cases} A \supset B \\ B \supset A \end{cases}$$

The brace reminds us that each of these two statements was derived from a single complex original statement.[6]

This symbolic representation brings out more clearly than the English version an interesting point about biconditional statements. While each of the constituent parts is a conditional statement, actually the biconditional as a whole is a complex *conjunctive* statement. We might have expressed it in English: "If A then B, *and* if B then A." Such a complex conjunctive statement is said to be a molecular statement of the SECOND ORDER. This means that it is itself molecular, and contains at least one element which is also molecular. Such statements are contrasted with the simpler molecular statements previously studied. These are said to be molecular statements of the FIRST ORDER, for although the statements themselves are molecular, their elements are atomic.

In symbolizing second-order conjunctive statements in this book, we shall always split them up into their first-order elements and write down the symbols for each element, as we did above. In adopting this procedure, we are really doing nothing more than we would in symbolizing the premises of any argument. For if you stop to think about it, it will be clear that any set of premises really constitutes a complex conjunctive statement. We understand that these premises are to be *taken together* to yield the conclusion, which is just another way of saying that they are conjoined.

SYMBOLIZING AN ALTERNATIVE STATEMENT

The standard symbol for the alternative connective is "V." The two prongs of this *fork* or WEDGE may be thought of as suggesting the either-

---

[6] We adopt the present procedure for handling second-order conjunctive statements, in preference to other available conventions, because it simplifies the writing of certain useful symbolic versions of these statements, called "zeroforms." (See Sections 11.2 and 15.4.)

or alternative, and the symmetrical shape of the symbol reminds us that the connective is a symmetrical one, the order of the elements making no logical difference. Thus our original alternative statement, "Either I don't go to the movies this evening or I'll not do well on the test tomorrow," is symbolized:

$$M' \lor T' \quad (\text{Read: "Either not-M or not-T, maybe both."})$$

Remember that this type of "either . . . or," which we have now symbolized by "$\lor$," always leaves open the possibility that *both* alternants should hold. In ordinary English, we tend to use an unqualified "either . . . or" indiscriminately, both for cases in which we mean to leave open this possibility and cases in which we mean to exclude it. In business and legal transactions, as well as in everyday conversation, it is often crucial to make it clear which of these two meanings we have in mind. The hybrid "and/or" is sometimes used to keep open the possibility of "maybe both." In ordinary English, the ambiguity is easily removed by adding one of the qualifying phrases, "maybe both" or "but not both," to our alternative statement. In logical analysis, we must clearly indicate which of these two meanings is intended. Ambiguity is avoided by defining the symbol "$\lor$" to mean *always* "either . . . or . . . maybe both." Get in the habit of reading it that way.

Contemporary logic treats this "$\lor$" type of alternative as the basic one, since as we shall see, the idea represented by the other type of "either . . . or" may be readily expressed in terms of "$\lor$" and disjunction. The simple alternative "$\lor$" is also basic in the sense that, in formal work, it is always the form used to express an "either . . . or" unless we have specific evidence that the more restricted "either . . . or . . . but not both" is intended.

One word more about getting ordinary English into standard logical form. We commonly use "either . . . or" not only to connect statements, but also to connect nouns. For example, instead of saying, "Either I'm going home Tuesday or I'm going home Wednesday," I might equally well say, "I'm going home either Tuesday or Wednesday." Since in the present context the connective "$\lor$" can be used only between *statements,* the latter version above would need to be recast in order to prepare it for logical analysis. In symbolizing an alternative statement, make sure that the letters you use really do stand for *statemental* elements.

SYMBOLIZING A DISJUNCTIVE STATEMENT

The disjunctive connective, "not both . . . and," is very compactly symbolized by a STROKE, "/." Thus our original disjunctive statement, "I cannot both go to the movies this evening and do well on the test tomorrow," is symbolized:

M / T (Read: "Not both M and T, maybe neither.")

Here again, ordinary English is often ambiguous. Sometimes when we say "not both," we mean "not both, maybe neither." This meaning is adopted as basic for logical analysis, and is precisely what is symbolized by "/." Unless we have clear evidence that more is meant, we shall always interpret a "not both" statement in this way. When we speak without qualification of a "disjunctive statement," this is what we mean.

SYMBOLIZING A DISJUNCTIVE-ALTERNATIVE STATEMENT

Sometimes, however, when people say "not both" they have a further meaning in mind. They mean "not both, *but at least one.*" If you think about it for a moment, you will see that this means precisely the same as "either . . . or . . . but not both," the second type of "either . . . or" that we distinguished above. You will recall that we have not yet developed a symbolic formulation of this type of "either . . . or." Since its meaning is identical with that of "not both, but at least one," we may consider these two forms together.

The type of statement we are now considering asserts that one and only one of two possibilities holds, without specifying which one it is. We have just seen that this meaning can be clearly conveyed by either of two English forms: "Either this or that, but not both" or "Not both this and that, but at least one." Such a statement is a second-order conjunctive which combines the meaning of the alternative and the disjunctive, and thus requires both an alternative statement and a disjunctive statement to give its full meaning.

Either A or B, but not both.
$$\begin{cases} A \lor B \\ A / B \end{cases}$$

SYMBOLIZING A FIRST-ORDER CONJUNCTIVE STATEMENT

A first-order conjunctive statement contains two atomic elements conjoined by "both . . . and." In symbolizing such a statement, we simply write the symbols of its elements side by side:

Both A and B.

AB

Some writers place a dot between the two elements to indicate the conjunction, thus: "A·B." [7] In everyday English, we of course commonly omit the "both" and simply conjoin the two statemental elements with "and." When one of the elements is positive and the other negative, this shift is often emphasized by the use of "but" in place of "and."

When we were studying the functions of language in Part I, we had occasion to note that the grammatical form of a sentence is not always a reliable indication of its function. Similarly, we shall have many occasions in Part II to find that the grammatical form of a sentence is not always a sure indication of its logical import. In analyzing molecular statements whose elements are connected by "and," for example, we must be on our guard. Sometimes such statements do not function conjunctively at all, but have a *conditional* force. "Drink to me only with thine eyes, and I will pledge with mine" looks conjunctive, but it really means something like "If you drink . . . then I will pledge . . ." It is thus correctly symbolized, not by "DP," but rather by "D ⊃ P."

Note carefully that on this interpretation, the antecedent "D" is not the original imperative, "Drink to me only with thine eyes," but rather a statemental element, "You drink to me with your eyes." An imperative itself is not a statement, since it is neither true nor false. An imperative thus cannot be symbolized by means of a capital letter, for such letters stand for statements.

SYMBOLIZING A BI-NEGATIVE STATEMENT

While they are not one of the basic types of statement used in logical analysis, "neither . . . nor" statements turn up occasionally and are likely

---

[7] In introducing a brace in our analysis of certain second-order conjunctive statements (biconditionals and disjunctive alternatives), we treated the brace merely as an informal device for reminding us that the two joined statements were derived from a single complex original. We may also think of the brace more formally as equivalent in function to the dot symbol.

to be quite troublesome for beginners. Consider, for example, "I want neither cake nor pie for dessert." Following a suggestion made when we were discussing alternative statements, we must first express this so that the "neither . . . nor" will connect statements, not nouns. This part is easy:

> Neither do I want cake for dessert nor do I want pie for dessert.

If we use "C" for the first element and "P" for the second, how shall we symbolize the statement as a whole? The "neither . . . nor" suggests both alternation and contradiction, but it is not obvious how these are to be combined. One of the most popular incorrect forms among beginners is "C' V P'." Do you see that this attempt fails to express the meaning of the original? These symbols mean, in English, "Either I don't want cake for dessert, or I don't want pie for dessert, maybe both." This interpretation is much too liberal. On this analysis, the possibility that I *might* want cake or that I *might* want pie is left open. Actually, doesn't the original mean that I don't want cake and I don't want pie either? What kind of statement is this? Simply a conjunctive statement, with both elements "primed":

$$C'P'$$

Following a suggestion of the logician, Rudolf Carnap, such "neither . . . nor" statements may be appropriately called BI-NEGATIVE STATEMENTS. Were we then mistaken in thinking earlier that "neither . . . nor" had something to do with both contradiction and alternation? No, we were not. As we shall see more clearly later, the statement "C'P'" is the *contradictory* of the *alternative* statement "C V P." In everyday English, "I want neither cake nor pie for dessert" is contradicted by the alternative statement, "I want either cake or pie for dessert, maybe both."

9.7. LOGICAL EQUIVALENCES BETWEEN A CONDITIONAL, AN ALTERNATIVE, AND A DISJUNCTIVE STATEMENT

If you have not by this time forgotten all about wanting to go to the movies this evening and to do well on the logic test tomorrow, you will remember that we saw that there were three different ways of stating your predicament. The conditional statement, the alternative statement, and the disjunctive statement all expressed precisely the same logical situation.

In other words, these three statements were LOGICALLY EQUIVALENT. Statements are logically equivalent when they *must* have the same truth-value, that is, when they are formally related in such a way that they must either *both* be false or *both* be true.[8] Note that we don't have to know whether the statements *are* true or whether they *are* false in order to determine their logical equivalence.

We do not at this time propose to *prove* that the three statements (1), (2), and (3) are logically equivalent. (We shall have a simple test of logical equivalence before long.) But you should at least examine them with care to see whether you cannot intuit or "see" their equivalence.

Using the familiar sign of equivalence, we may state these logical equivalences in our compact symbolism:

$$M \supset T' = M' \lor T' = M / T.$$

• SOME REMINDERS

9. While it might at first seem easier to conduct our analyses in "ordinary English," an appropriate symbolism proves useful in helping us discern logical form and in making possible the discovery and formulation of more general principles.

10. Molecular statements are symbolized by using capital letters for their elements and certain standard logical symbols for their connectives.

11. A situation expressible by means of a conditional statement may also be expressed by a logically equivalent alternative statement or disjunctive statement.

12. Two or more statements are logically equivalent when their forms are related in such a way that the statements *must* have the same truth-value.

APPLICATIONS

1. Express each of the following statements in appropriate logical symbols. If an atomic element is negatively expressed, remember to add a prime to the capital letter.

   a. If the north wind blows, then we shall have snow.

---

[8] By contrast, two CONTRADICTORY STATEMENTS are so related that they cannot both be false and cannot both be true; exactly one must be true, and exactly one must be false.

b. Black, black, black is the color of my true love's hair.
c. I do not agree with you, but I respect your opinion.
d. We shall not have a picnic if the weather doesn't improve.
e. Either he is lying or he is misinformed.
f. Neither of us is eligible to compete.
g. Cast your bread on the waters, and it will return to you.
h. Tomorrow will be Wednesday if and only if yesterday was Monday.
i. Either a statement is true or it is false.
j. All juniors and some seniors were invited.

2. First, express each of the following in English, in standard conditional form. Then symbolize. For the sake of uniformity, capitalize the bracketed letters and use them to symbolize *positively* expressed elements. If an element is negatively expressed, do not forget to add a prime to the letter.

a. I'll get there in time to [c]atch the train, provided I [h]urry.
b. You may [l]eave when the bell [r]ings.
c. "I can't [t]alk religion to a [s]tarving man." (Gandhi)
d. We'll [g]o regardless of whether it [r]ains or [s]hines.
e. We won't [s]hoot until we see the [w]hites of their eyes.
f. Jim will be in the [s]tarting line only if George is still in the [h]ospital.
g. Unless Piggy [g]oes over the stile, Old Woman won't get [h]ome tonight.
h. I not only always [s]ay what I [m]ean, but also always mean what I say.
i. "Chapel attendance is [r]ecognized at the rate of one-half credit for each semester providing the record shows the student has been [p]resent for 75 per cent of the chapel programs."
j. "Failure to [a]ttend 75 per cent of the Chapel periods will result in no Chapel credit being [r]ecorded."

3. Suppose that we were not permitted to introduce a special symbol for disjunction. Can you find a way of expressing a disjunctive statement in terms of other symbols already introduced?

4. We have already seen that a disjunctive-alternative statement may be symbolized by using "$\lor$" and "/." Can you discover a logically equivalent way of doing this by using "$\lor$" and "$'$"?

CHAPTER 10

ANALYZING MOLECULAR STATEMENTS

PREVIEW

Our work to date has suggested that the basic types of molecular statement are the conditional, the alternative, the disjunctive, and the conjunctive. Other molecular statements can always be analyzed in terms of one or more of these basic types. In the present chapter, we shall find that the conditional, the alternative, and the disjunctive have much in common, and that all three stand in opposition to the conjunctive statement.

10.1. THE LOGICAL IMPORT OF A CONDITIONAL STATEMENT

For six cents you can learn a lot about just what is involved in a conditional statement. It may cost you even less. Suppose you have a penny and a nickel. You say to me:

If I give you the penny, then I'll give you the nickel.

$$P \supset N \qquad\qquad (1)$$

How cheaply can you get out without going back on your word? Or more generally, what courses of action are consistent with this promise, and what ones are inconsistent with it? Let's consider the possibilities. You *might* give me both the penny and the nickel. We may symbolize this possibility by a conjunctive statement:

I give you the penny and I give you the nickel.

$$PN \qquad\qquad (a)$$

But suppose you gave me the nickel, but not the penny. This possibility can be expressed by the conjunctive:

I don't give you the penny, but I do give you the nickel.

$$P'N \qquad\qquad (b)$$

Could I, on the basis of your original promise, claim the penny too? Of course not. All you promised was that *if* you gave me the penny, you'd give me the nickel too. You didn't commit yourself in any way as to what you would or would not do if you gave me the *nickel.* You definitely did *not* say, for example,

If I give you the nickel, then I'll give you the penny.

N ⊃ P   (2)

If I thought you asserted (2), I was just mistaken. And if I were to urge that (1) and (2) mean the same thing, or that (1) warrants (2), you would be right in calling me badly confused.

Statements 1 and 2 are related in an interesting way, but they are neither logically equivalent, nor does one follow from the other. Can you describe their relation?

Statements 1 and 2 are conditional statements, containing the same elements, "P" and "N." But in (1), "P" is the antecedent and "N" the consequent, while in (2) these roles are interchanged. Two conditional statements related in this way are called CONVERSE STATEMENTS, and one is said to be the CONVERSE of the other.

With this fertile source of confusion cleared up, let us return to your promise and see if any other possibilities are open to you. Suppose you didn't give me either the penny or the nickel. This possibility may be symbolized:

P'N'   (d) [1]

Have you gone back on your word? Not in the least. All you said was, "*If* I give you the penny, then I'll give you the nickel." You didn't say what you'd do if you *didn't* give me the penny.

Does this mean that you can do anything you please and still keep your promise? No, it doesn't. There is still one possibility that we have not considered. Suppose you give me the penny but refuse to follow through with the nickel:

PN'   (c)

That's the one thing you can't get away with. Possibility (c) is inconsistent with your Statement 1. In fact, the following two statements are strict logical contradictories:

[1] The reason for skipping the letter "(c)" for the present will soon be apparent.

If I give you the penny, then I'll give you the nickel. **(1)**

I give you the penny, but I'll not give you the nickel. **(1′)**

We may draw together and systematize the results of our examination by setting up a table of the four conjunctive possibilities (a–d) and by indicating which are consistent and which inconsistent with "P ⊃ N." Such a presentation is called a CONSISTENCY TABLE.[2] Although any order would do, a standard order is adopted (see a–d above) for listing the conjunctive possibilities. This convention assures uniformity and simplifies reference. Note, then, that the first possibility listed never contains primes. The second has only the first letter primed; the third has only the second letter primed; the fourth has both letters primed. These four conjunctive possibilities are always written in the lower-left compartment of the consistency table, in the order specified:

$$
\begin{array}{c|c}
 & \\
\hline
PN & \\
P'N & \\
PN' & \\
P'N' &
\end{array}
$$

The expression to be analyzed is written above and to the right:

$$
\begin{array}{c|c}
 & P \supset N \\
\hline
PN & \\
P'N & \\
PN' & \\
P'N' &
\end{array}
$$

[2] A consistency table is a modification of the so-called TRUTH TABLE, which sets forth the possible combinations of truth values (truth or falsity) for various elements. The truth table which corresponds to the present consistency table is

P	N	P ⊃ N
T	T	T
F	T	T
T	F	F
F	F	T

The first two columns above correspond to our listing of the four conjunctive possibilities involving the elements "P" and "N." The third column tells us that "P ⊃ N" is false when (see first two columns) "P" is true but "N" is false. In the other three truth-value combinations for "P" and "N," the statement "P ⊃ N" is true (see third column).

Consistency tables have several important advantages over truth tables, if we are trying to move on toward a more general test of validity. Consistency tables, unlike truth tables, provide an immediate basis for zeroforms. While the truth table itself can be developed as a validity test, it is handicapped in this role by cumbersomeness when an argument contains (as it often does) three or more elements. Further, the

We next consider the given expression in relation to each of the four conjunctive possibilities. If a given conjunctive possibility is *consistent* with the expression, we place a "1" in the second column opposite that conjunctive possibility. If, on the other hand, a given conjunctive possibility is *inconsistent* with the expression, we write down a "0." The following table thus summarizes our previous work:

	P ⊃ N
PN	1
P'N	1
PN'	0
P'N'	1

Before going further, we should get clearer on the difference between *consistency* and *logical equivalence* and between *inconsistency* and *contradictoriness*. Two statements are CONSISTENT when they may both be true. Two statements are LOGICALLY EQUIVALENT when they must have the same truth-value; that is, either both must be true, or both must be false. (We needn't know which.) Two statements are INCONSISTENT when they cannot both be true. Two statements are CONTRADICTORY when they cannot have the same truth-value; that is, one must be false and the other must be true. (We needn't know which is which.) It is crucial to understand these distinctions clearly. It will help to note that two contradictory statements are always *inconsistent*, but that some pairs of inconsistent statements are not contradictory, since they might both be false. (Two inconsistent statements of this latter type are called CONTRARIES; they cannot both be true, but they may both be false.) Again, two *logically equivalent* statements are always *consistent*, but some pairs of consistent statements are not logically equivalent (since they need not have the same truth-value).[3]

The question now arises, how do logical equivalence and contradictoriness show up on the consistency table? The answer is simple: If exactly one "1" appears in the column, the conjunctive possibility to its left is *logically equivalent* to the expression being analyzed. If, on the other

truth table is of no use in testing syllogisms and other atomic arguments. The contraform test, which zeroforms make possible, suffers from neither of these handicaps (although it has certain limitations of its own), and puts us in possession of a simple elementary validity test of considerable generality. All this will be apparent in due time.
[3] For a further analysis of these distinctions as they apply to certain atomic statements, see Chapter 18.

hand, exactly one "0" appears in the column, the conjunctive possibility to its left is the strict *contradictory* of the expression being analyzed.[4]

If you are puzzled about the possibility of a logical equivalence turning up, consider the following example:

	NP′
PN	0
P′N	1
PN′	0
P′N′	0

Returning to our consistency table for "P ⊃ N," we have found that of the four conjunctive possibilities, three are consistent with our conditional statement, while the remaining one (PN′) *contradicts* it.

Since this result is completely general, we may easily set forth a maxim that will tell us how to form the conjunctive contradictory of a given conditional statement.

Maxim for contradicting a conditional statement:

Conjoin the antecedent and the contradicted consequent.

Before leaving the topic of conditional statements, it will be worthwhile to recall the *converse* of the statement we have been analyzing, and then to ask ourselves how this converse is to be contradicted. The converse of our original conditional statement is the statement we numbered "2" above: "If I give you the nickel, I'll give you the penny." In symbols, "N ⊃ P." Our maxim assures us that its contradictory is "NP′." Do you see that this is actually one of the four conjunctive possibilities we were considering above? It is possibility (b), represented by the second line of the consistency table, although it there was written "P′N." These two ways of writing it mean exactly the same. In a *conjunctive* statement, the order of the elements makes no difference. Conjunction is symmetrical. "NP′" and "P′N" are logically equivalent.

Here is the consistency table for "N ⊃ P," the converse of our original conditional statement:

---

[4] This paragraph is intended to apply only to the present use of consistency tables, where only one column is present to the right of the conjunctive possibilities. These comments do not apply in general for extensions of the consistency table.

	N ⊃ P
PN	1
P'N	0
PN'	1
P'N'	1

10.2. THE LOGICAL IMPORT OF AN ALTERNATIVE STATEMENT

When we were discussing the alternative statement, "Either I don't go to the movies this evening, or I'll not do well on the test tomorrow," we noticed that it left open the possibility that even though I don't go to the movies this evening, I still might not do well on the test tomorrow. This type of alternative, which leaves open the possibility that both alternants should hold, we agreed to treat as standard, and to symbolize by means of "V." We now want to explore more fully the logical import of a statement containing this connective.

Perhaps it is now my turn to furnish the six cents. Suppose I say to you: "Either I'll give you the penny, or I'll give you the nickel." [5] You will be glad to be assured that this is not a disjunctive alternative, but that I mean to leave open the possibility of giving you both coins.

Let us again set up the outline of a consistency table, listing the possibilities in standard order:

	P ∨ N
PN	
P'N	
PN'	
P'N'	

Since I have assured you that this is not a disjunctive alternative (Either . . . or . . . but not both), the first possibility is consistent with my promise, isn't it? I may consistently give you both the penny and the nickel. It is obvious that the second and third possibilities in the table are equally consistent with that promise, so that I might get by with giving you only the penny (see third line of the table). But the fourth possibility, "P'N'," which was open to you when you made your *conditional*

---

[5] Of course the "I" and the "you" now each refer to a different individual than before. But the logical form of the utterance remains the same, and that is what we are concerned with at present.

statement is clearly not open to me. If, having said that I'll give you either the penny or the nickel, I then go on to say that I won't give you the penny and won't give you the nickel, I shall have flatly contradicted myself. Here is the completed table:

	$P \vee N$
PN	1
P'N	1
PN'	1
P'N'	0

We may again formulate a simple maxim to guide us:

Maxim for contradicting an alternative statement:

Conjoin the *contradicted* alternants.

10.3. THE LOGICAL IMPORT OF A DISJUNCTIVE STATEMENT

Since you were able to fulfil your conditional promise without spending a cent, and since I am now out at least a penny, perhaps you will agree to put up the six cents for this final experiment. You tell me:

I won't both give you the penny and give you the nickel.

P / N

This immediately rules out the first possibility in our table, doesn't it? For that possibility is precisely that you *do* give me both the penny and the nickel. How about the other possibilities? You might consistently give me only the nickel (the second possibility), or give me only the penny (the third possibility). What about the fourth possibility? Might you consistently give me *neither?* You may have to think about this a moment, though we have discussed the general point before. All you said was that you wouldn't give me *both*. You told me what you would *not* do, but not what you *would* do. You really didn't commit yourself to giving me anything. Thus the fourth possibility, "P'N'," is perfectly consistent with your disjunctive statement.

Here again, then, we find that out of the four conjunctive possibilities, three are consistent with the given molecular statement, while the remaining one contradicts it. Here is the consistency table:

	P / N
PN	0
P'N	1
PN'	1
P'N'	1

And here is the maxim:

Maxim for contradicting a disjunctive statement:

Conjoin the disjuncts.

10.4. DEFINITIONS OF "LOGICALLY CONTRADICTORY"

We earlier saw that two statements are said to be *logically contradictory* when they are so related that one of them *must* be true and the other *must* be false. (Or we may say that two contradictory statements cannot *both* be true and cannot *both* be false.)

Our present explorations have provided the basis for another convenient definition. From this point of view, two statements are logically contradictory when each excludes precisely those possibilities which the other permits, and permits precisely those which the other excludes.

It is useful to keep these definitions in mind as our work proceeds. Which one we will use in a specific discussion is entirely a matter of convenience.

• SOME REMINDERS

The following table summarizes the results of our explorations. To emphasize the fact that these results are completely general, we shall use the variables "A" and "B" rather than the abbreviations "P" and "N" which stand only for two quite special statements.

FORM OF ORIGINAL STATEMENT	MAXIM FOR FORMING THE CONJUNCTIVE CONTRADICTORY	FORM OF CONJUNCTIVE CONTRADICTORY
A / B	Conjoin the disjuncts.	AB
B ⊃ A	Conjoin the antecedent and the	A'B
A ⊃ B	contradicted consequent.	AB'
A ∨ B	Conjoin the contradicted alternants.	A'B'

APPLICATIONS

1. Express each of the following in appropriate logical symbolism. Capitalize bracketed letters to stand for positively expressed elements. If an element is negatively expressed, be sure to add a prime to the capital letter.
   a. It is [s]nowing.
   b. Either [h]e is mistaken or [I] am.
   c. ". . . leave a [k]iss but in the cup and I'll not look for [w]ine."
   d. Fish can [s]wim.
   e. You can't [k]eep your cake and [e]at it too.
   f. Unless it [w]arms up, the pond will [f]reeze.
   g. The pond will not [f]reeze.
   h. I neither want to [f]orce the issue nor let it be [o]verlooked.
   i. John will [w]in the race only if he runs [f]aster.
   j. Although the [h]umidity is high, the [b]reeze keeps things comfortable.
2. Express in logical symbols the *contradictory* of each of the statements in 1 above.
3. With an eye on your work in 2, express in normal English the contradictory of each of the statements given in 1.
4. Give the form of the *conditional* statement which contradicts each of the following (use symbols). *Hint:* What is the maxim for contradicting a conditional statement? The present question can be answered by applying the maxim in reverse. The maxim is a very helpful temporary crutch, but we shall want to practice these operations until we can do them "automatically," without having to "think of the maxim" each time.
   a. A′B′   b. AB′   c. AB   d. A′B
5. Give in symbols the form of the *alternative* statement which contradicts each of the cases (a–d) given in 4.
6. Give in symbols the form of the *disjunctive* statement which contradicts each of the cases (a–d) given in 4.
7. The symbols "⊃," "∨," and "/" can all be defined in terms of "prime" and "and." For example, the disjunctive *stroke* can be defined as follows:

$$A / B \overset{\text{df}}{=} (AB)'$$

   (The symbol, "$\overset{\text{df}}{=}$", means "equals by definition.") Can you work out similar definitions for "⊃" and "∨"?
8. In order to clear up a point that is frequently confusing at first, explain why the expression "(AB)′" does *not* stand for a conjunctive statement, and why the expression "(A ⊃ B)′" does not stand for a conditional statement.
9. Explain, both in symbols and in normal English, the difference between contradicting each of two elements in a molecular statement and contradicting the molecular statement itself. Use as your example the statement, "If he [c]omes, then I will [g]o." Are the results of these two operations equivalent or not?
10. Using common-sense analysis and the relevant definitions given in Sections 10.1 and 10.4, examine each of the following pairs to determine how

the two statements are related. Are they contradictory, contrary, logically equivalent, or consistent but not equivalent? To decide, you will need to ask yourself such questions as: "Could they both be true?" "Could they both be false?" "Must they have the same truth-value?" "Must they have opposite truth-values?"

a. All freshmen are intelligent; no freshmen are intelligent.

b. Some people prefer Beethoven to Bach; some people prefer Bach to Beethoven.

c. No crimes go undetected; some crimes go undetected.

d. All men desire peace; some men desire peace.

e. No fish are mammals; no mammals are fish.

f. Some birds can fly; some birds cannot fly.

g. Today is cold and windy; today is cold but not windy.

h. If it rains, the grass grows; it doesn't rain but the grass grows.

i. He has either pneumonia or asthma; if he doesn't have pneumonia, he has asthma.

j. She loves me; I love her.

11. Construct a consistency table for "$A' \vee B$." Compare this with the consistency table for "$A \supset B$." What does this comparison reveal about the logical relation between these two statements?

12. Construct consistency tables for "$A' \supset B$" and for "A / B'." Do the tables show these two statements to be logically equivalent? In the next chapter, we shall learn a simpler way of testing the logical equivalence of such statements.

CHAPTER 11

TESTING LOGICAL EQUIVALENCE OF
MOLECULAR STATEMENTS

PREVIEW

This chapter explains a method for testing the equivalence of conditional, alternative, and disjunctive statements, and in the process introduces an important symbolic notation which will be useful to us later in determining the validity of arguments.

11.1. THE DESIRABILITY OF A MORE BASIC NOTATION

You will recall that when we were mulling over the problem of whether to go to the movies or prepare for a test, we felt that we could equally well express our predicament by means of a conditional statement, an alternative statement, or a disjunctive statement. These three statements had the following forms, and we urged that the three were logically equivalent, although we did not undertake to prove this at the time:

$$M \supset T'$$
$$M' \lor T'$$
$$M / T$$

How can we show that these three forms are logically equivalent? A simple analogy will suggest a possible approach. Suppose we are confronted with three sentences expressed in three different languages other than English. Are the three sentences equivalent in meaning or not? An experienced linguist, capable of "thinking" in all three languages, would probably feel no need of translating each of these three sentences into English in order to compare them and determine their equivalence or nonequivalence. But for many of us, this translation procedure would no doubt be the safest and clearest.

We face a somewhat similar situation in considering the logical equivalence of the three statements symbolized above. They are expressed in different "languages," the conditional, the alternative, and the disjunctive. The task of comparing them would be greatly simplified if we could somehow translate them all into a common language or notation. Such a language is the ZEROFORM NOTATION. It is easy to learn because it is based directly on our knowledge of contradictories, gained in the preceding chapter. This notation gives us a common language for dealing not only with the present problem of logical equivalence, but also with the central syntactical problem of testing the validity of arguments. We shall consequently find it very useful for further work.

11.2. ZEROFORMS OF CONDITIONAL, ALTERNATIVE, AND DISJUNCTIVE STATEMENTS

Let us first consider how to translate a conditional statement into zeroform notation. We know that a conditional statement of the form "A ⊃ B" is contradicted by a *conjunctive* statement of the form "AB'." Watch this next step carefully. If we proceed to contradict the conjunctive contradictory "AB' " what will happen? We'll either get back to our original statement "A ⊃ B" or to a logically equivalent expression, won't we? *The contradictory of the contradictory of a given statement is always logically equivalent to the given statement.* Now the zeroform of a conditional statement is the contradictory of its contradictory, and is hence logically equivalent to that statement.

The zeroform makes use of a special symbol for this *second* operation of contradiction. This symbol is "= 0" (read, "is equal to zero"). This, then, is the way to set up the zeroform of "A ⊃ B." First write down its conjunctive contradictory "AB' " (first contradiction), then set this equal to zero (second contradiction). The result is the expression "AB' = 0." This expression is called, for brevity, THE ZEROFORM OF "A ⊃ B." It could be described more fully by saying that it is the *conjunctive zeroform equation* which is logically equivalent to the original conditional statement. Note that in calling it a CONJUNCTIVE ZEROFORM, we do not mean that it is the zeroform of a conjunctive statement, but rather that the letters which form its left-hand side are conjuncts.

Observe how much this zeroform notation has in common with the consistency table.

ZEROFORM FOR	CONSISTENCY TABLE FOR
A ⊃ B:	A ⊃ B:

	A ⊃ B
AB	1
A′B	1
AB′	0
A′B′	1

AB′ = 0

The expression "= 0" which occurs in the zeroform has precisely the same force as a "0" in the consistency table, *when this zero is the only one in the column.* For this single zero indicates that the expression to its left is the contradictory of the expression being analyzed. In this case, it indicates that "AB′" is the contradictory of "A ⊃ B." So too, the zeroform notation "= 0" indicates that the expression written to *its* left is the contradictory of the expression being analyzed; in this case, that "AB′" is the contradictory of "A ⊃ B."

Remember that the expression written *to the left* of "= 0" is always the *contradictory* of the original statement, but that the whole zeroform, for example, "AB′ = 0," is always *logically equivalent* to the original. Whether, in a given case, we write "A ⊃ B" or "AB′ = 0" will depend on what we are trying to do; the two expressions represent precisely the same logical situation.

The zeroform of an alternative or of a disjunctive statement is formed in the same manner. Simply set the statement's conjunctive contradictory equal to zero. With a little practice, you will find that you can readily jot down the zeroform for a molecular statement of any one of these three types:

ORIGINAL MOLECULAR STATEMENT		CONJUNCTIVE ZEROFORM
Conditional	A ⊃ B	AB′ = 0
Alternative	A ∨ B	A′B′ = 0
Disjunctive	A / B	AB = 0

In the present book, the conjunctive zeroform is the only kind we shall admit for molecular statements. It is clear from our previous work that a conjunctive statement itself cannot have a zeroform of this kind. Why not?

11.3. EQUIVALENCE OF CERTAIN MOLECULAR STATEMENTS

Now that we know how to translate them into zeroform notation, it is a simple matter to establish the equivalence of the three statements given in Section 11.1. They each have the same zeroform, and hence are logically equivalent.

ORIGINAL STATEMENTS	ZEROFORMS
M ⊃ T′	MT = 0
M′ ∨ T′	MT = 0
M / T	MT = 0

The discerning student will notice that equivalence of these statements may also be established simply by comparing their contradictories. The principle involved here is that statements having the same contradictory are always logically equivalent. It is suggested, however, that you give yourself the benefit of practicing with the zeroforms for testing logical equivalence, because familiarity with this notation will greatly simplify future work. That is why zeroforms were introduced at this point.

APPLICATIONS

1. Where possible, give zeroforms for the following statements. Capitalize bracketed letters to symbolize positively expressed statemental elements. Add a prime for negative.
   a. Water will not [f]reeze unless it is [c]old enough.
   b. Today can't be [F]riday and [S]aturday too.
   c. The porridge in the middle-sized bowl was neither too [h]ot nor too [c]old.
   d. If winter [c]omes, spring can't be [f]ar behind.
   e. He will [r]etire from public life if he doesn't [w]in the election.
   f. Corn will [f]lourish only if it [r]eceives enough water.
   g. Either this [h]at has shrunk or my [s]kull has swollen.
   h. You can't [t]urn your paper in late and not [e]xpect to have your grade lowered.
   i. This statement may be treated either as [c]onditional or as [a]lternative.
   j. If two statements have the same [z]eroform, they are logically [e]quivalent.
2. Select groups of logically equivalent statements from the following list:
   a. A ⊃ B   e. A ∨ B   i. A / B
   b. A′ ⊃ B   f. A′ ∨ B′   j. A′ / B
   c. B ⊃ A   g. A ∨ B′   k. A′ / B′
   d. B ⊃ A′   h. A′ ∨ B   l. A / B′
3. We have seen that the same logical situation may be expressed by a conditional statement, an alternative statement, or a disjunctive statement. Using

appropriate symbols, express each of the following together with logically equivalent statements of the other two types. Capitalize bracketed letters to symbolize positively expressed statements. If an element is negatively expressed, add a prime.

a. If the bakers' strike [c]ontinues, there will be a [b]read shortage.

b. We [f]ail in our duty as citizens unless we [v]ote.

c. Either the car is [o]ut of gas or the fuel line is [c]logged up.

d. She cannot both be a Phi [B]ete and not [p]ass an easy course like that.

e. Her physician will let her [r]eturn to classes only if her temperature [s]tays normal.

4. For each of the original statements in (3) above, give logically equivalent statements of the other two types, using ordinary English.

5. Develop *maxims* for each of the following. (It is not suggested that you attempt to memorize these maxims and use them explicitly. It is better to learn to perform the operations directly. Working out these maxims will, however, clarify your own thinking about the relations involved; that is the purpose of the present exercise.)

Example: Maxim for deriving an equivalent alternative statement from a given conditional statement: "Alternate the contradicted antecedent and the consequent."

a. Maxim for deriving an equivalent conditional statement from a given alternative statement.

b. Maxim for deriving an equivalent alternative statement from a given disjunctive statement.

c. Maxim for deriving an equivalent disjunctive statement from a given alternative statement.

d. Maxim for deriving an equivalent conditional statement from a given disjunctive statement.

e. Maxim for deriving an equivalent disjunctive statement from a given conditional statement.

11.4. CONDITIONAL CONTRAPOSITIVES

To see how this same test of logical equivalence may be applied to two conditional statements, consider the following example. Suppose that, in a logical mood, we are discussing a large animal that has been cast up on the shore. I comment: "If it is a whale, then it's a mammal." You say, "If it's not a mammal, then it's not a whale." We certainly appear to be saying different things. Are we in agreement or not?

Let us compare our two statements by expressing them in symbols and then writing down their zeroforms:

My statement: $W \supset M$	*Zeroform:* $WM' = 0$
Your statement: $M' \supset W'$	*Zeroform:* $M'W = 0$

How do these zeroforms compare? They have exactly the same conjuncts, don't they? In each case the conjuncts are "W" and "M'." But they are written down in a different order each time. Does this make any difference? Think about it. We know that the conjunctive connective is symmetrical, not directional. The order in which conjuncts are written down is a matter of indifference, logically speaking. Thus our two statements, although verbally quite different, are strictly equivalent.

Our two statements illustrate an interesting logical relation between certain conditional statements. If we examine their forms, we find that the contradicted antecedent of one serves as the consequent of the other, and that the contradicted consequent of the one serves as the antecedent of the other. Two conditional statements related in this way are called CONTRAPOSITIVES. Conditional contrapositives are always logically equivalent.[1]

A maxim for deriving the contrapositive of any conditional statement is not difficult to formulate:

Maxim for forming contrapositive of a conditional statement:
Interchange the contradicted antecedent and the contradicted consequent.

Don't make the mistake of trying to apply this maxim to, say, alternative or disjunctive statements. Only conditional statements have antecedents and consequents.

11.5. EXPRESSING CONDITIONAL CONTRAPOSITIVES IN ENGLISH

As long as you are working with logical symbols, the formation of the contrapositive of a given conditional expression is quite mechanical. All you have to do is to contradict each element and interchange them. But when you are working, not with symbols, but with statements in English, care and ingenuity are sometimes required in order to express the contrapositive idiomatically, and without distorting the sense.

For example, take the conditional statement, "If the pond doesn't freeze, we won't go skating." Symbolizing this statement as:

$$F' \supset S'$$

we may readily form its contrapositive:

$$S \supset F$$

---

[1] While contrapositives of *conditional* statements are the only kind we shall discuss at present, it will help to avoid later confusion if we emphasize the fact that this statement about logical equivalence does not apply to some types of contrapositives.

But if we are to express this contrapositive in normal English, we shall have to watch our step in order to avoid misunderstanding. Suppose we went ahead in a mechanical fashion (as we can when we are working, not with everyday language, but with symbols). The contrapositive would then be:

> If we'll go skating, then the pond freezes.

The sequence of tenses here is curious, and the statement is not in good idiomatic English. Suppose we tried instead:

> If we go skating, then the pond will freeze.

This is better English, but the statement is likely to be confusing, for it might seem to suggest that our going skating would somehow *make* the pond freeze. But this is certainly not what we meant. If . . . then statements are frequently used to express causal relations (as when we say, "If you let go of it, it will drop") but we did not mean to suggest here that our going skating would *cause* the pond to freeze. To get across our point in an unambiguous way, we should have to say something like:

> If we go skating, then the pond will have frozen.

The choice of tenses in this last version eliminates the misleading suggestion of the previous version. The locus of the difficulty here is not in the logical form (which was simple enough to handle when expressed symbolically) but rather in the richness and suggestiveness of everyday English.

This problem is likely to crop up, of course, not merely when we are working with contrapositives, but whenever we are trying to express the results of logical transformations in English.

• SOME REMINDERS

1. The zeroform notation provides a common "language" for expressing certain different types of statement.
2. The contradictory of the contradictory of a given statement is logically equivalent to the given statement.
3. Statements having the same zeroform are logically equivalent.
4. Certain pairs of conditional statements are called "contrapositives" because of the special way in which they are related.
5. The contrapositive of a conditional statement is always logically equivalent to it.

APPLICATIONS

1. Give the contrapositive of each of the following:
   a. A ⊃ B
   b. C′ ⊃ D
   c. E ⊃ F′
   d. G′ ⊃ H′
   e. If it [r]ains, then I'll [w]ear rubbers.
   f. If this dress [s]hrinks, I'll not get [a]nother like it.
   g. If you're not [s]atisfied, we'll [g]ive you a new one.
   h. If he can't [s]ing a note, he can't be an [o]pera star.
   i. I won't [g]o to the door unless the doorbell [r]ings.
   j. Only if it does not [r]ain will the ceremony be held [o]utdoors.
2. Traditional logic distinguishes three LAWS OF THOUGHT, which may be expressed compactly in contemporary symbols:

The Law of Identity	A ⊃ A
The Law of Excluded Middle	A ∨ A′
The Law of Noncontradiction	A / A′

   Show that these laws, traditionally regarded as three separate and distinct principles of rational thought, are actually logically equivalent.
3. Give zeroforms for each of the following statements.
   a. If the door won't [o]pen, it must be [l]ocked.
   b. [K]eats wrote this, unless it is the work of a good [i]mitator.
   c. Either [K]eats wrote this or a good [i]mitator, but not both.
   d. This [t]able top will be smooth only if you [s]and it down properly.
   e. You will be [e]xcused from the test if and only if you are too [s]ick to take it.
   f. If John is [o]lder than Mary, then he can't be [y]ounger than Pat.
   g. Either Gregory has a [d]ouble larynx, or he can't sing [t]wo parts at once.
   h. There will not be [r]oom for all this baggage unless we [t]ie some on the roof.
   i. If she doesn't [a]nswer the next time I phone, I'll [c]onclude she's through with me.
   j. I can't [u]ndergo these constant rebuffs and still [b]elieve she really loves me.
4. Four boys are planning a fishing trip. Bill says, "Unless it's cloudy, the fish won't bite." Jack comments that either the fish will bite or it won't be cloudy. Hank argues that it can't be both that it is not cloudy and that the fish will bite. David insists that the fish will bite, provided it's cloudy. Sticking precisely to what each boy has asserted, determine which of them (if any) agree with David.

CHAPTER 12

TESTING A SIMPLE ARGUMENT BY MAXIMS

PREVIEW

In the last three chapters, we have been confining our attention to the analysis of individual statements and to certain simple logical relations holding between one statement and another. We now want to consider relations that hold between the premises and conclusion of an argument. How can we reliably determine whether the conclusion of an argument logically follows from the premises? In the present chapter we shall illustrate the way in which this question may be answered at the traditional level of maxims for one simple type of argument.

12.1. WHAT IS A SIMPLE CONDITIONAL ARGUMENT?

A SIMPLE CONDITIONAL ARGUMENT consists of two premises and a conclusion.[1] One of the premises is a conditional statement. The other is an element of the conditional statement or the contradictory of one of these elements.

Consider the following example:

If this is a potato, then it's a vegetable.	$P \supset V$	**(1)**
This is a potato.	P	
It's a vegetable.	V	

Does the argument make its point? Do the two premises, written above the line, guarantee the conclusion, written below the line? Could one accept

---

[1] In traditional terms, an argument which contains two or more premises is said to be a case of MEDIATE INFERENCE. Such arguments are contrasted with those simpler cases of IMMEDIATE INFERENCE, in which the conclusion follows directly or *immediately* from a single premise, without the mediation of a second. The inference involved in passing, for example, from a conditional statement to its equivalent alternative statement is in this sense *immediate*. Further immediate inferences will be studied in Chapter 18.

the two premises without also accepting the conclusion? Is Argument 1 valid or invalid?

Compare this argument with a rather similar one:

If this is a potato, then it's a vegetable.	P ⊃ V	**(2)**
This is a vegetable.	V	
It is a potato.	P	

What is the difference between these two arguments? Does this differ-ence in form affect the matter of validity? Suppose I were to urge that both these arguments are valid. How, at the common-sense level, would you go about showing me that I was mistaken? You would probably agree that the first argument is valid. But you would help me to see that the second argument fails to make its point. You might remind me that even if the first two premises are true, the conclusion that it is a potato might be false—the vegetable in question might be, say, a turnip or a bean. Thus the conclusion that it is a potato does not *necessarily* follow. The argument is invalid.

12.2. ANALYSIS OF VALID AND INVALID FORMS

To get a better insight into what is going on here, let us set up a con-sistency table, just as we did in exploring the logical import of different types of molecular statement.

		P ⊃ V
This is a potato, and it is a vegetable too.	PV	1
This is not a potato, but it is a vegetable.	P'V	1
This is a potato, but it's not a vegetable.	PV'	0
This is not a potato, and it's not a vegetable.	P'V'	1

Now let us see if we can go beyond the common-sense level of analysis, to discover *why* the first argument is valid, and the second invalid. Re-fresh your mind on what Argument 1 is. Our previous investigations assure us that the conditional premise, "P ⊃ V," rules out the third possibility, "PV'." This is shown by the above consistency table.

Now suppose we add our second premise, "P," and see what this addition does to the remaining possibilities. To assert "P," as we do in the second premise, is to rule out its contradictory "P'." Where does this contradictory element occur in the four possibilities? As the consistency table below shows, it occurs as one of the conjuncts in the second and fourth lines, so these two possibilities must be ruled out as inconsistent with our second premise "P."

	P ⊃ V	P
PV	1	1
P′V	1	0
PV′	0	1
P′V′	1	0

Our two premises *taken together* thus rule out three of the four abstract possibilities. We are left with the possibility "PV" as the only one open to us if we accept the two premises. This possibility is of course:

This is a potato, and it is a vegetable too.

Do you see that we are thus justified in asserting "V" as our conclusion ("It is a vegetable") on the basis of the given premises?

It is customary to describe the form of a particular simple conditional argument in terms of what the atomic premise "does" to one of the elements of the conditional premise. In the argument which we have just examined, the atomic premise ASSERTS THE ANTECEDENT of the conditional premise. We have just seen that this yields a valid argument if we go on and "do the same thing" to (that is, in this case, *assert*) the other element of our conditional premise as the conclusion.

The second argument above, which common-sense analysis shows to be invalid (since the premises could be true yet the conclusion false) has the form:

$$P \supset V$$
$$\frac{V}{P}$$

Following the custom just described, an argument of this form is said to be a case of ASSERTING THE CONSEQUENT. A simple conditional argument of this form is always invalid. Let us see if we can discover why. First, set up a consistency table for the two premises:

	P ⊃ V	V
PV	1	1
P′V	1	1
PV′	0	0
P′V′	1	0

As before, the conditional premise, "P ⊃ V," rules out the third possibility. What possibilities are ruled out by the atomic premise "V"? Look and see. To assert "V" is to rule out its contradictory "V'." Thus the third and fourth possibilities are both ruled out. The question is, what can we conclude from these two premises with respect to "P"? Are we warranted in concluding, "It's a potato"? Our premises eliminate two possibilities, but they leave two others open. In one of these (the first possibility) we find "P" along with "V." In the other (the second possibility) we find its contradictory, "P'." Thus the information given in our premises does not "pin down" a conclusion with respect to "P." Both "P" and its contradictory "P' " are consistent with these premises. No conclusion is dictated, so the argument is invalid.

Where did Argument 2 go astray? By asserting the consequent in our atomic premise, we doomed the argument to inconclusiveness. The argument, and any other argument of this form, is said to commit the FALLACY OF ASSERTING THE CONSEQUENT.

Let's try a third simple conditional argument, keeping the same conditional premise so that we may compare the arguments more readily:

If this is a potato, then it's a vegetable.	P ⊃ V	**(3)**
It is not a vegetable.	V'	
This is not a potato.	P'	

How does this argument differ from the preceding two? Here our atomic premise CONTRADICTS THE CONSEQUENT of the conditional premise, and the conclusion "does the same thing" to (in this case, contradicts) the other element in the conditional premise (in this case, the antecedent). Does this argument seem valid to you? If you accept the premises, must you also accept the conclusion? Could the premises be true without the conclusion also being true?

But don't trust your intuitions here. Consider the logical import of the premises in terms of the four conjunctive possibilities. See for yourself whether these premises dictate or "pin down" the conclusion. Don't take anyone else's word for it.

And here's one more form to try:

If this is a potato, then it's a vegetable.	P ⊃ V	**(4)**
This is not a potato.	P'	
It is not a vegetable.	V'	

Describe this argument in the traditional way, that is, by telling what happens in the atomic premise. Then explore the logical import of the premises, by considering the consistency table for the two premises, and determine whether the conclusion is dictated or not.

12.3. VALIDITY MAXIM FOR SIMPLE CONDITIONAL ARGUMENTS

When you have completed this exploration, you will be in a position to draw up a VALIDITY MAXIM for simple conditional arguments. It will specify valid procedure in the atomic premise.

Maxim for valid procedure in the atomic premise of a simple conditional argument:

A ssert the ntecedent   **OR**   **C**————————
                                                    ————————

Remember that, following this maxim, valid procedure requires you to "do the same thing" to the other element of the conditional premise for the conclusion.

You will now also be able to guard against two fallacious or invalid procedures in the atomic premise. The first we have already named. You name the second one.

Fallacious procedure in the atomic premise of a simple conditional argument:

1. Fallacy of asserting the consequent.
2. Fallacy of _____ the _____.

12.4. OTHER INVALID FORMS

It may have occurred to you that there are four other possible forms of simple conditional argument that we have not yet discussed. These forms result when, in passing from the atomic premise to the conclusion, we do not "do the same thing" (that is, assert or contradict) that we did in the atomic premise. Even at the common-sense level, all four forms are so obviously invalid that they require no particular discussion. The forms are as follows:

1. A ⊃ B	2. A ⊃ B	3. A ⊃ B	4. A ⊃ B
A	B	A′	B′
B′	A′	B	A

Forms 2 and 3 are, we may say, doubly fallacious, for they not only fail to "follow through" in the conclusion but also each commits in the atomic premise one of the two fallacies already discussed. You are unlikely ever to encounter actual cases of these four forms, as people rarely get *that* confused. If we were required to give a name for the fallacy illustrated by these four forms, we should be tempted to call it, with apologies to the *New Yorker* magazine, the FALLACY OF UTTER CONFUSION.

12.5. GETTING DOWN TO CASES

As you begin to apply all this to actual arguments you encounter in conversation and in your everyday reading, you will probably make two discoveries.

(1) Simple conditional arguments are so simple that in actual practice we seldom state them fully. Often the conditional premise is not expressed at all.

> "You can't be getting enough sleep."
> "What makes you think so?"
> "Why, just look at those circles under your eyes!"

This probably does not look like a conditional argument to you, because it isn't set up formally in traditional textbook fashion. But when we make the apparently intended assumptions explicit, don't we get something like this:

> [If you have circles under your eyes, you can't be getting enough sleep.]
> You do have circles under your eyes.
> _____
> You can't be getting enough sleep.

Don't expect people to present their lines of reasoning in a neat premise-premise-conclusion arrangement. They take a good deal for granted, including your ability to get the drift of the argument and to read between the lines.

(2) You are likely to encounter cases in which your common-sense intuitions do not agree with a judgment based on the maxim. When this happens, try to find out what it was about the example that led you astray. For instance, were you reading more into the premises than was actually asserted? Did your knowledge of the factual truth of the premises and conclusion make you consider the argument valid even though it was not? Were you perhaps confusing an "if" with an "only if"? Such a scrutiny of your common-sense reactions in the light of known validity maxims can do a good deal to sharpen up your thinking at the common-sense level.

Consider the argument:

> If I filled my pen this morning, it contains enough ink for this exam.
> I didn't fill my pen this morning.
> _____
> It doesn't contain enough ink for this exam.

I have found that many people will "swallow" this argument. Yet it clearly commits the fallacy of contradicting the antecedent. If it none the less seems plausible to you, can you discover why? Are you perhaps confusing the given conditional premise with the quite different one, "Only if I filled my pen this morning, will it contain enough ink for this exam"?

This same example will serve to illustrate a type of common-sense analysis which is often helpful when we lack a maxim to guide us. If an argument is to be valid, the conclusion must be true if the premises are. Thus, we can at the common-sense level show an argument to be invalid if we can think of a case in which the conclusion might be false, even though the premises are true. In the above example, let us concede the truth of the premises. Let us suppose that I didn't fill my pen this morning, but that if I had, it would contain enough ink for the exam. Even so, the conclusion that the pen doesn't contain enough ink for the exam might be false. Perhaps someone else filled it for me, or perhaps it already contained enough ink even without filling. Since the conclusion might be false, even though the premises were true, the argument is shown to be invalid.

• **SOME REMINDERS**

1. A validity maxim may be constructed which specifies correct procedure in a simple conditional argument.
2. Violations of the maxim constitute formal fallacies.
3. Arguments are seldom stated fully in everyday life; for formal analysis, assumptions must be made explicit.
4. Thinking at the common-sense level may be sharpened by analyzing cases in which our common-sense reactions differ from those prescribed by a validity maxim.

APPLICATIONS

1. First, express each of the following arguments in standard symbols. Capitalize the bracketed letters and use them as abbreviation symbols for positively expressed statements. If the given statement is negatively expressed, be sure to add a prime to the letter symbol. Second, test the validity of each argument by the appropriate maxim. If the argument is invalid, name the fallacy committed. Third, if the argument is invalid, show that it is by means of common-sense analysis of the type explained in the last paragraph of Section 12.5 above.

   a. If the fuel tank is [e]mpty, the car won't [g]o. The car doesn't go, so the fuel tank must be empty.
   b. If I can cut my three o'clock [c]lass, I can catch the [t]rain. But I cannot cut my three o'clock class. Thus I cannot catch the train.
   c. If you do not [u]nplug that iron, the [f]use will blow. The fuse blew, so evidently you did not unplug that iron.
   d. If I see [s]moke, I'll know there's a [f]ire. I don't see smoke, so I know there's no fire.
   e. If the north wind [b]lows, we'll have [s]now. But we'll not have snow. Thus the north wind won't blow.

2. Where a valid conclusion is possible, supply it. Where a valid conclusion does not follow, show what is wrong with the premises by pointing out the formal fallacy committed.

   a. If we have [s]now, poor Robin will [h]ide in the barn. Robin does hide in the barn. Therefore . . .
   b. If you don't see the [w]hites of their eyes, you will not [s]hoot. You do shoot. This shows that . . .
   c. You will not find this [e]asy if you have not studied [h]ard. But you have studied hard. Thus . . .
   d. If the polar caps on Mars are not [h]oar frost, they are [c]arbon dioxide. They are not carbon dioxide. Therefore . . .
   e. If the instructor is more than five minutes [l]ate, the class will not [b]e

there when he arrives. The instructor is not more than five minutes late. Hence . . .

3. Develop concrete examples of each of the four forms of argument which commit what we jokingly referred to as the Fallacy of Utter Confusion. After inspecting these, do you see why such forms are unlikely to occur in actual argument, or to fool you if they do?

CHAPTER 13

DEVELOPING A MORE GENERAL
VALIDITY TEST

PREVIEW

Complex arguments can usually, with varying degrees of ingenuity, be resolved into smaller units consisting of a relatively few simple types of argument. Following our approach in the last chapter, one can develop validity maxims for these simpler units, and analyze more complicated arguments by testing their component units. We shall later return to consider in more detail this traditional approach. In the present chapter, however, we shall move on to develop a more general analysis which dispenses with the need for special maxims for each separate type of argument unit. Our knowledge of zeroform notation will be immediately useful to us here.

13.1. THE SEARCH FOR A MORE GENERAL PATTERN

In the last chapter we formulated a validity maxim for the simple conditional argument. The maxim may be thought of as describing two valid patterns of simple conditional argument. As long as an argument conforms to either of these patterns, it is valid. But many arguments we might wish to test are not simple conditional arguments at all. Our achievement in developing a maxim for one type of argument is important, but obviously rather modest. How shall we proceed to test the many other types of argument that occur in thinking?

Two possible approaches suggest themselves. First, we might continue along the line followed in the preceding chapter, examining different types of argument one by one, and developing maxims which would describe the valid argument-forms of the several types. This is in the main the procedure of traditional logic, and we shall explore it more fully in later chapters. Second, we might take a quite different approach. Can we perhaps discover something distinctive about the formal pattern which *any* valid argument has? Or if this seems too ambitious, can we perhaps at least discover something distinctive about the patterns of some reasonably large range of arguments, including those arguments distinguished by traditional logic? This is the task which we set ourselves in the present chapter.

The successful completion of this task would give us a more general approach to the problem of validity than is provided by the traditional maxims. We should no longer need a separate maxim to describe the validity pattern of each separate type of argument (although these maxims would still retain their practical usefulness). Instead, we should have at our disposal a set of more general principles which would describe the validity pattern of many different types of argument. Such a set of principles would still not provide us with a completely general test of validity, for there are possible argument-forms lying beyond the scope of any single elementary test. Yet in spite of this limitation, we should clearly possess an analytical tool of considerable power and utility. The contraform test, to be described in this chapter, is such a tool, and is simple enough to be handled readily by beginners in logic.

13.2. EXPLORING THE ZEROFORM PATTERNS OF SIMPLE CONDITIONAL ARGUMENTS

Since a formal derivation of the contraform test would take us well beyond the scope of an elementary text, we shall adopt a simpler though theoretically less satisfying approach. We shall, for expository purposes, act as if the problem we face were an inductive one, and shall explore various valid arguments already known to us in order to determine the underlying logical pattern they have in common. We shall discover that the arguments we know to be *invalid* do not share this pattern. This approach will give us a clue to the more general principles which constitute the contraform test, and should give us some sense of sharing in their discovery.[1]

---

[1] If you wish to go beyond this approach to a more adequate analysis of the rationale of the contraform test, the first steps are indicated in the three *bracketed* footnotes in this chapter. These notes are necessarily somewhat technical, and a grasp of them is not essential to the use of the test. For comments on the historical antecedents of the test, see the Preface and Section 20.1.

Because at present we know intimately only the simple conditional argument, we shall start with it. We want, however, to deal with it in such a way that our results will be directly applicable to a wider range of arguments, of which the simple conditional type is only one example. The arguments to which we shall confine our attention in this and the next two chapters have three features in common. (1) They are entirely expressible in zeroforms, none of which contains more than two conjuncts. (2) They are all MOLECULAR ARGUMENTS, which means that they each contain at least one molecular statement.[2] (3) They contain no more than one atomic *premise*, although they may also have an atomic conclusion.

Simple conditional arguments reveal all three of these characteristics, and hence may be taken as typical of the larger group. Since, however, we want our results to apply to arguments that contain alternative and disjunctive statements as well as conditional and atomic ones, we shall need a notation that will reveal what they have in common. We faced a similar situation earlier, in seeking a way of testing the logical equivalence of certain molecular statements. We found that we could compare them directly by translating them into the common language of zeroforms. This approach will again prove helpful. We already know how to express conditional, alternative, and disjunctive statements in this notation: we take their conjunctive contradictories and set these equal to zero.

The ZEROFORM OF AN UNANALYZED ATOMIC STATEMENT is formed in the same general way: we simply set its symbolized contradictory equal to zero.[3] The resulting expression may be called a SIMPLE ZEROFORM, in contrast to the conjunctive zeroforms already studied.

UNANALYZED ATOMIC STATEMENT		SIMPLE ZEROFORM
Positively expressed	A	$A' = 0$
Negatively expressed	B$'$	$B = 0$

Let us now take four simple conditional argument-forms, two of which we know to be valid, and two of which we know to be invalid by maxim.

---

[2] Such arguments are to be contrasted with ATOMIC ARGUMENTS, which consist entirely of atomic statements. (See Chapters 19–22.)

[3] Actually, this procedure may be followed for any *unanalyzed* statement, whether it is atomic or not. If, for example, a conjunctive statement occurs as a constant element in a given argument, a single letter may be assigned for the whole unanalyzed conjunctive, and a simple zeroform given for it. This procedure sometimes makes it possible for us to handle in zeroform notation a conjunctive element that would otherwise cause trouble.

Then let us express each of them in zeroforms. Since a zeroform is logically equivalent to the statement from which it is derived, the zeroforms of each argument will also be logically equivalent to the original arguments.

(1)   A ⊃ B   AB′ = 0
      A   A′ = 0
      ‾‾‾   ‾‾‾‾‾‾
      B   Valid by maxim   B′ = 0

(2)   A ⊃ B   AB′ = 0
      B′   B = 0
      ‾‾‾   ‾‾‾‾‾‾
      A′   Valid by maxim   A = 0

(3)   A ⊃ B   AB′ = 0
      B   B′ = 0
      ‾‾‾   ‾‾‾‾‾‾
      A   Invalid by maxim   A′ = 0

(4)   A ⊃ B   AB′ = 0
      A′   A = 0
      ‾‾‾   ‾‾‾‾‾‾
      B′   Invalid by maxim   B = 0

What, if anything, have the zeroform patterns of the valid arguments in common which reliably distinguishes them from the zeroform patterns of the invalid arguments? In spite of, or perhaps because of, our narrow sample, certain features stand out. First, look at the zeroform equations derived from the premises. In the valid forms, each pair of equations contains a common letter, *which appears once primed and once unprimed.* In Example 1, it is the letter "A." It appears unprimed in the first equation, and primed in the second. For convenience, we shall say that these letters form a "pair," or that they "pair off." A PAIR consists of two occurrences, in different zeroform equations, of the same letter, once primed and once unprimed. In Example 2, "B′ " in the first equation and "B" in the second form a pair. This concept of *pairing* is a crucial one, so fix it clearly in mind.

Now consider the zeroforms which represent the premises of the two *invalid* forms. Neither set contains a pair in our defined sense, for in each case the common letter has the same sign in both its occurrences.

Next, let us observe a further characteristic which distinguishes the valid from the invalid forms. In the valid forms, the remaining letter in the premises, that is, the one which does not enter into the pair, recurs *with the same sign* (prime or lack of it) in the remaining zeroform. This is not the case in the invalid forms.

These two features which distinguish the above valid forms from the invalid ones are not happy accidents. They are characteristic marks of the zeroform patterns of valid arguments falling within the range indicated at the beginning of Section 13.2. The zeroform pattern of an invalid argument will lack one or both of these characteristics. In Section 13.4, we shall state these distinguishing marks more formally in terms of principles, and shall generalize them so that they will apply also to arguments having more than two premises.

13.3. SETTING UP A TEST FORM

If our interest were limited to molecular arguments, the manner in which we have stated the distinctive pattern of valid forms would be adequate, once we had taken account of arguments containing more than two premises. But since we shall later want to be able to deal with arguments which consist entirely of atomic statements, it is desirable to set up our validity test in such a way that it can later be applied to these forms also. What change is required in order to make this possible?

You will have noticed that, in describing the distinctive pattern of the valid forms above, "pairing off" involved the *premise* zeroforms, while the unpaired letter reappeared in the zeroform of the *conclusion*. In the valid atomic arguments which we shall later study, this will not always be the case. Hence it would be misleading to formulate our validity principles in terms of the contrast between premises and conclusion. The needed solution lies in stating the validity principles, not for the zeroforms of the argument being tested, but for *a closely related form in which the distinction between premises and conclusion no longer remains.*

This related form is called the TEST FORM, and is derived from the zeroform expression of the argument to be analyzed by doing two things: (1) We *contradict* the zeroform conclusion.[4] A zeroform equation is con-

---

[4] [If this does not seem strange to you, or if you are not the curious type, don't bother. But if you want to explore further the logical properties of the test form, this note will get you started. (The specific need for the test form will only become apparent later when we begin testing arguments consisting entirely of atomic statements.) You know that the zeroform expression of an argument is strictly equivalent to the original argument. If the original argument is *valid*, the statements composing it will constitute a CONSISTENT SET, and the same will be the case for the zeroform expression of a valid argument. To say that a set of statements is consistent means, as we have seen, that they may all be true. In fact, in a valid argument or its zeroforms, if the premises are true the conclusion *must* be true. Now think about the test form. In setting it up we

tradicted by changing its equation sign to an inequation sign. Thus the contradictory of "A = 0" is the inequation, "A ≠ 0" (read, "A is not equal to zero"). (2) Since we certainly do not want to claim that this contradictory of the zeroform conclusion *follows from* the given premises, we drop out the line (meaning "therefore") which is used to separate premises from conclusion. Compare carefully the zeroform equivalent of the simple conditional argument given below and the related test form:

ORIGINAL ARGUMENT	ZEROFORM EQUIVALENT	TEST FORM
$A \supset B$	$AB' = 0$	$AB' = 0$
B'	$B = 0$	$B = 0$
A'	$A = 0$	$A \neq 0$

Notice that in the test form, all references to premises and conclusion disappear, and the basis for distinguishing between the statements in the test form is whether the statement is an equation or an inequation. Note also that if, from the very first, you establish the habit of always dropping out the "therefore" line in the test form, you will never become confused about whether you are looking at the zeroform equivalent of an argument or at the related test form.

It is obvious that, in the types of argument we are now considering, the inequation will always appear in the last line of the test form. But it will help to remember that this will not necessarily be the case in the test forms of arguments we shall later study.

13.4. THE CONTRAFORM TEST

The contraform test of validity consists in setting up the test form of the argument in question, and then inspecting it to see whether it reveals the distinctive pattern which shows that the argument from which it was derived is valid. To put it another way, we inspect the test form to see whether it is a contraform. A CONTRAFORM is a test form which satisfies the three following requirements:

purposely *contradict* the zeroform conclusion. If the test form is a contraform, that is, if it satisfies the three contraform principles which we shall state in the next section, the original argument is shown to be valid. But if the original argument is valid, the test form is bound to be an INCONSISTENT SET; the zeroforms composing it cannot possibly all be true. A test form which satisfies the contraform principles is thus an inconsistent set of zeroforms which manifests a certain characteristic pattern, described by the principles. This pattern is a reliable symptom of the validity of the original argument.]

The contraform principles:

Principle 1: There is exactly one inequation.

Principle 2: At least one letter in each *equation* pairs off with a letter in another equation.

Principle 3: The unpaired letters in the equations reappear with their same signs (prime or lack of it) in the *inequation*.

Any argument which falls within the scope of the contraform test (see Section 13.6) but which fails to satisfy all three principles is invalid. Violations may be indicated by mentioning the number of the unsatisfied principle, or by naming the fallacy committed. Violations of Principle 1 lead either to the fallacy of NO INEQUATION or to the fallacy of MULTIPLE INEQUATIONS. When we violate Principle 2, we are guilty of the fallacy of INCOMPLETE PAIRING. Failure of a test form to satisfy Principle 3 constitutes the fallacy of FAULTY INEQUATION.

PRINCIPLE	FALLACY
1	No Inequation
	Multiple Inequations
2	Incomplete Pairing
3	Faulty Inequation

13.5. REMARKS ON THE CONTRAFORM PRINCIPLES [5]

It will help you fix these principles in mind if you note that Principle 1 deals with the inequation, Principle 2 with the equations, and Principle 3

[5] [By virtue of the way in which certain elements of the premises are related to each other, the conclusion of a valid argument asserts something directly about one or more other elements. This is apparent in a simple conditional argument such as:

$$A \supset B$$
$$\underline{A}$$
$$B,$$

where the "A" performs a bridging or relating function in the two premises which permits us to say something directly about "B" in the conclusion. This bridging or mediating role of certain elements in the premises of a valid argument is even more strikingly revealed in an argument of the form:

$$A \supset B$$
$$\underline{B \supset C}$$
$$A \supset C$$

Here, because of the mediating function of "B" in the premises, the conclusion is able to state a direct relationship between "A" and "C." But until a common nota-

with a certain relationship between the equations and the inequation.

As long as we are testing only molecular arguments, Principle 1 is bound to seem unnecessary, for our procedure in setting up the test form guarantees that we shall have exactly one inequation. Remember, however, that the principles are purposely stated in such a way that they can later be applied directly to atomic arguments as well.

Principle 2 describes the characteristic pattern of pairing which marks the test form of a valid argument. Remember that to "pair off," a letter must have *opposite* signs (prime or lack of it) in its two occurrences.[6] Note carefully how this principle is stated. If all test forms were as simple as those of the simple conditional arguments we have analyzed, there would be no need for inserting the expression, "at least." But many arguments have more than two premises, and we need to take account of this in formulating our principles.

Now a word about Principle 3. Here again, as in the case of Principle 2, we need to take account of more complex cases than those presented by the simple conditional argument. In a valid argument of that type, there is of course only one letter in the equations which does not pair off. In many arguments, however, there will be more than one unpaired letter in the equations. In accordance with Principle 3, they must reappear, with their same signs, as conjuncts in the inequation. If the same unpaired letter occurs twice in the equations, it need be written down only once in the inequation, for "AA" is just a complex way of saying "A."[7] There is one other point to notice about Principle 3, although we seldom have occasion to draw on it: there is nothing about this principle which rules out the possibility that some further letter might also appear in the inequation,

---

tion is available, no general description of the required mediating roles can be given. Once, however, the common language of zeroforms has been used to set up the test form of an argument, the contraform principles give us a generalized description of the bridging or mediating relationships essential for validity of a wide range of arguments. The upshot of this generalized description is that each constituent item (letter symbol) in the test form requires relating in one of two ways: (1) by pairing with an item in another equation or (2) by conjoining with other unpaired letters in the inequation.]

[6] A practical hint: In checking a test form by Principle 2, it will help you keep track of things better if you draw a light line through the letters which pair off. Make this a habit.

[7] This is a special form of what is called the SIMPLIFICATION RULE. We may express it more formally by saying that any argument of the following form is valid:

$$\frac{AA}{A}$$

even though it did not appear in an equation at all. This would be unusual, but we shall see in Section 14.2 why it would be a mistake to exclude this possibility.

If all this seems a bit complicated on first reading, be assured that with a little practice in applying the contraform test to concrete arguments, it will all be quite simple. If, in your first attempts to use these principles, questions of interpretation come up, turn back to this section to refresh your memory of just what the principles mean.

13.6. HOW GENERAL IS THE CONTRAFORM TEST?

There is no elementary test of validity which provides a uniform approach to all possible types of argument. The contraform test is no exception. While the contraform principles have a much broader scope than any traditional maxims, there are forms of argument to which they do not apply.

In this section we shall indicate the range within which the contraform principles in their present form reliably distinguish valid from invalid arguments. This problem does not need to be faced as long as we confine our attention to the argument forms of mediate inferences studied in this book, for these fall within the range of the test. An understanding of the scope of the test is needed, however, in order to decide whether the contraform principles are applicable to other forms of argument which may be encountered elsewhere. You may wish to postpone detailed study of this section until after you have become more familiar with the contraform principles themselves, and have gained some skill in applying them to concrete arguments.

We shall first give a compact summary of the range of the contraform test, and shall then discuss the matter in more detail.

Range of the contraform principles: The argument to be tested must
  a. have not less than two functional premises;
  b. be expressible entirely in two-conjunct or simple zeroforms;
  c. have a test form which does not contain more than one simple zero-form *equation*;
  d. have a test form which does not contain the same letter (primed, unprimed, or both) in more than two *equations*.

The most obvious limitation of the contraform test is that it cannot be applied to an argument unless that argument is entirely expressible in conjunctive zeroforms, or in a combination of conjunctive and simple zeroforms.

A second limitation of the contraform test in its present form is that it does not apply to an argument whose test form contains more than one simple (that is, single-letter) zeroform *equation*. Stating this limitation more specifically as it affects molecular arguments, the test does not cover a molecular argument which contains *more than one atomic premise;* in such cases we face a logical situation comparable to that in which a first-order conjunctive statement occurs. (These two limitations are summarized under (b) and (c) above.)

Even when an argument is entirely expressible in zeroforms, it may be either too simple or too complex to fall under the contraform test. On the side of simplicity, all *immediate inferences* fall outside its scope, for since they contain only one premise, Principle 2 has no meaning as applied to them. (Immediate inferences are handled, as we have seen, by simpler devices such as the direct comparison of two zeroforms.) You should perhaps also be warned about certain arguments which are deceptive in that they appear to have two premises, but actually have only one that plays a *functional role* in the inference. Consider, for example, an argument of the following form:

$$A \supset B$$
$$\frac{B}{A \supset B}$$

If you make the mistake of trying to apply the contraform test to this argument, you will think that it is invalid. Actually, it is perfectly valid, but only trivially so, for the conclusion merely repeats the first premise. The second "premise" is only window dressing, since the conclusion follows from the first premise alone. Thus the example, and others of its type, may for our purposes be considered a concealed form of immediate inference.[8] When such a unit is tucked away in a more extended argu-

---

[8] Such an argument may also be treated as falling under the general Simplification Rule of which a special form was mentioned in the preceding section. The general rule may be expressed symbolically:

$$\frac{AB}{A}$$

ment, it may give you trouble until you notice what is really going on. (The points discussed in this paragraph are summarized under (a) in the table above.)

Just as some arguments are too simple to fall within the scope of the contraform test, some are too complex. The test in its present form must be limited (1) to arguments whose zeroforms each contain no more than two conjuncts (see point (b) in the summary table above), and (2) to arguments whose test forms do not contain the same letter, whether primed, unprimed, or both, in more than two *equations* (see point (d) in the table). These two restrictions are related, although this may not be apparent on the surface. When argument-forms reach a certain level of complexity, it is sometimes possible to get a kind of excessive pairing in the test form. Thus, while most of the complex arguments which would test as valid by the contraform principles actually would be valid, the test does not reliably discriminate at this level, and would occasionally let an invalid argument slip through.[9]

One other restriction on the use of the test is only temporary. At the moment, we are purposely limiting its application to molecular arguments. There is nothing in the nature of the test itself which requires this limitation. In later chapters we shall see how these same three contraform principles will serve to check the validity of arguments consisting entirely of atomic statements. But before we can use the test for this purpose, we shall have to learn how to analyze such statements in terms of classes, and how to express the results in class zeroforms. This will be done in Chapter 16.

[9] [Consider, for example, an argument which lies beyond the first of these two limitations. To take a minimum case, suppose a test form contains one three-conjunct equation. Then, if the argument is valid, there should be left unpaired one, two, or *possibly three* letters to reappear in the inequation in accordance with Principle 3. In circumstances in which, to secure validity, three letters *should* reappear in the inequation, it would at times be possible to get an illicit pairing of two of the three, so that a single-letter inequation would mistakenly seem warranted. A similar situation would at times arise if the second limitation were ignored and Principle 2 were applied to pair a letter in one equation with its opposite in each of two other equations.

If an argument lies beyond the first limitation because the *inequation* contains more than two conjuncts, we encounter an opposite difficulty. Here the principles would on occasion (because of their inability to deal with conjunctive statements) lead us to reject as invalid a conclusion which is actually valid. Or, if the premises only were given and the conclusion were to be discovered by contraform principles, they would at times dictate a weaker (though valid) alternative conclusion, when a stronger *conjunctive* conclusion would actually also be warranted. Hence we limit the application of the test to the range within which it reliably discriminates.]

While you should not lose sight of the fact that the contraform test is not completely general in its applicability, you will find that it provides a useful tool for checking the validity of a great many arguments, including but not limited to the argument-forms distinguished by traditional logic. It thus serves as a convincing illustration at an elementary level of the power of contemporary symbolic analysis.

• SOME REMINDERS

1. The validity or invalidity of arguments expressible in zeroforms may, within limits specified in Section 13.6, be determined by contraform analysis.
2. Contraform analysis involves three steps:
   a. Express the original argument in zeroforms.
   b. Set up a test form by contradicting the zeroform conclusion and deleting the "therefore" line.
   c. Inspect the test form to see whether it is a contraform.
3. To be a contraform, a test form must satisfy the following principles:
   Principle 1: There is exactly one inequation.
   Principle 2: At least one letter in each equation pairs off with a letter in another equation.
   Principle 3: The unpaired letters in the equations reappear with their same signs in the inequation.

APPLICATIONS

1. Set up test forms for the arguments given in Application 1 of Chapter 12. Which of these test forms are contraforms? What does this show about the arguments from which they were derived?
2. Examine the following test forms to determine whether they satisfy the contraform principles. If one or more principles are violated, name the resulting contraform fallacies.

a. $AB' = 0$
    $B = 0$
    $A \neq 0$

b. $AB = 0$
    $A = 0$
    $B' \neq 0$

c. $AB' = 0$
    $BC' = 0$
    $AC' \neq 0$

d. $AB' = 0$
    $BC = 0$
    $CA = 0$

e. $AB' = 0$
    $D = 0$
    $BC' = 0$
    $CD' = 0$
    $A' \neq 0$

3. Which of the following situations are permissible in a contraform?
   a. more than two equations;
   b. pairing off a primed letter with another primed letter;
   c. pairing off a letter in an equation with a letter in an inequation;
   d. pairing off a primed letter in one equation with an unprimed letter in another equation;
   e. an inequation which was not derived from the conclusion of the original argument.

4. First, express each of the following arguments in standard symbols. Second, if you know a maxim that applies, test the argument by this maxim. If the argument is invalid, name the fallacy committed. Third, determine validity or invalidity of the argument by means of the contraform test. Fourth, if the results of applying the maxim or the contraform test disagree with your common-sense intuitions, follow suggestions made under (2) in Section 12.5.
   a. Either this paper will [c]hange its editorial policy, or I'll not [r]enew my subscription. The paper will change its editorial policy, so I will renew my subscription.
   b. If this lecture doesn't get more [i]nteresting, I'll get out my [k]nitting. I won't get out my knitting, because the lecture has gotten more interesting.
   c. He cannot both [m]arry that girl and not [l]ose the family inheritance. He will not lose the family inheritance. Thus he will not marry that girl.
   d. I can [g]o to Cleveland only if my allowance [c]omes in time. My allowance will come in time, so I can go to Cleveland.
   e. [I]'ll be glad to tell her, unless [y]ou'd rather tell her yourself. Since you wouldn't rather tell her yourself, I will be glad to do so.

5. Explain what it is about each of the following arguments that places it beyond the range of the contraform test.

   a. $A \supset (B \lor C)$
   $B \supset D$
   $C \supset E$
   $\overline{A \supset (D \lor E)}$

   b. $A \supset B$
   $\overline{A \ / \ B'}$

   c. $A \supset (B \lor C)$
   A
   $\underline{B'}$
   C

   d. $A \supset B$
   $A \supset C$
   $\underline{A}$
   BC

   e. $A \supset B$
   $B \supset C'$
   $\overline{C \supset B'}$

CHAPTER 14

APPLYING THE CONTRAFORM TEST

PREVIEW

We are now ready to examine more fully three practical uses to which the contraform analysis may be put in dealing with arguments falling within its scope. (1) As we saw in the last chapter, if we are given such an argument, the contraform test will determine whether it is valid or invalid. (2) If we are given certain premises, the contraform principles will determine what conclusion, if any, follows from them. (3) If we are given certain incomplete information and a conclusion, the principles will help us determine what additional information or assumptions are needed to validate the conclusion.

14.1. TESTING MORE COMPLEX ARGUMENTS FOR VALIDITY

Thus far we have used the contraform test to check the validity of only the simplest arguments. In the present section we shall illustrate the use of the test to determine the validity of more complex forms. The same three contraform principles apply, but we need to develop familiarity with their use in these more complex situations. Consider the following argument:

> The administration must not [p]ush this proposed legislation, or it will [a]lienate an important sector of the electorate. If the administration has the [i]nterests of the party at heart, it will not alienate an important sector of the electorate. But the administration cannot both [e]xpect to have the approval of the party and not have the interests of the party at heart. So if the administration pushes this proposed legislation, it cannot expect to have the approval of the party.

Not only have we no maxim for handling this particular form of argument, but also it is complex enough so that we should hesitate to trust our common-sense intuitions. Let us try the contraform test.

ORIGINAL ARGUMENT	ZEROFORM EQUIVALENT	TEST FORM
$P' \lor A$	$PA' = 0$	$PA' = 0$
$I \supset A'$	$IA = 0$	$IA = 0$
$E \, / \, I'$	$EI' = 0$	$EI' = 0$
$\overline{P \supset E'}$	$\overline{PE = 0}$	$PE \neq 0$

As you become more familiar with the contraform test, you may safely omit writing out the zeroform equivalent before setting up the test form. But it will be crucial to remember that the last line of the test form is always the *contradictory* of the conclusion, and not the zeroform equivalent of it.

When we examine the test form, what do we find? Of course there is exactly one inequation, so Principle 1 is satisfied. Principle 2 requires that at least one letter in each equation pair off with a letter in another equation. Inspection shows that the first two equations contain the pair "A'" and "A," while the second and third equations contain the pair "I" and "I'." Thus Principle 2 is satisfied. Principle 3 requires that the unpaired letters in the equations (in this case "P" and "E") appear with their same signs in the inequation. Since this principle is also satisfied, the test form is shown to be a contraform, and the original argument is now known to be valid.

The following example will help to clarify the application of Principle 3, for it illustrates the uncommon, but none the less permissible, occurrence of an "extra" letter in the inequation. This possibility was mentioned in discussing the third contraform principle in Section 13.5.

> If this cough medicine contains [c]odein, it may be [h]abit-forming. If it may be habit-forming, federal law requires that it be so [l]abeled. But federal law does not require that this cough medicine be so labeled. Hence, either it does not contain codein or it has a wild cherry [f]lavor.

ORIGINAL ARGUMENT	ZEROFORM EQUIVALENT	TEST FORM
$C \supset H$	$CH' = 0$	$CH' = 0$
$H \supset L$	$HL' = 0$	$HL' = 0$
L'	$L = 0$	$L = 0$
$\overline{C' \lor F}$	$\overline{CF' = 0}$	$CF' \neq 0$

The test form of this argument clearly satisfies the first two contraform principles. The unusual thing about it is that the inequation contains not only the unpaired letter "C," but a new letter "F'." There is nothing in the contraform principles which prohibits this, and in fact the argument is a valid one.

We shall want to see why it would be incorrect to interpret Principle 3 in such a way that it would exclude the possibility of an extra letter in the inequation. But this matter will be more readily understood after we have discussed a further way of using the contraform test. We shall therefore return to this problem at the end of the following section.

14.2. DERIVING VALID CONCLUSIONS

So far our use of contraform analysis has been limited to testing the validity of arguments. We now want to see that this analysis also gives us a way of finding out what conclusion, if any, follows from certain information.

Let's begin with a simple example in which the warranted conclusion will be obvious at the common-sense level:

> Either Mary is [p]resident or she is [s]ecretary.
> She is not president.
> _____

In a simple case like this, you will not hesitate to conclude that she must be secretary. Let's see how this conclusion is established by contraform analysis. Using appropriate symbols:

GIVEN PREMISES	ZEROFORM EQUIVALENT
$P \lor S$	$P'S' = 0$
P'	$P = 0$

We know that, if the argument is to be a valid one, our test form will have a zeroform *in*equation, representing the contradicted conclusion.

$$\text{TEST FORM}$$
$$P'S' = 0$$
$$P = 0$$
$$? \neq 0$$

But what will the left-hand side of this inequation be? Remember the requirements set forth by the contraform principles. In the test form, "P' " and "P" pair off to satisfy Principle 2. This leaves "S'." What becomes of it? We know that, to satisfy Principle 3, this "S' " must also appear in the inequation. Thus our completed test form will be:

COMPLETED TEST FORM

$$P'S' = 0$$
$$P = 0$$
$$S' \neq 0$$

Now what does this inequation mean, in terms of the conclusion we are seeking? We know that this inequation is the *contradicted* zeroform conclusion of the original argument. The zeroform conclusion itself is therefore "$S' = 0$," which is just a hard way of saying "S," or in everyday English, "Mary is secretary."

It would be outrageous to go to all this work to "discover" a simple conclusion that was obvious before we began, were it not for the fact that this exercise reveals an approach that can be used on much more complicated cases in which a warranted conclusion is by no means intuitively apparent.

Let us take a slightly more complicated example:

If the sun [c]omes out, we'll go on a [p]icnic.
We won't both go on a picnic and eat supper at [h]ome.

First we set up the zeroforms of the given premises, and then go as far as we can toward writing out the test form:

GIVEN PREMISES	ZEROFORM EQUIVALENT	TEST FORM
$C \supset P$	$CP' = 0$	$CP' = 0$
P / H	$PH = 0$	$PH = 0$
		$? \not\prec 0$

Inspection shows that the "P" and "P'" pair off in the equations, leaving "C" and "H" to be conjoined in the inequation, "$CH \neq 0$."

This inequation is the *contradictory* of the desired zeroform conclusion, hence that conclusion is "$CH = 0$." What does this mean? It may be expressed either as a conditional statement, or as an alternative statement, or as a disjunctive statement. These three statements are all logically equivalent, and it will be a matter of convenience which one we choose:

$C \supset H'$ If the sun comes out, then we won't eat supper at home.

$C' \vee H'$ Either the sun won't come out or we'll not eat supper at home (maybe both).

C / H Not both will the sun come out and will we eat supper at home (maybe neither).

In this example, we should probably tend to prefer the conditional form of conclusion, although the other two are each equivalent to it.

With this background, we may return to the question raised but not answered in the preceding section: "Why must we not exclude the possibility of an extra letter appearing in the inequation of a test form?" First, in terms of our cough medicine example, note what the situation would have been if the extra letter "F′" had not occurred. The inequation would have read simply "$C \neq 0$." If this had been the case, what would the original conclusion have been? The zeroform equivalent of this conclusion would be the contradictory of the zeroform inequation, in other words, "$C = 0$." This is of course equivalent to "C'," or in English, "This cough medicine does not contain codein." With the addition of the extra letter "F′" to the inequation, the zeroform equivalent of the conclusion will of course be "$CF' = 0$." This is a conjunctive zeroform equation, and as we saw above, any such zeroform may be interpreted indifferently as a conditional, a disjunctive, or an alternative. For our present purpose the alternative form makes it easiest to see what is going on. How does this alternative conclusion compare with the atomic conclusion "C'" that would have been indicated if the extra letter "F′" had not been present in the inequation? It contains the atomic conclusion "C'" as one of the alternants, along with the alternant "F."

Now comes the crucial point. Do you see that, no matter what "F" may be, if we were warranted in asserting the atomic statement "C'" we are also warranted in asserting the alternative statement "$C' \lor F$"? If we were warranted in concluding from the given premises, "This cough medicine does not contain codein," could we possibly be mistaken in asserting the weaker alternative statement, "Either this cough medicine does not contain codein or it has a wild cherry flavor"? We could not be. If we accept a given statement, we are always logically committed to accepting also an alternative statement having the given statement as one alternant, and any conceivable statement as the other alternant.[1]

Let us note the logical relationship between such a given statement

---

[1] This is technically called the ADDITION RULE, and may be summarized by saying that any argument of the following form is valid:

$$\frac{A}{A \lor B}$$

While this consideration by itself would permit the introduction of an indefinite number of "extra" letters in the inequation, we shall not in the context of contraform analysis consider cases where the total number of conjuncts in the inequation exceeds two. Otherwise we have moved beyond the specified scope of this elementary test. (See Section 13.6.)

and such an alternative statement. They are so related that (1) if the former is true, the latter is necessarily true also, but from the truth of the latter, nothing may be inferred about the truth-value of the former, and (2) if the latter is false, the former is necessarily false also, but from the falsity of the former, nothing may be inferred about the truth-value of the latter. Of two statements related in this way, the former is called SUPERALTERN and the latter SUBALTERN.[2]

Let us summarize the results of this exploration. Since an alternative statement (such as we have been examining) is always equivalent to a certain conditional, and to a certain disjunctive statement, an extra letter in an otherwise single-letter inequation of a test form is justified, no matter whether the resulting conclusion is expressed as an alternative or as a conditional or disjunctive.

14.3. SUPPLYING ASSUMPTIONS NEEDED FOR VALIDITY

Thus far we have used the contraform principles for two purposes: (1) to determine the validity of a given argument and (2) to derive a valid conclusion, if one is possible, from given premises. In the present section, we shall note how these principles may be used on enthymemes to determine what assumptions must be supplied for validity. It should be clear that the question of whether such needed assumptions are actually justified by the facts will have to be decided not on formal, but on empirical grounds. Our present concern, however, is not with the factual truth of the supplied assumptions, but rather with their form.

Let us set up the zeroforms and the test form of the following enthymeme:

I can't get that [E]nglish theme finished this evening, because I have to do my [l]ogic.

ZEROFORM EQUIVALENT	TEST FORM
$L' = 0$	$L' = 0$
$E = 0$	$E \neq 0$

[2] These names, despite appearances, have nothing to do with the fact that the latter statement in our pair happened to be an *alternative* statement. The logical relationship with respect to truth-values would hold equally if, in place of the alternative statement, we had used its conditional or its disjunctive equivalent. For examples in which both the superaltern and the subaltern are atomic, see Section 18.4.

Obviously, the conclusion does not follow from the given information. But we can determine what additional assumption would validate the argument. The situation is simple enough so that we could supply such an assumption either by common sense or by means of the maxim for a simple conditional argument. But instead, let us work it out by means of the contraform requirements.

Inspection of the test form indicates that an additional premise is needed. The "L'" must pair off with an "L" in another equation, and the "E" in the inequation must recur unchanged in an equation. Clearly, the way to meet these requirements is to supply a further premise as follows:

SUPPLEMENTED TEST FORM
$$[LE = 0]$$
$$L' = 0$$
$$E \neq 0$$

The contraform principles are now satisfied, and it only remains to translate the supplied premise into English. This can be done in a number of different ways, one of which is, "If I have to do my logic, I can't get that English theme finished this evening." In what other ways might this zeroform be expressed in English?

Now let us consider a somewhat more complex example. Some time ago we examined a simple conditional argument: "If it's a potato, then it's a vegetable. It is not a vegetable. Therefore, it is not a potato." Suppose we had argued instead:

> If this is a [p]otato, then it's a [v]egetable.
> This is a [f]ruit.
> _____
> It's not a potato.

If we try to treat this as a complete simple conditional argument, it is clearly invalid, for the atomic premise does not contradict the consequent. (Why not?) Yet most of us would accept this as a good argument. Why? Because we are all in a position to supply the further premise needed to make this argument a valid one. We all know that if this is a fruit, then it's not a vegetable. We take this assumption for granted in judging the argument to be a good one.

If we approach this problem in terms of the contraform principles, what do we find? Symbolize the given argument and set up the test form:

ORIGINAL ARGUMENT	TEST FORM
$P \supset V$	$PV' = 0$
F	$F' = 0$
$\overline{P'}$	$P \neq 0$

In applying the contraform principles, we find that there is exactly one inequation. We also note that the "P" in the equation reappears in the inequation. But as it stands, we can't regard this as "left over" because as yet nothing has been paired off in the equations. If this were a purely formal problem, we should probably have no hesitation in rejecting the argument as invalid and letting it go at that. Since, however, we are analyzing an actual argument which we are reluctant to reject, it is of interest to see whether we can formally justify our considering the argument as prevalid. When the test form is inspected from this point of view, it is clear that if "F'" and "V'" were paired off with an "F" and a "V" in another equation, all three principles would be satisfied.

SUPPLEMENTED TEST FORM

$$PV' = 0$$
$$[FV = 0]$$
$$F' = 0$$
$$P \neq 0$$

If we express this supplied premise as a conditional statement, we shall get either "If this is a fruit, then it's not a vegetable" or its contrapositive, "If this is a vegetable, then it's not a fruit."

• SOME REMINDERS

1. For arguments falling within its scope, the contraform test can be used to determine validity or invalidity, to derive warranted conclusions, or to supply further assumptions needed for validity.
2. The contraform principles permit the appearance of an extraneous letter in the inequation of the test form.

APPLICATIONS

1. Apply the contraform test to each of the following arguments. Indicate whether the argument is valid or invalid. If invalid, name contraform fallacy committed.

a. Captain John Smith will be [e]xecuted by the Indians unless Pocahontas [i]ntervenes. She will intervene only if she [l]oves him enough to risk her father's displeasure. She apparently does love him that much, for John Smith is not executed.

b. The wolf didn't eat both [R]ed Riding Hood and her [g]randmother. If he had eaten Red Riding Hood, she wouldn't ever have [a]rrived at her grandmother's house. She did, however, arrive there, so he must have eaten the grandmother.

c. This specimen is either [g]old or [i]ron pyrites. If it's gold, I'm [r]ich. On the other hand, if it's iron pyrites, I've been [d]uped. So if I'm rich, I haven't been duped.

d. If the prof is sick on [T]uesday, our exam will be [p]ostponed. But either he will be sick on Tuesday or I'll cut class [M]onday. If the exam is postponed, I'll have time to [s]tudy for it. But I cannot both stay in [b]ed on Tuesday and have time to study for the exam. Therefore either I'll cut class Monday or I'll not stay in bed on Tuesday.

e. If he wasn't [w]atching where he was going, he was in no [p]osition to avoid the crash. Either he was [b]linded by the bright lights or he wasn't watching where he was going. He was in a position to avoid the crash. If he was blinded by the bright lights, the accident wasn't his [f]ault. Hence he was watching where he was going. (*Hint:* Is all the information needed?)

f. If the American Indians came from [S]iberia, they must have crossed by a land [b]ridge to Alaska. If they did this, the [g]eography of the region has changed. If they did not come from Siberia, they must be [i]ndigenous to America. But it is false that they are. Hence either the geography of the region has changed, or they did not come from Siberia. (*Hint:* Watch interpretation of Principle 3.)

g. Voters will [a]pprove the bond issue only if they are [c]onvinced that a new school building is imperative. If taxes go [u]p, some people will have to [r]etrench on luxuries. Either voters will not approve the bond issue or taxes will go up. Hence, if voters are convinced that a new school building is imperative, some people will have to retrench on luxuries.

h. If John is to be a [d]octor, he'll have to go to [m]edical school. If he's to do that, he'll [n]eed more funds than he has. If so, someone will have to [h]elp him out financially. But, unfortunately, no one will help him in this way, so either he can't be a doctor, or one of our [p]remises is false.

i. [C]ondensation will gather inside this underground fuel tank unless it is kept [f]illed during the warm weather. The tank will [r]ust if this condensation occurs. It won't rust, however, if it's kept filled during the warm weather. If the tank develops a [l]eak, the oil will run out into the [g]round. In this case, it will be [w]asted. I won't have to buy a [n]ew tank if this one doesn't develop a leak. If the oil is wasted, I'll have to buy [m]ore. So I'll either have to buy a new tank or more oil, maybe both.

    j. Unless Alice goes to the movies with [m]e, [J]ack can go to the movies with her. If I [b]reak out with an allergic rash, Alice will be [a]nnoyed. If I buy her some [p]opcorn, she'll [o]ffer me some. Jack will [c]atch cold if he doesn't put his sweatshirt on after the [r]ace. Either Alice won't be annoyed, or I'll be annoyed [t]oo. Not both will Alice go to the movies with me and I not buy her some popcorn. If I'm annoyed too, I'll [s]tutter. If Jack catches cold, he can't go to the movies with Alice. Alice will offer me some popcorn only if I'll [e]at it. If I eat it, I'll break out with an allergic rash. So if Jack doesn't put his sweatshirt on after the race, I'll stutter.

2. Using contraform principles, complete the following enthymemes by deriving a valid conclusion if none is given, or by supplying an assumption which, together with the given premises, will validate the given conclusion.

    a. It can't be that he has a wooden [l]eg. If he had, he couldn't [d]ance that well.

    b. He couldn't [p]ass the exam without [s]tudying more than he admits he did. So he must really have studied more than he admits.

    c. Unless he [r]eports the fire promptly, it is likely to get [o]ut of control. He can do so only if the phone is not [b]usy. But it is.

    d. If Mary [e]nters the beauty contest, she is sure to [w]in, because if she enters it, the judges will find her [i]rresistible.

    e. This tree is either a [s]pruce or a [l]arch. If it's a larch, it will shed its needles in [a]utumn. So either it will shed its needles in autumn or its needles are [f]our-sided.

    f. If we are to see the sun come [u]p, we'll have to get up [e]arly. If we have to do that, I'll be too sleepy to stay [a]wake until sunset. So it can't possibly be both that we see the sun come up and I see it go [d]own.

    g. Jane will be a more [a]ttractive girl if she will use [c]osmetics with more subtlety. She will do so, provided her roommate is [p]ersuasive enough. We may be sure that Jane will be more attractive, because her roommate is on the [d]ebating team.

    h. If [J]ones made a two-base hit, then [B]rown was forced to run. Either [G]reen did not get home safely or [M]iller was on second. So Green did not get home safely unless Jones did not make a two-base hit.

    i. It can't be both that the [a]ltitude here is less than 7000 feet and that these are [P]onderosa pines. But either these are Ponderosas or some [o]ther kind of pine. And unless this topographic map is [w]rong, the altitude here is less than 7000 feet.

    j. Only if the Spanish missionaries had lots of [h]elp could they have [b]uilt these New Mexican churches. They didn't have lots of help, unless they got it from the [I]ndians. If the missionaries could not have built these New Mexican churches, then we don't [k]now who did. So either the missionaries [g]ained the Indians' confidence, or we don't know who built these churches.

CHAPTER 15

FURTHER MOLECULAR ARGUMENTS

PREVIEW

If we were to limit ourselves to analysis in terms of maxims, we could at this stage test only one type of argument, the simple conditional argument. In the present chapter we shall become further acquainted with analysis in terms of maxims, by considering other basic types of molecular argument and the maxims by which their validity may be determined. Note, however, that even before this exploration, the contraform principles developed in Chapter 13 provide a general test of validity for any of the arguments to be discussed.

15.1. SIMPLE ALTERNATIVE ARGUMENTS

A simple conditional argument, the nature of which we have already explored, is one of the commonest units of reasoning. Another very common unit, at the same level of complexity, is the SIMPLE ALTERNATIVE ARGUMENT. Like the simple conditional argument, it consists of two premises, one molecular and the other atomic, and an atomic conclusion. It differs from the simple conditional argument in that the molecular premise is alternative. How does this change affect valid procedure in the atomic premise and conclusion?

Now that we are in possession of the contraform test, this question might be explored directly in terms of contraform analysis. Perhaps you would like to try out that approach before reading further.

In the present section, we shall carry through an analysis at the levels of common sense and maxims.

In a certain college, the freshmen men are normally required to wear frosh caps throughout the first semester. By showing their prowess in various ways, however, they may win the privilege of abandoning their caps at Thanksgiving time. One condition that must be met, among others, is that they be victorious over the sophomores in a traditional tug of war. Since other conditions must also be fulfilled, winning the tug of war does not necessarily insure that they may doff their caps at Thanksgiving time. One thing is sure, though:

> Either the frosh win the [t]ug of war or $T \lor C$
> they wear their [c]aps the whole semester.

From what has been said, it is clear that this is an alternative statement, not a disjunctive alternative. We are therefore justified in symbolizing it simply as "$T \lor C$." This statement leaves open the possibility that the frosh will win the tug of war and still have to wear their caps the whole semester. Since this possibility is left open, the further information that the frosh this year won the tug of war does not warrant the conclusion that they will not have to wear their caps throughout the semester. Thus it would be *invalid* to argue:

> Either the frosh win the tug of war or they $T \lor C$ **(1)**
> wear their caps the whole semester.
> The frosh win the tug of war. T
> ─────────────────────────────────
> The frosh do not wear their caps the whole C'
> semester.

Similarly, if with this same alternative premise we had been given instead the additional information that the frosh will have to wear their caps the whole semester, we should be unwarranted in concluding from this that they lost the tug of war. Perhaps they won but failed to meet certain other conditions. Thus the following form must also be rejected as *invalid*:

> $T \lor C$ **(2)**
> C
> ──────
> T'

When we explored simple conditional arguments, we found that certain procedures in the atomic premise were fallacious. We distinguished the fallacy of asserting the consequent and the fallacy of contradicting the antecedent. Can you describe the fallacious procedure in the two examples of simple alternative argument we have just considered? They both commit the FALLACY OF ASSERTING AN ALTERNANT.

But perhaps it is not always fallacious to assert an alternant in the atomic premise of a simple alternative argument? Perhaps things would have come out all right if we had followed through in the *conclusion* by asserting (rather than by contradicting) the other alternant? No, that would not have helped. In fact the resulting forms would be obviously invalid, even at the common-sense level of analysis. Try expressing such forms in ordinary English, and see what you think.

Why does asserting an alternant as our atomic premise always lead to an invalid conclusion? The alternative premise merely tells us that either or both of the alternants hold. The additional information that a given one of the alternants holds does not warrant any conclusion at all about the other one. Consider the consistency table for an alternative argument, the atomic premise of which asserts one of the alternants:

	$A \vee B$	A
AB	1	1
A'B	1	0
AB'	1	1
A'B'	0	0

The alternative premise of course rules out the fourth possibility. Our second premise "A" rules out the possibilities which contain the contradictory "A'" as a conjunct, namely, the second and fourth. The trouble is that two possibilities (the first and the third) remain, both of which are consistent with the given information. In one of these, "A" occurs along with "B," and in the other, it occurs along with the contradictory "B'." Thus no conclusion is dictated, and the procedure of asserting an alternant as our atomic premise is seen to be invalid. The outcome would have been the same, of course, if we had used "B" instead of "A" as the atomic premise.

If we now return to our concrete example about the freshmen, it should be easy to see how we might have proceeded validly. If we were told that the freshmen did *not* win the tug of war, we could safely conclude that they would wear their caps the whole semester:

$$T \vee C \qquad\qquad (3)$$
$$\underline{T'}$$
$$C$$

Or if we had been told instead that they were *not* going to wear their caps the whole semester, we could have correctly inferred that they won the tug of war:

$$T \lor C \qquad\qquad \textbf{(4)}$$
$$\underline{C'\qquad\qquad\qquad}$$
$$T$$

Given an alternative premise, an additional premise which *contradicts* one of the alternants always permits us to conclude by *asserting* the other alternant. Explore the four conjunctive possibilities in a consistency table to see how such an atomic premise always makes it possible to pin down a specific conclusion.

Validity maxim for simple alternative argument: Contradict one alternant in the atomic premise, and conclude by asserting the other alternant.

15.2. EQUIVALENCE BETWEEN SIMPLE ALTERNATIVE AND CONDITIONAL ARGUMENTS

You will recall that, when we were studying the simple conditional argument, we found that valid procedure involved "doing the same thing" (asserting or contradicting) in the conclusion that we did in the atomic premise. In a simple alternative argument, however, valid procedure involves contradicting one alternant in the atomic premise, and then "doing the opposite," that is *asserting* the other alternant, in the conclusion. This shift of procedure seems to be sanctioned by our common-sense "feelings," and its necessity can be shown by more analytical methods, for example by considering the conjunctive possibilities in relation to the premises, or by contraform analysis. If you are like most other beginners in logical analysis, however, this shift may still seem puzzling to you until you get at it in another way.

This further way is to compare a given valid alternative argument with the logically equivalent conditional argument. For the sake of familiarity, let us reconsider Argument 3 above:

> Either the frosh win the tug of war or they
> wear their caps the whole semester.
> The frosh do not win the tug of war.
> _____
> The frosh wear their caps the whole semester.

Can you express the alternative premise in logically equivalent conditional form? You may first need to state the zeroform of the alternative statement, and then derive the appropriate conditional statement from this zeroform. Or perhaps now you can go directly from the above alternative statement to a logically equivalent conditional statement:

> If the frosh do *not* win the tug of war, then they
> wear their caps the whole semester.

Let us keep the atomic premise and the conclusion just as they are, and draw up two parallel and logically equivalent arguments, one the alternative argument above, and the other a simple conditional argument using the conditional statement we have just derived. The resulting forms will be:

$$
\begin{array}{rcl}
T \lor C & = & T' \supset C \\
\underline{T'} & = & \underline{T'} \\
C & = & C
\end{array}
$$

First, convince yourself that these two arguments really are logically equivalent. (If you are hard to convince, write out the zeroforms of both these arguments and compare them. What do you discover?) Then inspect the conditional argument above to see whether it observes the maxim for validity. Yes, the atomic premise asserts the antecedent (and the conclusion "does the same thing" to the consequent, namely, asserts it). The logically equivalent alternative argument, having the identical atomic premise and conclusion, also observes the appropriate maxim for valid procedure: the atomic premise contradicts an alternant, and the conclusion "does the opposite" to the other alternant, namely, asserts it.

15.3. SIMPLE DISJUNCTIVE ARGUMENTS

By this time we have had enough experience with the analysis of simple arguments at the level of maxims so that it should be relatively easy to explore valid procedure in a simple disjunctive argument. If we begin with a disjunctive premise, how must we proceed in the atomic premise and in the conclusion to complete the argument validly?

In a simple *alternative* argument, we found that we must contradict one alternant in the atomic premise, and conclude by asserting the other alternant. But if we recall the logical import of a disjunctive statement, we shall see that this procedure will certainly not work here. Why not? A *disjunctive* statement merely asserts that not both of the disjuncts hold. If we tried to proceed by adding the information that a given disjunct does not hold, we would be left in the dark about the other one; it might or might not hold. Thus it is always invalid to proceed in a disjunctive argument by contradicting a disjunct in the atomic premise.

Suppose instead that our atomic premise asserts one of the disjuncts. This makes an important difference. The molecular premise asserts that *at most* one of the disjuncts holds. Thus when we are given the additional information that a particular one of the disjuncts holds, we are certainly on safe ground in concluding that the other one does not hold. Try this out on a concrete case and see.

Validity maxim for simple disjunctive argument: Assert one of the disjuncts in the atomic premise, and conclude by contradicting the other disjunct.

Given a simple conditional, alternative, or disjunctive argument, a logically equivalent argument of each of the other two types is derivable. If one of the three is valid, the others will be too, and each will be found to conform to its appropriate validity maxim.

The following table will help you compare the valid procedures for simple conditional, alternative, and disjunctive arguments.

REFERENCE TABLE OF VALID PROCEDURES IN SIMPLE MOLECULAR ARGUMENTS

If Molecular Premise Is:	Do This in Atomic Premise:	Then Do This in Conclusion:
conditional	assert antecedent ----or---- contradict consequent	assert consequent ---- contradict antecedent
alternative	contradict an alternant	assert the other alternant
disjunctive	assert a disjunct	contradict the other disjunct

15.4. SIMPLE BICONDITIONAL ARGUMENTS

In many cases of reasoning, we have on hand more information than we need to establish the desired conclusion. A simple example is:

> If this banana is rotten, I won't eat it.
> I don't like rotten food.
> This banana is rotten.
> _____
> I won't eat it.

The argument is of course valid, although it contains unneeded information. Even though the second premise may throw some light on why I won't eat the banana, it is extraneous to the logic of the argument itself. The first and third premises alone are sufficient to dictate the conclusion. But note carefully that the extraneous information given in the second premise does not *invalidate* the argument; it merely clutters it up.[1]

In order to think clearly about this, you will need to distinguish sharply between two possible situations. The first is the present situation.

> *Situation 1.*   Having all the information needed to validate a certain conclusion, and having in addition some further information not needed for this particular purpose.
> *Situation 2.*   Not having all the information needed to validate a certain conclusion, but having instead certain other information that does not serve this purpose.

These remarks have a direct bearing upon the analysis of a simple biconditional argument. A valid argument of this type always confronts us with Situation 1 above. Consider the following example.

The package of razor blades I am now using bears the statement: "Guaranteed eight perfect shaves per blade or your money back." The meaning of the guarantee is quite clear, and may be expressed in standard logical form by means of either a biconditional statement or a disjunctive-alternative statement. In biconditional form, the guarantee means:

> If and only if I do not get eight perfect shaves per blade, will they give me back my money.

Since, as we saw earlier (Section 9.6), a biconditional is a second-order conjunctive, it yields upon analysis two conditional statements:

> If I do not get eight perfect [s]haves per blade, $S' \supset M$
> then they will give me back my [m]oney.
> If I do get eight perfect shaves per blade, then $S \supset M'$
> they won't give me back my money.[2]

Such a biconditional statement may be used in any one of four different valid simple biconditional arguments:

---

[1] In discussing the scope of the contraform test (Section 13.6) we noted that an argument cannot be tested if its test form contains the same letter in more than two equations. In the light of the present discussion, it is clear that an argument which seemed to violate this restriction would actually not do so, provided the "offending" equation merely represented extraneous information.

[2] We could of course have used the equivalent contrapositive here, although the English would be somewhat more awkward to handle in the resulting argument.

1. $\begin{cases} S' \supset M \\ S \supset M' \end{cases}$
   $\dfrac{S'}{M}$

2. $\begin{cases} S' \supset M \\ S \supset M' \end{cases}$
   $\dfrac{M'}{S}$

3. $\begin{cases} S' \supset M \\ S \supset M' \end{cases}$
   $\dfrac{S}{M'}$

4. $\begin{cases} S' \supset M \\ S \supset M' \end{cases}$
   $\dfrac{M}{S'}$

State each of these arguments in English, so you'll see what's going on.

ANALYSIS BY MAXIM

No new maxim is needed to validate these arguments. Each of the four may be tested in terms of the validity maxim for simple conditional arguments. Arguments 1 and 2 conform to this maxim by drawing on the first component of the biconditional premise. For these two arguments, the second conditional element, "$S \supset M'$," is quite irrelevant, and is not drawn upon. Arguments 3 and 4, however, draw upon this second conditional element in accordance with the maxim, ignoring the first conditional element upon which the first two arguments were based. With this in mind, describe in terms of the maxim the procedure followed in each of these four arguments.

Analysis of simple biconditional arguments by maxim is easy if you remember that the biconditional premise contains more information than is needed for any one argument. This point should also be kept in mind as we turn to the contraform analysis of such arguments.

ANALYSIS BY CONTRAFORM PRINCIPLES

Here are the test forms of the four arguments given above. The starred equations represent extraneous information not drawn upon in satisfying the contraform requirements.

1. $\begin{cases} S'M' = 0 \\ SM = 0 \end{cases}$ *
   $S = 0$
   $M' \neq 0$

2. $\begin{cases} S'M' = 0 \\ SM = 0 \end{cases}$ *
   $M = 0$
   $S' \neq 0$

3. $\begin{cases} S'M' = 0 \\ SM = 0 \end{cases}$ *
   $S' = 0$
   $M \neq 0$

4. $\begin{cases} S'M' = 0 \\ SM = 0 \end{cases}$ *
   $M' = 0$
   $S \neq 0$

15.5. SIMPLE DISJUNCTIVE-ALTERNATIVE ARGUMENTS

As we noted above, the guarantee on my package of razor blades might equally well have been expressed by means of an equivalent disjunctive-alternative statement:

> Either I get eight perfect [s]haves per blade or they will give me back my [m]oney, but not both.

$$\begin{cases} S \lor M \\ S \mathbin{/} M \end{cases}$$

Here again, four valid simple disjunctive-alternative arguments are possible. Following procedures that parallel those used in analyzing the above simple biconditional argument, we may show these four forms to be valid in either of two ways. We may at the level of maxims apply the validity maxim for simple alternative arguments or for simple disjunctive arguments, in each case drawing upon only one half of the disjunctive-alternative premise. At the level of principles, we may show these four forms to be valid by means of the contraform test, in each case drawing upon only one of the braced equations.

In the light of our previous work, it should be apparent that for any simple biconditional argument, a logically equivalent simple disjunctive-alternative argument can be given, and vice versa.

• SOME REMINDERS

1. By means of common-sense analysis and consistency tables, maxims may be derived for simple alternative and for simple disjunctive arguments.
2. For every simple conditional, alternative, or disjunctive argument, there is a logically equivalent argument of each of the other two types.
3. Simple biconditional and simple disjunctive-alternative arguments do not require any new maxims for their testing.
4. Valid arguments of either of these two types, whether analyzed by maxims or contraform principles, will be found to contain superfluous information.
5. For any simple biconditional argument, a logically equivalent simple disjunctive-alternative argument may be given, and vice versa.

APPLICATIONS

1. For each of the arguments given in Application 1, following Section 12.5, give in English a logically equivalent (a) simple alternative argument and (b) simple disjunctive argument.
2. Check each of the arguments developed in 1 above by the appropriate maxim.
3. By means of consistency tables, show why the *conclusion* of a simple alternative argument can never validly contradict an alternant.
4. By means of consistency tables, show why the *conclusion* of a simple disjunctive argument can never validly assert a disjunct.
5. In each of the arguments below, the conclusion follows validly from the information. This fact is somewhat concealed by the presence of one or more logically extraneous or superfluous premises. Identify these premises by marking them with a star, and show that the conclusion validly follows from the remaining premises alone.

a. $A' \lor B$	c. $A \supset B$	e. A / D
$B' \lor A$	$B' \supset C$	$B \supset D$
A	B'	$C \supset B'$
$\overline{B}$	$C' \supset A$	$A \lor B$
	$\overline{A'}$	$\overline{C' \lor D'}$
b. A / B'	d. $A' \lor B'$	
$B' \supset C$	$A' \supset C$	
$C' \lor A$	B	
$\overline{A \lor B}$	$B' \supset C'$	
	$\overline{C}$	

15.6. PURE CONDITIONAL ARGUMENTS

In contrast to a *simple* conditional argument, which contains only one conditional statement, a PURE CONDITIONAL ARGUMENT is composed entirely of conditional statements. Such arguments may, of course, be readily tested by contraform analysis. At the level of maxims, two rules for a valid form of pure conditional argument having two premises may be set up.

Validity maxims for two-premise pure conditional argument:

1. The conditional premises have a common element, occurring in one of the premises as antecedent, and in the other as consequent.
2. The two other elements in the premises recur, each in its same role (antecedent or consequent), in the conditional conclusion.

Here is a form which satisfies the maxims and two which violate them.[3]

VALID FORM	INVALID FORM	INVALID FORM
A ⊃ B	A ⊃ B	A ⊃ B
B ⊃ C	C ⊃ B	B ⊃ C
A ⊃ C	A ⊃ C	C ⊃ A

A pure conditional argument which does not, as it stands, conform to these maxims may sometimes be shown to be logically equivalent to an argument which does conform, and hence valid. This is shown by taking the contrapositive of one or more statements in the original argument.

ORIGINAL ARGUMENT		EQUIVALENT VALID FORM
A ⊃ B		A ⊃ B
C′ ⊃ B′	contrapositive	B ⊃ C
C′ ⊃ A′	contrapositive	A ⊃ C

When contraform analysis is used instead, the original argument above shows itself to be valid as it stands, with no need to derive contrapositives.

There is nothing to limit a valid pure conditional argument to two premises. Extended arguments can be readily analyzed by contraform principles. At the level of maxims, analysis of an extended pure conditional argument involves breaking it up into units of two premises each, and testing these against the two rules stated above. For example:

ORIGINAL ARGUMENT	TRADITIONAL ANALYSIS
A ⊃ B	A ⊃ B
B ⊃ C	B ⊃ C
	[A ⊃ C]
C ⊃ D	C ⊃ D
	[A ⊃ D]
D ⊃ E	D ⊃ E
A ⊃ E	A ⊃ E

[3] A curious case of no practical importance but of considerable theoretical interest arises if we treat a conditional statement and its converse as the sole premises of an argument:

A ⊃ B	AB′ = 0
B ⊃ A	BA′ = 0
?	? ≠ 0

If we were to proceed to apply the contraform principles in the usual way, everything would pair off and there would be nothing left to reappear in the inequation. In this special case, by treating only one of these sets as a *pair*, we could satisfy Principle 2 and have the other set left over to use as conjuncts in the inequation. Depending on which set we selected, one or the other of the following valid but tautologous conclusions (or its logical equivalent) would be derived: "A ⊃ A" or "B ⊃ B." In either case, the resulting argument conforms to the validity maxims given above.

The traditional analysis above first derives the intermediate conclusion "A ⊃ C" from the first two premises in accordance with the maxims. This derived statement is then used as a premise along with the third original premise to obtain a further intermediate conclusion, and so on, until the original conclusion is reached and shown to be valid.

15.7. THE DILEMMA

When we say that someone is "in a dilemma," we sometimes mean merely that he is in doubt about what he should do and is wrestling with the problem. Often, however, the phrase carries a further meaning, and suggests that he is faced with a choice between two or more alternatives,[4] each of which seems to have unpleasant consequences. In the sport of debating, forcing your opponent into a dilemma is often an impressive tactic. If you can get him to admit that the only alternatives open are such-and-such, and if you can then show that whichever alternative is accepted, the results are damaging to his position, you have scored an important point.

When we consider a dilemma, not from the psychological point of view of its unpleasantness nor from the rhetorical point of view of its effectiveness in debating, but as a logical argument-form, we make an interesting discovery. We find that the dilemma is a much commoner pattern of reasoning than we had supposed. It is, in fact, the typical pattern of deliberation, of weighing alternative possibilities, of deciding upon a course of action.

To be intelligent about our choices involves considering their consequences, and making up our minds not merely in the light of immediate inclination, but with an awareness of the probable results. One practical reason for not following the advice of the proverb to eat, drink, and be merry is that it is really quite unlikely that we shall die tomorrow. Instead, we shall have to live and pay the price of today's indulgences. When we consider the choices before us and try to envisage the consequences of alternative courses of action, our thinking takes the logical form of a dilemma. What is this form?

A dilemma contains an alternative premise which sets forth the choices before us. It then uses each of these alternatives as antecedents in condi-

[4] The *alternants* of an alternative statement express "alternatives" in this sense of the word.

tional premises which explore the consequences of each alternative. The conclusion is again alternative, facing us with the consequences of each choice. A dilemma thus has the following form:

$$A \lor B$$
$$A \supset C$$
$$\underline{B \supset D}$$
$$C \lor D$$

The argument whose function and pattern we have been analyzing is traditionally called a COMPLEX CONSTRUCTIVE DILEMMA. In addition to this basic form, three others are traditionally distinguished. A closely related form, the SIMPLE CONSTRUCTIVE DILEMMA, results when the two antecedents have the same consequent. Such premises of course permit a simple atomic conclusion which asserts this consequent.

$$A \lor B$$
$$A \supset C$$
$$\underline{B \supset C}$$
$$C$$

Two other forms are traditionally classed as dilemmas, but are labeled DESTRUCTIVE rather than constructive. Examine these two forms (complex and simple, respectively) to determine the appropriateness of this label.

$$
\begin{array}{cc}
C' \lor D' & \qquad C' \lor D' \\
A \supset C & \qquad A \supset C \\
\underline{B \supset D} & \qquad \underline{A \supset D} \\
A' \lor B' & \qquad A'
\end{array}
$$

The validity of all four forms is readily established by the contraform test, or suitable maxims may be devised for the purpose.

15.8. INDIRECT ARGUMENT

There is another interesting argument-form that sometimes crops up as we consider a possible course of action.[5] Suppose you are thinking of going home for a big dance this week end. Let us also suppose that your funds are at a low point, and that you have no way of supplementing them. Much as you would like to attend this dance, the more you think about

---

[5] I am indebted to Max Black for my awareness of the practical aspects of this argument-form. See his *Critical Thinking*, Second Edition, New York, Prentice-Hall, Inc., 1952, p. 88.

it, the more you see it can't be done in the present circumstances. For your fare home will exhaust your resources, and you'll have no money left for the dance. If we have correctly analyzed your predicament, this is the way it looks:

> If I can go to the [d]ance, I must go [h]ome.
> If I must go home, the [f]are will cost x dollars.
> If the fare costs x dollars, I'll be [b]roke.
> If I'll be broke, I can't [p]ay for the dance.
> If I can't pay for the dance, I can't go to the dance.
> _____
> I can't go to the dance.

The premises of this argument are those of a pure conditional argument. As we have seen, such premises would clearly warrant the *conditional* conclusion, "If I can go to the dance, then I can't go to the dance." But in the above argument, the conclusion is not conditional, but *categorical* or atomic. How can such a conclusion be justified? Let us apply the contraform test and find out.

$$
\begin{array}{ll}
D \supset H & DH' = 0 \\
H \supset F & HF' = 0 \\
F \supset B & FB' = 0 \\
B \supset P' & BP = 0 \\
P' \supset D' & P'D = 0 \\
\hline
D' & D \neq 0
\end{array}
$$

In the test form there is exactly one inequation. Everything in the equations pairs off except two cases of "D." And this "D" reappears with the same sign in the inequation. The argument is shown to be valid.

Why, in this type of case, is it possible to have an atomic conclusion, while the usual pure conditional premises would permit only a conditional conclusion? Let us look at this normal conditional conclusion once more:

> If I can go to the dance, I can't go to the dance.
>
> $$D \supset D'$$

As Max Black has pointed out (*ibid.*), it is important not to confuse this conditional statement with the self-contradictory conjunctive statement, "DD'." Far from being self-contradictory, the conditional statement immediately dictates the conclusion, "D'." If you accept "$D \supset D'$," you are logically committed to accepting "D'." The quickest way to see this is to compare the zeroforms for these two expressions. When we do so, we discover that the second zeroform is directly derivable from the first by the special form of the Simplification Rule. (See Section 13.5, note 7.)

$$D \supset D' \qquad\qquad DD = 0$$
$$D' \qquad\qquad\quad D = 0$$

On the basis of this investigation, we may set up the following valid argument-form, containing only one premise:

$$\frac{A \supset A'}{A'}$$

An argument based, like ours about the dance, upon this logical form may be called an INDIRECT ARGUMENT. It establishes a conclusion ("I can't go to the dance") *indirectly*, by showing that it is the consequent of its contradictory. We begin by exploring the consequences of accepting its contradictory ("If I can go to the dance, then what?") and show that the consequences include rejecting the contradictory.

• SOME REMINDERS

6. A pure conditional argument consists entirely of conditional statements.
7. A dilemma is a valid logical form for presenting alternative possibilities and for exhibiting their consequences.
8. From the information that a given statement implies its contradictory, we may validly conclude by asserting its contradictory.

APPLICATIONS

1. By analogy with pure conditional arguments, define "pure alternative argument." How could one go about setting up validity maxims for two-premise pure alternative arguments? State such maxims.
2. Do the same for pure disjunctive arguments.
3. Develop validity maxims for the complex constructive dilemma.
4. Work out concrete examples of each of the four forms of dilemma described in Section 15.7. Then test each by contraform principles.
5. Set up validity maxims for the simple constructive dilemma, the simple destructive, and the complex destructive.
6. Develop an indirect argument to show why you can't graduate from college at the end of your freshman year.
7. Consider the nursery rime, "Who Killed Cock Robin?" By means of an indirect argument, supplying any needed assumptions, develop an alibi which will show that the fly was not guilty.

8. Develop an indirect argument out of your own personal experience.
9. Exhibit the logical form of each of the following, supplying any needed assumptions. If the form has a name (for example, "indirect argument," "simple alternative argument") give it. Then derive conclusion (if not already given) and check validity by contraform principles.

   a. "As it was the first nation to develop and use atomic explosives, the United States could not escape the responsibility for taking the first step toward international control. If it did nothing, an atomic armament competition was inevitable, and the American government would be directly responsible for the resulting war. If, on the other hand, the United States released its technical knowledge of how to construct the bombs without effective guarantees against misuse of the knowledge, it would incur the grave risk of hastening the development of atomic explosives by governments that might employ their new-found power to destroy the United States." (Cord Meyer, Jr.: *Peace or Anarchy*, Boston, Atlantic Monthly Press and Little, Brown & Company, 1947, Copyright 1947 by Cord Meyer, Jr., p. 131)

   b. "A Nebraska district court ruled last week that no Communist is entitled to unemployment compensation checks. The court's reasoning: Under the law, an unemployed person must be 'available for employment,' and 'No one in this part of the country will hire a Communist.'" (*Time*, May 8, 1950, p. 20)

   c. "We find it hard, in thus pointing to the need to rescue Christmas for its true purpose, to be very critical of the merchants. It is easy enough to see the crass commercialism in their exploitation of the season, and to deplore it. But the merchant is caught in a dilemma. Frequently he is a devout Christian who would like to exalt the religious significance of the festival, if that could be done without exposing his business to the peril of ruin. But to many a retailer, extravagant Christmas buying by his patrons has become the difference between a year of profit and of loss." (Reprinted by permission of *Christian Century* from the issue of December 21, 1949, p. 1510)

   d. "In a press conference on March 17, 1947 in Tokyo, Gen. MacArthur said: 'Democracy is a relative thing. It's a question of the degree of freedom you have. If you believe in the Anglo-Saxon idea you believe this will stay here. If you are a cynic or believe in totalitarianism you may doubt it is here to stay. I believe sincerely and absolutely that it is here to stay.'" (*World Report*, April 1, 1947, p. 43)

   e. "In court for trial today, he [Willie Smith] told City Judge John J. Walsh:

      "'I was sitting in a car double parked in front of a grill. An officer told me to move the car and I explained to him that the owner was in the grill. The officer told me to move the car. Then I moved it just under twenty feet and the officer asked for my license. I didn't have any so he locked me up.'

      "Mr. Smith said he had pleaded innocent on arraignment because 'I figured due to the circumstances I wasn't guilty.' The officer, Sgt.

Michael Grazidei, interrupted, 'But he moved the car and he didn't have a license.'

"Mr. Smith changed his plea to guilty and was sentenced." (*New York Times,* December 20, 1951)

f. "It was from him we learned that we were known all over the town as the 'Anglees with the shiny boots.' In that part of the world they only recognized two categories of foreigner: Russians and Anglees (or Englishmen). Any idiot could see that we were not Russian, and so we were English." (Wilfred Skrede: *Across the Roof of the World,* New York, W. W. Norton & Co., Inc., 1955, p. 45)

g. "A recent survey showed that roughly two-thirds of all fishermen never eat fish. This should surprise nobody. Fish is brain food. People who eat fish have large, well-developed brains. People with large, well-developed brains don't eat fish. It's that simple." (W. T. Webster and Ed Zern: *To Hell With Fishing or How to Tell Fish from Fishermen,* New York, D. Appleton-Century Co., 1946, Copyright 1946 by Ed Zern, p. 7)

h. "Next, they said, 'if a handful of Jews could ever stand off the hordes of Arabs it would be nothing short of a miracle.' But the Jews fought. And won. And lo! a miracle." (Advertisement for United Jewish Appeal, October, 1949)

i. "A New York Supreme Court Justice will have to decide whether Bedloes Island, home of the Statue of Liberty, is in New York or New Jersey.

"At issue is the claim of Mrs. Evelyn Hill, who operates the island's refreshment and souvenir shop, for the return of $1,949 in sales and other taxes paid to the City of New York.

"Victor Wolder, attorney for Mrs. Hill, told Justice Thomas L. J. Corcoran yesterday that inasmuch as Bedloes Island was not even in New York State it certainly was not in New York City, and therefore this city could not tax his client." (William M. Farrell in *New York Times,* December 11, 1953)

j. "Premier Georgi M. Malenkov's claim that the Soviet Union had 'mastered' the hydrogen bomb must be treated seriously whether it represents fact or fiction.

"If it is true, the world has reached another crossroads of history with the future dark and uncertain.

"If it is false, the Communist claim will nevertheless find acceptance in the minds of many, particularly in neutral nations, and will have important political and psychological repercussions, as it was undoubtedly intended to do." (Hanson W. Baldwin in *New York Times,* August 9, 1953)

k. " 'Well, I don't know what he expects of her—after all, she isn't a genius,' one of our friends heard on a Madison Avenue bus the other afternoon. And then, 'Of course not. If she was a genius, she'd be asking fifty dollars a week.' " (*The New Yorker,* May 16, 1953, pp. 25–26)

l. "The proposal that public school children sing the first and fourth stanzas of the patriotic hymn 'America' in lieu of a daily prayer suggested by the New York State Board of Regents, was opposed yesterday by

Jerome Nathanson, a leader of the New York Society for Ethical Culture.

"Taking issue with Arthur Levitt, Brooklyn member of the Board of Education who recommended the singing of the hymn, Mr. Nathanson said:

" 'If Mr. Levitt were proposing that "America" be sung as a matter of American patriotism, there could be no objection to the proposal. Obviously, this is not what he is proposing. He is proposing that it be sung as an alternative to prayer.

" 'In this sense, it is no alternative at all, for the words of the fourth stanza of "America" constitute a prayer and nothing else. Taken as a prayer, accordingly, all the objections which have been urged against the New York State Regents' proposal hold also with respect to this.' " (*New York Times,* November 3, 1952)

m. "While a missionary among the headhunters of northern Luzon, I was one day riding along a narrow trail and, rounding a sharp turn, saw before me several of my female parishioners taking a shower under a roadside waterfall. Not wanting to embarrass them, I began talking loudly to my pony, proceeding slowly enough for them to scramble behind some bushes.

"Instead, with one accord they cupped their hands over their faces and stood there glistening in their naked beauty. They were apparently working on the theory—justified in this instance—that I would not recognize them, and that if I did not recognize them they couldn't be embarrassed." (Charles Norris in *Reader's Digest,* December, 1953, p. 111)

CHAPTER 16

ANALYZING ATOMIC STATEMENTS

PREVIEW

Up to now, we have treated atomic statements as unanalyzed units, except for noting whether they were positively or negatively expressed. In this chapter we shall see why further analysis is needed, and shall learn how it may be done by means of zeroforms. By the end of the chapter, you will be ready to test the validity of an argument consisting entirely of atomic statements, by applying the already familiar contraform principles.

16.1. NEED FOR FURTHER ANALYSIS OF ATOMIC STATEMENTS

Consider the argument:

No imbeciles can reason.	**(1)**
Some college students can reason.	**(2)**
Some college students are not imbeciles.	**(3)**

If you are one of these college students who can reason, it will probably seem clear to you that the above argument is valid. But if you are asked why it is valid, you will at this stage of the game have to be content with an analysis at the common-sense level. We have not yet discovered any maxims that will apply to arguments of this type. Nor does the contraform test appear to give any guidance here. We shall soon see, however, that this is another one of those cases where you can't trust appearances.

How does the above argument differ from those we have previously analyzed? For one thing both the premises and the conclusion are atomic statements, aren't they? Unlike a conditional statement or an alternative statement, for example, they are not molecular. They are not analyzable

198

into statemental elements joined by such connectives as "either . . . or," "if . . . then," or "both . . . and."

We have, of course, already made considerable use of atomic statements as elements in arguments. Thus far, though, we have treated atomic statements as unanalyzed units, representing them by single letters with or without primes. Such a treatment proved adequate for arguments such as:

> If this college student is an imbecile, he can't reason.
> He can reason.
> _____
> He is not an imbecile.

16.2. GETTING AT THE INTERNAL STRUCTURE OF ATOMIC STATEMENTS

When we turn from such arguments to consider the new type of argument with which this chapter opened, we see the need for an approach that will get at the internal structure of atomic statements.[1] The argument clearly has a discernible form. The premises say something about the relation between imbeciles and ability to reason, and the relation between at least some college students and ability to reason. The conclusion asserts a relation between some college students and imbeciles.

Let me suggest a way of looking at Statement 1 above:

> No imbeciles can reason.   **(1)**

Suppose we restate it:

> There are not any imbeciles who can reason.

Does this accurately preserve the sense of the original? If you agree that it does, will you let me state it this way too:

> imbeciles who can reason $= 0$.

This is not normal English, but I do not think you will have any difficulty in understanding it. I am here talking about a certain type or kind or CLASS of being, namely, beings who are *both* imbecilic *and* able to reason. And what I am saying about this class is that it is EMPTY, that is, it has no

[1] In this chapter, we shall deal specifically with the analysis of general statements. Later, in Section 17.2, we shall consider the handling of singular statements. For the distinction between these two types of atomic statement, see Section 9.4.

members. If this seems a perversely complicated way of saying a simple thing, be patient, for we are really getting somewhere now.

We have already encountered "both . . . and" (conjunction), but only as a logical connective between *statemental* elements, yielding a molecular (conjunctive) statement. We now want to get acquainted with the notion of a CONJUNCTIVE CLASS, a class which is named by conjoining the names of two other classes.

Thus we may speak of the class of woolen things, and also of the class of neckties. Conjoining the names of these two classes gives us the name of a third class, the class of woolen neckties. Note very carefully that this conjunctive class is *not* the class of things which are *either* woolen *or* neckties. Rather it is the class of things which are *both* woolen *and* neckties. There happen to be such things as woolen neckties, in other words, the conjunctive class has members. If there were no woolen neckties, we should have to say that this conjunctive class is empty, or equivalently, that it has no members. (Note that we can refer to a class, whether or not it happens to have any members. You might like to relate this point to our earlier recognition that we can talk about mermaids, even though there aren't any.)

In our earlier work, we agreed to use capital letters as abbreviations for atomic statements. Let us now agree to use small letters as abbreviations for class-names. For the class-name "imbeciles" let us substitute the lower-case letter, "i." And for "beings who can reason" let us substitute the letter "r." Let us follow our earlier convention of indicating conjunction by writing the symbols side by side. Our previous statement that

$$\text{imbeciles who can reason} = 0$$

will now be abbreviated:

$$ir = 0$$

Thus "$ir = 0$" symbolizes our original Statement 1, "No imbeciles can reason." If this has seemed a rather difficult transition from everyday English to logical symbols, you should at least be encouraged to see that we have ended up with what is certainly a conjunctive zeroform equation. The lower-case letters remind us that this zeroform, unlike those we have used up to this time, was derived from an atomic statement rather than from a molecular one. This new type of zeroform may be called a

CLASS ZEROFORM, since it involves a class analysis of atomic statements.[2]

This looks encouraging, doesn't it? If we can carry through along this line, finding out how to express other atomic statements in zeroforms, we should be able to check the validity of our new type of argument by the contraform test.

Let's have another look at Statement 2, the second premise of the argument with which we began:

Some college students can reason.   **(2)**

It should be a simple matter to name the conjunctive class involved here. It is the class of things that are both college students and beings capable of reasoning. Let us symbolize this conjunctive class by "sr." Now what are we saying about this class? That it is empty? Certainly not. We are saying that there *are* some members of this conjunctive class. In other words, we are saying that this class is *not* empty.

The statement that the class in question is *empty* would, as we know, be symbolized:

$$sr = 0$$

and in normal English this would be "No college students can reason." Statement 2, which we are trying to analyze, is the strict logical *contradictory* of this statement. We can accurately symbolize Statement 2 thus:

$$sr \neq 0.$$

You will recall that we have already made use of this inequation sign, when contradicting the zeroform conclusion in setting up the test form for the contraform test.

As a third example, let us look at the conclusion of the argument with which we began, Statement 3:

Some college students are not imbeciles.   **(3)**

In order to handle this one, we shall need one more concept, that of the COMPLEMENT of a given class. Consider the given class, birds. Do you see that there will be another class, the class of nonbirds? If a narrower context is not specified, this class of nonbirds will contain a curious assortment of things: telephone poles, ice cream cones, the smell of lilacs, the middle of next week, and everything else in the universe *except* birds. In a con-

---

[2] Zeroform notation, as applied to classes, is derived from the work of George Boole (1815–1864).

crete discussion, however, there would probably be some more or less clearly understood limits. For example, in a discussion in biology, the understood limits (or UNIVERSE OF DISCOURSE) might be the class of organisms, and "nonbirds" would be understood to name, not the class of literally everything else except birds, but rather the class of organisms-that-are-not-birds.

The logical symbol used to indicate this "non-" is the familiar *prime*. Hitherto we have used the prime to form the contradictory of a given statement. Now we shall use it to name the complement of a given class. Thus if the class of birds is symbolized by "b," its complement (the class of nonbirds) will be symbolized by "b'."

Now let's get back to the college students who are not imbeciles. When we say that some college students are not imbeciles (Statement 3) this is logically equivalent to the statement that there are members of a certain conjunctive class: the class of beings who are *both* college students *and* nonimbeciles. As in the case of Statement 2 above, what we are saying about this conjunctive class is that it has members, in other words, is not empty. Here it is in symbols:

$$si' \neq 0$$

Note that here, as in our previous work, the prime applies only to the element to which it is attached, in this case to the "i," and not to the whole conjunctive "si."

Now you know how to express in zeroforms all three statements in our new argument. Just to see how far you've come, try out the contraform test on this argument. Set up the test form in the usual way, and apply the three contraform principles. Is the argument valid or invalid?

The three forms we have distinguished are all you need in order to analyze the given argument, but there is another form that we need in order to round out the picture. Actually, you will encounter this form yourself when you set up the test form. For in setting up this test form, you will have to contradict the zeroform conclusion, won't you? This zeroform conclusion and its English original are:

Some college students are not imbeciles. $si' \neq 0$ **(3)**

When you contradict this, you will get a new statement:

$$si' = 0 \qquad\qquad \textbf{(4)}$$

In applying the contraform test, there is of course no need for stating this in English, but let's try to do it for another reason. We are clearly saying here that a certain conjunctive class is empty. What class is it? The class of beings who are both college students and nonimbeciles. How can we express this in normal English?

Remember that (4) is the contradictory of (3). Would it be enough to assert simply that *some* college students are imbeciles? Recall what we mean by saying that two statements are contradictory. Of a contradictory pair, exactly one must be true, and exactly one false. In order to contradict (3) in English, we must assert:

$$\text{\textit{All} college students are imbeciles.} \qquad si' = 0 \qquad \textbf{(4)}$$

16.3. TRADITIONAL BASIC TYPES OF ATOMIC STATEMENT

We have now analyzed four different atomic statements by means of class zeroforms. These four were not picked at random, nor simply because three of them occurred in the argument we wished to analyze. The four numbered statements illustrate the four basic types of atomic statement distinguished by traditional logic.

Even before we go further, it will be useful to explore briefly some of the relationships among these types. A fuller analysis will be given later. You will note that two of the statements refer to "all" or to "none" of the subject class; such statements are called UNIVERSAL. The other statements refer to "some" of the subject class; such statements are called PARTICULAR. Universal and particular statements are said to differ in QUANTITY, and the words ("all," "some," and so on) which indicate the quantity of the statement are called QUANTIFIERS. Two of the four statements are positively expressed, and are hence called POSITIVE (or *affirmative*), while two are negatively expressed and are therefore called NEGATIVE. This difference between positive and negative is referred to as a difference in QUALITY.

By a convention of long standing (that is, since the middle of the eleventh century), each of these four types may be compactly referred to by means of one of the four vowels, "A," "E," "I," "O." Thus a universal positive statement is conveniently called an "A-statement," a universal negative an "E-statement," a particular positive an "I-statement," and a particular negative an "O-statement." [3]

---

[3] The letters "A" and "I," used as labels for the two types of positive statement, are said to have been derived from the first two vowels of the Latin word, *affirmo* (I affirm). The letters "E" and "O" may be similarly drawn from *nego* (I deny).

The table below summarizes the results of this analysis. Note especially how clearly the logical contradictories stand out when the statements are expressed by zeroforms. Zeroform contradictories, as we know, are alike in all respects except that one is an equation and the other an inequation. The zeroforms clearly reveal that an A-statement and the corresponding O-statement are contradictories, as are also an E-statement and the corresponding I-statement.

TYPE	NORMAL ENGLISH	CLASS ZEROFORM
A-statement *Universal* *Positive*	All a is b.	$ab' = 0$
E-statement *Universal* *Negative*	No a is b.	$ab = 0$
I-statement *Particular* *Positive*	Some a is b.	$ab \neq 0$
O-statement *Particular* *Negative*	Some a isn't b.	$ab' \neq 0$

16.4. THE SIMPLEST ATOMIC STATEMENTS

The commonest types of atomic statement are those we have just considered. We have seen that they may be analyzed by means of a zeroform whose left-hand member names a conjunctive class.

There are, however, even simpler atomic statements which, when analyzed by zeroforms, have only a single letter on the left-hand side. Consider the following two groups of atomic statements:

There are stars.	There aren't any mermaids.
Something is a star.	Nothing is a mermaid.
Stars exist.	Mermaids are nonexistent.

The first three statements are, for logical purposes, equivalent. They are called SIMPLE EXISTENCE STATEMENTS. How shall we analyze them by means of a class zeroform? At first we are tempted to hunt for a conjunctive class. One might try, for example, to think of these as A-statements, and to propose a zeroform to the effect that the class of things which are both stars and nonexistents is empty. Actually, the situation is simpler than this. All we are trying to say is that the class of stars is nonempty, in other words, that the class of stars has members. And we already know how to express this idea of a class having members. We simply set the class-name not-equal to zero. The result is a simple (that is, single-letter) class zeroform:

$$s \neq 0$$

The remaining three statements may also be treated as simply three ways of saying the same thing. But here, instead of expressing existence, the zeroform must express nonexistence. All we need to do is to symbolize the class of mermaids by "m" and set this equal to zero:

$$m = 0$$

Such statements may be called SIMPLE NONEXISTENCE STATEMENTS.

- **SOME REMINDERS**
1. In terms of the following concepts, it is possible to set up zeroforms which reveal the internal structure of many atomic statements.

CONCEPTS	SYMBOLS
classes	a, b, . . .
conjunctive class	ab
complement of class b	b′
is empty, has no members	$= 0$
is nonempty, has members	$\neq 0$

APPLICATIONS

1. Using the bracketed letters as abbreviation-symbols for positively expressed class-names, symbolize the following classes. If a class-name is negatively expressed, add a prime to the letter-symbol.
   a. [s]tudents
   b. [g]irls who are not [s]tudents
   c. [r]ed-headed [f]reshmen
   d. those who are neither [g]irls nor [s]tudents
   e. [d]ragons with [g]reen eyes but no [c]laws
2. Give class zeroforms for each of the following statements:
   a. Some [p]eople [o]ught to know better.
   b. There aren't any [w]itches.
   c. Anyone [o]ver twenty-one may [v]ote.

     d. [P]lums are a kind of [f]ruit.

     e. [T]ables exist.

     f. No [m]an lives [f]orever.

     g. Some [p]oliticians are [h]onest.

3. Name, in English, the conjunctive classes involved in the zeroforms worked out for Application 2.

4. Develop maxims which will tell you how to get from the normal English form to the appropriate zeroform. Refer to the table of A-, E-, I-, O-types given above. These maxims should be thought of only as a temporary aid, and as a means of helping you notice relationships you might otherwise overlook.

5. Now that you know how to set up class zeroforms, apply the contraform test to each of the following arguments. Is the argument valid or invalid?

     a. No [i]mbeciles can [r]eason, but some college [s]tudents can. Therefore, some college students are not imbeciles.

     b. Some [f]ootball players are also [b]asketball players, and some basketball players are over [s]ix feet tall. Therefore some football players are over six feet tall.

     c. All [t]respassers will be [p]rosecuted. All trespassers are law-[v]iolators. There are some trespassers. Therefore, some law-violators will be prosecuted.

     d. All really [u]npleasant days are [d]espised by vacationers. Some [J]uly days are very [h]ot days. No days that are despised by vacationers are good [b]usiness days for resort owners. All very hot days are really unpleasant days. Therefore, some July days are not good business days for resort owners.

16.5. PICTURING CLASSES BY VENN DIAGRAMS

The British logician, John Venn (1834–1883), devised a convenient and vivid way of picturing information about classes. The circle diagrams which we shall use in this book are, with slight modifications, based on his work.

Let a circle represent a given class, named "a":

If we want to indicate that this class is empty (that is, that it has no members), we may do so by marking the area with a zero: [4]

---

[4] Note carefully the difference between these two diagrams. The first merely calls attention to a class; the second is a way of picturing *a statement about* the class.

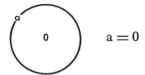

a = 0

This is a "geometrical" representation of the simple nonexistence statement that can be represented "algebraically" by the zeroform written at the right above.

Suppose instead that we want to indicate that the class in question is nonempty, in other words, that it has members (at least one). We may picture this information by placing a check-mark within the area. At the right of this picture you will find the equivalent zeroform, which is that of a simple existence statement.

a ≠ 0

If the area within the circle represents class *a*, what will the area *outside* the circle represent? It will stand for the complement of this class, namely, *a'*.

To consider a class *a*, in relation to another class *b*, we draw two over-lapping circles, one to represent class *a*, the other to represent class *b*.

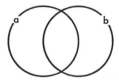

Now let's consider a further question. What class will the area outside *both* these circles represent? If there is anything out there, how can we describe it in terms of "a" and "b"? It won't be an "a," will it? But for that matter, it won't be a "b" either. The area outside both circles represents the conjunctive class *a'b'*. Label this area in the diagram above. We can follow out this approach and name the three subregions *within* the circles too:

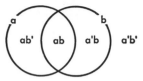

Anything within the *a*-circle will be an "a," and anything outside it will be a "non-a." Similarly, anything within the *b*-circle will be a "b," and anything outside it, a "non-b." Note that the above diagram does not assert that there actually is anything that meets these descriptions. The diagram as it stands merely analyzes the universe in terms of the classes *a*, *b*, their complement classes, and the conjunctive classes formed from *a*, *b*, and their complements.

The overlapping region in the middle, that is the region common to the two circles, represents the conjunctive class *ab*. The left-hand crescent is an area which lies within the *a*-circle but outside the *b*-circle, and thus represents the conjunctive class *ab'*. The right-hand crescent lies within the *b*-circle, but outside the *a*-circle. It represents the conjunctive class *a'b*.

Once we see how this works, there is no need to write in the labels for the conjunctive classes. If the circles themselves are properly labeled, a little practice will make it possible to call off the name of any region.

16.6. PICTURING ANALYZED ATOMIC STATEMENTS

We have already learned that a statement asserting that a particular class is empty may be pictured by putting a zero in the appropriate region. We also know that the assertion that a given class has members (at least one) may be indicated by inserting a check-mark in the proper place. We are thus in a position to picture the four types of zeroform developed in Section 16.2 above.

We saw that an atomic statement of the form, "No a is b," has as its zeroform the expression, "ab = 0." Picture this statement by placing a zero in the appropriate region, thus:

No a is b.

ab = 0

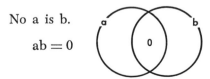

The contradictory of the above atomic statement is, in English, "Some a is b," or in zeroform, "ab $\neq$ 0." Note how contradictories show up in these geometric diagrams. The same region is marked in each case, but in the one it is marked empty, and in the other occupied.

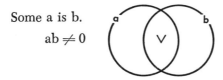

Some a is b.

ab $\neq$ 0

The following diagrams picture the remaining basic forms, "All a is b" and its contradictory, "Some a isn't b." Note that the region ab' is involved in both cases.

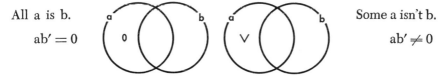

All a is b.

ab' = 0

Some a isn't b.

ab' $\neq$ 0

We shall later see that, by adding a third overlapping circle, we may diagram many two-premise atomic arguments, such as the one about college students, imbeciles, and reasoning ability. Furthermore we shall find that such a diagram also provides a simple check on the validity of the argument being diagrammed.

• SOME REMINDERS

2. The various conjunctive classes making up a given universe of discourse may be represented by means of overlapping circles, appropriately labeled.
3. With certain additional markings, such circle diagrams also represent *statements* about classes. Such diagrams are "geometric" equivalents for "algebraic" zeroforms.
4. Diagrams of A-, E-, I-, and O-statements are given, along with other information, in the combined Reference Table at the end of the next chapter.

APPLICATIONS

1. Picture the classes mentioned in Application 1, following Section 16.4 above. Use circles, as we have been doing, to represent *positively* named

classes. Shade-in the areas to which you wish to call attention. (Note that shading-in, in this use, is equivalent to pointing. It is not as here used equivalent to asserting the existence or nonexistence of members in a given region.)

2. Diagram, by means of circles and appropriate check-marks or zeros, each of the statements given in Application 2, following Section 16.4 above.

16.7. INTERPRETING UNIVERSAL STATEMENTS

You must have noticed by this time that the zeroforms of universal statements are always equations, asserting that a given conjunctive class is empty. You are probably not bothered by the use of an equation to express an E-statement. It seems normal enough to interpret a statement such as "No men are angels" in terms of the emptiness of the class of men-angels.

But if your reactions are typical, you have probably been troubled by the fact that we treat an A-statement such as "All women are beautiful" in terms of the emptiness of the class of nonbeautiful women. You probably feel that we should really be saying something about a particular class's being occupied. You have a point, but we must be careful to see exactly what it is. This will take a little investigation.

It will not do to argue that the zeroform for the A-statement is incorrect. We have the strongest formal reasons for adopting this particular form as our standard interpretation. The simplest way to see this is to recall the zeroform for the *contradictory* of an A-statement. But first, what *is* the contradictory of an A-statement? Contradictories, we have many times noted, are two statements so related that exactly one must be true, and exactly one must be false. An A-statement is contradicted by the corresponding O-statement. For example:

A: All [c]hildren are [p]olite.   *Contradictory* O: Some
                                     children aren't polite.

The zeroform for this contradictory O-statement does not usually give trouble. It states that the class of nonpolite children has members:

$$O: cp' \neq 0$$

When we recall that any zeroform is contradicted by changing it from an inequation to an equation or vice versa, leaving everything else just as it is, it becomes clear that the correct zeroform for the A-statement which contradicts this O-statement is:

$$A: \; cp' = 0$$

A further very important reason for adopting this type of zeroform equation as the basic interpretation of an A-statement will be more apparent if we select a new example:

> A: All students who get [p]erfect scores on the next test will be [e]xcused from class for a week.

Would we be warranted in inferring, from this English statement, that there actually will be anyone who gets a perfect score? Clearly not. We simply do not know whether the subject class, the class of those who will get a perfect score on the next test, has members or not. The *form* of the A-statement could not decide this point. The matter can be settled only in terms of additional *factual* information. The following standard zeroform and circle diagram correctly set forth all the information inferable from the *form* of the given statement:

$$pe' = 0$$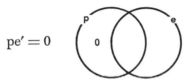

This last remark applies equally well to any statement having the same A-form, for example, "All cows are ruminants." But here the relevance of the remark is obscured by the fact that we all know perfectly well, *on other grounds,* that there really are such things as cows.

In many cases, of course, the "richer" interpretation of a universal statement is warranted. We frequently know, on factual grounds, that a class about which we are talking in a universal statement really does have members. But the above MINIMUM INTERPRETATION, which contemporary logic treats as basic, has the great virtue of making us distinguish between what is being actually stated and what is being merely assumed. This is not to say that we have no right to make assumptions, nor that our assumptions are not often factually sound. It merely means that, as we have seen before, precision in thinking requires that we make our assumptions explicit. Let us see how this can be done.

Suppose I am optimistic enough to assert:

> A: All who [r]ead this section carefully will [u]nderstand it.

The *minimum* or basic meaning of this statement may be expressed explicitly in English by the following sentence, and symbolically by the following zeroform and diagram:

A: All who read this section carefully (if anyone does) will understand it.

$$ru' = 0$$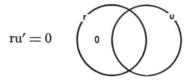

If I make the further assumption, as I do, that someone will read it carefully, I am quite clearly going beyond the above minimum meaning. The additional assumption which I make is made explicit in the following English sentence, and by the following zeroforms and diagram:

A_e: All who read this section carefully (and someone will) will understand it.

$$\begin{cases} ru' = 0 \\ [r \neq 0] \end{cases}$$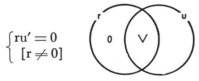

When this assumption of the nonemptiness of the subject class has been made explicit, the resulting enrichment of the minimum or basic meaning is called the EXISTENTIAL INTERPRETATION of the A-statement. I have indicated this existential interpretation by adding a subscript "e" to the "A" which labels a basic universal positive statement. Note how this existential assumption is expressed in zeroform, and how it is represented on the circle diagram. With respect to the latter, do you see that I placed the "∨" in the only place I could? The basic meaning of the A-statement assured me that the class ru' is empty. Any existing r must be in the ru region.

Three further remarks will round out the present discussion.

(1) In the present section, we have confined our illustrations to one of the types of universal statement, namely, the A-statement. Similar remarks apply to the interpretation of E-statements, for these are also universal.

(2) You may recall that in Section 9.6 we noted that a general condi-

tional statement, for example, "If anyone wants to be a concert violinist, he will need to practice," was not a molecular statement. It is now clear that such a statement is equivalent to an A-statement, and that we can preserve the significance of the "if" by confining ourselves to the minimum interpretation. In terms of our example:

> All who want to be concert violinists (if anyone does) will need to practice.

(3) In nearly all cases, the basic or minimum interpretation of universal statements gives us all we need for the validity of arguments in which those statements occur. Contemporary logic therefore adopts the convention of treating all universal statements minimally *except* in cases where a *particular* conclusion is being derived from premises all of which are universal. In such cases, the question of whether the richer existential interpretation is legitimate must be faced. But remember that even here this question cannot be answered on purely formal grounds. Our decision in such cases must rest on further factual information which we may possess. We shall meet this problem again when we come to consider *particularized syllogisms* in Chapter 21.

16.8. NOTE ON AN ALTERNATIVE ANALYSIS OF GENERAL STATEMENTS

General statements may be analyzed in two different ways. For the purposes of this book, we have adopted the class analysis. In the light of the foregoing account of universal statements, we are now in a position to see the possibility of a different analysis. Let us briefly note its nature.

On this analysis, general statements are treated as quantified statement-forms. The universal quantifier is represented by the expression, "For every *x*." The A-statement, "All who want to be concert violinists will need to practice," is analyzed as follows:

> For every *x*, if *x* wants to be a concert violinist, then *x* will need to practice.

The corresponding E-statement, "No one who wants to be a concert violinist will need to practice," is analyzed:

> For every *x*, if *x* wants to be a concert violinist, then *x* will not need to practice.

Note that this analysis, like our basic zeroforms, treats universal statements minimally, and does not make any existential assumption.

Particular statements, on the other hand, have an existential import, as in our zeroform analysis. The particular quantifier is the expression, "There exists at least one x such that . . ." The I-statement, "Some who want to be concert violinists will need to practice," is analyzed:

> There exists at least one x such that x wants to be a concert violinist and x will need to practice.

The corresponding O-statement, "Some who want to be concert violinists will not need to practice," is analyzed:

> There exists at least one x such that x wants to be a concert violinist and x will not need to practice.

It is with the possibility of this type of analysis in mind that some logicians regard general statements as neither molecular nor atomic, but as constituting a third distinct type.

• SOME REMINDERS

5. A distinction must be made between the minimum and the existential interpretation of universal statements.
6. Contemporary logic treats the minimum interpretation as basic, and requires that the existential assumption, when made, be explicitly stated.
7. An alternative to the class-relation analysis of general statements is an analysis in terms of quantified statement-forms.
8. When this latter analysis is used, general statements are often treated as neither molecular nor atomic, but as a third distinct type.

APPLICATIONS

1. Suppose someone were to challenge our position that an A-statement is contradicted by an O-statement, and were to assert instead that the contradictory of an A-statement is the corresponding E-statement. Select a concrete example, and show him why he is wrong.
2. Consider the E-statement, "No students like long assignments." Distinguish between the basic and the existential interpretation of the statement by means of (a) English sentences, (b) zeroforms, (c) circle diagrams.
3. Explain why this question of basic vs. existential interpretation does not also arise in the case of I-statements and O-statements.

4. Give five universal statements for which the existential interpretation would not be factually justified, and five for which it would. Give zeroforms and circle diagrams for all ten.

5. In discussing the Venn diagram for the existential interpretation of "All r is u," we saw that the check-mark had to go in the *ru* region, because the minimum meaning had already asserted that the *ru'* region was empty. Express this line of reasoning in zeroforms, then submit the argument to the contraform test.

CHAPTER 17

TRADITIONAL SUBJECT-PREDICATE ANALYSIS

PREVIEW

In this chapter we shall consider more fully the traditional standard subject-predicate forms of certain atomic statements. We shall see how such statements may be unambiguously symbolized, and how various nonstandard English forms may be restated to reveal more clearly their logical structure.

17.1. STANDARD SUBJECT-PREDICATE FORMS

Along with our zeroforms and circle diagrams, we have been presenting "normal English" versions of the four types of atomic statement being analyzed. You are by this time sophisticated enough in semantical matters to know that there is no single "normal" way of expressing things in English. We did, however, have a special reason for using those particular forms. They are the forms adopted as standard by traditional analysis.

We have already made some preliminary comments on the standard forms. In the present section, we shall examine them more closely. Such an examination will serve at least three purposes: (1) it will familiarize us with the traditional approach to the analysis of atomic statements, (2) it will give us standard forms for expressing atomic statements in everyday English, and (3) it will show the usefulness of certain refinements to be introduced in the next section in symbolizing such statements.

We shall begin with concrete examples of the four basic types of atomic statement recognized by tradition:

> A: All seniors are geniuses.
> E: No seniors are geniuses.
> I: Some seniors are geniuses.
> O: Some seniors aren't geniuses.[1]

[1] The contracted form "aren't" (or "isn't") is adopted as standard, not for colloquial effect, but because it shows clearly that the negative is interpreted as belonging to the

An atomic statement expressed in one of these four forms is said to be in STANDARD SUBJECT-PREDICATE FORM. Many atomic statements not in one of these forms may be restated in standard form without much difficulty. Others can be put into standard form if we are willing to make certain sacrifices of style, emphasis, or meaning. Later on we shall have to face this problem of getting nonstandard expressions into standard form, just as we did when dealing with conditional statements.

The elements of such atomic statements are class-names. They are traditionally referred to as TERMS. The terms in the above examples are "seniors" and "geniuses." The terms are distinguished by their grammatical roles *in the standard form.*[2] In the above examples, "seniors" is the SUBJECT TERM, while "geniuses" is the PREDICATE TERM.

In standard subject-predicate form, the terms are always joined by a form of the verb "to be." This verb is called the COPULA because it is a bond or tie relating the two class-names.

All four examples above have the same subject term and the same predicate term. But each statement obviously has a different form. Traditional analysis handles these differences in terms of the two concepts mentioned earlier, *quantity* and *quality.* In each of the four statements, the subject term is quantified. The quantifiers "all" and "no" are both called *universal,* because they indicate that the statement is about each and every member of the subject class. The quantifier "some" is called *particular,* and is always interpreted to mean "at least one." It leaves open the possibility that "all" might also be asserted. In this it differs from the interpretation of "some" as meaning "at least one but not all."

The three quantifiers, "all," "no," and "some," are the only ones admitted as standard for traditional analysis. Statements about most, or many, or a few of the subject class are treated as particular, and are standardized by using the particular quantifier "some." In a given case, we merely decide whether all or none of the subject class is referred to. If so, the statement is universal; otherwise it is particular.

The remaining concept needed for the traditional analysis is that of *quality.* Whereas the quantifier applies, strictly speaking, to the subject

---

verb, rather than to the predicate class-name. The statement "Some seniors are non-geniuses" is, as we shall later see, logically equivalent to our present form, but it is an I-statement (with negatively expressed predicate class) rather than an O-statement.

[2] The italicized qualification is necessary, because in a few nonstandard forms the grammatical subject is actually the logical predicate. See Section 17.5 below.

term, the notion of quality has to do with the copula. This is clearly revealed when an O-type statement ("Some a *isn't* b") is expressed in standard form, but is concealed by the traditional form of E-statement ("No a is b"). In such statements, the word "no" is really doing double duty. On the one hand, it serves as a universal quantifier of the subject term; on the other, it indicates the negative quality of the copula. O-statements also have a negative copula. A- and I-statements have positive copulas.

17.2. TRADITIONAL TREATMENT OF SINGULAR STATEMENTS

A singular statement is, of course, not really a statement about how two *classes* are related. Rather, it states that an individual has a certain property or is a member of a certain class. Traditional logicians, however, adopted a convenient fiction which made it possible to treat singular statements in the same way as general statements. This analysis makes believe that a statement about an individual is a statement about a single-membered *class*. Hence to refer to an individual is to refer (according to this fiction) to *all* (each and every member) of a class which has only one member. "The Fourth of July is a national holiday" is accordingly treated as an A-statement, while "George Washington is not our present chief executive" is regarded as an E-statement.

• SOME REMINDERS

1. The traditional subject-predicate analysis of atomic statements is conducted in terms of the following concepts:

   A. TERMS (Class-names)   C. QUANTITY (of subject term)
      subject term   universal
      predicate term   particular
   B. COPULA   D. QUALITY (of copula)
                                       positive
                                       negative

2. Singular statements are traditionally treated as a special type of universal statement.

3. Standard subject-predicate forms for A-, E-, I-, and O-statements are given, with other information, in the combined Reference Table at the end of this chapter.

17.3. SYMBOLIZING SUBJECT-PREDICATE STATEMENTS

In order to appreciate the problem we shall now discuss, it will be helpful to recall a parallel situation faced earlier in connection with molecular statements. We found, for example, that "either . . . or" may have one of two meanings in English, and is often ambiguous. For formal analysis, it is crucial to adopt an unambiguous symbolism, and we did so by defining "V" to mean "either . . . or . . . , maybe both." We then symbolized the other type of "either . . . or" by means of "V" and "/." We face similar problems in symbolizing typical subject-predicate statements.

Many of these problems are cleared up, once we express the statements in the standard subject-predicate forms we have been studying. At two points, however, these traditional forms still fall short of our contemporary standards of logical clarity and precision. We shall consider each point in turn, together with its symbolic remedy.

First, we have already noted that the word "no" in an E-statement is serving two functions at once. It serves as a universal quantifier and indicates a negative copula. A symbolic form should clearly separate these two functions. The traditional form of O-statement is quite adequate from this point of view, for it has separate words for the particular quantifier ("some") and the negative copula ("not"). It might at first seem that we could easily remedy this fault of the standard subject-predicate E-statement by adopting a similar procedure. We might use "all" as our universal quantifier, and attach a "not" to the copula. This would result in the form: "All a isn't b." One needs only to think about this form to realize that it is really no improvement. It has overcome one fault, only to introduce another: it is ambiguous. It may mean "No a is b" (universal negative), but in ordinary English this form more commonly means "Some a isn't b" (particular negative). For example, when we say "All students are not going to the game," we probably do not mean that none are, but rather that some are not. In other words, the colloquial function of the "not" in this statement is probably to *contradict* the universal positive statement, "All students are going to the game," rather than to serve as a negative copula in an E-statement. When the "not" is taken in this colloquial way, the statement means "Some students are not going to the game," for this is the contradictory of the corresponding universal positive statement. The refinement which we shall consider in this section avoids ambiguity by introducing a special symbol for the negative copula, while adopting "all" as the standard quantifier for universal statements, whether those statements happen to be positive or negative.

A second contemporary objection to the traditional subject-predicate form is that the copula "is" or "are" does not clearly indicate the precise nature of the relation between subject and predicate. It may seem perverse to raise questions about the meaning of an apparently simple little word like "is." But present-day logicians are impressed by the variety of meanings which this little word has, and commonly distinguish at least six different ones, all with differing logical properties. The kind of "is" involved in these traditional forms is not in general the "is" of identity, for example, but rather the "is" of class-inclusion. We therefore prefer to adopt an unambiguous symbol for this relation of class-inclusion.

Note that there is only one universal quantifier, "all." The copula and its quality are handled in terms of two class-relations: (1) INCLUSION, symbolized by "$<$" (which stands for the positive copula), and (2) EXCLUSION, symbolized by "$\not<$" (which stands for the negative copula). The four symbolic forms are adequately differentiated by mentioning quantifier (universal or particular) and class-relation (inclusion or exclusion).

As in our work with class zeroforms, we symbolize positively named classes by means of lower-case letters. The following table summarizes the results.

CLASS-RELATION SYMBOLS			
Universal Positive (Inclusion)	*Universal Negative (Exclusion)*	*Particular Positive (Inclusion)*	*Particular Negative (Exclusion)*
A-statement	E-statement	I-statement	O-statement
All a $<$ b	All a $\not<$ b	Some a $<$ b	Some a $\not<$ b

We shall retain the traditional subject-predicate forms as standard when we are "talking English," but we shall always *symbolize* them in the above class-relation symbolism. The above four forms are to be read, respectively, "All a is included in b," "All a is excluded from b," "Some a is included in b," and "Some a is excluded from b."

As always, the universal quantifier "all" is to be understood as meaning each and every member of the class named. The particular quantifier, "some," is to be understood in the sense of "at least one," not in the narrower sense of "at least one, but not all."

APPLICATIONS

1. Express each of the following in standard subject-predicate form, then indicate its type (A, E, I, O) and name its quantity and quality.
    a. Bats are mammals.
    b. Many students were not in class yesterday.
    c. God loveth a cheerful giver.
    d. People who live in glass houses shouldn't throw stones.
    e. Man is a strange creature.
    f. Apples are red.
    g. The senator gave a stirring address.
    h. Movies are entertaining.
    i. The dog is man's best friend.
    j. Jack Spratt could eat no fat; his wife could eat no lean.
2. Express each of the above in class-relation symbols. Then describe each in terms of quantifier and class-relation.
3. Express each of the following class zeroforms in class-relation symbols.
    a. $ab' \neq 0$ c. $b'a = 0$ e. $ab' = 0$
    b. $ab = 0$ d. $a'b \neq 0$

17.4. RESTATING IN STANDARD SUBJECT-PREDICATE FORM

When we were dealing with molecular statements, we found it convenient to adopt certain forms of expression as standard, and to "reduce" or restate variant expressions in these standard forms. Thus, by seeing that "unless" meant the same as "if not," we were able to put a molecular "unless"-statement into the standard conditional ("if . . . then") form.

A similar problem, for which a similar solution is appropriate, faces us now in connection with the variety of ways in which atomic statements are expressed in ordinary English. Many atomic statements may be reexpressed in standard subject-predicate form in such a way that their logical import is preserved. Such restatement usually involves more or less damage to such nonlogical factors as style, and also purposely abstracts from the various *degrees* of particular quantification expressed by such words as "most," "many," "a few," and "lots."

From the point of view of subject-predicate analysis, a statement such as "Cats like milk" presents three types of difficulty. First, it has no quantifier expressed. Second, it has no copula. Third, the predicate, "like milk," is quite clearly not the name of a class. Let us consider these difficulties in turn.

QUANTIFYING THE SUBJECT CLASS

When no quantifier for the subject term is given, we have to supply one as best we can from the context or from our knowledge of relevant facts. When someone says, "Mice are rodents," we understand him to mean that *all* mice are, so we supply the universal quantifier. When someone says, "Cats like milk," the intended quantifier is not so clear. People have a way of making sweeping statements even when they know them to be false. A person is likely to talk as if *all* cats like milk, even though he can be led under pressure to admit that some cats don't like milk. If we interpret the unquantified statement, "Cats like milk," to mean "All cats like milk," the statement will, as a matter of fact, be false. (This is, of course, an empirical rather than a formal question.) We must not overlook the likelihood that the speaker really did intend to make this broad universal statement, even though he will later admit, if questioned, that the statement is false if "taken literally."

The rejected suitor who moans, "Women are fickle," probably really does mean, in his present mood, that *all* women are. But when the mood passes, he may be willing to admit that it would have been more accurate to assert merely that *some* women (that is, at least one) are fickle. Unfortunately, it often makes a big difference whether we take a statement universally or not. If all women are fickle, and Jane is a woman, it follows that she is fickle, even though she has not yet revealed any indication of being so.

SUPPLYING THE COPULA

The statement "Cats like milk" does not contain a form of the verb "to be," functioning as a copula. Standard subject-predicate form requires that such a copula be supplied. Merely supplying the copula "are" will not be enough, for the statement, "Some cats are like milk," does not preserve the sense of the original. We must also restate the predicate so that it names the class that is being related by the copula to the class of cats. This is our third point, to which we now turn.

NAMING THE PREDICATE CLASS

"Like milk" is clearly not the name of a class. Yet it is not difficult to see what class we are talking about. We might call it the class of "animals that like milk," or more broadly, "things that like milk," or more compactly but less colloquially, "milk-likers." For the purposes of formal analysis, make sure that the predicate of your statement really does name a class.

When these three difficulties have been solved, our original statement, "Cats like milk," will appear in standard form something like this: "Some cats are milk-likers," or, if we believe the more sweeping but inaccurate statement was intended, "All cats are milk-likers."

17.5. COMMON NONSTANDARD EXPRESSIONS

Some of the most frequent nonstandard expressions which need restating are the following:

"A FEW," "MOST," "MANY," "NEARLY ALL," ETC.

These quantifiers, and others like them, indicate that *some* rather than *all* of the subject class is being explicitly mentioned. Hence, as we know, we must substitute the standard particular quantifier, "some." It is important to notice that we have lost something in the process. Remember also that "some," used in this way, means at least one, and leaves open the question of whether what is being asserted about some of the class might also be asserted about all of the class.

"NOT ANY," "NONE OF," ETC.

Such expressions, like the standard "no" of the traditional subject-predicate forms, serve two roles at once. They indicate a universal quantifier and a negative copula.

"NOT ALL"

This expression raises an important special problem, for it is frequently ambiguous, unless sufficient context is provided. It most often means "some are not." Review the earlier discussion of "all are not" in Section 17.3.

"FEW" vs. "A FEW"

The logical import of "few" must be carefully distinguished from that of the apparently similar expression, "a few." The sentence, "A few students went to church last Sunday," is a particular positive statement, and is readily reduced to standard form by substituting the particular quantifier, "some," supplying a positive copula, and naming the predicate class. The word "few," used alone without the preceding "a," has a *negative* import which it is important not to overlook. In ordinary (nonstandard) language, we could bring out this negative aspect by saying, "Many students did *not* go to church last Sunday, but *a few* students did." To give this complex meaning in standard form requires both a particular negative statement and a particular positive statement. What are they?

"ONLY SOME"

Reflection will show that "only some" is like "few" in this respect, and yields both an O-statement and an I-statement. Think this over, and try it out with a few examples.

"ONLY," "NONE BUT," ETC.

The situation is quite different when "only" appears without the particular quantifier. Then it has a function similar to that of "none but." Consider the force of the statement:

Only men are on the varsity football team.

A moment's thought will make it clear that this does *not* mean that all men are on the varsity team. The correct standard form for this statement is of course:

A: All who are on the varsity football team are men.

Perhaps it will help you remember this if we call attention to the fact that the *grammatical* subject of such statements is really the *logical* predicate, and the order of the class-names must be changed in putting the expression into standard form. (It might even help to note that there is a certain analogy here with the case of "only if" in analyzing conditional statements. "Only if" does not introduce the antecedent, as we might hastily suppose, but always introduces the consequent; similarly, "only" as used in the examples we are now considering, does not introduce the logical subject, as we might mistakenly think, but always introduces the logical predicate.)

Occasionally you will encounter expressions involving "only" or "none but" which, in the light of the context or other information possessed by you, may legitimately be given a fuller interpretation. Consider, for example, the intended import of a sign which reads, "Employees only." We might reasonably urge that this means something like, "Only employees may enter this room." As we saw from our example about football players, this means at least:

> A: All who may enter this room are employees.

But in this somewhat special case, we would presumably have grounds for interpreting this sign as meaning *also:*

> A: All employees are people who may enter this room.

To summarize: Although the context will occasionally permit us to interpret a statement of the form, "Only s is p," as meaning both "All p is s" and "All s is p," we are usually entitled to assert only the first of these.

• SOME REMINDERS

4. As in the formal analysis of molecular statements, certain subject-predicate forms are adopted as standard, and variant expressions are restated in terms of them.
5. Many atomic statements in ordinary English require one or more of the following changes to put them in standard form: the quantifier must be expressed, the copula must be supplied, and the predicate must be rephrased so that it names a class.
6. A number of common but nonstandard expressions are analyzed in the text.

APPLICATIONS

1. Restate the following in standard subject-predicate form, then express in class-relation symbols, using the bracketed letters as abbreviation-symbols for positively expressed class-names.
   a. Only a [b]oor would [t]alk that way to a lady.
   b. Almost every [w]oman [s]eems beautiful to someone.
   c. Every [c]loud has a [s]ilver lining.
   d. Old Mother [H]ubbard went to the [c]upboard.
   e. None without [t]ickets was [a]dmitted.

f. Few [p]rofessors wear [b]eards.
g. None but [e]arly birds [c]atch worms.
h. A few [l]ate-comers [m]issed the excitement.
i. He who [h]esitates is [l]ost.
j. All except [f]reshmen may [r]egister for this course.

CLASS ANALYSIS REFERENCE TABLE

	A	E	I	O
Standard Subject- Predicate Statements	*Universal Positive* All [a]pes are [b]ipeds.	*Universal Negative* No apes are bipeds.	*Particular Positive* Some apes are bipeds.	*Particular Negative* Some apes aren't bipeds.
Class- Relation Symbols	*Universal Inclusion* All a < b	*Universal Exclusion* All a ≮ b	*Particular Inclusion* Some a < b	*Particular Exclusion* Some a ≮ b
Zeroforms	$ab' = 0$	$ab = 0$	$ab \neq 0$	$ab' \neq 0$
Circle Diagrams				

CHAPTER 18

SOME RELATIONS BETWEEN SUBJECT-PREDICATE STATEMENTS

PREVIEW

In exploring molecular statements, we came upon such relations as converses and contrapositives of conditional statements, and learned how to derive conditional, alternative, and disjunctive statements that are logically equivalent. We also noted such relationships as contradictories, contraries, and subalterns. In the present chapter we shall examine certain similar relations between atomic statements of the four traditionally distinguished forms.

18.1. SUBJECT-PREDICATE CONVERSES [1]

Thus far, our use of the term "converse" has been confined to conditional statements. We know that "A ⊃ B′" is the converse of "B′ ⊃ A." We also know that conditional converses are not logically equivalent.

The term "converse" is also applied in relation to atomic statements of the types we have been examining. The CONVERSE of a subject-predicate statement is derived by interchanging the elements (terms or class-names), leaving everything else just as it is. The process of deriving the converse of a given statement is called CONVERSION.

Maxim for converting a subject-predicate statement: Interchange the terms.

Let us try converting atomic statements of each of the four traditional types. Zeroforms and circle diagrams are valuable supplements here, so

---

[1] Some instructors may wish to consider this topic in the light of the traditional concept of *distribution*. If so, Section 19.2 may be assigned at this time.

let us work them out too. In labeling the circles for the converse of the given statement, the left-hand circle will be assigned to the subject term of the *original* statement, even though this term becomes the predicate in the converse. This procedure will simplify direct comparison of the two forms.

Original A: All [r]oses are   *Converse* A: All flowers are
[f]lowers.   roses.

All r < f   All f < r
rf' = 0   fr' = 0

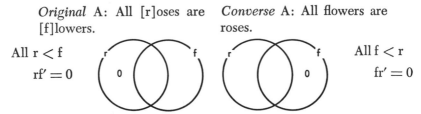

It is easy to see that the converse of an A-statement is not logically equivalent to the original. This is obvious enough from the subject-predicate form alone, and our common-sense reaction to these forms is confirmed by looking at the zeroforms and the circle diagrams for these two statements.

We have just seen that the strict converse of an A-statement is not logically equivalent to it. There is a traditionally recognized form, called the LIMITED CONVERSE, which we shall now examine. The limited converse of an A-statement is formed from the strict converse by "limiting" the quantifier to *some* rather than *all*. Thus the limited converse of "All roses are flowers" is "Some flowers are roses." The following comments are in order: (1) The limited converse is obviously not logically equivalent to the original, although it would commonly be held to *follow from* the original. (2) This common view can be accepted only on the *existential* interpretation of the original A-statement. The limited converse does not follow from an original which is given the minimum interpretation. This difference may be readily verified by inspection of zeroforms and by means of the contraform test. (3) On neither interpretation can you "get back to" the original by converting the limited converse (an I-statement) itself. For the converse of an I-statement, see below.

Next, consider an E-statement and its converse:

Original E: No [r]oses are   *Converse* E: No birds are
[b]irds.   roses.

All r ≮ b   All b ≮ r
rb = 0   br = 0

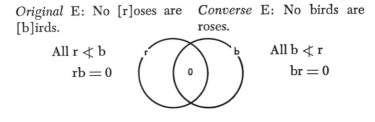

The converse of an E-statement, as the above analysis shows, is logically equivalent to the original. The two subject-predicate statements, quite apart from our further analysis, certainly appear to be logically equivalent. But if we suspected that this was only an appearance, dependent upon the particular content we happened to choose, we could easily remove this suspicion by examining the zeroforms and the circle diagram. I assume that by this time you know that "rb" means exactly the same as "br."

Now how about the converse of an I-statement?

Original I: Some [f]lowers   *Converse* I: Some roses are
are [r]oses.   flowers.

Here I purposely picked an example where the content *would* get in the way. You probably feel rather dissatisfied with this converse, and wish that I'd said instead, "*All* roses are flowers." Now this latter statement happens to be true, but it is not the converse of "Some flowers are roses," nor is it logically equivalent to this original, nor does it follow from it. You will perhaps feel better when you remember that the "some" in the converse is to be interpreted as meaning at least one, maybe all, for you will admit that in this sense some roses are flowers. Where do we come out? "Some roses are flowers" really is the converse of the original I-statement, and it is logically equivalent to the original. Let us verify these claims by recalling the maxim for conversion and by looking at the zeroforms and diagram below. The diagram represents both statements equally well:

Original I: Some flowers are   *Converse* I: Some roses are
roses.   flowers.

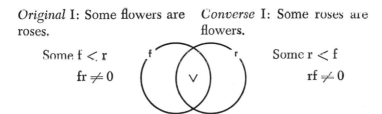

Some f < r   Some r < f

fr ≠ 0   rf ≠ 0

It remains to examine the converse of an O-statement:

Original O: Some flowers   *Converse* O: Some roses
aren't roses.   aren't flowers.

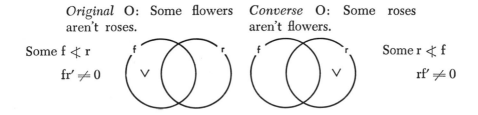

Some f ⊀ r   Some r ⊀ f

fr′ ≠ 0   rf′ ≠ 0

Here, as in the case of an A-statement, the converse is not logically equivalent to the original, nor does it follow from the original. Any doubts we may have at the common-sense level are removed by setting up the appropriate zeroforms and diagrams.

Before leaving this topic, note that the strict converse of a statement is always another statement of the same logical type. An A-statement converts to another A, and so on.

18.2. OBVERSES

Traditional logic also explores another basic relation between subject-predicate statements, called OBVERSION. The process of obversion is somewhat more complex than that of conversion, for it involves two steps:

Maxim for obverting a subject-predicate statement:

a.   Change the quality of the copula.
b.   Replace the predicate term by its complement.

Let's see how this maxim for obversion works.

A: All [d]ucks are [s]wim-   *Obverse* E: No ducks are
mers.   nonswimmers.

Perhaps the first thing you notice here is that, unlike conversion, this process of obversion yields a statement of different type from that of the original. The obverse of an A-statement is an E-statement.

Are the above obverses logically equivalent? It may help us better to see what is going on if, here again, we symbolize the statements in standard class-relation form before we derive their zeroforms and diagrams.

A: All $d < s$ *Obverse* E: All $d \nless s'$

$ds' = 0$ $ds' = 0$

Is the obverse of an A-statement logically equivalent to the original, even though the obverse is itself an E-statement?

Now, how about *beginning* with an E-statement, and obverting it:

E: No [c]rows are
[s]wimmers.

Obverse A: All crows
are nonswimmers.

All c ⊀ s

All c < s′

cs = 0

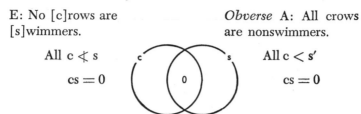

cs = 0

Do you see how I got that zeroform for the obverse A-statement? And is the obverse of an E-statement logically equivalent to the E-statement?

Next, let's try to obvert an I-statement:

I: Some [b]oys are
[s]wimmers.

Obverse O: Some boys
aren't nonswimmers.

Some b < s

Some b ⊀ s′

bs ≠ 0

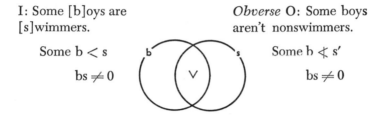

bs ≠ 0

With this much practice, go ahead and work out the obverse of the following O-statement:

O: Some [b]oys aren't
[s]wimmers.

Obverse: ————————.

———————

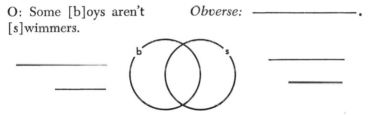

————

———————

————

When you have completed your analysis, you should have adequate grounds for accepting the following statement: *Obverses are always logically equivalent.*

18.3. SUBJECT-PREDICATE CONTRAPOSITIVES

Do you remember how to derive a *conditional* contrapositive? You interchange the contradicted antecedent and the contradicted consequent. The contrapositive of "A ⊃ B" is "B′ ⊃ A′." The heading above should lead you to expect something similar for subject-predicate statements.

Let's start out with an A-statement. And let's agree never to perform an operation unless it will yield a logically equivalent statement.

Original A: All Quakers are pacifists.

We know that if we *convert* this A-statement, we will get a statement which is not logically equivalent to it. Let's not follow that line, for it leads nowhere and violates our agreement to derive only logically equivalent forms. Instead, let us obvert this A-statement. We know that any obverse is equivalent to its original.

Obverse E: No Quakers are nonpacifists.

Now, for the fun of it, let's *convert* this obverse. Since it is an E-statement, we know that its converse will be equivalent to it.

Converse of Obverse: No nonpacifists are Quakers.

If you're still enjoying this, let's obvert once more, to get another logically equivalent statement:

Obverse of the Converted Obverse:
All nonpacifists are non-Quakers.

How does this compare with our original statement? Write them down together so we can see:

Original A: All Quakers are pacifists.
Resulting A: All nonpacifists are non-Quakers.

Are you willing to accept these two statements as subject-predicate contrapositives? That's what they are. The terms of one are simply interchanged and negated (that is, their complements are substituted) to get the other. We have taken the long way around to secure this result, but we have learned something along the way: the contrapositive of an A-statement is the obverse of the converse of its obverse. We know that these two are logically equivalent, because we have proceeded from the one to the other by a series of logical equivalences. We can also prove that they are logically equivalent by comparing their zeroforms. Do it.

A-statements and O-statements are the only atomic types that have *logically equivalent* contrapositives. In the Applications below, you will have an opportunity to show that this is so, and to discover why it is.

Maxims for deriving the contrapositive of a subject-predicate statement:

1. *The Long Way:* Obvert, then convert, then obvert.
2. *The Short Way:* Replace the original terms by their interchanged complements.

APPLICATIONS

1. In each case, tell how the second statement is related to the first, and indicate whether the two are logically equivalent. You will sometimes need to combine two terms to describe the relationship, for example, a statement may be the obverted converse of another.
   a. Some brunettes have curly hair. Some curly-haired people are brunettes.
   b. No diamond can be scratched by copper. All diamonds are things that cannot be scratched by copper.
   c. All tardy students will be marked absent. Some tardy students will not be marked absent.
   d. Some radishes taste strong. Some things that don't taste strong are things that aren't radishes.
   e. All skyscrapers are over four stories high. Some things over four stories high are skyscrapers.
   f. Some chairs are uncomfortable. Some chairs are not comfortable.
   g. All men are mortal. No immortals are men.
   h. Some movies aren't worth seeing. Some things worth seeing are non-movies.
   i. No cowbirds raise their own young. All who don't raise their own young are cowbirds.
   j. Some who aren't afraid of water aren't non-Polynesians. Some Polynesians aren't afraid of water.
2. Explain why the *limited* converse of "All [o]ranges are [r]ound" does not follow from the minimum interpretation of the original A-statement. Then show, by means of the contraform test, that this limited converse does follow from the existential interpretation of the original statement.
3. Obvert each of the following. Check by zeroforms to establish logical equivalence of obverses.
   a. All horses like hay.
   b. Some students are always late to class.
   c. No true poets write doggerel.
   d. Some people aren't as clever as they think they are.
4. Derive, step by step, the contrapositive of "All $a < b$" (using standard class-relation forms). Label each step, and write the appropriate zeroform beside each step. What does an examination of the zeroforms reveal?
5. Start from the statement, "Some a is b," and apply first obversion, then conversion, alternating one with the other until you are stopped by a nonequivalent form or reach the contrapositive.
6. Do the same for the statement, "Some a isn't b."
7. Do the same for the statement, "No a is b."
8. Use the "short way" maxim to derive contrapositives for each of the following. Then set up zeroforms and draw circle diagrams to determine which of the contrapositives are logically equivalent to their original.
   a. All $a < b$.   c. Some $a < b$.
   b. All $a \not< b$.   d. Some $a \not< b$.

18.4. THE TRADITIONAL SQUARE OF OPPOSITION

Certain further relations between pairs of the four basic types of subject-predicate statement are conveniently exhibited by a traditional diagram called the SQUARE OF OPPOSITION. Two subject-predicate statements are said to be OPPOSED in this sense when they (a) have the same subject class and the same predicate class, but (b) differ in quantity or quality or both. The names of some of these opposing relations are already familiar to us from an earlier and more general account (see Section 10.1).

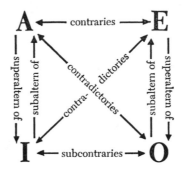

As we know, the A-statement and its opposing O-statement are *contradictories;* they cannot both be true, and cannot both be false. Thus from the truth of one of them the falsity of the other logically follows, and vice versa. The same holds for an E-statement and its opposing contradictory I-statement.

All the remaining relations on the square of opposition hold only if the universal statements involved as well as the particular are interpreted *existentially,* that is, only if the subject class is understood to have at least one member. On this traditional assumption, the A-statement and its opposing E-statement are *contraries;* that is, they cannot both be true, although they may both be false. Thus, from the truth of one of them, the falsity of the other logically follows. But from the falsity of one of them, nothing can be inferred about the truth-value of the other.

Again on the usual existential interpretation, the I-statement and its opposing O-statement are SUBCONTRARIES. Two statements are subcontrary if they cannot both be false, but may both be true. Thus from the falsity of one of them, the truth of the other logically follows, although from the truth of one of them, nothing can be inferred about the truth-value of the other.

When universal statements as well as particular ones are interpreted existentially, opposing statements of the same quality but different quantities stand in the relation of SUBALTERNATION. The particular statement is called the SUBALTERN of its corresponding universal statement, which in turn is called the SUPERALTERN of the particular statement. This relation, like the others on the square, is defined in terms of truth-values. The truth of a subaltern follows from the truth of its superaltern, but not vice versa. On the other hand, the falsity of a superaltern follows from the falsity of its subaltern, but not vice versa. Compare the earlier discussion of this relationship in Section 14.2.

18.5. THE CROSS OF CONTRADICTION

For reasons adequately explored earlier (Section 16.7), contemporary logicians regard the minimum, rather than the existential, interpretation of universal statements as basic. When we no longer assume that a universal statement implies that members of the subject class exist, the traditional square of opposition undergoes a marked transformation. All the relations indicated around the perimeter of the diagram disappear, leaving only the central CROSS OF CONTRADICTION.

On the minimum interpretation of universals, the A-statement and its corresponding E-statement are not contraries, for they might both be true. In fact, they will both be true whenever the subject class is empty. This is readily seen in terms of zeroforms. If $a = 0$ (that is, if there isn't any a at all) then obviously $ab' = 0$ (there isn't any a that is non-b), and $ab = 0$ (there isn't any a that is b). Since on this minimum interpretation, the A- and E-statements may both be true, it follows that their respective contradictories, the opposing O- and I-statements, may both be false. Hence they can no longer be regarded as subcontraries. Finally, the relation of subalternation also disappears, for on the minimum interpretation of universal statements, the truth of a particular statement no longer follows from the truth of its corresponding universal statement. Why not? Because the particular statement clearly has an existential import, while the universal statement does not. Thus, if the subject class is empty, the universal will (as we saw above) be true, but the corresponding particular cannot possibly be.

It is important to understand that the purpose of this section has been to show what happens to the traditional square of opposition when we interpret universal statements minimally, not to show that traditional logicians were mistaken in discerning the relations they did. As long as universal statements as well as particular ones are interpreted existentially, the traditional square correctly pictures the relations which hold between opposing subject-predicate statements. But it is still worth remembering that it is not in all cases *factually* sound to interpret a universal statement existentially.

• SOME REMINDERS

1. When applied to subject-predicate statements, the logical operations of conversion, obversion, and contraposition yield other subject-predicate statements.
2. Depending upon the logical operation involved and the type of statement to which it is applied, the resulting statements are or are not logically equivalent to the originals.
3. The Square of Opposition illustrates further relations between certain subject-predicate statements.
4. When universal statements are interpreted minimally, the relations around the perimeter of the Square no longer hold.

APPLICATIONS

1. Given that "All opossums are marsupials" is true, and that there are opossums, which of the opposing statements on the square of opposition are true, which false, and which indeterminate?
2. Given that "No apes are edentates" is true, and that there are apes, which of the opposing statements are true, which false, and which indeterminate?
3. Given that "Some horses are mammals" is true, which of the opposing statements are true, which false, and which indeterminate?
4. Given that "Some organisms aren't vertebrates" is true, which of the opposing statements are true, which false, and which indeterminate?
5. For each of the following statements in turn, assume that the statement is false, but that the subject class contains at least one member. In each case, what can be inferred about the truth-value of the opposing statements on the square?

a. All students are lazy.
b. No professors are human.
c. Some sophomores are wise.
d. Some alumni are not educated.
6. Explain how your analyses of the above eight examples would be affected if it were not known that the subject classes are nonempty.

CHAPTER 19

TRADITIONAL ANALYSIS OF SYLLOGISMS

PREVIEW

An important traditionally distinguished form of atomic argument is the syllogism. We have already used numerous examples of this type for illustrative purposes. In this chapter we shall examine four maxims by which the validity of such arguments may be determined.

19.1. WHAT IS A SYLLOGISM?

Classical logicians regarded the syllogism as the central form of argument.[1] This form has been the subject of detailed study for over two thousand years. Other forms of argument were in general forced, with varying degrees of violence and ingenuity, into the pattern of the syllogism, and were then tested by a set of validity maxims. While contemporary logic does not give the syllogism the central place accorded it by traditional logic, the form is an interesting and important one which repays study. Many of the arguments we encounter in everyday life may be readily analyzed in its terms.

An argument is a syllogism if it meets the following two requirements:

1. The argument has exactly two premises and a conclusion, each expressible as a standard A-, E-, I-, or O-statement.
2. The argument contains exactly three terms (class-names), each term occurring twice, each time in a different statement.

---

[1] The type of argument here called simply a "syllogism" is sometimes referred to more fully as a *categorical* syllogism. In traditional logic, this adjective serves to distinguish arguments of the present type from simple conditional arguments, which are sometimes called "hypothetical syllogisms," and from simple alternative arguments, which are sometimes called "alternative syllogisms."

An argument which satisfies the first requirement but contains a fourth term which is the complement of one of the other terms, can sometimes be restated so that it satisfies the second requirement. This is done by obverting one of the statements, or by first converting (if this yields an equivalent form) and then obverting it.[2] An argument which contains a fourth term which cannot be so eliminated is traditionally said to commit the FALLACY OF FOUR TERMS. It might be better to say that such an argument is simply not a syllogism, for it cannot be restated to meet the second of the two requirements which together define this form.

If you think about this second requirement, it will be apparent that in a syllogism there is one term common to both premises. The traditional name for this term is MIDDLE TERM. This term functions as a middleman or mediator or bridge between the other two terms. Having performed this mediating function in the premises, it drops out in the conclusion, leaving the other two terms directly related. These other terms also have traditional names. The one that serves as the logical predicate of the *conclusion* is called the MAJOR TERM, and the premise in which it occurs is called the MAJOR PREMISE. The subject term of the conclusion is called the MINOR TERM, and the premise in which it also appears is called the MINOR PREMISE. In traditional analysis, the major premise is customarily written first, but the order of the premises does not, of course, affect validity.

In general discussions like the present one, where no specific content is being analyzed, it is customary to use "s" as the symbol for the minor term, "p" for the major term, and "m" for the middle term. When a concrete argument is being analyzed, it is usually more convenient to follow our previous practice of picking abbreviation-symbols which remind us of the specific class-names.[3]

---

[2] There are other irregular forms that can be shown to be logically equivalent to a standard syllogism. One of the most important of these is the general conditional argument, discussed in Section 19.6 below.

[3] Traditional logicians developed a compact way of specifying the pattern of any syllogism by mentioning its mood and figure. MOOD is the pattern of the syllogism with reference to its quantity and quality; it is given by mentioning, in order, the vowel symbols (A, E, I, or O) of the major premise, minor premise, and conclusion. FIGURE is the pattern of the syllogism with reference to the position of the middle term. Four figures are possible, and a number is assigned to each as follows:

Figure	1		2		3		4	
Major Premise	m	p	p	m	m	p	p	m
Minor Premise	s	m	s	m	m	s	m	s

19.2. DISTRIBUTED AND UNDISTRIBUTED TERMS

The validity or invalidity of a syllogism may be readily established by means of the contraform test, using class zeroforms. We shall now, how-ever, examine the traditional way of testing such arguments by maxims. Once a syllogism has been expressed in standard form, its validity may be determined by four maxims. Two of these have to do with matters of inclusion and exclusion, and will be readily understood. The other two deal with what is called DISTRIBUTION.

Consider the symbolic forms of the two universal types of subject-predicate statement:

A: All s $<$ p   E: All s $\not<$ p

In both cases, the quantifier of the subject term is "all," and refers to each and every member of the class named. Whenever such reference occurs, the term is said to be DISTRIBUTED. Subject terms of universal statements are thus always distributed. But how about the two particular forms?

I: Some s $<$ p   O: Some s $\not<$ p

In both these cases, the quantifier of the subject term refers merely to *at least one* of the class. Although, as you will recall, this does not rule out the possibility that the relation may also hold for each and every member as well as for some of the class, yet the particular quantifier does not refer to all of the class. Hence the subject terms of particular statements are UNDISTRIBUTED.

But how about the *predicate* terms? Are they distributed or not? It might at first seem that we would have no way of telling, inasmuch as no explicit quantifiers are given. But if you will think over the manner in which two classes are related in an exclusion (E or O), you will find that, quite clearly, the subject class is excluded from the *whole* of the predicate class. When we say that no flowers are vertebrates, or that some flowers are not vertebrates, we are in each case excluding the flowers referred to from the entire class of vertebrates. The predicate terms of exclusions are always distributed. But the situation is otherwise with the predicates of *inclusions.* When we say, "All bees are insects," we make no claim that bees are all the insects there are; we do not refer to the whole class of insects. And the claim made by the particular inclusion, "Some bees are insects," is even weaker. Thus we see that the predicate terms of *inclusions* are undistributed. Our findings may be compactly summarized:

DISTRIBUTED TERMS
subjects of universals
predicates of exclusions

Other terms are undistributed. (Be sure to note that, in listing distributed terms, we are *not* grouping universals and particulars together, nor inclusions and exclusions, but rather the subject terms of *universals* and the predicate terms of *exclusions*.)

A simple and convenient way of indicating distributed terms is to draw a CAP above their symbols, thus:

A: All $\hat{s} < p$ E: All $\hat{s} \not< \hat{p}$
I: Some $s < p$ O: Some $s \not< \hat{p}$

You may find it helpful in remembering the function of this cap to think of it as a "roof" sheltering each and every member of the class.

19.3. VALIDITY MAXIMS FOR THE SYLLOGISM

Four maxims suffice for determining the validity of most of the syllogisms we encounter. The exception is the *particularized syllogism*, in which a particular conclusion is drawn from two universal premises.[4]

The first two maxims have to do with distribution of terms.

Maxim 1: The middle term must be distributed at least once.

This rule is required in order to assure that the middle term can perform its mediating function. If the class named by the major term is related merely to *some* of the mediating class, and the class named by the minor term is also related merely to *some* of this class, we have no assurance that these two "somes" overlap in membership. Thus we are not warranted in concluding anything about the direct relation between minor and major classes.

---

[4] Do not at present attempt to use these maxims for testing a particularized syllogism. Their significance in this connection will be explained in Section 21.2, note 2.

> *Maxim 2:* If a term is distributed in the conclusion, it must also be distributed in its premise.

If this maxim is violated, we assert more than we are entitled to in the conclusion. If our information in the premises involves merely *some* of a class, we are not warranted in asserting something about *all* of the class in our conclusion.

The other two maxims have to do with the permissible combinations of inclusions and exclusions.

> *Maxim 3:* If the conclusion is an *exclusion*, exactly one premise must also be an *exclusion*.

The above maxim is required to eliminate two situations, one in which we might attempt to draw an exclusion from two inclusions, and the other in which we might try to derive an exclusion from two exclusions. The first case must be ruled out, because two inclusions give us no information on which to base an assertion to the effect that one of the given classes is excluded from another. The second case must be ruled out also, because two exclusions give us no information which would justify any assertion about the relation between "s" and "p" in our conclusion. The above rule prohibits our deriving an *exclusion* from two premises, both of which are exclusions. The following rule will also prohibit our deriving an *inclusion* from such premises:

> *Maxim 4:* If the conclusion is an *inclusion*, both premises must also be inclusions.

You should study Maxims 3 and 4 together, to see clearly that the only situations they permit are the following:

       a. *Premises:* one exclusion, one inclusion
          Conclusion: an exclusion
       b. *Premises:* two inclusions
          Conclusion: an inclusion

19.4. SYLLOGISTIC FALLACIES

Violation of any of these maxims constitutes a formal fallacy, and makes the syllogism invalid. We may always indicate the general nature of the fallacy by specifying the maxim which is being violated. It is, however, often more convenient and informative to have specific names for these different possible violations.

The traditional name for the formal fallacy resulting when the first maxim is violated is UNDISTRIBUTED MIDDLE. The second maxim requires that if a term is distributed in the conclusion, it must also be distributed in its premise. We may specify which term is involved in the violation of this maxim, by speaking of an ILLICIT MAJOR where the major term is illicitly distributed in the conclusion, and of an ILLICIT MINOR when the minor term in the conclusion is so distributed. When the premises are both exclusions, we may refer to the fallacy of TWO EXCLUSIONS. When we illicitly attempt to derive an exclusion from premises both of which are inclusions, we may refer to ILLICIT EXCLUSION. The fallacy of ILLICIT IN-CLUSION is analogous to this last, and results when, in violation of Maxim 4, we attempt to derive an inclusion without having two inclusions as premises. We may summarize our results by listing the possible violations of each of the four validity maxims:

MAXIM	FALLACY
1	Undistributed Middle
2	Illicit Major Illicit Minor
3	Two Exclusions Illicit Exclusion
4	Illicit Inclusion

19.5. COMMENT ON TWO COROLLARIES

The above four maxims, as we have already indicated, are sufficient to establish the validity of any syllogism except the special type (two universal premises and particular conclusion) called a particularized syllogism.

The maxims already given, however, can be shown to imply certain others; given these four rules, we can prove that certain other maxims also hold. Should we incorporate these derived rules, the COROLLARIES, in our list? There are things to be said on both sides of this question.

IN FAVOR OF SUCH INCORPORATION	AGAINST SUCH INCORPORATION
We might point to the logical interest in recognizing that these rules are implicit in the others, and to the practical point that violations of the corollaries may sometimes be easier for the beginner to spot than violations of the related basic rules.	We might urge both the greater logical simplicity of using only the necessary minimum of rules, and the greater practical or psychological simplicity of not bothering ourselves with extra rules when four will do the job.

Let us, however, at least note two corollaries, and then make use of them or not as we find convenient.

Corollary 1: At least one of the premises must be universal.

The maxims already given are sufficient to prove that this corollary must hold. Consider a case in which we have, in violation of this corollary, two particular premises:

$$\text{Some m} < \text{p}$$
$$\underline{\text{Some s} < \text{m}}$$

Now let us mark the distributed terms. But there aren't any. In the example we have chosen, where both premises are affirmative, it is clear that the middle term is *not* distributed at least once, so Maxim 1 is violated. Let us try to improve the situation by considering another argument which differs from this one in that the middle term is distributed in the minor premise. This will of course require that the minor premise be an exclusion:

$$\text{Some s} \not< \hat{\text{m}}$$

Now, unless we are to violate Maxim 4 and commit the fallacy of illicit inclusion, our *conclusion* will have to be an exclusion, won't it? But in that case we shall get into trouble, too, for our major term, "p," will then be distributed in the conclusion, although it was not distributed in its premise. Hence we shall have violated Maxim 2, and have committed the fallacy of illicit major.

If we should try to patch things up by distributing "p" in its premise,

$$\text{Some } m \not< \hat{p}$$

we should then have two exclusions, which is a fallacy resulting from violation of Maxim 3. Are there any other possibilities? You will find that any syllogism with both basic premises particular will violate at least one of the rules already given.

The practical value of being acquainted with this corollary is, of course, that the minute you spot a syllogism with two particular premises, you can be assured that it is invalid. It may take a little further thought to determine which of the four basic maxims is being violated in the particular example. Let us now look at a second corollary:

Corollary 2: If one of the premises is particular, the conclusion must be particular.

This second corollary may be investigated along lines similar to those used in examining the first. We shall not undertake this investigation here (though you might enjoy doing it yourself) but shall merely consider one example which illustrates the violation of this corollary, and hence also the violation of one of the four basic rules already presented.

$$\text{All } \hat{m} < p$$
$$\underline{\text{Some } \ m < s}$$
$$\text{All } \hat{s} < p$$

Here the fallacy of illicit minor is committed through violation of Maxim 2. A complete investigation would disclose that, no matter what else we try, so long as we attempt to derive a universal conclusion from premises one of which is particular, we shall be violating one of the four basic maxims.

The practical value of being acquainted with this second corollary is that, the moment we spot a syllogism which attempts to derive a universal conclusion when one premise is particular, we know that the argument is invalid.

Following the pattern of naming fallacies resulting from the violation of the four basic maxims, we may assign special names to violations of the corollaries. When Corollary 1 is not satisfied, we have a case of the fallacy of TWO PARTICULARS. When Corollary 2 is violated, the fallacy is that of ILLICIT UNIVERSAL. Rather than rest content with these two labels, however, it is good practice to trace the difficulty back to the four basic maxims, and to name the fallacy committed in relation to them.

19.6. ARGUMENTS CONTAINING GENERAL CONDITIONALS

An argument containing a general conditional, along with atomic statements, may of course be analyzed by restating the general conditional in equivalent atomic form. The simplest argument of this type is like the simple conditional argument, except that it contains a general conditional in place of the molecular conditional. For example:

> If anything is a parallelogram, then it is four-sided.
> This figure is a parallelogram.
> ――――――――――――――――――――――――――――――
> This figure is four-sided.

When the general conditional premise is restated in subject-predicate form, the result is a standard syllogism:

> All parallelograms are four-sided.
> This figure is a parallelogram.
> ――――――――――――――――――――――――
> This figure is four-sided.

This syllogism may be shown to be valid by the traditional maxims. Hence the original general conditional argument, which is equivalent to it, is also valid.

It is sometimes convenient to refer to the pattern of such a general conditional argument without first restating it as a syllogism. How can this be done? We are tempted to use the terminology with which we became familiar in discussing simple conditional arguments, and to say that the above argument "asserts the antecedent." This would be inaccurate, however, for the antecedent of a general conditional is not a statement at all and cannot be asserted. It is instead a statement-form, containing the variable, "anything." What the second premise really asserts is a statement which is called a SUBSTITUTION INSTANCE of this statement-form. This statement results from substituting the constant "this," which refers to a specific object, for the variable, "anything." The argument is thus correctly described as one which *asserts a substitution instance of the antecedent.*

By testing the validity of the corresponding syllogisms, it can be shown that the valid and invalid patterns of general conditional arguments parallel those of simple conditional arguments. Valid forms either assert a substitution instance of the antecedent or contradict a substitution instance of the consequent.

• SOME REMINDERS

1. A syllogism is an atomic argument containing two premises and a conclusion, all expressible in subject-predicate or class-relation form. Such an argument must, when expressed in standard form, contain exactly three terms.
2. The validity or invalidity of all syllogisms except particularized ones is reliably determined by four maxims.
3. Two corollaries to the four maxims have some practical value.
4. Some arguments containing general conditionals may be restated as standard syllogisms and then tested by the syllogistic maxims, or may be tested directly by a maxim paralleling that for the simple conditional argument.

APPLICATIONS

1. First, mark the distributed terms. Then test each of the following arguments by the four traditional maxims. Indicate whether the syllogism is valid or invalid. If it is invalid, name *all* the fallacies committed.

a. All m ≮ p
   Some m < s
   ―――――――
   All s < p

b. All p ≮ m
   All s < m
   ―――――――
   All s ≮ p

c. All m < p
   All s ≮ m
   ―――――――
   All s ≮ p

d. All p < m
   Some m ≮ s
   ―――――――
   Some s ≮ p

e. All m ≮ p
   All s < m
   ―――――――
   All s ≮ p

f. All m < p
   Some m ≮ s
   ―――――――
   Some s < p

g. All p ≮ m
   Some m < s
   ―――――――
   Some s ≮ p

h. All p < m
   All s < m
   ―――――――
   All s ≮ p

i. All m ≮ p
   Some s ≮ m
   ―――――――
   Some s ≮ p

j. All m < p
   Some m < s
   ―――――――
   Some s < p

2.   Name the mood and figure of each of the syllogisms in Application 1 above.
3.   First, locate the conclusion. Then name in English the classes to be sym-
      bolized by the bracketed letters. (For example, in the first syllogism be-
      low, [q] = May Queen candidates, [e] = those who will be elected, [d] =
      those who deserve to be elected.) Next, express the syllogism in standard
      class-relation symbols, using these letters. Finally test by the maxims, de-
      termine validity or invalidity, and name all fallacies committed.
      a.   Since not all May [Q]ueen candidates will be [e]lected, and since every
            May Queen candidate [d]eserves to be elected, it follows that some who
            deserve to be elected will not be.
      b.   Nobody who takes [l]ogic has to take [m]ath. Thus some who have to
            take math are not [f]reshmen, for some freshmen take logic.
      c.   All [p]re-meds have to take [b]iology, so some [A]lpha Alpha Alphas
            must be pre-meds, for some Alpha Alpha Alphas have to take biology.
      d.   Inasmuch as all the [p]hones in this building are [o]ut of order, every
            phone in this building [n]eeds to be repaired, because any phone that
            is out of order needs to be repaired.
      e.   I am sure that everyone at the [c]arnival was [h]aving a good time, for
            although [w]eeping people are not having a good time, no one there was
            weeping.
      f.   No [s]tudents will study during the [h]olidays. Some students are going
            home by [b]us. Hence at least some people who will study during the
            holidays are not going home by bus.
      g.   All [a]lumni have been [i]nvited for Alumni Day. Thus some alumni
            must be [p]rominent people, for many prominent people have been
            invited.
      h.   It is evident that if anything is a [c]ircle, it is not also a [t]riangle, for
            if anything is a triangle, it is three-[s]ided, and if anything has three sides
            it is not a circle.
      i.   Naturally, [I] don't [b]elieve in witches! Only [s]uperstitious people do,
            and you know perfectly well that I am anything but superstitious.
      j.   Since it is false that none but the [b]rave [d]eserve the fair, it follows
            that some [m]en deserve the fair, for some men are not brave.
4.   What rules are broken by syllogisms composed of the following types of
      proposition (the first in each case being the major premise and the last
      the conclusion)? [5]
      a. EOA.   c. III.   e. AIA.
      b. OEE.   d. IEO.
5.   Determine what type of valid conclusion can result from the following types
      of premises (the first being the major premise in each case). [5]
      a. AI.   c. AA.   e. AO.
      b. EI.   d. EA.   f. IO.

[5] These two exercises are reprinted by permission of the publisher from Max Black:
Critical Thinking, Second Edition, (Copyright 1946, 1952 by Prentice-Hall, Inc., New
York), p. 153.

CHAPTER 20

CONTEMPORARY ANALYSIS
OF SYLLOGISMS

PREVIEW

In this chapter we shall comment on the use of the contraform test for establishing the validity or invalidity of syllogisms, and shall then explore the use of Venn diagrams for this purpose.

20.1. APPLYING THE CONTRAFORM TEST TO SYLLOGISMS

Ever since we learned, in Chapter 16, to express atomic statements by means of class zeroforms, we have had at our disposal a validity test for syllogisms. The use of contraform principles in testing this type of argument presents no new problems of theory. One practical matter perhaps calls for brief comment.

As long as you were dealing with molecular arguments, you found that the satisfaction of Principle 1 was automatic. The items in the test form that were derived from the premises were always equations, and the last line of the test form was always an inequation. In atomic arguments, however, the required inequation may turn up anywhere in the test form. This may constitute a slight psychological hurdle until you get used to it. But note carefully that it in no way calls for a restatement of the basic contraform principles. From the very first, these principles have been stated, not in terms of premises and conclusion, but in terms of equations and inequation, wherever the latter may occur in the test form.

Historically, the distinctive validity pattern which the contraform principles describe was first noticed in connection with the analysis of syllogisms. In the early 1880's, Christine Ladd-Franklin discovered this symptomatic pattern and based what she called an ANTILOGISM TEST upon it. This test turns out, in the light of later work, to be a restricted form of our present contraform test. Our test is indebted to her pioneer work, but is more comprehensive in two respects. First, it is not limited to arguments having only two premises. Second, it is not confined to arguments consisting of analyzed atomic statements, but has been given an interpretation for molecular arguments as well. The contraform test brings together in generalized form certain basic features of the truth-table analysis for molecular arguments and the antilogism test for atomic syllogisms.

Even when restricted to the two-premise syllogism, the contraform test has certain advantages over the traditional maxims. The most important lies in the ease with which it handles an argument which as it stands does not contain three and only three terms, but which is logically equivalent to a standard syllogism which does. Consider this example:

> No ungrateful people are righteous.
> No grateful people are sanctimonious.
> No sanctimonious people are righteous.

First note the traditional approach to analyzing this argument. One might too hastily assert that this argument commits the fallacy of two exclusions, but this would be a mistake, for the argument is not yet in the standard form to which the traditional maxims apply. The relevant point to note is rather that the argument contains four terms, two of which are complements.[1] The question then arises, as explained in Section 19.1, whether we cannot get rid of the extra term by some such process as obversion. We find that we can validly convert the first premise and get "No righteous people are ungrateful." We get rid of the fourth term by then obverting this converse, thus: "All righteous people are grateful." The result is the standard syllogism:

> All righteous people are grateful.
> No grateful people are sanctimonious.
> No sanctimonious people are righteous.

When we now apply the maxims to this resulting form, we find that it is valid. This shows that the original argument, to which it is logically equivalent, is also valid.

[1] This interpretation is possible only if we understand *ungrateful* and *grateful* to exhaust the possibilities, so that a person would have to be one or the other. Otherwise the terms are not complements, and the proposed solution is inapplicable.

This type of ingenuity is not required in testing the original argument by the contraform test. We simply follow the standard procedure of setting up the test form of the argument as given, and check it against the contraform principles.

Again, if the original argument had been such that the fourth term could not have been eliminated in this way, or if its elimination would have given rise to some other formal difficulty, a certain amount of trial and error might have been required to determine this by the traditional approach. By contraform analysis, however, setting up the test form in the usual way and checking it by the principles would have revealed the invalidity of such an argument directly, without the need for experimentation.

APPLICATIONS

1. By means of the contraform test, determine the validity or invalidity of each of the following.

    a. All m $<$ p
        All s $\not<$ m
        _____
        All s $\not<$ p

    b. All p $<$ m
        Some m $\not<$ s
        _____
        Some s $\not<$ p

    c. All m $\not<$ p
        All s $<$ m
        _____
        All s $\not<$ p

    d. Some p $<$ m
        All m $<$ s
        _____
        Some s $\not<$ p

    e. All m $<$ p
        Some m $<$ s
        _____
        Some s $<$ p

    f. Some m $<$ p
        All m $<$ s
        _____
        Some s $<$ p

    g. All p $<$ m
        All m $<$ s
        _____
        All s $<$ p

    h. All p $\not<$ m
        All s $<$ m
        _____
        All s $\not<$ p

    i. Some m $<$ p
        Some s $<$ m
        _____
        All s $<$ p

    j. All m $<$ p
        Some s $<$ m
        _____
        Some s $<$ p

2. In each of the following arguments, first locate the conclusion. Then name in English the classes to be symbolized by the bracketed letters. (For example, in the first argument below, [b] = bridge-players, [k] = people who knit Argyle socks, [t] = people who take this course.) Next, express the argument in standard class-relation symbols. Finally, set up the test form and apply the contraform principles. Is the argument valid or invalid?

    a. No [b]ridge-players [k]nit Argyle socks, and some people who [t]ake this course do not knit them either. Thus some who take this course do not play bridge.

    b. It is clear that some [c]ar owners do not [r]ide bicycles, since some car owners are [p]rofessors, and no professors ride bicycles.

    c. Some who [s]ing in the *Messiah* also [p]lay in the band. Therefore some music [m]ajors do not play in the band, because no one who sings in the *Messiah* is a music major.

  d. Inasmuch as everything written by [S]chopenhauer is fundamentally [p]essimistic, it follows that "The Wisdom of [L]ife" was written by him, for it is certainly fundamentally pessimistic.

  e. Who can doubt that only a [c]ourageous person would have [d]one what John did? For we all know that [J]ohn did what he did, and that he is clearly a courageous fellow.

  f. Some [a]ppetizers I like, for they contain [W]orcestershire sauce and I like anything containing Worcestershire sauce. (*Hint:* use "things [l]iked by me" as one of the terms.)

  g. [A]rson is a [c]rime, so it is never [j]ustifiable, because it simply is not the case that crimes are ever justifiable.

  h. Surely you must admit that [h]igh tariffs are [d]esirable. For only such tariffs adequately [p]rotect infant industries, and to fail to protect them is clearly undesirable.

  i. Many of [L]ongfellow's poems are too [s]entimental for present-day tastes. Anything that is will be [n]eglected by most readers. So it is not surprising that most readers neglect many of his poems.

  j. A [b]ox kite is the only type that will [s]tay up in a strong wind and not need a tail. This [k]ite is not a box kite, so it will need a tail if it is to stay up in a strong wind. (*Hint:* How is "This will stay up in a strong wind and not need a tail" related to "If this will stay up in a strong wind, it will need a tail"?)

20.2. TESTING VALIDITY BY VENN DIAGRAMS

By introducing a third overlapping circle to represent the middle term, John Venn discovered that we can use circle diagrams to provide a pictorial check on the validity of a syllogism.

Let us familiarize ourselves with this expanded diagram by naming each of its subregions. To name a subregion adequately, we shall need three letters, either primed or unprimed, written conjunctively. Study this labeled diagram carefully.[2]

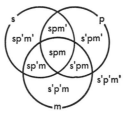

[2] Get in the habit of letting the left-hand circle represent the subject of the *conclusion* (that is, the minor term), the right-hand circle the predicate of the conclusion (that is, the major term), and the lower circle the middle term. This convention makes it much easier for you to compare your results with those of your classmates and instructor.

How can this setup be used to check the validity of a syllogism? Here is what you do:

To *check a syllogism by Venn diagram:*

1. Plot the two *premises* on this diagram.
2. Then *inspect* the diagram to see whether, in plotting the two premises, you have actually already pictured the conclusion.

That's all there is to it. If the conclusion is thus pictured, the syllogism is valid; otherwise, it is invalid. The following pointers will be helpful:

(1) Remember that you do not plot the conclusion as such. You plot the premises, and then just *look* at the result to see whether the conclusion is represented. The purpose of the test is to check validity, in other words to discover whether the premises, taken by themselves without appeal to further information, really do dictate the conclusion. You would not want to "beg the question" by *separately* marking in the conclusion as an additional step.

(2) Note that, because of the third circle, each premise will involve two subregions. Thus, for example, to plot the premise "All s ⊀ m," you must indicate that the whole "sm" region is empty. This "sm" region consists of two parts or subregions, "spm" and "sp'm." Each subregion must be marked with a zero:

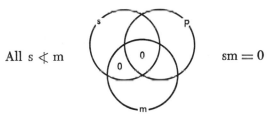

All s ⊀ m   sm = 0

(3) You will need to watch your step when you plot a *particular* premise such as "Some m < p." This premise doesn't really claim very much, merely that there is at least one "m" which is also a "p." The statement merely asserts that there is something *somewhere* in the "mp" region. It is an open question whether there is just some "spm," or just some "s'pm," or both some "spm" and some "s'pm." Therefore it would be incorrect to place a check-mark in *each* subregion, for this would claim too much. Place the check-

mark on the curve between the two subregions involved, with one tip pointing into each subregion. It may help you to think of this check-mark, when so placed, as the familiar sign of the alternative, "V," meaning:

either
something
HERE

or
something
HERE

or
BOTH

Study the following diagram:

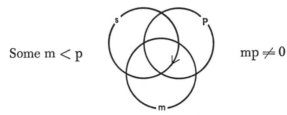

Some m < p

mp ≠ 0

(4) Note that a zero in a subregion is "stronger" than a check-mark on the curve between two subregions. The zero definitely indicates that the subregion in which it is placed is *empty*. It takes precedence over the tip of a check-mark that also points into this subregion. All this tip indicates is that, in the absence of further information, there *may* be something in this subregion. If we have the further information, given by a zero, that this subregion is empty, the check-mark has no force in this subregion. The effect of the zero is to drive the check-mark out of this subregion, and to make it apply exclusively to the other subregion. Consider the following example:

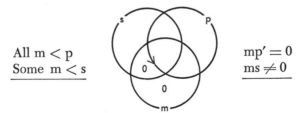

All m < p
Some m < s

mp′ = 0
ms ≠ 0

(5) Now reconsider the situation pictured in the above diagram. The universal premise informs us that the subregion "sp′m" is empty. Do you see that this information, along with the information given by the check-mark, assures us that there *must* be something in the

subregion "spm"? And do you see that this combined information warrants the conclusion, "Some s < p"? This is typical of what we find when we plot the premises of a valid syllogism; the combined information given by the two premises pictures a conclusion that could not have been inferred from either of the premises taken alone.

(6)   We have seen that a check-mark placed on the border between two subregions merely informs us that there is something somewhere in the region as a whole. It does not assure us that a given one of the subregions is occupied. How does this affect your interpretation of the following diagram?

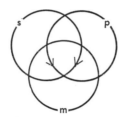

Does the information plotted here warrant the conclusion, "Some s is p"? It would be "leaping to conclusions" to think so. The left-hand check-mark merely assures us that there is something somewhere in the "sm" region as a whole, and the right-hand check-mark merely informs us that there is something in the "mp" region as a whole. There *may* be something in the "sp" region, but the given premises are too weak to dictate the conclusion that there actually is something there. The fact that the tips of two check-marks point into the subregion "spm" does not alter the case.

The above six points deal with typical problems of interpretation that one encounters in using Venn diagrams as a test of validity. If you understand these points, the rest will be easy.

• SOME REMINDERS

1.   Contraform principles readily determine the validity or invalidity of syllogisms.
2.   Three-circle Venn diagrams provide a pictorial means of testing the validity of syllogisms.

APPLICATIONS

1. Establish by Venn diagrams the validity or invalidity of each of the following syllogisms:

    a. All m < p
        Some m < s
        _____
        Some s < p

    b. All p < m
        All m < s
        _____
        All s < p

    c. Some m < p
        Some s < m
        _____
        Some s < p

    d. All m ≮ p
        Some m < s
        _____
        Some s ≮ p

    e. All p < m
        All s < m
        _____
        All s < p

    f. All m ≮ p
        All s < m
        _____
        All s ≮ p

    g. Some m < p
        All m < s
        _____
        Some s < p

    h. All m < p
        All s ≮ m
        _____
        All s ≮ p

    i. All p < m
        Some m ≮ s
        _____
        Some s ≮ p

    j. All p ≮ m
        All s < m
        _____
        All s ≮ p

2. Test the arguments in Application 3, following Section 19.6, by Venn diagrams.

3. Test the arguments in Application 2, following Section 20.1, by Venn diagrams.

CHAPTER 21

THE PARTICULARIZED SYLLOGISM

PREVIEW

Thus far we have purposely avoided the consideration of syllogisms having two universal premises and a particular conclusion. We shall now consider the special problem raised by such "particularized syllogisms," and shall see how the problem may be met by special maxims and by the contraform test.

21.1. THE PROBLEM OF THE PARTICULARIZED SYLLOGISM

If a syllogism derives a particular conclusion from two universal premises, we shall call it a PARTICULARIZED SYLLOGISM. Such arguments are to be distinguished both from UNIVERSAL SYLLOGISMS, which derive a universal conclusion from two universal premises, and from PARTICULAR SYLLOGISMS which have a particular premise as well as a particular conclusion.

Consider the following example of a particularized syllogism:

> All [r]eaders of this page understand [E]nglish.
> All readers of this page are [s]tudents of logic.
> Some students of logic understand English.

Does the conclusion follow? Both by common sense and by the traditional maxims such an argument would appear valid. Certainly, common sense urges, if we accept the premises we must admit that at least *some* students of logic understand English. Careful common sense will agree that the corresponding *universal* conclusion, "All students of logic understand English," goes too far. But there seems no reason for questioning the particular conclusion. As for the traditional maxims, the given argument violates none of them.

When, however, we test the argument either by circle diagrams or by the contraform principles, we must give a different verdict. On the Venn diagram, the two universal premises will be represented by appropriately placed zeros. If the particular conclusion were to be represented, there would have to be a check-mark in an appropriate subregion. Hence the analyzed argument is invalid. This agrees with the result obtained by the contraform test. For it is clear that the test form of a particularized syllogism will violate Principle 1, because it will contain nothing but equations.

Once we have gone this far, the source of the difficulty is clear. Our common-sense analysis was making certain unexpressed assumptions, while our more precise and cautious symbolic analyses limited themselves to what was explicitly stated. Common sense was quite properly assuming that of course this page does have some readers. It was interpreting the universal premises not in their minimum sense, but existentially. Note that the argument did not assert, in so many words, that there are readers of this page. On the basis of available factual information, however, it is implicitly understood that there are some. Precise analysis requires us to make such assumptions explicit. When we do, we see that the first premise was no doubt intended to mean not merely, "All [r]eaders of this page, if there are any, understand [E]nglish," but rather, "All readers of this page, and of course there are some, understand English." In zeroforms, the statement was intended to mean not merely:

$$re' = 0$$

but rather:

$$\begin{cases} re' = 0 \\ [r \neq 0] \end{cases}$$

Notice that the existential assumption, given in square brackets, has a different form from that of the basic universal premises. It is a simple existence statement, not a subject-predicate statement at all.

21.2. THE SUPPLEMENTARY EXISTENTIAL PREMISE

Now that we have made this assumption explicit, we may use it as a supplementary premise in our argument. We shall call such a premise a SUPPLEMENTARY EXISTENTIAL PREMISE. It supplements the two basic premises and asserts the existence of members (at least one) of a certain class mentioned in the basic subject-predicate premises.

There is some question of the propriety of calling this expanded argument a *syllogism,* for it no longer fits the traditional definition. In spite of this, the argument is so intimately related to the traditional syllogism that its treatment as part of a contemporary analysis of syllogisms seems highly desirable.

It should be clear that whether we are, in a given case, actually warranted in introducing such an existential premise, will depend upon factual rather than upon formal considerations. In the present case, it will depend upon our empirical knowledge that there is at least one reader of this page.

When we add this supplementary information to our Venn diagram and to our test form, we find that the argument is now valid:

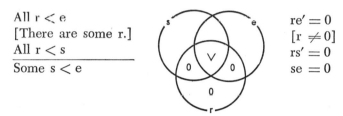

All r $<$ e   re$'$ = 0
[There are some r.]   [r $\neq$ 0]
All r $<$ s   rs$'$ = 0
——————————   se = 0
Some s $<$ e

On the Venn diagram, we first plot the basic universal premises by appropriately placed zeros. We then proceed to indicate by a check-mark that there is some *r.* Notice that there is only one possible subregion within the *r*-circle in which this check-mark can be placed. All the others have been marked empty in representing the basic universal premises. It is apparent that in thus indicating that there is some *r* we have at the same time represented the conclusion, "Some s $<$ e." The supplemented argument is thus seen to be valid.[1] As for the contraform test, the supplemented test form now contains an inequation, thus satisfying Principle 1. Inspection reveals that Principles 2 and 3 are now also satisfied, and the argument is shown to be valid.

Our original example, strictly interpreted, is now seen to be an example of what we earlier called a *prevalid* argument. It was not valid as it stood, but became so when an intended assumption was brought out into the

---

[1] Our immediate concern is in noting that the original syllogistic conclusion, "Some s $<$ e," is represented. But it is interesting to note also that certain nonsyllogistic conclusions may be read off from the information plotted on this diagram. For example, "Some r $<$ e," and "Some s $<$ r." The first of these follows from the plotted premises, "All r $<$ e" and "There are some r." The second follows from the plotted premises, "All r $<$ s" and "There are some r." These arguments may also be shown to be valid by the contraform test. For a further discussion of nonsyllogistic atomic arguments, see Section 22.3.

open. For convenience, we shall introduce a special term for such a pre-valid particularized syllogism. If a particularized syllogism is such that it becomes valid with the addition of an appropriate existential premise, we shall say that it is PENEVALID in its original form. The term *penevalid* is formed in the same way as the words *peninsula* and *penultimate* and means literally, "almost valid." Observe that penevalidity is not a special type of validity, but of prevalidity. A penevalid argument is not valid as it stands.[2]

21.3. DISCOVERING THE NEEDED ASSUMPTION BY SPECIAL MAXIMS

In the example just considered, we found that we needed to assert that $r \neq 0$. Two points are of interest here: (1) This is *all* the additional information we needed for validity. (2) Similar information about the non-emptiness of s alone, or of e alone, or even of s and of e would not have helped at all. This second point can be most readily seen by consulting the Venn diagram once more.

This general situation holds for all penevalid particularized syllogisms. In each case validity requires the addition of one specific existential premise, asserting that a specific class has members. Corresponding information for one or both of the other two classes is neither sufficient nor necessary for validity. It is also interesting to note that when we go to plot the minimum existential supplement on the Venn diagram of a *penevalid* particularized syllogism, we always find that there is precisely one subregion of the required class which has not already been marked empty on the basis of the original premises. When a check-mark is placed in this remaining subregion, the original conclusion will be found to have been thereby represented.

The crucial question, of course, is: Just *which* class must be asserted to be nonempty? Various hypotheses to the effect that it must be, say, the class named by the major term, or by the minor, or by the middle term are readily confuted. To make progress toward formal maxims to guide us, we must consider the zeroforms. When we express a particular-

---

[2] Let us here note the bearing of the traditional maxims for the syllogism upon the problem raised by the particularized syllogism. If a particularized syllogism satisfies the maxims, this shows not that the argument is valid, but rather that it is *penevalid*. These maxims are of no help, however, in determining the minimum supplementary existential assumption needed for validity.

ized syllogism in zeroforms, it will of course have two equations as basic premises, and an inequation for the conclusion. (Note that we are not now talking about the test form, which has three equations.)

There are, of course, many ways for an argument to fall short of validity, and some particularized syllogisms are defective quite apart from their lack of a proper supplementary existential premise. It is not the case that every particularized syllogism can be made valid simply by selecting an appropriate existential assumption, and it is well to keep this fact in mind. This is only another way of saying that some particularized syllogisms are not penevalid, but just plain invalid.

Analysis shows that every particularized syllogism that becomes valid with the addition of an appropriate existential premise possesses a distinctive zeroform pattern. This pattern not only reliably distinguishes particularized syllogisms that are penevalid from those that are not; it also reveals precisely what minimum existential assumption is required for validity.

Let us consider the zeroforms of three typical *penevalid* particularized syllogisms. The first form is that of our earlier example about readers of this page.

$$mp' = 0 \qquad\qquad pm' = 0 \qquad\qquad pm' = 0$$
$$\underline{ms' = 0} \qquad\qquad \underline{ms' = 0} \qquad\qquad \underline{sm = 0}$$
$$sp \neq 0 \qquad\qquad\; sp \neq 0 \qquad\qquad\; sp' \neq 0$$

These and all other *penevalid* particularized syllogisms have a zeroform pattern that provides the basis for three maxims. The first maxim is nothing new; it is simply the defining rule for particularized syllogisms whether penevalid or not, expressed in terms of zeroforms. The second maxim determines penevalidity. The third maxim specifies the minimum existential supplement needed for validity.

1. *Defining maxim:* The basic premises are both equations; the conclusion is an inequation.
2. *Penevalidity maxim:* Exactly one of the three letters involved has the same sign (prime or lack of it) in both its occurrences.
3. *Existential supplement maxim:* A supplementary premise is required for validity, stating that the class named by the twice-same letter (see Maxim 2) has members.

The way this all works out may be readily seen by inspecting the second and third zeroform examples given above. Both clearly satisfy the first maxim, and are hence shown to be particularized syllogisms. In the second example, the letter "p" alone appears twice with the same sign, and in the third form, the letter "s" alone so appears. Thus both these forms satisfy Maxim 2 and are hence penevalid. In the second example, the required supplementary premise is "$p \neq 0$." In the third example, it is "$s \neq 0$." The supplemented zeroforms and Venn diagrams for these two examples are as follows:

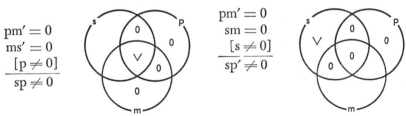

$$pm' = 0$$
$$ms' = 0$$
$$\underline{[p \neq 0]}$$
$$sp \neq 0$$

$$pm' = 0$$
$$sm = 0$$
$$\underline{[s \neq 0]}$$
$$sp' \neq 0$$

Each diagram shows the argument in question to be valid, once the required supplementary premise is added.

21.4. DISCOVERING THE NEEDED ASSUMPTION BY CONTRAFORM PRINCIPLES

If the result seems somewhat mysterious, the mystery may be easily dispelled by showing that the treatment by maxims conforms to the requirements of the contraform principles. We have already applied the contraform test to our first example, but then we used it only to show that we were right in picking the existential assumption we did. We know, however, that the contraform principles may be used not only to test an argument that is completely presented, but also to determine what additional premises are needed for validity. Let us now, without reference to our previous work, use the contraform principles for this second purpose. The zeroform equivalent of our original example and the resulting test form are:

ZEROFORM EQUIVALENT	TEST FORM
$re' = 0$	$re' = 0$
$rs' = 0$	$rs' = 0$
$se \neq 0$	$se = 0$

When we refer to the contraform principles, it is obvious that the first one is not satisfied. There isn't any inequation at all. But suppose we go ahead and *introduce* an inequation into the test form. This inequation will represent a possible additional premise:

$$[? \neq 0]$$
$$re' = 0$$
$$rs' = 0$$
$$se = 0$$

We have now of course satisfied the first principle; we have exactly one inequation. Now for the second principle. Does at least one letter in each equation pair off with a letter in another equation? Yes, this second principle is satisfied. But how about the third? It requires that the remaining letters be conjoined to form the left-hand side of the inequation. Now the only remaining letter in this case is "r." So we introduce it as the left-hand member of the inequation, and all three principles are satisfied. To translate back into English, this contraform analysis has shown that our original argument becomes valid with the introduction of the supplementary premise, "There are some readers of this page." And this, of course, is what our earlier analysis in terms of the special maxims also showed. Similar results may be obtained for any penevalid particularized syllogism.

• SOME REMINDERS

1. On the strict interpretation of the universal premises, a particularized syllogism can be no more than penevalid.
2. With the addition of an appropriate existential premise, some particularized syllogisms become valid.
3. Penevalid particularized syllogisms all exhibit a characteristic zeroform pattern which provides the basis for three maxims.
4. One maxim is merely a defining rule for the particularized syllogism. The second maxim determines penevalidity, and the third specifies the minimum existential supplement needed for validity.
5. Results obtained by applying these maxims agree with those obtained by applying the contraform principles.

APPLICATIONS

1. Express each of the following arguments in zeroforms, then test by (1) the special maxims for the particularized syllogism, if applicable, (2) the contraform test, (3) Venn diagrams. In each case, decide whether the argument *as given* is valid, penevalid, or invalid-but-not-penevalid. If the argument is penevalid, supply the required minimum in the way of supple-

mentary existential premise. Do the results of the three tests agree? If not, find out what is wrong.

a. All m $<$ p
   All s $<$ m
   ―――――――
   Some s $<$ p

b. All p $\not<$ m
   All m $<$ s
   ―――――――
   Some s $\not<$ p

c. All p $<$ m
   All s $\not<$ m
   ―――――――
   Some s $<$ p

d. All m $\not<$ p
   All s $<$ m
   ―――――――
   Some s $\not<$ p

e. All p $<$ m
   All m $<$ s
   ―――――――
   Some s $\not<$ p

f. All p $\not<$ m
   Some m $<$ s
   ―――――――
   Some s $\not<$ p

g. All p $<$ m
   All m $<$ s
   ―――――――
   Some s $<$ p

h. All m $\not<$ p
   All m $<$ s
   ―――――――
   Some s $\not<$ p

i. All p $\not<$ m
   All s $<$ m
   ―――――――
   Some s $\not<$ p

j. All p $<$ m
   All s $\not<$ m
   ―――――――
   Some s $\not<$ p

2. Using the directions given for Application 1 above, analyze each of the following arguments:

a. No [s]even-day library books may be [r]enewed, and all the books in this [d]isplay are seven-day library books. Hence some of the books in this display cannot be renewed.

b. All [l]iars are [s]coundrels, and no liars are [d]ependable. Hence some scoundrels are not dependable.

c. No [r]obins can [s]wim, but all [f]ish can swim. Hence some fish aren't robins.

d. No [f]ree man [l]oves tyranny, but [s]laves are not free men. Hence some slaves love tyranny.

e. All who [s]it in the front row have last [n]ames beginning with "A." Everyone whose last name begins with "A" will [r]eceive an "A" in the course. It follows that some of those who will receive an "A" in the course sit in the front row.

f. All students who [s]leep in class are [e]ither tired or bored. Anyone who is either tired or bored [n]eeds counseling, so some who need counseling sleep in class.

g. No [f]aculty members wore [m]asks at the Hallowe'en party, but everyone who wore a mask [l]ooked like a faculty member. So some who looked like faculty members really were not.

h. We may be sure that at least some who attended the [d]ance did not go to [c]hurch, because although everyone who was up for [b]reakfast went to church, no one who attended the dance was up for breakfast.

i. Although all who do not have their buttons [p]olished will get a [d]emerit, some in our [s]quad will not get one, because all in our squad have their buttons polished.

j. All who [f]avored creation of a duchy [s]tayed away from the polls. Only members of the [P]eople's Party did not favor creation of a duchy. Hence at least some members of the People's Party must not have stayed away from the polls.

CHAPTER 22

FURTHER ATOMIC ARGUMENTS

PREVIEW

Outside of logic textbooks, syllogisms are seldom fully expressed. In this chapter we shall note how the traditional maxims and the contraform principles may be used to supply missing elements required for validity. We shall also analyze certain extended atomic arguments, and certain nonsyllogistic arguments to which the traditional maxims do not apply.

22.1. ANALYZING SYLLOGISTIC ENTHYMEMES

Actual everyday arguments of a syllogistic type are (like other arguments) usually expressed incompletely. One premise may be assumed rather than stated, or the premises may be given and the hearer left to draw his own conclusion. Such incompletely expressed arguments or enthymemes pose no new problems for contraform analysis. We have already had practice in using this analysis to discover what statement must be supplied in order to yield a valid argument. It may be helpful to review Sections 14.2 and 14.3 on deriving conclusions and on supplying missing premises needed for validity. Whether such supplied premises are factually justified would, of course, have to be decided on empirical, not formal, grounds.

The traditional maxims may also be used for completing syllogistic arguments. It might, of course, be found that the given material already involved a fallacy which could not be remedied by supplying an appropriate premise. This would be the case, for example, if the given premise was negative, while the given conclusion was positive. Such an enthymeme would have to be rejected as invalid. Many enthymemes, however, may be shown to be prevalid by use of the maxims.

First, set up the enthymeme and determine how far it goes toward satisfying the validity maxims. Consider an enthymeme having the following form:

$$[\qquad ? \qquad]$$
$$\text{Some } s \not< m$$
$$\overline{\text{Some } s \not< p}$$

Inspection shows that the middle term is distributed at least once, so Maxim 1 is satisfied. The conclusion is an exclusion, and thus far exactly one of the premises (the given one) is an exclusion. So Maxim 3 is satisfied, if we do not spoil things by supplying the wrong type of additional premise.

The next thing to do, then, is to consider what form the missing premise must have to complete the validity requirements. We know that it must contain the terms "m" and "p." Since "p" is distributed in the conclusion, we must satisfy Maxim 2 by seeing that "p" is also distributed in its premise. This could be achieved either by using "p" as the subject of a universal, or as the predicate of an exclusion. The latter possibility, however, must be ruled out, for this would commit the fallacy of two exclusions. Thus we shall need to use the "p" as the subject of a universal inclusion. This will leave the "m" to serve as predicate of the major premise. In this position the "m" is undistributed, but this need not concern us, for it is already distributed in the other premise.

$$[\text{All } p < m]$$
$$\text{Some } s \not< m$$
$$\overline{\text{Some } s \not< p}$$

The resulting syllogism satisfies the traditional maxims, and is hence valid.

APPLICATIONS

1. By means of contraform analysis, complete each of the following enthymemes to yield a *valid* syllogism if possible. Enclose in square brackets the statements you supply.
    a. All $m < p$, hence All $s < p$.
    b. All $m < s$, hence Some $s < p$.
    c. Some $s \not< m$, hence Some $s \not< p$.
    d. All $m \not< p$, hence Some $s \not< p$.
    e. All $m < s$, hence All $s \not< p$.
    f. Some $m \not< p$, and All $m < s$, so what?
    g. Some $m \not< p$, hence Some $s \not< p$.

    h. All s ≮ m, hence All s ≮ p.
    i. All p < m, and Some m ≮ s, so what?
    j. Some s < m, hence Some s < p.
2. Check your work in Application 1 by Venn diagrams.
3. By means of traditional maxims only, complete each of the following enthymemes to yield a valid syllogism if possible. If not possible, explain why not. Enclose in square brackets the statements you supply.
    a. Some s < m, hence Some s < p.
    b. All p ≮ m, hence Some s ≮ p.
    c. All p < m, hence Some s ≮ p.
    d. Some m < p, hence Some s < p.
    e. All m ≮ p, hence All s ≮ p.
    f. Some p < m, hence Some s ≮ p.
    g. Some s < m, hence Some s ≮ p.
    h. All p < m, hence Some s < p.
    i. All m ≮ s, hence All s ≮ p.
    j. All s < m, hence All s ≮ p.
4. Check your work in Application 3 by Venn diagrams.
5. Using your choice of methods, complete each of the following enthymemes to yield a valid syllogism if possible. Enclose in square brackets the statements you supply.
    a. It is obvious that some college [s]tudents aren't [m]arried, for no married person [l]eads a carefree life.
    b. All [Z]ionists approved the [e]stablishment of the state of Israel. Quite clearly some [A]rabs are not Zionists.
    c. Some [l]ogic classes will not have a [q]uiz this week, for some logic classes do not [m]eet on Tuesday.
    d. Of course [H]aggie cannot be Junior Prom [Q]ueen, since none but [b]eautiful girls can be.
    e. The fact that all [c]hapel speakers are [w]ell-known shows that not all well-known people can [k]eep students awake.
    f. Inasmuch as some [s]ophomores are not [D]emocrats, it follows that some [m]en students are not.
    g. At least some [b]uildings are [w]orthy of preservation for posterity, for all structures of [h]istoric significance are worthy of such preservation.
    h. Even an un[i]ntentional blunder [c]alls for an apology, for a blunder, though unintentional, is still a [b]lunder.
    i. Of course [h]e should have [k]nown better. After all, he's [o]ver twenty-one.
    j. I am sure that [M]ary, like all [y]oung people away from home for the first time, will occasionally [f]eel twinges of homesickness.
6. Where possible, construct a *valid* syllogism in the *figure* specified in parentheses, having the given statement as conclusion. (For the meaning of "figure" in this sense, see Section 19.1, note 3.) If a valid syllogism is not possible, explain why not.
    a. Some [b]ites of the black widow spider are [f]atal. (1)
    b. No presidential [c]andidates should [k]iss babies. (4)

   c. Only a [s]killed driver could have [a]verted that accident. (1)
   d. Some very [i]ntelligent people do not [l]ook particularly bright. (4)
   e. Female [c]owbirds seem like rather [i]rresponsible parents. (2)
   f. Not all [h]airbrushes have [n]atural bristles. (3)
   g. Nobody [s]uspected of subversive tendencies will be given a [p]assport to travel abroad. (2)
   h. Some [v]alid arguments have only [o]ne premise. (4)
   i. Some [p]latitudes are not [w]orth repeating. (2)
   j. No logic [e]xercises last [f]orever. (1)

22.2. EXTENDED SYLLOGISTIC ARGUMENTS

A syllogism has, by definition, only two premises. But there is nothing in the nature of class relations which would rule out the possibility of valid class arguments with more premises. Such extended arguments have long been recognized. But because of the limitations of traditional analysis, it seemed necessary to justify such arguments by showing how they could be "reduced" to a series of syllogisms.

THE TRADITIONAL APPROACH

One of the commonest forms of such extended argument is the SORITES. In traditional terms, it may be viewed as a connected chain of syllogisms, with all conclusions unexpressed except the final one. Consider the following sorites:

All chairs are made to sit on.	**(1)**
All things made to sit on are tangible.	**(2)**
All tangible things are material.	**(3)**
All material things occupy space.	**(4)**
All chairs occupy space.	**(5)**

This argument seems quite clearly valid at the common-sense level. We may check its validity, however, by syllogistic analysis in terms of the four maxims. Statements 1 and 2 may be used as premises to derive the syllogistic conclusion:

All chairs are tangible.   **(6)**

This intermediate conclusion may now be used as a premise along with Statement 3 to obtain a further conclusion:

All chairs are material.   **(7)**

This new Statement 7 may then be used along with Statement 4 as premises for the final conclusion (5). The sorites may be shown to be valid by establishing that each of the constituent syllogisms conforms to the syllogistic validity maxims.[1]

COMPARISON WITH THE CONTRAFORM APPROACH

In the above example, the statements were presented in the order in which they would be needed for syllogistic analysis. In actual practice, of course, these statements might have been set forth in some other order. In such a case, traditional procedure would require us to begin with two premises containing a common term, to derive an intermediate conclusion by maxims, then to select as our next premise the statement which shared a term with this intermediate conclusion and so on.

From our present point of view, all this seems unnecessarily cumbersome. A sorites may be tested directly by contraform analysis, without rearranging premises and without working out intermediate syllogistic conclusions. Try testing the above argument by contraform analysis.

APPLICATIONS

1. The sets of premises in this and the following application are taken, with minor changes, from Lewis Carroll's *Symbolic Logic*. First, restate the premises in standard class-relation symbols. This will require some ingenuity. Watch especially for terms which, in the context of the argument, may be treated as *complements*. (For example, "lunatics" is here being used as the complement of "sane people," and can hence be symbolized as "s'.") Then supply a *valid* conclusion by traditional maxims.

    a. Everyone who is [s]ane can [d]o logic;
       No lunatics are [f]it to serve on a jury;
       None of [y]our sons can do logic.

    b. The only articles of food that my [d]octor allows me, are such as are not very [r]ich;
       Nothing that [a]grees with me is un[s]uitable for supper;
       [W]edding-cake is always very rich;
       My doctor allows me all articles of food that are suitable for supper.

[1] Once the rationale of a particular form of sorites had been justified by this type of syllogistic analysis, it was of course possible to formulate special maxims for the specific form in question. Traditionally, this was done for only two types of sorites, both in the first figure. In one, the ARISTOTELIAN SORITES, the minor premise was stated first; in the other, the GOCLENIAN SORITES, the major premise was stated first. The special maxims for the Aristotelian form were (1) all premises must be positive except the last which may be negative, and (2) all premises must be universal except the first, which may be particular.

    c. When I work a logic-example without [g]rumbling, you may be sure it is one that I can [u]nderstand;

These [s]orites are not [a]rranged in regular order, like the examples I am used to;

No [e]asy example ever [m]akes my head ache;

I can't understand examples that are not arranged in regular order, like those I am used to;

I never grumble at an example, unless it gives me a headache.

    d. I call no day "un[l]ucky," when Robinson is civil to [m]e;

[W]ednesdays are always [c]loudy;

When people take their [u]mbrellas, the day never turns out [f]ine;

The only days when Robinson is uncivil to me are Wednesdays;

Everybody takes his umbrella with him when it is [r]aining;

My "lucky" days always turn out fine.

    e. All the [d]ated letters in this room are written on [g]ray paper;

None of them are in [b]lack ink, except those that are written in the [t]hird person;

I have not [f]iled any of them that I can [r]ead;

None of them that are written on [o]ne sheet, are undated;

All of them that are not [c]reased, are in black ink;

All of them written by [J]ones begin with "Dear [S]ir";

All of them written on gray paper are filed;

None of them written on more than one sheet are creased;

None of them that begin with "Dear Sir" are written in the third person.

2.   Follow the directions for Application 1, except this time supply valid conclusions by contraform analysis. These two applications will enable you to compare the relative merits of traditional and contemporary modes of analysis as applied to sorites.

    a. [B]abies are [i]llogical;

Nobody is [d]espised who can [m]anage a crocodile;

Illogical persons are despised.

    b. Things [s]old in the street are of no [g]reat value;

Nothing but [r]ubbish can be [h]ad for a song;

[E]ggs of the Great Auk are very valuable;

It is only what is sold in the streets that is really rubbish.

    c. No [i]nteresting poems are un[p]opular among people of real taste;

No [m]odern poetry is [f]ree from affectation:

All [y]our poems are on the subject of [s]oap-bubbles;

No affected poetry is popular among people of real taste;

No ancient poem is on the subject of soap-bubbles.

    d. Every idea of mine that cannot be [e]xpressed as a Syllogism, is really [r]idiculous;

None of my ideas about [B]ath-buns are [w]orth writing down;

No idea of mine, that fails to come [t]rue, can be expressed as a Syllogism;

I never have any really ridiculous idea that I do not at once refer to my [s]olicitor;

My [d]reams are all about Bath-buns;
I never refer any idea of mine to my solicitor, unless it is worth writing down.

e. The only animals in this [h]ouse are [c]ats;
Every animal is [s]uitable for a pet, that [l]oves to gaze at the moon;
When I [d]etest any animal, I [a]void it;
No animals are [f]lesh-eaters, unless they prowl at [n]ight;
No cat fails to [k]ill mice;
No animals ever [t]ake to me, except what are in this house;
[G]iraffes are not suitable for pets;
None but flesh-eaters kill mice;
I detest animals that do not take to me;
Animals that prowl at night always love to gaze at the moon.

22.3. NONSYLLOGISTIC ATOMIC ARGUMENTS

The atomic arguments thus far studied have, with the exception of the particularized syllogism, been adequately analyzable by traditional maxims. The handling of extended arguments by the maxims is somewhat cumbersome and time-consuming, but it can be done. We now want to note certain nonsyllogistic atomic arguments which lie beyond the scope of the maxims, but can readily be tested by the contraform principles.

As an example of such a nonsyllogistic argument, consider the following:

> All [s]nakes are [r]eptiles.
> There are some snakes.
> _____
> There are some reptiles.

The given argument is clearly not a syllogism, in spite of the fact that it has two premises and a conclusion, all atomic. Only two classes are involved, and the second premise and the conclusion are simple existence statements. The maxims give us no guidance here. The validity of the argument is of course readily established by the contraform test:

$$sr' = 0$$
$$s \neq 0$$
$$r = 0$$

Here is a more complex example of atomic argument which falls outside the scope of the traditional syllogistic maxims:

Although no [b]asketball player is on [p]robation, there are some basketball players. Only those on probation are on this [l]ist. All students now in the [d]ean's office are on this list. Hence some basketball players aren't students now in the dean's office.

The validity of this argument is readily established by the contraform test:

$$bp = 0$$
$$b \neq 0$$
$$lp' = 0$$
$$dl' = 0$$
$$bd' = 0$$

The following nonsyllogistic argument illustrates the permissible appearance of an extraneous letter in the inequation of the test form:

All the [a]nimals in this cage are [c]entaurs.
Centaurs are nonexistent.

No animals in this cage are [f]leet-footed.

$$ac' = 0$$
$$c = 0$$
$$af \neq 0$$

Note that without the appearance of this extra "f" in the test form, the simple nonsyllogistic conclusion, "There aren't any animals in this cage," would result.

As long as such nonsyllogistic arguments contain no more than three letters and their primes, they may also be readily checked by means of Venn diagrams. Try checking the first and last examples above by this method.

• SOME REMINDERS

1. Syllogistic enthymemes may be completed by use of the traditional maxims or the contraform principles.
2. The traditional maxims may be used for testing extended syllogistic arguments by deriving intermediate conclusions which are then used as premises.
3. The contraform principles may be used for testing extended syllogistic arguments without the need for rearranging premises or deriving intermediate conclusions.
4. Certain nonsyllogistic atomic arguments which lie beyond the scope of the traditional maxims may be readily tested by contraform principles.

APPLICATIONS

1. Determine the validity or invalidity of the following nonsyllogistic atomic arguments by means of the contraform principles.
    a. There are some [n]ovels. All novels are works of [f]iction. Therefore there are some works of fiction.
    b. All [m]ermaids are [i]maginary beings, but imaginary beings do not exist. Thus there are no mermaids.
    c. Some of her [f]riends don't [o]wn cars. Those who don't own cars have to [w]alk. Therefore, there are some who have to walk.
    d. All [m]agicians can [p]ull rabbits out of a hat, and anyone who can do so is [c]leverer than I. Some are cleverer than I. Thus some who are cleverer than I are magicians.
    e. No [e]lephants [l]ive on the Antarctic continent, but some [o]rganisms live there. Therefore there must be some nonelephants.
    f. Although some sonatas by Joe [D]oakes aren't [m]asterpieces, all of [B]eethoven's are. Hence there are some masterpieces.
    g. All the pipes in this [c]ollection are made of [i]mported briar. But of course not everything is made of imported briar. All [m]y pipes are in this collection. Hence my pipes aren't all there is. (*Hint:* Express the second and fourth statements by simple zeroforms.)
    h. All the [p]lants in this garden are [w]eeds, and some plants in this garden are [d]andelions. Thus weeds are (unfortunately) not nonexistent.
    i. None but non[v]iolent people are [p]acifists, but there are some violent people, so some violent people are nonpacifists.
    j. If there are any figures on this [p]age, they're all [t]riangles. Although no [e]ight-sided figures are triangles, there are some eight-sided figures. Hence there are no figures on this page.
2. Check the arguments in Application 1 by Venn diagrams.

PART III

EMPIRICS

THE LOGIC OF

FACTUAL INQUIRY

CHAPTER 23

THE STUDY OF EMPIRICAL INQUIRY

PREVIEW

In order to concentrate on important questions of logical form, syntactics purposely sets aside considerations of empirical truth. It is concerned with validity, not with truth; with answering the question, "So what?" rather than the equally important question, "What's what?" In thinking things through, we cannot stop with considerations of meaning and of logical form. The third area of logic, empirics, considers the principles and problems of fact-finding, and seeks to determine the ways in which our claims to factual knowledge are supported. We shall find ourselves drawing constantly on what we have learned in the previous two areas about meanings and logical form. In the present chapter, for example, we shall need to deal largely with certain semantical questions which face us as we begin to talk about empirics and factual inquiry. Since common sense and science are both concerned with determining what the facts are, we shall also note some basic similarities and differences between these two modes of factual inquiry.

23.1. EMPIRICS, "INDUCTIVE LOGIC," AND "SCIENTIFIC METHOD"

Empirics has traditionally been called "inductive logic," and such logic has been sharply contrasted with the "deductive logic" which is the concern of syntactics. You will see before long that this suggestion of an antithesis between the two is somewhat misleading. For one thing, deduction plays an important and indispensable role in empirical inquiry, whether at the level of common sense or in the sciences. Furthermore, as our empirical knowledge in a given field becomes more and more comprehensive and adequate, our reasoning approaches more and more the pattern of deduction. Then too, confusion is likely to result when all empirical inquiry is called "inductive," for "induction" is also used in a narrower and more specific sense, as the name for the process by which empirical generalizations are inferred from a number of instances. In this narrower sense (which, by the way, is the only one we shall use in this book) it is obviously false to equate the logic of empirical inquiry with "induction." For the inferring of generalizations from instances is only one aspect of empirical inquiry.

Empirics has also been commonly described as the study of "scientific method." Quite apart from the fact that a number of reputable scientists like to insist, for one reason or another, that "there is no such thing as scientific method," the traditional description is misleading. For it either assumes that we are all scientists without knowing it, or it overlooks the fact that the basic methods of empirical inquiry are present, and are used with considerable success, at the everyday level of common-sense thinking. Investigators in "the sciences," to be sure, apply such methods with greater rigor than common sense demands in everyday inquiry. Furthermore, the scientist's use of empirical inquiry is enriched by a variety of special procedures and "techniques" which make the general method more effective. We need to avoid both the extreme of thinking that scientific method is "nothing but common sense," and the extreme of supposing it to be something radically different from anything we find at the common-sense level of inquiry.

The layman is sometimes both surprised and amused when he discovers that scientists, philosophers, and other specialists who "ought to know" are in disagreement over the answers to such questions as whether there *is* such a thing as scientific method and whether such-and-such a discipline is "really" a science or not. What the layman as well as the specialist often overlooks is the extent to which such disagreement is verbal, involving interpersonal ambiguity of the type discussed in Chapter 5. There is more to it than that, but it will be helpful to consider here some of the verbal issues.

One of the most central difficulties arises from the ambiguity of the name "science" itself. If we consider the word with an eye to its Latin derivation and in its generic sense, we shall tend to call any systematic knowledge-seeking "scientific," and any organized body of knowledge a "science." For *scientia* means "knowledge" and *scientific* in this sense means simply "knowledge-making."[1] In this broad sense, it may be urged that such diverse undertakings as physics, sociology, psychology, philosophy, and theology are "sciences." We seldom use the term this broadly. But even if everyone were agreed to use the term in this generic sense, there would still remain a rich source of verbal dispute, for the battle would now shift to the words "knowledge" and "knowledge-making." Add to this the further nonverbal problem of determining whether a given field actually reveals certain characteristics and is hence a "science" in some agreed-upon sense, and you will have a better insight into why such diverse things are said on the subject.

There are many different ways to narrow down this generic sense of "science." If, for example, we stipulate that anything to which we shall apply the name must be characterized by a laboratory approach, or by the quantification of data and results, we shall by definition have eliminated a number of knowledge-seeking enterprises from the realm of "science." A physicist, from the somewhat special perspective which his own subject gives him, may object to his colleagues in, let us say, sociology, calling themselves "scientists"—even "social scientists."[2] They are rather, he may stipulate, "students of society," and what they are doing is "not science at all" but rather "social studies." By this time, we may suspect that the proposed definitions have lost their purely cognitive function and have assumed certain persuasive features. To take a different type of example, a psychologist of a particular school may decline to call his field a "science." His reasons may range all the way from the belief that psychology is as yet too youthful an enterprise to have achieved the status of "a true science," to the belief that the study of "the psyche" requires a special brand of insight not to be found in "the sciences." Such reasons may, of course, rest on more than verbal grounds,

---

[1] Compare our earlier example in Section 5.3, of an argument over whether mathematics is a science or not. See also C. J. Ducasse: *Philosophy As a Science*, New York, Oskar Piest, 1941, p. 114.

[2] Such a stand may, of course, involve nonsemantical issues as well. A natural scientist might, whether correctly or not, doubt that his methods can be adapted to other areas. A paper which was read at an international Conference on Science and Freedom, held in Hamburg, Germany, discussed the applicability of "the scientific method" to studies other than the natural sciences. It was reported that "physical scientists were strongly critical of this approach and the . . . thesis did not appear to find favor with the conference." (Special dispatch by M. S. Handler, *New York Times*, July 26, 1953.)

but we can scarcely get to the remaining factual and evaluational matters until the verbal difficulties are recognized and alleviated.

When we turn to the question of "scientific method" we encounter similar problems. We noted above the claim of some competent scientists that there is, after all, nothing that can properly be called *the* scientific method. One may have a number of different reasons for speaking in this way as a scientist. Often it is merely that the scientist has in mind the great diversity of specific TECHNIQUES from science to science, and even from one problem to another in his own field. To study animal tissue, you may place it in paraffin, slice off very thin sections with a microtome, mount them on a slide, insert the slide under a microscope, and so on. This is something quite different from what you do if you are going to determine the temperature of the Martian polar regions, or the age of some seeds found in a prehistoric burial. A person impressed by this diversity may exclaim, "How could there possibly be *a* scientific method?" He is of course right in insisting that we shall find no unity at this level of specific *techniques*. But this is of course not the sense in which logicians and philosophers of science or scientists themselves have urged that there *is* a general rationale of inquiry which may be called "the scientific method."

Some scientists have a rather different reason for not liking to talk about a scientific "method." As they approach their own problems and reflect upon their results, they are in one sense not aware of having used any *method* at all. They have "simply" sized up the problem and then have waded into it with everything at their command. How can we speak here of a "method"? The eminent physicist, P. W. Bridgman, while not sharing so extreme a view, insists that "the so-called scientific method, as far as it is a method, is nothing more than doing one's damnedest with one's mind, no holds barred." [3]

What, then, shall our own approach to the study of empirics be? For one thing, we must keep these semantical difficulties before us, and try to avoid confusing a verbal matter with one which is nonverbal. Our earlier work in semantics will be of help to us here.

In the second place, it will help if we consider what we can rea-

[3] P. W. Bridgman in *Yale Review*, XXXIV (1945), p. 450, quoted by James B. Conant: *On Understanding Science*, New York, New American Library (Mentor Book), 1951, p. 116.

sonably hope to get out of an elementary investigation of empirics. Either your career will lie in one of the sciences, or it will not. If it does, your understanding of your special field and its specific problems and techniques will of course be gained from extended studies in that field. An elementary consideration of empirics will of course not make a scientist out of you. What then can you hope to get from it? Such a study may give you a perspective from which to appreciate your own specialized work, and some sense of how your specialty is a part of the larger human enterprise of finding out what's what. But suppose you do not plan to go ahead in some science. Perhaps you even think you "don't like science." What then? Here again, our study of empirics will not make you a scientist, but it should help you appreciate your undergraduate courses in science more. It should help you see the sense in which the sciences you are studying as part of your general college course extend and refine the somewhat casual procedures of common-sense inquiry. A study of empirics may help you to avoid the feeling that science is something essentially mysterious and remote. It should make you aware of the continuity between your own best efforts to make sense out of the world, and science's similar concern.

Finally, as for "scientific method," perhaps we should not care too much whether we use that term or not. Perhaps, for our present purposes, we shall get along better if we think rather in terms of exploring some of the principles and problems of empirical inquiry, whether in "the sciences" or at the level of everyday living. Our central aim here is not to become scientists, but to deepen our understanding of what we may call the rationale of factual inquiry, the logic of fact-finding. As we proceed with our work in this area, we should try to keep in mind the warning implicit in Bridgman's words. There is considerable danger that in discussing "factual inquiry" or "scientific method" we shall make it sound more logical than it really is. "Guesses," "insights," "lucky breaks," and "strokes of genius" all have their role in empirical discovery, but such things elude analysis. The stage at which a hypothesis dawns upon one, for example, often seems mysterious; we speak of "bolts from the blue" and "intuitions." Again, the innumerable judgments of relevance and irrelevance ("Might this factor be important, or can I just disregard it?") required in any empirical investigation, while they reflect previous knowledge, cannot be reduced to "rules." Granting all this, let us explore the extent to which an analysis of empirical inquiry reveals logical principles at work, and the extent to which empirical inferences may be logically justified.

23.2. SOME BROAD DIFFERENCES BETWEEN COMMON SENSE AND SCIENCE

Up to this point, our remarks have perhaps served to stress continuities between common sense and scientific inquiry, rather than to recognize differences. These differences are more striking when we compare, say, an advanced science such as physics with "crude" common sense, than when we compare a less highly developed science and "enlightened" common sense. To avoid unrewarding verbal controversy so far as possible, let us for the moment consider as examples of "sciences" only those fields of inquiry which would almost universally be called by that name, namely such "natural" sciences as physics, chemistry, geology, and biology. We should warn ourselves in advance that this procedure will tend to emphasize differences rather than continuities. Yet even these differences turn out to be largely differences of degree.

AWARENESS OF BIAS AND NEED FOR SAFEGUARDS AGAINST IT

We never start thinking "from scratch." Even when embarking on a new and unexplored field of inquiry, we bring as background a certain general outlook which includes presuppositions, basic attitudes, vague expectations, and analogies drawn from other areas of our experience. This is as true of a human thinker in his role of scientist as in his role of common-sense individual. But the trained scientist is much more aware of the importance of getting his presuppositions out into the open, and of the need for being continually on the alert to safeguard against presuppositions which may have a distorting or prejudicial effect upon his inquiry. We cannot avoid having presuppositions, but we can learn to scrutinize them and to distinguish between those that are a fruitful source of suggestions and hypotheses, and those that are likely to bias or prejudice our work. Charles Darwin was so impressed by our human tendency to let our biases and hopes get in the way, that he took elaborate precautions. When he was working on his theory of natural selection, he found that it was much easier for him to remember cases which confirmed his thesis than those which went against it. He set up for himself the stringent rule that he would put down in writing every exception or contrary instance that occurred to him or that he encountered in his researches. Only so, he felt, could he hope to control the distorting effect of his own hopes and biases. To do this, more of course was needed than merely to keep a note-book. Yet this instance illustrates the alertness with which a careful investigator watches his own prejudices.

A MORE ANALYTICAL APPROACH

The investigations of a scientist are typically carried on at a much more analytical level than our usual common-sense inquiries. A simple illustration will suggest the difference without ignoring the continuity. Unsophisticated common sense may note that both robins and bats have wings and fly through the air, and may on these grounds classify both as "birds." More sophisticated common sense would note certain differences which underlie this obvious similarity, for example, the fact that the robin, like many other flying things, has feathers, while a bat is quite unusual in having fur instead. This would suggest a relation to other fur-bearing animals. Science, carrying the analysis still further, would focus attention upon more detailed anatomical and physiological matters (such as the bat's possession of mammary glands and the robin's egg-laying). The outcome, of course, is that the more analytical approach results in a deeper knowledge of fundamental relationships, and provides the basis for classifying bats with other mammals. This scientific classification tells us more about bats than does the primitive common-sense classification.

The analyses of science are greatly enriched by the application, where possible, of mathematical procedures for the quantification and manipulation of data and the precise expression of results. Here again, while recognizing the importance of mathematics to science, and its prominence in such fields as physics, we must not ignore the continuities with enlightened common sense. The housewife gains precision in keeping track of her household expenditures by analyzing them mathematically, and the farmer discovers how much lumber he will need for the new chicken coop through elementary mathematical analysis. On the other hand, there are many aspects of, say, geology, in which mathematical analysis plays little or no role. In spite of a widely held view to the contrary, it does not seem that the quantification of data and results is a distinguishing characteristic of science. This mathematicizing aspect of much science seems rather to be an aspect of science's general concern for analytical precision.

Science is also more analytical than common sense in its approach to the circumstances accompanying a factor under investigation. While common sense tends, for example, to develop rough causal generalizations which ignore important qualifications and variations in the circumstances, science typically seeks causal generalizations which will express precisely what will happen under precisely what type of conditions when some specific type of event occurs. In these and other matters we find that science is characteristically dissatisfied with the cruder and more superficial formulations of common sense, and seeks to carry the analysis to a deeper level.

A MORE RIGOROUS CONCEPT OF EXPERIMENTATION

In everyday speech, when we speak of "experimenting" we mean little more than just trying something out. The scientific concept of experimentation is more involved, and marks one of the sharpest differences between scientific and typical common-sense analysis. If, as a common-sense individual, you find that you have that "tired, run-down feeling" of which advertisers are so fond, you may decide to try taking supplementary vitamins for a while. So, in the common-sense meaning of the term, you "experiment." After a week or so of taking the pills, you find you are feeling much less tired, so you decide that vitamins must have done the trick. "That proves it!" you may say. "Vitamins are certainly wonderful. I'm glad I went ahead and experimented." Our point here is not to criticize your language, but rather to examine your procedure in the light of the scientific concept of experimentation. The scientist would deny that, in the scientific sense, you were really "experimenting." To him, a procedure is not an *experiment* unless it reveals certain characteristics of control.

In a SCIENTIFIC EXPERIMENT, something is done on purpose under *controlled conditions* in order to see what will happen, and the result is carefully noted for the light it throws on a specific question stated in advance. The element of control is conspicuously lacking from your trial of vitamins. You tried something out, and then noted what "happened," but you have no clear grounds for the conclusion that it happened *because* of the vitamins. One of the commonest fallacies of empirical thinking is that of supposing that, just because Event B happens *after* Event A, it was *caused* by Event A. So common is this fallacy that it has had a standard name ever since the days when people spoke Latin. It is the POST HOC FALLACY, or to give its full name, the fallacy of *post hoc ergo propter hoc,* "after this, therefore on account of this."

Your so-called "experiment" was conducted under such varying and uncontrolled conditions that there is no way of telling what part, if any, the vitamins played in your improvement. Perhaps the week before you began the trial, you were staying up late night after night working on a term paper. Maybe all you needed was a little sleep, which you got the following week. Or perhaps, to stretch a point, all you needed was a little exercise away from the books. Walking down the hall three times a day to get water to swallow your pills may have been the secret of your new lease on life. Or perhaps the mere fact that you were at last "doing something about it" gave you the psychological boost you needed at the time and improved the way you felt. There are any number of things other than the vitamins that might account for your feeling better, but your "experiment" was not set up in such a way that you could take these possibilities into account and get some light on them.

By contrast, the IDEAL OF SCIENTIFIC EXPERIMENTATION is to isolate a situation in such a way that all the relevant factors are known and are under control, and *only one factor is permitted to vary at a time,* so that any change can be attributed with some probability to this varying factor. In many cases, even the scientist is unable to attain this ideal fully, but at least he has a clear conception of what he is working toward. When he finds that adequate control is not possible, he holds his results much more tentatively and dubiously than the common-sense individual would in similar circumstances. Even when it is impossible for him to bring some of the variable factors under direct control, the scientist has ways of taking them into account. At times, he can do no more than use large numbers of cases, in the hope that the uncontrolled "random" variations from case to case will cancel each other out. At other times, he will have all the relevant factors under such complete control that a single case, or a very few, will be all he needs in order to decide the point at issue with a high degree of probability.

In the summer of 1952, large-scale experiments were conducted in epidemic areas to throw light on the possible effectiveness of gamma globulin, a blood derivative, in combatting paralysis in poliomyelitis. One of the best ways of seeing the difference between the common-sense and the scientific meanings of "experiment" is to compare a case like your vitamin "cure" with a case like the gamma globulin experiment in Houston, Texas. We shall not take time to discuss the careful studies which preceded this large-scale experiment, but will note some of the precautions taken in carrying out the experiment itself. Instead of just giving gamma globulin injections to a lot of children in order to "see what would happen," half the children (the EXPERIMENTAL GROUP) were given the globulin and half (the CONTROL GROUP) were not. Stop to consider why this was a good idea from the point of view of finding out what was really happening and why.

But further controls were set up. If some children were given an injection and some were not, psychological factors *might* have an important influence on the result. In a similar fashion, your mere awareness that you were "taking pills" might, as we saw, have had something to do with your feeling better. How could this possibility be minimized or eliminated? The experimenters gave injections not only to the children in the experimental group, but also to the children in the control group. The difference was that the injections given to the control group consisted of a harmless gelatin that looked like gamma globulin; its physiological effect was roughly equivalent to eating a spoonful of Jello. Think over the ways in which this procedure helped to bring certain factors under control.

Still further precautions are described in the following report of preparations from the *New York Times* for April 28, 1952. It will pay you to ask yourself why each of these precautions was taken, and how it helped to give better control of the experimental situation:

> The youngsters receiving the gamma globulin will be selected by chance. Not even the researchers conducting the tests will know until later which children did receive it.
>
> Syringes containing the two substances have been prepared by a pharmaceutical manufacturer. The syringes were taken for packaging and numbering from stockpiles of the two.
>
> The children will be injected as they appear for the experiment with similar-looking syringes picked from the container at random. The serial number on each one will be entered on the child's record card. The factory record of syringe serial numbers has been locked away until the study has been completed.

Similar procedures were used two years later in the field trials which were conducted to determine the efficacy of the Salk vaccine.

HIGHER STANDARDS OF CONFIRMATION AND SUSPENSE OF JUDGMENT

If you are jilted by two red-headed girls in a row, you may decide that there is just something about redheads that does not agree with you. This may be a sound common-sense decision, but it will not satisfy a scientist. You mustn't, he will urge, generalize from so few cases. He is of course right, if what you were trying to do was to be "scientific."

To put it more technically, science insists on a higher degree of confirmation than we ordinarily demand at the common-sense level of inquiry. Intimately associated with this characteristic of science is suspense of judgment. In general, we must not as scientists accept a conclusion until the evidence in support of it is strong enough to confirm it with a high degree of probability. Just how high a degree will be required is a somewhat conventional matter, and differs from science to science and from problem to problem. But in any case, science is much more rigorous in its standards here than common sense.

It is sometimes urged that, as scientists, we must not accept a conclusion until "all the evidence is in." Once we recognize that we can seldom if ever be sure that the evidence is complete, and that in most cases it cannot possibly be, we realize that the above advice is rather curious. The phrase "accept a conclusion" is ambiguous, and the advice is absurd or of some merit depending on how we interpret that phrase. If it is taken to mean that, as scientists, we must not incorporate into the body of scientific knowledge any conclusion for which the evidence is not complete, and that we must not proceed to build upon such conclusions, the advice is silly. What is more, the advance of science would be impossible on this basis, and no practicing scientist takes such advice seriously. If, however, the phrase merely means that we must, as scientists, hold our conclusions tentatively, and be ready to modify them in the light of what further inquiry may reveal, then the advice is sound. For, recognizing as he does that the evidence is seldom if ever complete, and that he probably won't know it if it is, the scientist must hold all his scientific conclusions subject to modification.

Is this one sense in which we might reasonably seek to become "more scientific" in our ordinary thinking? Is this attitude one which might benefit us at the common-sense level too? Yes, in so far as the attitude is really applicable. We need to note that, as scientists, we often confront a much simpler situation than we face in everyday life. A scientist may, on a theoretical issue, suspend judgment throughout his lifetime if necessary, content in the knowledge that he is doing what he can to extend human understanding, and that what he cannot do, someone else may eventually do. On many theoretical issues we, whether as laymen or as scientists, really don't have to "make up our minds." But there are other issues of a practical nature where we must, willy-nilly, make up our minds, even though the evidence is inadequate to provide the basis for a "scientific conclusion." For, as the American philosopher William James pointed out, there are some situations in which *not* to decide *is* to decide.[4] If, for example, you refuse to marry a person until "all the evidence is in" that this person will be a good life-partner, you will die a bachelor or a spinster. Your refusal to decide in the face of inconclusive evidence will have decided for you. The swimmer who refuses to decide whether to attempt a rescue, when no one else is around to do it, will by his indecision have committed himself to an irrevocable decision. Even to linger too long over such questions as "What are the chances that I will drown too?" or "Is this person really worth saving anyway, or would the world be better off without him?" will have the effect of having made a decision. To do nothing is sometimes an extremely significant way of doing something.

It is worth noting that when an important practical issue is involved, scientists will in their own work sometimes be forced to make decisions of this type. A striking example was the decision, made in the spring of 1955, to undertake a nationwide program of mass inoculations with the Salk polio vaccine. Purely theoretical considerations might have led instead to further laboratory work or to another year of field trials.

Common sense can learn much from science about refusing to make snap decisions and about reticence in claiming truth for conclusions which have little to support them. But common sense will always be confronted with many practical urgencies requiring decision and action in the absence of evidence adequate to meet "scientific" standards.

---

[4] William James: *The Will to Believe and Other Essays*, New York, Longmans, Green and Company, 1927, p. 11.

GREATER STRESS ON SYSTEM AND INTERRELATIONS

The knowledge which constitutes a given science is expected to be not merely more objective and free from bias than common-sense knowledge, more analytical in nature, and more highly confirmed. It is also expected to fit into an orderly and logically coherent system with other items of knowledge. At an uncritical level, the same individual who believes that all redheads are unreliable may decide, on similarly scant evidence, that girls by the name of "Lucy" are highly dependable. These two generalizations may be held with equal tenacity, in spite of the fact that some redheads are named "Lucy." At a more critical level of common sense and in the sciences, such an inconsistency will present a challenge and will indicate that the competing generalizations call for further scrutiny. A particular science, however, goes much further than common sense in systematizing its results, and in working out the logical interrelations among them. The same is less true for science considered as a whole. Here, both because of the magnitude of the task and because modern science perhaps necessarily produces specialists rather than experts in synoptic vision, relatively little has as yet been done. Within a given science our understanding of interrelations is relatively advanced; between science and science it is as yet fragmentary. How far such systematizing and interrelating across scientific subject matters can go remains to be seen. Some scientists, however, hold up the ideal of a single unified body of scientific knowledge, into which the knowledge gained by our now largely separate disciplines will be integrated.

23.3. BUT WHAT DO YOU MEAN, "FACTS"?

Empirics, we have said, is the logic of factual inquiry. It is that branch of logic which investigates the principles involved in finding out "what's what," and in justifying our claims to factual knowledge. Such preliminary attempts to explain the nature of empirics, however, are inevitably handicapped by the diversity of ways in which we commonly use words like "fact" and "factual" and their synonyms. It will be helpful to distinguish several different usages of the word "fact." All of these are common enough, and all are in accordance with "good English." We shall note a generic sense of "fact," in which a fact is whatever is the case. We shall note that this generic sense embraces three specific senses: semantical, syntactical or formal, and empirical. We shall examine the empirical sense more fully, since it is particularly relevant to our present study. Finally, we shall note a divergent popular use which we shall avoid.

"FACT" AS WHATEVER IS THE CASE

The most general way in which we use the word "fact" is in expressions having the form: "It is a fact that so-and-so is such-and-such." It is in this sense of "fact" that we may correctly say that every true statement expresses a fact, and that a statement is true precisely because it *does* express a fact. Consider the four following examples of this usage:

    a. "It is a fact that two plus two equals four."
    b. "It is a fact that a 'skillet' is a pan used for frying."
    c. "It is a fact that ice melts when heated sufficiently."
    d. "It is a fact that Abraham Lincoln was assassinated."

To understand the great range of this first usage, note that example (a) deals with a *formal* or syntactical matter, (b) with a *semantical* matter, (c) with a general empirical "law" and (d) with an empirical matter concerning a single individual. In this generic sense, then, a fact is anything that is the case.

Before considering other usages of "fact," let us note how the two expressions, "It is a fact that . . ." and "It is true that . . . ," are related in ordinary English. We would ordinarily regard it as a matter of indifference whether we said, "It is a fact that two plus two equals four" or "It is true that two plus two equals four," and so on for the other three examples above. This everyday equating of the two expressions is logically justified in that a given true statement reports a fact, and a given fact is reportable by means of an appropriate true statement. The two members constituting such a pair of statements strictly satisfy our definition of "logically equivalent," for they must always have the same truth-value. If, for example, the statement, "It is a fact that Abraham Lincoln was assassinated" is *true,* the following statement must also be true and vice versa: "It is true that Abraham Lincoln was assassinated."

In spite of this logical equivalence, however, we do not want to confuse a true statement with the fact which it expresses. To do so is to commit the elementary semantical blunder of confusing a sign (in this case, a statement) with what it stands for (in this case, a fact).[5] In cases where precision requires it, we can readily distinguish these two cases by writing, for example:

1. "Ice melts when heated sufficiently" is true.
2. That ice melts when heated sufficiently is a fact.

In (1), the words within the quotes are a statement. The whole Statement 1 asserts that this quoted statement is true. Statement 2, on the other hand, asserts that something (*expressed* by the words, "ice melts when heated sufficiently") is a fact.

Since we have throughout this book been considering truth as a property of *statements*, it is important to note that truth is determined by the facts, not vice versa. A statement is shown to be true by showing that it expresses a fact. We do not examine the *statement*, "This stone is granite," in order to determine whether the statement is true. Rather, we examine the stone, to see whether it has, as a matter of fact, the characteristics which the name "granite" signifies.

"FACT" AS WHAT IS THE CASE IN EXPERIENCE

One species of the generic type of fact we have just discussed is empirical fact. This more specific sense of "fact" is the one that is most important for our present purposes. It is the sense we have in mind when we say that empirics is the logic of factual inquiry, or more colloquially, the logic of fact-finding. When we speak of facts in this sense, we mean not simply whatever is the case, but more specifically, whatever is the case in sense experience or is inferable from sense experience. That ice melts when heated sufficiently, and that Abraham Lincoln was assassinated are both facts in this empirical sense. Instances of empirical fact range all the way from cases which may be determined by direct observation to cases where an elaborate process of inference from observations is involved. The simpler type includes facts such as would be expressed by the statements, "I am now hearing a bell" and "I am now seeing a table."

[5] In everyday speech, people sometimes say things like: "These are the true facts of the case." In this harmless colloquial usage, "true" seems merely for emphasis, like the word "really," or the word "are" in italics: "These really are the facts" or "These *are* the facts."

(For convenience, we may call such statements OBSERVATION STATEMENTS, since they report observations or perceptions.) The more complex type of case includes facts such as may be expressed by the statements "The earth's orbit is an ellipse" and "Man evolved from earlier forms of life." The facts to which such statements refer are facts of the empirical kind, but they cannot be known directly from observation. Our knowledge of them is based on a complex set of observations, but requires in addition some fairly involved interpretations and inferences.

We have already noted that a fact in the senses thus far distinguished may be either general or individual. That is, it may on the one hand deal with all or some of a class and hence be expressible by means of a universal or a particular statement. Or it may on the other hand deal with a single individual and hence be expressible by means of a singular statement. Some writers on empirics restrict the name "fact" to states of affairs reportable by singular statements, and refuse to apply it to cases which require a particular or universal statement for their expression. In this restricted usage, one could say that it is a fact that *this* piece of ice melted when heated sufficiently. But it would on this usage be incorrect to say that it is a fact that ice (that is, ice in general, any instance of ice) melts when heated sufficiently, or that most living plants contain chlorophyll. This restriction is somewhat inconvenient, and we shall not adopt it.

A DIVERGENT POPULAR SENSE: "FACT" AS CONCRETE OBJECT

This final sense we shall mention only because it is rather common in everyday speech, and because we want to avoid confusing it with other usages. In this sense, which we shall avoid, "fact" is used to mean a concrete individual object, as when people say that a stone is a fact. You should note the difference between calling a stone a "fact" and saying that it is a fact *that* a certain object is a stone. The latter is the empirical sense of "fact" discussed above.

Sometimes when people appear to be using "fact" in this concrete-object sense, they are really only speaking elliptically. Thus when they say, "This stone is a fact," they may merely be calling attention, in a condensed form, to the empirical fact *that* there is a stone here-now.

• SOME REMINDERS

1. We do not equate empirics with inductive logic or with the study of scientific method. Various reasons for not doing so are considered.
2. There are important continuities between factual inquiry at the common-sense level and in the sciences. There are also important differences, although these differences are mostly matters of degree.
3. The word "fact" is commonly used in several different senses which we need to distinguish if we are to understand what is meant by saying that empirics is the logic of factual inquiry.

APPLICATIONS

1. Comment on the specific meaning of "science" (and derivative words) in each of the following:
   a. Clean your teeth the scientific way: use Toofyglint.
   b. "To trust the soul's invincible surmise
      Was all his science and his only art." (George Santayana)
   c. It is a scientific fact that dinosaurs once roamed the earth.
   d. The struggle between science and religion
   e. What we need is a more scientific understanding of human relations.
   f. Science proves that Fluffotex towels absorb 32% more water.
   g. Einstein was a scientist; he left the practical applications to others.
   h. Bachelor of Science
   i. In the Middle Ages, theology was considered the queen of the sciences.
   j. Politics is not a science but an art.
2. Give some examples from your own experience in which it was, or would have been, wise to suspend judgment until more evidence was available.
3. Give some examples from your own experience in which practical urgencies made it unwise or impossible to suspend judgment, even though evidence was not complete, and in which "not to decide" would have been a kind of deciding.
4. Explain the function and importance of a control group in each of the following investigations:
   a. "Coconut milk contains a still-unidentified substance that is a sort of 'embryo juice' and is exceedingly potent in stimulating growth in certain plant tissues. This discovery was announced by Dr. S. M. Caplin and Prof. F. C. Steward of the University of Rochester in the journal, *Science* (Dec. 10).

   "In their experiments they used tiny pieces of carrot tissue, kept under sterile conditions and supplied with a standard nutrient solution. To some of the cultures they added heat-sterilized, filtered coconut milk; to others the well-known growth-promoting chemical, indole acetic acid; still other cultures received no additions and served as controls.

"The bits of carrot in the control cultures remained alive but failed to grow. Those receiving indole acetic acid showed slow growth, while those receiving coconut milk grew quite rapidly. Their average increase in weight, over a three-week period, was 23 times that of the pieces receiving indole acetic acid.

"Although the substance has not yet been identified or isolated, there is some suggestion that it has some relation to the formation or utilization of vitamin A. Further experiments looking into this are now in progress." (*Science News Letter,* December 25, 1948, pp. 403–404)

b. "A three-month study at Boston University on the effect of three antihistaminic drugs in the treatment of the common cold, has failed to reveal 'any effect of the drugs in the dosage used that differed significantly' from a placebo of milk sugar, according to the report on the study published today in The New England Journal of Medicine.

"The placebo, or inactive preparation, consisted of a sugar pill given to one-fourth of the 1,214 persons studied, none of whom knew the nature of the drug he was taking. . . .

"After the questionnaires 'deemed invalid for a number of reasons had been discarded,' the report stated, 'those remaining totaled 729.' . . .

"Of these, 163 reported that the cold 'became worse'; 110 that it 'remained the same'; 163 that it was 'slightly improved'; 211 that it was 'improved markedly,' and 82 that the cold had 'disappeared completely.' . . .

"In the third group of 163, those 'improved slightly,' there were 130 from the drug group and 33 who had taken the sugar pill.

"Of the fourth group of 211, those who 'improved markedly,' a total of 155 had taken one of the three drugs, while 56 had had only the milk sugar tablet. In this group the sugar pill did better than any of the three antihistaminics.

"In the last group of 82, which reported that the colds had 'disappeared completely,' there were 60 who had taken one of the drugs, while 22 had taken the sugar pill. In this group the sugar pill 'worked' better than two of the antihistaminics and nearly as well as the third." (*New York Times,* January 26, 1951)

5. Consider the relative value of the two different types of control group used in the Salk vaccine field trials in 1954:
   a. The first and third graders were used to constitute an "observed control group" in certain areas in which vaccine was given to second graders.
   b. In certain other areas in which about half of the children in the first three grades were given the vaccine, the other half were given a *placebo* (a dummy injection).
   Can you see why the statisticians who evaluated the trials gave more weight to the results from the placebo study areas? (Data from *U. S. News and World Report,* April 22, 1955, p. 39)
6. In each case, try to determine whether the word "fact(s)" is being used in the semantical, syntactical, empirical, or concrete-object sense. If empirical,

indicate whether it is general or individual. If in doubt, explain why.

a. The aim of natural science is to determine what the facts are.
b. It may be a fact that there is plant life of some kind on Mars.
c. It is a fact that vertebrates all have spinal columns.
d. Arithmetic is not concerned with facts but with numerical concepts.
e. It is a fact that the square erected on the hypotenuse of a right triangle is equal to the sum of the squares of the other two sides.
f. Give me facts, not theories.
g. As a matter of fact, "big" is not the same as "huge."
h. The brute facts are these: You haven't done the work, so you fail the course.
i. The fact of the matter is, people don't like to admit defeat.
j. It is not a fact that he must be bald simply because he is over forty and some men over forty are bald.

CHAPTER 24

FACT-FINDING AND PROBABILITY

PREVIEW

For reasons that we shall explore more fully later on, considerations of probability play an important part in empirical inquiry. In the present chapter, we shall note some central characteristics of probability, and shall try to clarify the semantical difficulties arising out of our varied uses of words like "probable" and "certain."

24.1. CAN WE REALLY GET AT THE FACTS?

At the common-sense level, all of us are confident that we know a great many empirical facts. We feel that we can readily express many of these facts by means of statements that are completely true. Impressed as we are with the achievements of the empirical or natural sciences, it seems obvious to us that in the sciences, too, we have knowledge of large bodies of both singular and general facts. It is consequently difficult for us to take seriously the contention that virtually all of our empirical knowledge, even in the sciences, is at best only highly probable, not certain. Yet this contention has been defended by many students of empirics and scientific method. We may suspect that the difficulty is in part semantical. As our own study of empirics proceeds, we shall be in a better position to understand and evaluate the grounds for the contention that little if any of our empirical knowledge is certain. At present, we may simply note some of them in a preliminary way.

(1) We often confuse PSYCHOLOGICAL CERTAINTY (or perhaps better, "certitude") with factual certainty. That is, we confuse "I feel certain that . . ." with "It is certain that . . ." To have no doubts about the truth of a given statement is one thing; to be in possession of evidence adequate

to establish, with certainty, the truth of a statement is another thing. The Tewa Indians feel certain that the earth is flat, and yet we would have no hesitation in saying that they do not have adequate evidence to establish this belief with certainty. It is then perhaps also reasonable to suppose that some things about which you and I feel certain are not really certain.

(2) We often discover later that we have made a mistake in observation or in reasoning, although we felt confident enough about it at the time.

(3) Some of our best established generalizations hold only "on the whole" or "in most cases." Hence, when we make use of such generalizations in reasoning about a particular case, we must recognize that the conclusion which we derive is at best only probable.

(4) Sometimes the pattern of our inference is such that, even if our premises were known to be true, the conclusion can be known only to be probably true. (Inductive, diagnostic, and analogical arguments, to be examined later on, are all examples of this kind.)

(5) Frequently we have to make up our minds on the basis of incomplete evidence. Conclusions arrived at in this manner can at best be known only to be probably true.

What are we to make of these observations? They at least serve to call our attention to the fact that we probably know with certainty a good deal less than we ordinarily suppose. Again, they help us to understand why so much of empirical reasoning is concerned with judgments of probability, and why the concept of probability is a central one in empirics. On the other hand, let us note that even if we accept these observations at their face value, we have no reason to deny that the aim of empirical inquiry is to determine what is really the case. We may fall short of realizing this aim in its fullness, but it is still our aim.

24.2. SOME SEMANTICAL CONSIDERATIONS

We shall find it easier to think clearly about probability if we first deal with certain semantical issues. We shall note how the word "probable" is used in everyday English, and shall then examine the extent to which customary technical usage departs from this.

"PROBABLE" AS APPLIED TO STATEMENTS AND TO EVENTS

We usually speak indifferently about (a) the probability of a statement and (b) the probability of an event or state-of-affairs. In most cases, no confusion results from this practice, and we shall feel free to adhere to this dual usage in our subsequent discussions. To see why we can afford to be liberal about this matter, consider the statement:

It will probably rain before nightfall.

This probability statement may be readily interpreted as a statement about a *statement*, to the effect that this latter statement is probably true:

"It will rain before nightfall" is probably true.

Or, with equal ease, it may be interpreted as a statement about the probable occurrence of a particular event:

Rain-before-nightfall will probably occur.

Note that when we speak of a *statement* as "probable" in the light of evidence set forth by other statements, we simply mean that on this evidence the statement in question is probably *true*. Thus, as applied to *statements*, "probable" is equivalent to "probably true." Events or states-of-affairs, on the other hand, are not the kind of things that can be either true or false; they simply are or are not. Thus, when we speak of an *event* as "probable" on such-and-such evidence, we mean that, in the light of this evidence, the event is likely to happen.

EVERYDAY USAGE TENDS TO CONCEAL AN IMPORTANT FACT ABOUT PROBABILITY STATEMENTS

Statements of probability are always relative to a particular body of evidence. This fact is often obscured at the common-sense level by our tendency to speak, as in the above example, of a statement as "probable" without bothering to mention the evidence which makes it probable. We shall deal with this matter of evidence later. At present, we merely call attention to the problem created by our ordinary manner of speaking.

RANGE OF APPLICATION OF "PROBABLE" IS NARROWER IN COMMON USAGE THAN IN TECHNICAL

In ordinary English, we do not call a statement "probable" unless we think its chances of being true, on available evidence, are greater than 50-50. In other words, we do not ordinarily call a statement "probable" unless we think there is more reason to believe it than not. At just this point, the usage common in more technical discussions of probability is at first confusing to the layman. In statistical theory, our everyday limitation of the range of application of "probable" proves inconvenient. In technical discussions of probability, therefore, the range of application is extended to include all cases where there is favorable evidence at all, even though the chances are less than one-half. It will help to notice that this broader technical usage covers cases which, in everyday English, we should rather describe by such words as "improbable" or "possible but not probable." This broadened usage will not bother you once you understand how it departs from our ordinary usage. The context should make it clear which usage is being followed.

TECHNICAL USAGE ADMITS DEGREES OF PROBABILITY, BUT NOT DEGREES OF CERTAINTY

At one other point, also, everyday usage departs from that found in more technical discussions. Epistemologists (specialists concerned with theory of knowledge) and statisticians usually make a very sharp distinction between "probability" and "certainty." In their usage, probability is subject to degrees, but certainty is not. In their usage, a statement may be more or less probable, but cannot be more or less certain; either it is certain or it is not. In statistical work, degrees of probability are represented either by fractions, or by decimals falling between "0" and "1." Using this latter notation, some writers refer to "1" as "certainty." For convenience, we may call this STATISTICAL CERTAINTY.

Everyday usage differs from this special statistical usage in permitting us to speak of varying degrees of certainty. We commonly say such things as: "It is fairly certain that he will propose to her," or "It is reasonably certain that there will not be an economic recession this year," or "He most certainly has whooping cough." In everyday usage, these degrees of certainty are roughly equated with the *higher* ranges of probability.

A good semi-technical term for certainty in this everyday sense might be "practically certain" or PRACTICAL CERTAINTY. Such usage could be understood as combining two meanings of "practical" and "practically": (a) *"practically* certain" in the sense of *almost* certain, and (b) *"practical* certainty" in the sense of the kind of certainty we need in order to proceed in practice, that is, probability high enough to warrant our acting *as if* it were certain.

Since this everyday type of certainty admits of degrees, we commonly think of it as capable of progressive heightening until it passes from the range of practical certainty to an ultimate and unassailable type of certainty not admitting of degrees. We may, for want of a better name, call this latter type COMPLETE CERTAINTY.

While this notion of complete certainty may function as a meaningful ideal against which to measure our attainments at the level of practical certainty, there are good reasons for questioning whether we ever reach it in empirical matters.

PRACTICAL CERTAINTY DISTINGUISHED FROM SYNTACTICAL CERTAINTY

Practical certainty may also be contrasted with what we may call formal or SYNTACTICAL CERTAINTY. This is the kind of certainty possessed by statements which are necessarily true because of their logical form. Examples include: "If no a is b, then no b is a," "If A ⊃ B and B ⊃ C, then A ⊃ C," "All people who are both short and fat are fat," and "Everything is either a watermelon or not a watermelon." Such statements are incontrovertible; they cannot be denied with consistency; to reject them is to contradict oneself. It is important to note that even when such a statement has (like the last two examples above) empirical content, it is true not because of the specific content, but because of the form of the statement.

The contradictory of any syntactically certain statement is self-inconsistent, and hence necessarily false. By contrast, the contradictory of a practically certain statement is not self-inconsistent. It may be false, but it is not necessarily false. It may be unreasonable in the light of available empirical evidence, but one can assert it without contradicting oneself.

We must guard against the temptation of thinking of the "necessarily so" nature of syntactical certainty as setting forth a perfect pattern which our practical certainties are imperfectly trying to copy. These two types of certainty belong to logically different realms and apply to different subject matters, the first to formal relationships and syntactical structures, the second to the stuff of experience and the world of empirical fact.

FIVE DIFFERENT SENSES OF "CERTAINTY"

Since we have now had occasion to use the word "certainty" in five different senses, it will be helpful to summarize these distinctions all in one place, where we may refer to them later if need be.

(1) PSYCHOLOGICAL CERTAINTY: The feeling that a given statement is true (or false), whether or not the feeling is justified by adequate evidence. Certainty in this psychological sense is perhaps better called "certitude."

(2) STATISTICAL CERTAINTY: Probability of 1.

(3) SYNTACTICAL CERTAINTY: The kind of certainty possessed by a statement which is necessarily true because of its logical form.

(4) PRACTICAL CERTAINTY: A degree of probability high enough to justify acting upon it, more or less as if the statement were actually known to be unqualifiedly true.

(5) COMPLETE CERTAINTY: An ideal limit conceived as lying beyond the highest ranges of practical certainty.

Later we shall find it necessary to distinguish one further sense of "certainty" which we shall call *immediate certainty*. (See Section 25.2, note 1.)

24.3. PROBABILITY DEPENDS UPON EVIDENCE

No statement, considered in isolation, is either probable or improbable.[1] The probability of a statement is always relative to a body of evidence. As we have already noted, this fact is often obscured by our tendency to speak of a statement as probable without bothering to mention the evidence which makes it probable.

When, for example, I say that it is probable that it will rain before

---

[1] Here and in what follows, we purposely leave out of account statements having syntactical certainty, for the concept of probability does not properly apply to them.

nightfall, I commonly fail to state explicitly the evidence upon which my judgment of probability is based. Quite likely I am not even very clear myself about just what evidence I am drawing upon. It is only when you ask me, "What makes you think so?" that I am forced to make the evidence explicit.

"Why," I may reply, "just look at those dark clouds moving in from the west!" This may satisfy you, but if it does, it will only be because both of us are making certain further assumptions and drawing upon certain further evidence which neither of us has bothered to make explicit. We both know from past experience, for example, that clouds of this general type contain moisture that commonly falls as precipitation. And we are both aware, let us suppose, that it is too warm for this moisture to fall as snow instead of as rain.

This is good enough for many everyday purposes. Often we are concerned only with the roughest estimates of probability; we want merely to know whether the evidence makes it "more probable than not" that a given statement is true or that a given event will occur.

24.4. DEGREE OF PROBABILITY DISTINGUISHED FROM DEGREE OF CONFIDENCE

Once we understand clearly that probability is a relation between a statement and a body of evidence, it is easy to avoid certain common confusions. In the first place, it is then easy to see that the probability of a statement is one thing, and our subjective feeling of confidence in a statement is another. It is quite possible for a person to feel confident that a given statement is true, even though he has no evidence to support his feeling, or even though the available evidence indicates that his confidence is unjustified. It is of course easier to detect cases of this disparity in others than in ourselves. We all know the type of student who is highly confident that he is going to pass a given course, even though all the available evidence indicates that it is highly probable he is not going to pull through. And we all know the type of student who keeps worrying about whether he will, let us say, make a "B" in a course, when all the available evidence makes it highly probable that he will. This does not of course mean that we never proportion our feeling of confidence to the evidence, but it reminds us that confidence and probability are two different things. The extent to which our degree of confidence in a statement *is* proportioned to the available evidence is a good index of how rational we really are.

24.5. PROBABILITY SHIFTS WITH THE EVIDENCE

In the second place, since probability is dependent upon evidence, it should not surprise us to find the probability shifting as the evidence changes. A statement which is quite improbable (in the everyday sense of the term) on a given set of evidence may be highly probable on another set of evidence.

If all the information we have about a given individual is that he is twenty years old, we will, on this evidence, regard it as quite highly probable that he will live until his next birthday.[2] If we have the additional evidence that he will be twenty-one day after tomorrow, we will consider it almost certain that he will live until his next birthday. If, however, we are now told that he is engaged at the moment in bitter hand-to-hand front-line fighting, our previous estimate of his chances of living until his next birthday may be revised downwards. And when we learn that he has just been shot through the heart, we may on this new evidence judge it to be improbable that he will survive until his birthday.

This example helps us see that a question of the form: "What is the probability that so-and-so is such-and-such?" is incomplete. In practice, it is a convenient shorthand form for the question, "What is the probability, *on the available evidence,* that so-and-so is such-and-such?"

24.6. A STATEMENT THAT IS HIGHLY PROBABLE ON GIVEN EVIDENCE MAY BE FALSE

There is a third way in which recognition of the fact that probability depends upon evidence clarifies our thinking. Once we understand this relationship, it no longer seems paradoxical that a statement which is highly probable on the basis of available evidence may none the less be false. A weather forecaster, for example, makes up his forecast on the basis of his general knowledge of meteorology and the specific data provided by reports from stations scattered across the country. Occasionally, all the

[2] A similar example is used by Ernest Nagel: *Principles of the Theory of Probability,* Chicago, University of Chicago Press, 1939, pp. 23, 45.

available evidence may support a prediction which is falsified by the combined effect of small local disturbances about which the forecaster had no reports.[3] On the evidence, the prediction was highly probable, yet it turned out to be mistaken.

In the area of human relations, too, we find many examples in which the evidence points one way and the truth turns out to lie in the other. Once the wedding date has been set and the invitations sent out, it is highly probable that the engaged couple will go through with the ceremony. But we all know of cases in which, in spite of the probabilities, things have turned out differently: Joe gets hit by a truck, or Mary decides to enter a convent after all, or they both decide in the nick of time that the whole thing was a terrible mistake.

On the other hand, we all know cases in which something that, on the available evidence, is highly improbable, none the less actually happens. A desperately sick person, for example, who on the basis of the best medical evidence should have died long ago, may surprise the doctors by staying alive and eventually recovering.

24.7. INCREASED PRECISION IN PROBABILITY ESTIMATES REQUIRES INCREASED ATTENTION TO EVIDENCE

When we are called upon to be more specific in our estimates of probability, explicit attention to the available evidence becomes increasingly important. Even here, however, as long as we remain at the common-sense level of discussion and inquiry, rough estimates are all that are possible and all that are expected of us. These estimates are expressed by such phrases as: "The chances are quite good that . . . ," "It is highly probable that . . . ," "It is fairly likely that . . . ," and so on.

In scientific and technical inquiries, it is often desirable or necessary to be more specific about the degree of probability attaching to a given statement on given evidence. In such cases, provided the data meet certain requirements and our knowledge of the evidence is detailed enough, statistical procedures are available for expressing probabilities in numerical terms.

In many phases of scientific work, however, the scientist too has to get

[3] This perhaps accounts for the difficulties of a U. S. Weather Bureau meteorologist reported in *Time*, May 11, 1953. He arrived late for a speaking engagement, confessing that his plane had been held up by "unexpected weather."

along with rougher, nonnumerical estimates of probability. When, for example, he is confronted with two possible solutions to a problem, and is wondering which is worth investigating first, or when he is in doubt about which of two alternative procedures will work better in a given case, or when he is trying to decide whether he will be able to solve a problem by a given date, he too is limited to the less precise, nonnumerical estimates of probability familiar to all of us at the common-sense level.

24.8. A NOTE ON THE FREQUENCY ANALYSIS OF PROBABILITY

By this time you should be accustomed to thinking of probability as a relation between a statement and a body of evidence. Is this the last word on the subject? Or is it possible to give a more analytical account of this relationship? One motive that leads us to seek such an analysis is our desire to be able, in certain cases at least, to give a precise and if possible numerical estimate of the probability of a given statement on the available evidence.

It turns out that, in many cases, the evidence on which a given statement is probable may be readily interpreted in terms of *relative frequencies*. Some contemporary students of probability theory are hopeful that all cases can be so interpreted, but this point is, at the present stage of research, still controversial. For our own purposes, it will be sufficient to see, without prejudging the issue, what is involved in a frequency interpretation of examples similar to those we have been using.

Why, for example, do we think it highly probable that a twenty-year-old will live until his next birthday? Isn't it because experience shows that most twenty-year-olds have done so? Or, to put it in actuarial jargon, isn't it because the "life expectancy" of the average twenty-year-old is known to be more than one year? If we consider the class of twenty-year-olds, we find that the *frequency* with which members of this class survive until their twenty-first birthday is far greater than the frequency with which they do not.

Or again, why did we think that it would probably rain before nightfall? Wasn't it because experience had taught us that under similar conditions in the past, it had rained more frequently than not?

These examples reveal the ease with which many probability statements may be interpreted as statements about relative frequencies. They also suggest that our common inability to give a precise numerical value to a probability has two possible sources. (1) Our information may be too vaguely formulated or our knowledge of the data too meager to afford grounds for numerical treatment. For example, just how many twenty-year-olds per thousand do live until their next birthday? Common-sense experience assures me that most of them do, but I am ignorant of the exact proportion. I am not even clear about just what group or REFERENCE CLASS of twenty-year-olds I mean to base my judgment on. Do I mean twenty-year-old Americans? Or twenty-year-old American men? Do I mean twenty-year-old American men over the past ten-year period? Or over a longer period? Or a shorter period? How long or how short? As long as I am merely trying to make the rough kind of estimates common to everyday dealing with probabilities, these refinements may be irrelevant. For it may be that, whichever of these classes I mean, it is the case that the great majority of the members of each of them survive until their next birthday. But when I am concerned to give a precise numerical value to the probability, these are questions which I must face and settle. (2) The second source of inability, at the common-sense level, to assign numerical values is more easily dealt with. It is our ignorance of an appropriate mathematical formula. Such a formula has long been known to scientists, mathematicians, and logicians. It is fortunately very simple:

$$\text{probability} = \frac{\text{favorable cases in the reference class}}{\text{total cases in the reference class}}$$

or, in customary symbols:

$$p = \frac{f}{n}$$

The FAVORABLE CASES are those which manifest the special characteristic in question, for example, survival until the twenty-first birthday. Suppose we have made up our minds about precisely what question we mean to ask: "How probable is it, on the basis of the evidence for the past ten-year period, that an American man now twenty years old will survive until his next birthday?" Even now our question is not altogether precise, for we have not specified just what evidence of the past ten-year period we have in mind. But to simplify matters, let us suppose that this evidence shows that 980 out of 1000 in the reference class do survive. Substituting these values in our formula, we conclude that the probability, on this evidence, is $^{49}\!/_{50}$, or in decimal notation, .98. In more colloquial English, we may say that, on this evidence, and assuming that the ratio will continue to hold during the present year, the "chances" that an American man now twenty years old will survive until his next birthday are 98 out of 100, or 49 out of 50.

In order to see how this frequency interpretation fits in with our general approach to probability, note the following points:

(1) The frequency interpretation is not a rival to the view that probability is a relation between a statement and a body of evidence, but a further analysis of this view. Thus, on the frequency analysis, the statement, "Jack Smith will live until his next birthday" is highly probable on the evidence that Jack is a twenty-year-old American and that 980 out of 1000 twenty-year-olds in our reference class have lived until their next birthdays.

(2) In accordance with our earlier discussion of semantical preliminaries, the result of this frequency analysis may be interpreted either as a statement about the probable occurrence of an event:

> "The probability of Jack's living until his next birthday is .98,"

or as a statement about the probable truth of a second statement:

> "The probability that the statement, 'Jack will live until his next birthday,' is true, is .98."

Or, to put it more colloquially in terms of "chances," we may say equivalently:

> "Jack's chances of living until his next birthday are 98 out of 100."
> "The chances that the statement, 'Jack will live until his next birthday,' is true, are 98 out of 100."

(3) As we have seen, statements like the four just quoted are elliptical or incomplete. "The probability . . . is .98" must be understood in all these cases to mean, "The probability *on the evidence referred to* . . . is .98."

In terms of the frequency analysis, this general point is often developed in a special way. Any statement, it is urged, which attributes a probability to a *single case* must involve an at least implicit reference to a *class* of which the single case is a member.

On the frequency analysis, to say that the probability is such-and-such that a given single case (for example, Jack Smith) has a given characteristic, is thus to be understood to mean:

> In the reference class (for example, the class of twenty-year-old American men) on which the singular probability statement is based, the ratio of cases having the specified characteristic (for example, living until their next birthday) is such-and-such (for example, .98).

On the frequency analysis, as in our general account, we need to understand that a change in the evidence will usually lead to a change in the probability of the singular statement. Thus, for example, if we refer the case of Jack Smith, not to the class of twenty-year-old Americans, but to the class of twenty-year-old Americans with bullets in their hearts, we shall presumably find the ratio of survival to be much less than .98.[4]

(4) There is at present, as we have remarked, a lively disagreement among experts as to whether all probability statements are subject to the frequency interpretation. This problem has no crucial importance at the common-sense level of inquiry, since at this level we seldom have precise enough information to permit a numerical treatment of our data. But at the level of scientific inquiry, the question of how far we can carry the frequency interpretation is of practical as well as theoretical importance. The practical importance is this: it happens that we have available a well-developed branch of formal mathematics, the probability calculus. Once we are able to express our data numerically and to show that the problem is subject to the frequency interpretation, the problem can be handled with great precision in accordance with the principles of the mathematical theory of probability.

It may be that your life-work or the types of problem in which you become interested will lead you into the technical intricacies of probability theory and its application to empirical problems. Or perhaps you will never feel called upon to go much beyond the everyday estimation of rough probabilities of the type we all continually make at the common-sense level. In any case, our present purposes do not require a further pursuit of this particular question.

[4] Cf. Ernest Nagel, *op. cit.*, p. 23.

Our concern with probability is to get a clearer idea of the role of probability judgments in empirical inquiry, and an understanding of the ways in which the probability of a statement may be increased through inquiry. You will find that virtually every topic with which we shall be concerned in the rest of the book has some bearing on these central questions. We shall understand them best if we consider them not in isolation, but in intimate connection with specific aspects of inquiry and an analysis of concrete examples of factual investigations.

• SOME REMINDERS

1. There are a number of reasons for thinking that much that we ordinarily suppose to be certain is only highly probable.
2. To avoid semantical confusions, we need to distinguish various senses of "certainty" and of "probability."
3. Statements of probability are always relative to a body of evidence. Recognition of this fact clarifies in three important ways our thinking about probability.
4. The frequency analysis makes possible a numerical treatment of probability. It is not clear that this analysis is always pertinent.

APPLICATIONS

1. How would you answer someone who argued this way: "If what you say about probability is true, how can we really know anything? We want to get at what is the case. But if all we can get at is what is *probably* the case, and if a probably true statement may none the less be actually false, how can we ever trust any item of so-called knowledge?"
2. Here is an exercise in judging probabilities at the common-sense level. In each case, consider whether (on the basis of available evidence) the statement is improbable, more probable than not, or practically certain. Indicate the evidence upon which your estimate is based.
   a. Some of you will pass this course.
   b. A rocket will be sent to the moon this year.
   c. There are mice on the moon.
   d. There will be snow on the campus in December.
   e. There will be snow on the campus in April.
   f. There will not be snow on the campus in June.
   g. You will marry a classmate.
   h. The Democrats will win the next national election.
   i. A person will be injured if he falls out of a third-story window.
   j. A person will be killed if he falls out of a third-story window.

3. In the light of the following passage from his *An Enquiry Concerning Human Understanding*, do you think that David Hume (1711–1776) would have approved or disapproved the view of probability set forth in Section 24.8? Give reasons for your answer.

   It seems evident that when we transfer the past to the future, in order to determine the effect which will result from any cause, we transfer all the different events in the same proportion as they have appeared in the past, and conceive one to have existed a hundred times, for instance, another ten times, and another once. As a great number of views do here concur in one event, they fortify and confirm it to the imagination, beget that sentiment which we call belief, *and give its object the preference above the contrary event, which is not supported by an equal number of experiments, and recurs not so frequently to the thought in transferring the past to the future. Let anyone try to account for this operation of the mind upon any of the received systems of philosophy, and he will be sensible of the difficulty. For my part, I shall think it sufficient if the present hints excite the curiosity of philosophers, and make them sensible how defective all common theories are in treating of such curious and sublime subjects.*

4. List ten statements which you consider to be certain. Then determine which, if any, of the five senses of "certainty" distinguished in this chapter is relevant to each statement.

5. The English philosopher John Locke (1632–1704) once wrote to his friend Stillingfleet:

   With me, to know and to be certain is the same thing: what I know, that I am certain of; and what I am certain of, that I know. What reaches to knowledge I think may be called certainty; and what comes short of certainty, I think cannot be called knowledge.

   Evaluate critically (favorably or unfavorably) the view here expressed, being careful to distinguish semantical from nonsemantical aspects of the problem.

6. Could a person be certain of something and yet turn out to be mistaken? If there are semantical difficulties in this question, clarify them before giving your answer.

CHAPTER 25

FINDING THE FACTS BY OBSERVATION

The ultimate appeal in any question of empirical fact is to experience. In the simplest cases, the appeal is quite direct, as when we answer the question, "What's that?" by looking and seeing. In other cases, the appeal may be quite indirect, as when we appeal to the testimony of others or make predictions by reasoning out the logical implications of present knowledge and observation. How probable are the judgments we make in these different cases, and how may their probability be increased? What obstacles do we face in trying to make well-grounded empirical statements, and how are these obstacles to be overcome? What patterns of reasoning have we available for determining what is probably what? With such questions we shall be concerned in the following chapters. In the present chapter, we shall consider a relatively simple type of empirical statement, one which reports an observation. We shall consider how the probability of such statements can be increased, and shall ask whether such statements can ever be not merely probable but completely certain.

25.1. EMPIRICAL KNOWLEDGE, "DIRECT" AND "INDIRECT"

The knowledge we derive from the testimony of others may be called "indirect" or "derivative." So, also, may the knowledge which we get through *reasoning from* data provided by the testimony of others or experiences of our own. In contrast, the knowledge we gain by observation, that is, through our own sense-experience, may be called relatively "direct." This does not of course mean that the process of observation or "sense perception" is physically or physiologically simple. We all know enough about such matters to realize that the apparently simple act of seeing, let us say, an apple, involves such things as light waves impinging upon the retina, excitation of the retinal rods and cones, neural currents to the brain, and so on. Nor do we mean to overlook the fact that observation involves the interpretation of various sensory cues. By calling knowledge through observation relatively direct, we mean rather to emphasize that (1) it is based on our own experience, not someone else's, and (2) it is for the most part nonreflective, and does not involve an explicit process of inference. In the first respect, observation differs from testimony as a source of factual knowledge; in the second, it differs from reasoning.

25.2. THE SIMPLEST CASES OF FACT-FINDING

In many cases we make a direct appeal to observation: Is the sun shining? Look out of the window and see. Is my fountain pen on my desk? Look and see. Is this piece of sandpaper rougher than that one? Feel them and decide. Is this milk sour? Smell it, taste it, and find out. Various philosophers and psychologists have been concerned to argue that even such relatively "direct" cases of observation are much less direct than we commonly suppose, involving varying amounts of interpretation and inference. Be that as it may, there is no good reason for denying that the simple act of "looking and seeing" is often an adequate means of establishing, beyond reasonable doubt, that such-and-such is the case.

In such relatively simple cases, it would be rather far-fetched to claim that an actual process of inference or reflection is involved. Our responses here have of course been learned, but they proceed for the most part at an habitual, nonreflective level. The details of the process of sense perception are the concern, not of logicians, but of psychologists and physiologists. Our concern as logicians, interested in the principles and problems of factual inquiry, is of a different sort. We want to examine how statements which report observations are justified. We want to note how people defend observation statements when someone challenges them. We want to have a look at the evidence for observation statements.

Suppose, for example, that I point to this object lying here beside my typewriter and say, "This is an apple." Surely it would seem strange to say that I have had to reason this out. If you were to ask me how I know that it is an apple, I might even be inclined to be impatient. "Why," I might reply, "any fool knows it's an apple. Look and see for yourself." At the common-sense level, this would be an appropriate reply. But your question was not intended at this level, and my reply does not satisfy you.

You are asking the question in your role as logician, and you want to know what logical grounds I have for my assertion. While it seems true that I did not have to reason in order to decide that this is an apple, yet it is reasonable to ask how I can defend this claim if it is challenged.

When we examine this matter, what do we find? On what evidence did I base my claim that this was an apple? Simply that it looked like an apple.[1] The maxim to which I would have to appeal to justify my original claim would be something like: If anything looks like an apple, then it is an apple. If you push me a little, I will have to admit that this maxim itself is only fairly probable. But let us grant it for a moment. Granting it, I can validate my observation statement by asserting a substitution instance of the antecedent (see Section 19.6).

> If anything looks like an apple, then it is an apple.
> This looks like an apple.
> ───
> This is an apple.

Does the fact that this conclusion follows necessarily from the premises show that it is itself necessarily true? Or does the syntactical certainty of the argument-form in which it appears show that the conclusion is itself, as a matter of empirical fact, certain? Of course not. A valid conclusion can be no more probable than the premises from which it is derived. It may be claimed that I know the second premise, "This looks like an apple," to be true, since it is immediately certain to me. But I can make no similar claim for the first premise, "If anything looks like an apple, then it is an apple." In fact, I have enough evidence to lead me to doubt that this is true. For I have learned from experience that "looks" are sometimes deceptive. The maxim on which I was drawing admits of some exceptions.

[1] Here we must make an important distinction. The observation statement, "This is an apple," makes a greater claim than the statement "This looks to me like an apple" or "This appears to me to be an apple." For in the case of an observation statement I claim to report how or what something *is*, while in the latter type of case I am merely reporting how something *appears* to me at the moment. This latter type of statement may be called for convenience an APPEARANCE STATEMENT. Unless I am wilfully lying, or do not know what the word "apple" means, it is difficult to see that I could possibly be mistaken in the claim made by such an appearance statement uttered at the time things appeared that way to me. If something looks like an apple to me, then it does look like an apple to me. My appearance statement is for me *immediately certain*. IMMEDIATE CERTAINTY may be defined as follows: the type of certainty possessed by an appearance statement for the person who is making it at the time things appear to him as the statement reports. (For other basic senses of "certainty" see Section 24.2.) Having gratified ourselves by finding a type of empirical statement that is immediately certain, we must now note that such statements are for the most part quite trivial. We need to return to the problem of whether more significant empirical statements, such as *observation statements*, can ever be certain.

Once it occurs to me, for example, that you may have placed a cleverly contrived wax "apple" on my desk for the express purpose of fooling me, I will be willing to modify my maxim. Its application to a given case is only probable. Let me then restate it more cautiously:

If anything looks like an apple then it *probably* is an apple.

Now, however, when I add that this looks like an apple (an appearance statement which asserts a substitution instance of the antecedent), the most I am justified in concluding (by asserting the same instance of the consequent) is, "This *probably* is an apple." In this particular case, you may be willing to agree that the probability is so high that it would be unreasonable to doubt the simpler related statement, "This is an apple." In other words, you may be willing to admit that the probability is high enough to justify proceeding *as if* the statement, "This is an apple," were known to be true. This, of course, is just another way of saying that, on the available evidence, you agree that the statement, "This is an apple," is *practically certain*. But this still falls short of complete certainty.

25.3. HOW THE PROBABILITY OF OBSERVATION STATEMENTS IS INCREASED

We are both, perhaps, thoroughly convinced that this really is an apple. If we push the inquiry further in so simple a case, it will not be so much to reassure us that this is an apple, as it will be to understand more clearly how we can increase the probability of observation statements. The advantage of taking a simple example is considerable, for we can pay attention to the structure of the problem without being distracted by complicated or unfamiliar details.

Let us therefore push our sceptical questioning further. Granted that this looks like an apple, is it really? This question is an appeal for more evidence, and we both know how to proceed.[2] Let's look again.[2a] Let's turn the object around and look at all sides of it.[2b] Let's cut it open and look inside.[2b] If necessary, let's put on our glasses and look again.[2c] Yes, we agree, all these looks are apple-ish.[2d] But we are not through yet. Thus

[2] This simple example illustrates certain general procedures of observational inquiry:
  a. repetition of the observation
  b. extension of the observations
  c. use of instruments to improve or extend powers of unaided sense organs
  d. checking personal perceptions against those of other competent observers.

far we have been limiting our inquiry to a single sense, that of sight. Our folk adage, "Seeing is believing," rightly reflects the priority which most human beings assign to the evidence of sight. Often, such visual evidence is all we need. But let us go further. Let us smell the alleged apple. Yes, it smells like an apple. Let's feel it. Yes, it feels like an apple. Let's eat it. As we bite into it, we hear a pleasant "crunch." Yes, it even sounds like an apple. And now, as we savor the object, we agree that it also tastes like an apple. Here, with the core before us, we come to the end of our observational inquiry. "If this isn't an apple," we say, "I'll eat my hat."

It is now time to turn our attention from the apple to the logic of the situation. It is clear that our rigorous inquiry has amassed overwhelming evidence. The probability of our original observation statement has been increased to the point where, from any common-sense point of view, we should maintain that the statement is not merely "highly probable" but certain. Many epistemologists have held that such an empirical statement can never be completely certain, and that all knowledge derived from experience is at best only highly probable.

In terms of the logical structure of our inquiry, this is what has been happening: We have been progressively replacing our original empirical maxim, "If anything looks like an apple, then it probably is an apple," by maxims of increasingly higher probability. We might briefly indicate some of these in the order in which we drew upon them: [3]

> If anything keeps looking like an apple, then it probably is an apple.
>
> If anything both keeps looking like an apple and also smells like an apple, then it more probably is an apple.
>
> If anything keeps looking like an apple, smells like an apple, and feels like an apple, then it very probably is an apple.
>
> If anything keeps looking like an apple, smells like an apple, feels like an apple, sounds like an apple, and tastes like an apple, then it most probably (almost certainly) is an apple.

It is clear that if we take this last statement as one premise, we may add to it a premise summarizing our appearance statements about the alleged apple:

[3] This example is a good illustration of the PRINCIPLE OF CONVERGENCE. A statement becomes increasingly probable as varied lines of evidence all turn out to support it.

This does keep looking like an apple, smells, feels, sounds, and tastes like an apple.

We thus conclude validly:

This almost certainly is an apple.

25.4. FEW, IF ANY, OF OUR EMPIRICAL ASSERTIONS ARE COMPLETELY CERTAIN

We have been purposely singling out a relatively simple type of empirical statement, namely one which reports an observation. We have seen that even in such cases, there may be reasons for calling such statements into question. We can scarcely claim that even such statements are completely certain.

Once we have left such simple cases, the claim to more than practical certainty is even less plausible. By far the greater number of our empirical assertions are at best only probable. But this "best" is, as experience shows, often adequate for our needs. The purpose of urging, as we have, that our knowledge of empirical facts involves probability is not to argue that such knowledge is unsound, but rather to remind us that such knowledge is always open to correction and improvement in the light of further experience. Our analysis in this chapter should help us understand what Ernest Nagel meant when he wrote that "conclusions of factual inquiry are not in principle incorrigible, because the formal conditions for assuring the logical validity of those conclusions are not completely realized, and because statements having factual content are not logically necessary." [4] Many empirical assertions are so highly probable that it would be unreasonable to doubt them. Even when the probabilities are less overwhelming, it is reasonable, when action is needed, to act upon the highest probabilities available at the time.

These considerations have an important bearing on the whole problem of ascertaining the facts. Finding out what's what involves an appeal to experience, and such appeals result in general only in the establishment of what is probably the case. In these terms, the aim of empirical inquiry is to increase the probability to the point where it is fully adequate to our needs and purposes. This is an aim which it is often possible to achieve

[4] Ernest Nagel, *op. cit.*, p. 5.

in spite of our human limitations. One of the main values we may hope to get from a study of empirics is a clearer understanding of the principles and methods by which the probability of empirical statements may be increased to the point of adequacy.

• SOME REMINDERS

1. Our analysis has not been aimed at showing that, in deciding that something is an apple, we actually go through the process of inference here set forth. Our perceptual responses are, in simple cases, habitual and nonreflective.
2. The analysis rather explores the manner in which an observation statement may be justified if it is called into question.
3. The analysis has set forth the logical structure of this justification, showing it to be a case of a general conditional argument, proceeding validly by asserting a substitution instance of the antecedent.
4. The probability of an observation statement is increased by amassing further empirical evidence by means of the same and different senses.
5. These additional items of evidence are all substitution instances falling under empirical generalizations of increasingly high probability.
6. Our example illustrates the Principle of Convergence.
7. Although most of our empirical statements are only highly probable, this probability is often high enough to justify acting upon it.
8. Empirics seeks a clearer understanding of the principles and methods by which our factual knowledge becomes adequate for our needs and purposes.

APPLICATIONS

1. In each case, indicate whether you believe the statement to be psychologically certain, practically certain, completely certain, syntactically certain, immediately certain, or not certain in any of these senses. Give reasons for your answers. In the following, "I" means you, the person reading these words.
   a. A straight line is the shortest distance between two points.
   b. I am now seeing black marks on a white background.
   c. I am over ten years old.
   d. There is someone here in the room with me.
   e. My mother is older than I am.
   f. God exists.
   g. When I shut my eyes, the book before me no longer exists.

   h. All square objects are either round or square.
   i. I am now sitting on a chair.
   j. If I jump on the floor, it will not collapse.
2. List as many types of significant factor as you can which help account for the fact that people differ in what they observe in a given situation.
3. Why does a scientist typically average a set of measurements rather than take just one?
4. To what extent and in what ways does a clearly conceived purpose (a) make for more thorough and accurate observations? (b) introduce elements which may distort or hinder observations?
5. What problems and limitations of observation are suggested by the following?
   a. Six persons were called before an investigating panel of the Civil Aeronautics Board as eyewitnesses to the crash of a commercial airliner in a residential district. One witness reported that, prior to the crash, the plane had been flying level, but then had nosed down. Another, who had been about the same distance away but was viewing the plane from a different angle, thought that the plane was flying on a level as it crashed into a house below the second floor. A third witness reported that the plane had nosed up just before the crash and had then dived down into the house. Still another witness declared that the landing wheels had been down at the time of the crash, while another, who claimed he had a clear view of the belly of the plane, asserted that the wheels were not down. (Data from *New York Times,* March 5, 1952)
   b. "Astronomers in seeking to build ever greater precision into their instruments were warned by certain curious incidents that the limiting factor was the uncertainty of the human observer. One standard observation in which great precision is desirable is that of timing the transit of a star across the meridian of a given observatory. The telescope is pointed straight north or south (at the necessary elevation); the star enters the field and passes over a grid of vertical hair lines, the middle line being the exact meridian. At what exact time does the star pass this middle line?

   "An old standard procedure is the 'eye and ear method.' The observer first reads the time to the second from his clock and counts additional seconds by listening to the strokes of the pendulum. He notes the exact position of the star at the stroke just before and at the stroke just after it crosses the meridian. From these two positions he computes the time of transit to the tenth of a second.

   "The first indication of unreliability in this method came in 1795 when Maskelyne, head of the Greenwich observatory, discharged an otherwise capable assistant because of a habit of recording all transits about half a second too late. The only way the chief had of estimating the error of his assistant was by comparison with his own observations which he naturally assumed to be correct. A note of these facts in the Greenwich observatory report caught the attention of the German astronomer, Bessel, some decades later, and led him to test astronomers against each other, with the result that no two agreed precisely on the time of a given transit. Usually the difference between two skilled observers was well under a second. It seemed at first to be a constant difference between any two specified individuals, so that their observations could be harmonized by use of a constant correction or 'personal equation,' such as Jones — Smith = 0.35 sec. Further investigation showed that it was by no means constant. It varied with the magnitude of the star and with its rate of movement across the telescope field, and its constancy as between two observers was only temporary." (Robert S. Woodworth: *Experimental Psychology*, New York, Henry Holt and Company, 1938, p. 300)

c. "Somewhere on this planet there was an earthquake shortly after 5 A.M. yesterday. Of this much the staff of the new seismograph at City College is certain.

"Because of 'lack of operational experience,' Prof. Daniel T. O'Connell, chairman of the department of geology, explained, it was 'impossible to make even an approximate estimate of where the earthquake took place.'

"At Fordham University, veteran quake-recorders issued the following bulletin: 'An earthquake of medium intensity, 3,850 miles from New York, in a southerly direction and probably in Peru, was recorded on the Fordham seismograph at 5:32 A.M., New York time.'" (*New York Times*, May 12, 1948)

CHAPTER 26

FINDING THE FACTS BY REASONING FROM EXPERIENCE

PREVIEW

In the preceding chapter, we considered simple cases of fact-finding by observation, where little or no explicit inference was involved. Reasoning entered only when we were called upon to substantiate our observations, or to consider what grounds might be brought forth to make an observation report more probable. We now turn to consider cases where inference is involved in the very process of determining what the facts are. We discover many facts, not by direct observation, but by reasoning from our previous knowledge and from data supplied by observation. In the present chapter we shall distinguish different types of argument by which we reason from experience to determine further facts and probabilities. We shall then note the typical stages through which an empirical inquiry of the problem-solving variety proceeds to a solution.

26.1. DETERMINING THE FACTS OFTEN INVOLVES EXPLICIT INFERENCE

In the type of case thus far considered, finding out what's what is a relatively direct matter, involving observation but no explicit process of inference. Inference comes into the picture in such a case only when we are challenged as to the grounds for our observation statement. I look at something, find that it looks like an apple, and report: "This is an apple." In so far as no one challenges me, and in so far as further experiences with the object sustain my original report, I have no occasion to reflect or reason about the matter. Our analysis has shown, not that such observation statements are groundless, but rather that we ordinarily have no need to think about these grounds or to make them explicit.

Many cases of fact-finding are much more complex. While they, too, involve an appeal to observation somewhere along the line, the inferential aspect bulks larger. Consider, for example, even so relatively simple a matter as the rotundity of the earth. The fact that the earth is round is not one that can be determined by observation alone. Our usual unreflecting acceptance of its rotundity rests, not on the fact that we have directly perceived that the earth is round, but rather upon the fact that we are willing to accept the reasoning of previous thinkers and investigators who have looked into the matter.

26.2. VALID DEDUCTION
NOT THE ONLY TYPE OF SOUND ARGUMENT

The statemental expression of a process of inference is, as we know, an *argument*. At the outset of our discussion of syntactics, we noted briefly that not all sound arguments are conclusive. We saw that some perfectly good arguments, such as that of the butter inspector who certified a carload of butter on the basis of inspecting a sample of it, do not even aim at validity, but are concerned with establishing the probability of a conclusion on the basis of given evidence.

The type of inference involved in a deductive argument (such as those we studied in Part II) is sometimes called *necessary inference*. This label reminds us that, in a sound (i.e. valid) deductive argument, if the premises are true, the conclusion *must* also be true. To accept the premises of a valid argument as true, but to reject the conclusion as false, is to contradict oneself. In contrast, the type of inference involved in nondeductive arguments may be called *probable inference*, in the sense that, even in a sound nondeductive argument, the truth of the premises does no more than establish a probability that the conclusion is also true.

It is difficult for the beginning student to avoid the feeling that there is something inferior or defective about nondeductive arguments. He tends to contrast unfavorably the probability of a nondeductive conclusion with the necessity of a valid deductive conclusion.

One source of this common feeling that nondeductive arguments are inferior to deductive ones lies in a confusion between the *necessity* of a deductive conclusion and its factual *truth*. To say that the conclusion of a valid argument is necessary is only to say that it is strictly implied by the premises, so that *if* the premises are true, the conclusion will be true also. But the validity of the argument does not, of course, establish by itself that the conclusion is true, any more than it establishes that the premises are true. Some of the premises can be false and the corresponding conclusion true or false without impugning the validity of the argument. (Recall the examples given in Section 7.4.) If one asserts that the premises are true, one must then on logical grounds assert that the conclusion is true, but no more certainty of truth is inherent in the conclusion as a statement than inheres in the statements from which it was validly deduced.

If we could know with complete certainty that the premises of a given valid argument were true, then we would also be in a position to know with complete certainty that the conclusion was true. But when we are dealing with empirical matters, such premises are usually known, at best, only to be probably true. This fact is often concealed by our practice of asserting premises dogmatically and without qualification, as if they were known with complete certainty to be true. Actually, we often do not even really know that they are more probable than not.

Such considerations help us to see that the mere fact that the conclusion of a nondeductive argument is only probable, does not make such a conclusion inferior to those of typical deductive arguments concerning empirical matters.

In fact, one may urge that a deductive argument by itself is not a very serviceable device for fact-finding or establishing new empirical truths. Its utility is plain where one wishes to exhibit the logical consequences of some empirical hypothesis, or to demonstrate rigorously how some fact may confute some hypothesis. But the formally required relationship between the content of the conclusion and the content of the premises of a valid argument eliminates the possibility of there being factual information in the conclusion that was not already at least implicitly present in the premises.

If we are to expand our knowledge of the world of empirical fact, we must also expand our modes of reasoning beyond deduction. Much of our best attested knowledge, namely that to be found in the natural sciences, has been established in large part by nondeductive procedures.

26.3. TYPES OF ARGUMENT ESTABLISHING WHAT IS PROBABLY THE CASE

Our preceding discussion has given us a basis for understanding the extent to which factual inquiry involves the determination of probabilities. We want now to make a preliminary survey of four different types of argument, commonly used in empirical inquiry, that aim at the establishment of factual probabilities. These four types are: (1) analogy, (2) inductive argument, (3) diagnosis, and (4) deductive argument involving probability. In later chapters, we shall analyze such arguments more fully and shall consider the principles and special problems involved in each of them.

For our first look at these types of argument, we want some specimen examples that will be as simple as possible in form. It will also be advantageous to keep their content as similar as possible. To achieve both simplicity of form and similarity of content unfortunately involves sacrificing strength in some of the arguments. But we shall have ample opportunity later to see the difference between weak and strong arguments of these various types.

Suppose that by "chicken eggs" we mean merely the ovoid objects produced by certain chickens. I say "merely" because we want here to block out a problem for inquiry, not to assume that we have already solved it. Now assume that we have a good supply of two things: eggs and curiosity. We break open one chicken egg and observe that it contains, among other things, a globular yellowish object, which we shall name a "yolk." Remember, this is *all* we know about chicken eggs up to this point:

1. Chicken eggs exist.
2. Here are some chicken eggs.
3. Object A is a chicken egg, and it contains a yolk.[1]

Now let us proceed to inquire further:

Argument from Analogy
 Object A is a chicken egg, and it contains a yolk.
 Object B is also a chicken egg.
 --[2]
 Object B contains a yolk.

[1] I find that I have picked up this example of an egg having a yolk from Max Black. He mentions the analogical conclusion, "This egg, like the last, will have a yolk" and the generalization that all eggs have yolks, but does not develop the example further. See Max Black, *op. cit.*, p. 321.
[2] The relation between premises (or evidence statements) and conclusion in the first three types of argument we shall now consider is not deductive. The arguments, even if sound, are not such that the evidence guarantees the conclusion; the conclusion might be false even if the premises were true. The relation between them is not "therefore." We indicate this difference by using a broken line in such cases (to be read: "So probably") instead of the solid line used for deductive arguments.

In this argument, on the basis of a *known* similarity between two objects, and a known further characteristic of one of the objects, I conclude that probably the other object will possess this characteristic too. Note that this conclusion may be viewed as a *prediction* based on the evidence provided by a single similar case. If this is really all we have to go on, it should be clear that the inference is a precarious one, even though Object B, when opened, turns out to contain a yolk too. When we observe that it does, the prediction is said to be verified. Not all arguments from analogy, of course, are as precarious as this one. We shall later want to consider more fully just what makes the difference. At present, let us note merely one factor.

Suppose I find upon investigation that not only Eggs A and B contain yolks, but also the next two eggs I open. Suppose I then argue about a fifth Object E:

> Object A is a chicken egg, and it contains a yolk.
> Object B is a chicken egg, and it contains a yolk.
> Object C is a chicken egg, and it contains a yolk.
> Object D is a chicken egg, and it contains a yolk.
> Object E is a chicken egg.
> --
> Object E contains a yolk.

This too is an analogical argument of the type called *compound,* but you will have no hesitation in recognizing it as a stronger argument than the preceding one (called a *simple analogy*). Explain what makes the difference in strength.

When I break open Object E and find that it really does contain a yolk, I may feel that I am beginning to get the idea. So I proceed next time to reason, not to a *singular* conclusion about an as-yet-unexamined Egg F, but to a *universal* conclusion about chicken eggs in general, that is to a *generalization.*

> *Inductive Argument*
> Object A is a chicken egg, and it contains a yolk.
> Object B is a chicken egg, and it contains a yolk.
> Object C is a chicken egg, and it contains a yolk.
> Object D is a chicken egg, and it contains a yolk.
> Object E is a chicken egg, and it contains a yolk.
> --
> If any object is a chicken egg, then it contains a yolk.

This probable conclusion might, of course, have been expressed in terms of the equivalent A-statement: "All chicken eggs contain a yolk." Note also that I might have shifted to this generalized type of conclusion earlier, say, after having examined only Egg A. In that case, the argument would still have been inductive in form, but we would have no hesitation in labeling the conclusion a RASH GENERALIZATION. What is the difference between these two cases? Why is the conclusion rash in the one case and fairly reasonable in the other? The obvious answer is that in the one case the sample upon which we base our conclusion consists of a single item, while in the other it consists of several. As we shall see in more detail later on, size of sample is one of several factors which determine the probability of an induction.[3]

Now, suppose that in the light of considerable experience, I regard the generalization as pretty well established. I might then use it as a premise for an argument of a quite different type:

> *Diagnosis*
> If an object is a chicken egg, then it contains a yolk.
> Object X contains a yolk.
> --
> Object X is a chicken egg.

The singular premise of a diagnosis always states a possible *symptom* (see Section 2.2) though not necessarily a reliable one. As in the analogical and inductive arguments above, the truth of the conclusion is not guaranteed, even if the premises are known to be true. In the present example, Object X might actually be a goose egg or a mixing bowl. Yet the premises do provide evidence that lends some probability (in this case, perhaps rather slight) to the conclusion. If we mistakenly regarded this argument as a case of deduction, we should have to classify it as invalid and as a case of the fallacy of asserting a substitution instance of the consequent. But this is not intended as a deductive argument, and it is not claimed that the conclusion is dictated, but only rendered somewhat probable, by the premises. The argument is of the same general pattern

---

[3] By a SAMPLE we shall mean a subgroup of members (one or more *but not all*) of a given reference class. A sample is what mathematicians call a PROPER PART of a class, that is, a part which is less than the whole. This usage will stress the fact that an inductive conclusion in an important sense always *goes beyond* the evidence. An inductive argument always proceeds from the known constitution of a sample to the probable constitution of the class from which the sample was taken.

as the one by which a physician decides that someone has appendicitis on the basis of abdominal pain and a high white-corpuscle count. We shall later want to explore why some diagnoses are so much more probable than others.

Before considering the fourth type of argument by which we seek to establish what is probably the case, let us look once more at the general conditional premise of our diagnosis. As it stands, it is stated dogmatically, as if it were known to be true. On the available evidence, of course, this premise is known only to be probably true. It would have been more accurately expressed in the form:

> If any object is a chicken egg, then it probably contains a yolk.

It is clear that this introduces a second source of probability in the diagnostic conclusion. Our conclusion is at best only probably true, for two different reasons: (1) the argument has the *form* of a diagnosis, and (2) at least one of the premises is only probably true. In presenting this example in the first place, I purposely omitted this complication. It was important to emphasize first of all that the conclusion of a diagnostic argument would be only probable *even if* the premises were known with complete certainty to be true.

Let us now take this probable general conditional premise and use it in another type of argument, the form of which is already familiar to us:

> *Deductive Argument of Probability*
> If any object is a chicken egg, then it probably contains a yolk.
> Object Y is a chicken egg.   ₄
> ───
> Object Y probably contains a yolk.

This argument is, of course, a valid deduction which proceeds in the atomic premise by asserting a substitution instance of the antecedent. The conclusion validly asserts a substitution instance of the consequent. Here the "probably" of the conclusion derives not from the *form* of the argument, but solely from the fact that at least one of the premises is only probably true. In this important respect it differs from the diagnostic argument just considered. Apart from this point, the deductive argument

---

₄ Here, for obvious reasons, we return to the use of a solid line, read "therefore," to separate premises from conclusion.

calls for no special comment, for our study of syntactics dealt extensively with deductive arguments, and we are by this time well acquainted with their nature. The deductive argument of probability is here included to remind us that (1) a deductive conclusion may be a conclusion of probability, in fact most that we use in actual reasoning are, although our dogmatic way of asserting premises obscures this fact; (2) we can extend our empirical knowledge by deducing the consequences of factual information in our possession; [5] in the present case, we learned through deduction that the object before us probably contains a yolk.

There are, then, four basic patterns by which we reason from experience to what is probably the case: analogy, induction, diagnosis, and deduction of probability. Analogy will be analyzed more fully in Chapter 30, diagnosis in Chapter 27, and induction in Chapters 28 and 29.

26.4. TYPICAL STAGES OF AN EMPIRICAL INQUIRY

An awareness of the four types of argument outlined in the preceding section is one valuable aid to understanding the logic of fact-finding. Another is a sense of the various stages through which a typical problem-solving inquiry proceeds to a solution. Let us consider a concrete case of problem solving at the common-sense level. The problem happens to be a diagnostic one, but the general phases which the inquiry reveals are characteristic of most empirical investigations.

I woke up one winter morning not long ago to find the house abnormally cold. What could be wrong? Here, in contrast to some problems we face, was one that had immediate practical bearing. It was not the type of problem about which one can suspend judgment, waiting to see what will turn up. As husband, father, and superintendent of buildings and grounds, I had to do something about it. But what had happened?

My previous experience and general knowledge were adequate to suggest readily a number of possibilities or hypotheses. A HYPOTHESIS is a suggestion which offers a possible answer to a question or solution of a problem. Perhaps the oil burner had gone off. If so, why? Was there (as had happened once before) an air lock in the supply line, so that oil

[5] This is not to overlook the fact, noted in the preceding section, that the conclusion of a valid argument can contain no more information than was already implicit in the premises. But deduction may add to our actual knowledge by drawing out implications of which we might otherwise have been unaware.

could not get to the burner? Had the electrical power failed, so that the whole mechanism had shut off? Or, to take another tack, was the difficulty not in the furnace at all? Had there been a sharp drop in outside temperature? If so, was the difficulty merely that I had perhaps opened the windows too wide last night? Or had I sleepily turned down the thermostat too far? You see, I was full of hypotheses. In the light of previous experience and knowledge, they occurred to me rapidly as I shivered into my clothes. We are not always this fortunate. Often, in both scientific and common-sense inquiry, the hardest part of all is to find even one hypothesis that seems adequate to account for the difficulty. In general, the more background knowledge and experience we have, and the more the present problem resembles others we have solved, the easier it is to think of relevant hypotheses.

It was easy to check up on some of the hypotheses at once, and to narrow the field for investigation. A flick of the light switch assured me that the current was on. A glance at the narrowly opened windows as I shut them tight made it seem quite unlikely that I had merely opened them too wide the night before. I held my hand to the nearest register and found that no heat was coming out, and the metal of the register was cool to the touch. Apparently the furnace had gone off. I walked to the kitchen, on the way to the basement, glancing at the thermostat as I passed. It was set at 63°, its usual nighttime setting, but the attached thermometer read only 48°. I shoved the thermostat up to 70°. As I passed the kitchen register, which is located not far from the furnace, I thought I heard something. Yes, it was the characteristic whirr of the burner. Had it just gone on, or had I been too far away back in the bedroom to hear it before? I felt the kitchen register. Yes, a certain amount of warm air was coming out, though it seemed there should have been more. Perhaps (as had happened once before) the electrical contacts on the thermostat were dusty, so that it was not working right. Perhaps my just shoving the thermostat up to 70° had made an adequate contact, so that everything would now be all right. I went back to the bedroom to reassure my wife. But when I felt the bedroom register, it was as cold as ever. This was strange, since I had felt heat coming out of the kitchen register. Then a sudden idea hit me, that seemed to make sense of everything. The blower! Perhaps there was something wrong with the blower! If so, this in itself would account for the house being cold, even though the burner was operating. A certain amount of heat would probably rise through the kitchen register, which was near the furnace, even though the blower was not on. But no heat would be pushed down to the other end of the house, where the bedroom was. If I was right, there wouldn't need to have been anything the matter with the thermostat after all. I rushed down to the basement, removed the door on the blower, and sure enough: the blower motor was running at full speed, but the pulley on the blower fan was slipping, so that the fan itself stood motionless. A moment's work with a wrench, and the problem was solved.

This Case of the Cold House, which we shall analyze more fully in the following chapter, illustrates the typical stages of an empirical inquiry. Let us at present simply call attention to the general pattern which it reveals. You will find a knowledge of this pattern useful in analyzing a wide variety of cases.

Typical Pattern of a Factual Inquiry:
1. Awareness of a difficulty
2. Clarification and formulation of the difficulty through observation and use of previous knowledge
3. Formulation of hypotheses and supporting assumptions
4. Derivation of the consequences
5. Testing of the consequences through observation or experimentation
6. Resulting confirmation or confutation of the hypothesis

This general pattern of empirical inquiry is what some writers have in mind when they speak of "the scientific method." This label, if used, must not be taken in an exclusive sense, for the pattern is characteristic of intelligent problem-solving inquiry wherever it occurs. This does not mean that the pattern is inviolable or that the order of the "steps" is rigidly fixed. At any point we may find it necessary, for example, to make further observations. Again, hypotheses do not occur to us at any fixed stage that can be numbered "3." In general, some at least vague hypothesis is present from the start, else we should not know what observations might be worth making. Also, in simple inquiries, we may not consciously derive the consequences, but merely "look and see." Or again, some of the steps may be absent in a given case because we have become tired and given up, or have switched our interest to something else.

• SOME REMINDERS

1. Many cases of fact-finding require explicit inference.
2. Necessary inferences are to be distinguished from probable inferences. Our common feeling that there is something inferior about probable inferences may rest in part upon a confusion between logical necessity and factual truth.
3. Probabilities may be established by analogy, by induction, by diagnosis, and by deduction.
4. Six "steps" may be distinguished in a typical factual inquiry. These steps indicate a general pattern or rationale, but they are not inviolate, their order is not rigidly fixed, and in simple inquiries, certain steps may not be explicit.
5. In unfamiliar cases, where our background knowledge is limited, discovery of a plausible hypothesis may be the most difficult part of an inquiry. In other cases, where our background knowledge and previous experience are considerable, many hypotheses may be available at once.

APPLICATIONS

1. In each case, determine whether the line of reasoning is deductive, inductive, diagnostic, or analogical. Justify your answers, for some cases may be interpreted in more than one way.
   a. I doubt that any cows are purple, because although I've seen a lot of cows, none of them was purple.
   b. Margaret is a freshman, for no one who had been here longer could be so ignorant of campus traditions.
   c. There will be a game tomorrow, because there is to be a pep rally this evening.
   d. Bill has given up smoking because the doctor told him that smoking was bad for one's health.
   e. Janet and Grace are probably twins; they look so much alike.
   f. I'll bet Janet is a good dancer, because Grace is, and they're twins, you know.
   g. Agnes will probably fail the course because she hasn't cracked a book yet.
   h. A fellow with lots of meat on him makes the best center on a football team. Just think of all the great centers of the past.
   i. There can't be any animal life on the moon, because there is no oxygen there.
   j. Since living animals on earth require oxygen, it is reasonable to suppose that living animals on the moon would require it too.
2. Select a recent personal example of problem-solving inquiry, and analyze it in terms of the general pattern described in Section 26.4.

3. Analyze each of the following accounts to show which stage or stages of problem-solving inquiry are exhibited.

   a. "Tooth decay can be caused by the action of bacteria within a tooth as well as by acid attack on the enamel surface, a New York City research doctor said today.

   "Dr. William Lefkowitz based his assertion on a continuing study at Montefiore Hospital, where he is a research associate. He spoke at the annual meeting of the Dental Society of the State of New York.

   "In the past, the general belief was that tooth decay always was caused by an acid attack. But, said Dr. Lefkowitz, the new studies revealed decay despite an alkaline mouth condition that resisted acid attack. The bacterial attack, he said, destroyed the substance that holds a tooth's enamel rods together.

   "The fact that teeth decay most in childhood, when the enamel is alkaline, suggests that acid is not the sole cause of decay, Dr. Lefkowitz said. That is supported, he added, by the discovery that in adults tooth enamel is slightly acid, yet tooth decay is less severe than in children." (*New York Times*, May 10, 1951)

   b. "Scientists have long disagreed whether the mysterious way bees tell time, as indicated in the clocklike regularity by which they can be trained to leave hives for food, depends on an inner time signal or outer influence. Tests had ruled out all outer factors but one: the influence of celestial changes resulting from the 24-hour turning of the earth.

   "Dr. Renner meant to shift the bees suddenly to a new time zone, in effect partly canceling the earth's rotation. After feeding the bees in Paris he rushed them to New York for the next meal. Then he wanted to see if the five hours' difference would affect the bees' sense of time . . . The bees stuck to their old schedule, proving to Dr. Renner's satisfaction that a bee's feeding habits are prompted from within." (LIFE, July 11, 1955. Excerpted by permission from LIFE Magazine, (c) TIME, Inc. 1955)

   c. "I met Gavin and Alan as arranged, and we made our usual journey along Whitehall to the Abbey. It was now certain that if we were to be successful [in stealing the Stone of Scone], we should have to break in from the outside. We marshalled the facts that we knew. Firstly, the door to the Poet's Corner, the most secluded door to the Abbey, was of pine and could possibly be forced. Secondly, there was at least one watchman inside, and if the information given to me when I was captured on Saturday night were correct he kept up a patrol all night and could reasonably be expected to hear the noise we made forcing the door.

   "These were the relevant facts. The rest was a matter of deduction. None of us could really believe that a watchman, unsupervised as he would necessarily be, would pad continuously about the dim corridors of the Abbey. Knowing what we did about human nature, we were certain that the most he could be expected to do was to patrol at regular intervals, and whether or not he did this would be a matter for his own diligence. For my own part, I could not see him doing his rounds oftener than every two hours." (Ian R. Hamilton: *No Stone Unturned, The Story of the Stone of Destiny,* New York, Funk & Wagnalls Company, 1952, p. 70)

d. "When his young son was afflicted with asthma four years ago, Dr. [Ernesto] Escudero [a chest surgeon of Buenos Aires], to whom the subject had been only professional until then, began an intensive study of the disease and its treatments. He had tried the conventional treatments of altitude, airplane flights, tests for allergies and others. He knew how often they brought little or no relief.

"The doctor remembered that in all chest operations on asthmatic patients he had noted that the upper part of the lung showed a lack of blood. Perhaps that was one of the causes of asthma, he reasoned. Instead of being starved for air, the sufferer perhaps was being smothered by an excess; he was not breathing properly.

"While continuing the traditional treatments on his small son, Dr. Escudero began experimenting with his new theory. Instead of propping the boy on pillows at night, so that the struggle for breath might be easier, he had him lie flat on his stomach. He started to walk him around in the old game of human wheelbarrow, holding the boy's legs high in the air while the youngster walked on his hands.

". . . He told the boy to lie down for several minutes each morning, half in [and half] out of bed, with his head cradled on his arms on the floor. He had the youngster change his normal breathing habits and inhale in short gasps, instead of deeply and slowly. An almost immediate and radical improvement was noted. Today, the doctor's son has been free of all asthmatic symptoms for more than three years.

"Since his first experiments with these revolutionary treatments, Dr. Escudero has had more than 400 asthmatic patients. Some of them were extreme cases that other doctors had given up as hopeless. He has not had complete cures in all cases. Where tissue already was destroyed his treatments did not help. But those who faithfully followed his advice were helped. Children especially responded almost instantly to his treatment." (Foster Hailey in *New York Times,* January 1, 1952)

e. "During the past few years, the sale of raw popcorn has skyrocketed 500%. Leaving no stone unturned to find out why, the National Association of Popcorn Manufacturers sent pollsters to question 200 families living in & around Chicago. Last week they had their answer: television. Of TV-owners, 4% eat hot, buttered, homemade popcorn every single night of the week. Another 10% eat it five or six nights a week; 63% indulge one to four nights a week." (*Time,* November 13, 1951, p. 85)

f. A form of yellow fever called "jungle yellow fever," which occurs in certain regions of South and Central America, strikes newly married men more frequently than any other group. Why should this be so? It was discovered that howler monkeys were also frequent victims. These monkeys live in the tree tops. This in itself seemed to throw no light on the high incidence of the fever among men who had recently been married. It was found that the disease was transmitted by a certain mosquito which also frequented the tree tops, but this still did not seem to solve the problem. Then it was remarked that among the first things a bridegroom of the region would do was to clear an area of the jungle for his new home. Felling the trees brought the mosquitoes to earth, and they bit the first person they met. (Data from *New York Times,* June 8, 1955)

g. "A black and white chow-and-police dog named Jackie did everything but take the witness stand yesterday in Mid-Manhattan Court in its efforts to testify against one of two persons who claimed to own it.

"The dog arrived in court with Jose Rodriquez . . . and his 13-year-old stepdaughter Zoraida Santini. But Mrs. Inocencia Feliciano said that Jackie had been stolen from her two weeks ago by Mr. Rodriquez, who used to be the superintendent in the building . . . where she lives and operates a grocery store. . . .

"Mrs. Feliciano showed the magistrate a dog license dated last October, listing Jackie's name and description.

"Mr. Rodriquez insisted he, too, had a license for Jackie, only he did not have it with him. He said he was an automobile mechanic and had taken the dog two and one-half years ago in return for a $100 repair job for a man who was unable to pay him.

"Magistrate Andrews . . . told Mrs. Feliciano to go to one wall of the courtroom and Mr. Rodriquez to go to the opposite wall. He instructed the 13-year-old Zoraida to unleash the dog and told Mrs. Feliciano to call it to her.

"The animal leaped to her and for more than a minute licked her hands and snuggled against her.

"It was Mr. Rodriquez' turn.

"The dog headed across the courtroom. But he ran right past Mr. Rodriquez and out the door into the corridor.

" 'I haven't the slightest doubt the woman owns the dog,' Magistrate Andrews said. . . ." (*New York Times,* January 10, 1952)

h. "Two supersonic pilots have demonstrated how the 'mystery explosions' which jolted Los Angeles were caused.

"The Los Angeles area, about 100 miles south of this base, was aroused three times during the weekend and early this week by blasts accompanied by a rumbling roar.

"Jet propulsion experts said that shocks were caused when power-diving supersonic planes set up waves in the air.

"Maj. Pete Everest and Lieut. Col. F. J. Ascani showed yesterday how it was done by diving at speeds faster than 660 miles per hour. About twenty-five seconds after each pilot pulled out of his dives below 30,000 feet the air base was shaken by blast-like detonations. Together they made six dives." (*New York Times,* January 13, 1951)

i. "With tongue-in-cheek, a scientific laboratory has offered a somewhat dubious explanation of the barley and corn that rained upon the Empire State Building Tower, and upon no other place, last August. The answer —pigeons, simply pigeons. . . .

"According to the publication, the 'Wallerstein Laboratories Communications,' chemists and assistants in their office, a few hundred feet from the world's tallest structure, are kindly disposed toward pigeons.

"Accordingly, they scatter on the sills of their windows the many samples of barley malt, corn and other grains that come to them for analysis. However, the pigeons are foresighted and do not eat this food. Instead they carry it to the Empire State Tower, where it is put by for difficult times. . . ." (*New York Times,* April 16, 1951)

j. "British scientists are engaging in a controversy over what makes a star appear to twinkle. . . .

"British ophthalmologists H. Hartridge and R. Weale started the controversy by reporting that their experiments showed minute movements in the eye gave rise to the twinkling effect. Neither bright nor very dim lights seem to twinkle, they said, but lights of in-between strength would hit a few of the little rods and cones which receive light impressions in the eye. As the eye moves ever so slightly, the light hits first one cone and then the other, thus making it appear to twinkle.

"In the *Nature* [British scientific journal] article, three astronomers take issue with the two eye men. One of them, C. C. L. Gregory of the University of London Observatory, points out that star twinkle diminishes when the atmosphere is calm and gets worse when hot and cold air currents are acting up.

"An American ophthalmologist, who refused to allow his name to be used, said that both sides in the British star-twinkle controversy were probably right. 'Either the optical effects of the air currents or what happens to a light image inside the eye, or both of them together, might cause a star to appear to twinkle,' he said. 'And I'm rather sure that neither side will ever prove its case.'" (*Science News Letter,* March 4, 1950, p. 137)

CHAPTER 27

ESTABLISHING A SPECIFIC FACT
BY DIAGNOSIS

PREVIEW

In the preceding chapter, we briefly examined the Case of the Cold House as an illustration of the general pattern of empirical inquiry. Now we shall submit this example to a more extended analysis, both to explore certain aspects of this pattern more fully and also to get at the specific nature of a diagnosis. Through such reflective study of concrete examples, you will get a more intimate insight into empirical inquiry than is possible from reading a generalized account. Pay particular attention to the central role which hypotheses play in inquiry, and to the uses of deductive reasoning in an empirical investigation.

27.1. ANTECEDENT PROBABILITY OF A HYPOTHESIS

As we begin a more detailed analysis of the Case of the Cold House set forth in the last chapter, let us recall the situation as it was at the start of the inquiry. At the outset, the only specific evidence at hand was that the house was cold. Any of a considerable number of rival hypotheses could account for this. This does not mean, though, that even at the start of our inquiry all rival hypotheses were *equally* probable. For in addition to the specific knowledge that the house was cold, we also had on hand considerable background knowledge of a more general sort. This is a point that is easily overlooked. That we were drawing upon such background knowledge seems clear from our very choice of hypotheses that seemed worth investigating.

It did not occur to us, for example, that the house might be cold because the oil had frozen and could not flow from the tank to the furnace. Nor did we stop to consider that an army of mice might have clogged up all the registers by building nests in them during the night. Either of these hypotheses would adequately account for the house being cold. The point is not that I was too sleepy or too lacking in ingenuity to think of them, nor that I just hadn't thought about the problem long enough and intensively enough to have these hypotheses occur to me. My background knowledge of the behavior of oil and of mice, even though this knowledge was not brought to the focus of attention, was sufficient to predispose me against considering either of these hypotheses. To summarize in slightly more technical language: in the light of my background knowledge, the *antecedent probability* of these two hypotheses was so low that they did not even occur to me, in fact *should* not have occurred to me, and would not have been worth considering at the time even if I had thought of them.[1] Don't forget, though, that an antecedently improbable hypothesis may become highly probable if the right kind of evidence turns up in the course of the investigation. Remember also that an antecedently improbable hypothesis, which in the light of previous knowledge doesn't even seem worth investigating, may none the less be true.

Even among the significant hypotheses that did occur to me, there were differences in antecedent probability. It was not, for example, antecedently very probable that the tank was empty. I did let it get empty once, but since then I have been smart enough to measure its contents more frequently. Similarly, it was not antecedently highly probable that the electrical supply had failed, though this has been known to happen on infrequent occasions.

You might suppose that the best approach to an inquiry would be to investigate first those hypotheses that had the highest antecedent probability. In actual practice, particularly at the everyday level, things seldom work out that way. For one thing, our estimates of relative antecedent probabilities are so rough that we would often be quite unable to say which of two hypotheses, both probable enough to warrant investigation, had the higher antecedent probability. Even more important, some hypotheses can be investigated so readily, that it is often wise to have a look at them first, even though they may seem somewhat less probable ante-

---

[1] This *empirical* notion of antecedent probability should not be confused with the formal concept of prior probability as it occurs in mathematical theory, for example, in Bayes' theorem. ANTECEDENT PROBABILITY, as we are using the term, means simply the probability based on what we know from previous experience *before* we embark on a particular inquiry.

cedently than some others. For example, even though it was rather unlikely that the electrical supply had failed, this was the first hypothesis investigated. It was a simple matter to turn on the bedroom switch. If the lights went on when I flicked the switch, the hypothesis would be confuted, and I would no longer need to consider it. This in itself marked an advance in my knowledge, for it narrowed down the area within which a solution was to be found. (Compare Section 27.3 below.) This type of progress by indirection is as characteristic of scientific research as of common-sense inquiry. "Science advances," writes the physicist L. L. Whyte, "mainly by its ability to prove certain assumptions wrong and to cast them aside." [2]

27.2. THE CENTRAL ROLE OF HYPOTHESES

The hypotheses put forth in dealing with the problem of the cold house may be grouped under two alternative possibilities. Either (Possibility A) the oil burner has gone off or (Possibility B) it has not gone off:

POSSIBILITY A: *Oil burner has gone off.*
Hypothesis 1: Supply tank is empty.
Hypothesis 2: Air lock has formed in supply line.
Hypothesis 3: Electrical supply has failed.
Hypothesis 4: Contacts in thermostat are dusty.

POSSIBILITY B: *Oil burner has not gone off.*
Hypothesis 5: Windows were opened too wide.
Hypothesis 6: Thermostat was mistakenly turned down farther than usual.
Hypothesis 7: Something is wrong with the blower.

The whole example illustrates the central role which hypotheses have in empirical inquiry. Much more is needed than merely to "observe the facts." Without some guiding hypothesis, we do not even know what facts are worth observing. A hypothesis, when used in conjunction with our previous knowledge, tells us what to look for, and helps us separate out those facts that may be relevant to the inquiry.

In order to see what is meant by "deriving the consequences" of a hypothesis (Step 4 of our general pattern), and in order to see how this furthers the inquiry, let us consider a specific example, Hypothesis 3: The electrical supply has failed. If this hypothesis is true, what else will

[2] L. L. Whyte: *The Next Development in Man,* New York, New American Library (Mentor Book), 1950, p. 10.

be true? For one thing, the furnace will have shut off. In other words, the
hypothesis will account for the difficulty:

> If the electrical supply has failed, the furnace will
>   have shut off.
> If the furnace has shut off, the house will be cold.
> _____
> If the electrical supply has failed, the house will be cold.

To put it another way, if a hypothesis is to be RELEVANT to a particular
inquiry, we must be able to assert a true or reasonably probable conditional statement having as its antecedent the hypothesis, and as its consequent, a statement of the difficulty which the inquiry is seeking to solve.

The above argument does not *confirm* our hypothesis; it merely shows
the hypothesis to be *relevant* to this inquiry. We also need to have some
way of testing the hypothesis. It is not enough to know that the house will
be cold if the electrical supply has failed, for there are a number of other
hypotheses which will equally well account for the house being cold. So
we ask, what else will be the case if the electrical supply has failed? On
the basis of previous knowledge, we know that if the electricity is off, the
bedroom light will not go on when I flick the switch. So what do I do?
I flick the switch. What happens? The light goes on. So what? The electrical supply has not failed, and the hypothesis that it has has been confuted. The logical pattern here, of course, is a valid simple conditional
argument which proceeds by contradicting the consequent, and concludes by contradicting the hypothesis which forms the antecedent:

> *Confutation of Hypothesis 3:*
>   If the electrical supply has failed, then the bedroom light
>   will not go on when I flick the switch.   (Prediction
>   based on previous empirical knowledge)
>   But the bedroom light does go on when I flick the switch.
>   (Experiment and observation)
> _____
>   The electrical supply has not failed.   (Valid deduction)

This may seem a negative kind of progress, but since the possible sources
of the difficulty are presumably finite in number, the elimination of a possible source narrows the field of investigation. (See Section 27.3 below.)

Probable Confutation of Hypothesis 5: The case is somewhat different
with the hypothesis that I may have opened the windows too wide. Here,
I merely proceeded in terms of a casual observation and a rough estimate
of the probabilities. Glancing at the windows before I closed them, I

found that they had been open only slightly, and on the basis of previous experience I decided that it was rather unlikely that this could be an important factor in accounting for the cold house.

> If the windows are open only slightly, they are probably not
>   responsible for the cold house. (Previous experience)
> The windows are open only slightly. (Observation)
> _____
> They are probably not responsible for the cold house.
>   (Valid deduction of probability)

Of course, if I had not come upon new evidence which confirmed one of the other hypotheses, I might have had to come back to this matter of the windows and consider it more carefully. This is typical even of scientific inquiries: some hypotheses that occur to us seem, on the basis of our general knowledge, to be less likely than others.[3] We may either set them aside for the time being, or investigate them just far enough to reassure ourselves on our previous estimate of their relative probability. It is, of course, essential to recognize that a hypothesis that has only a low probability on given evidence may none the less be true.

Confutation of Hypotheses 1 and 2: If I had ever got around to it, I could have investigated in a fairly direct manner the hypothesis that the oil supply was exhausted. I could have gone outdoors, removed the intake cap projecting up from the underground storage tank, and inserted the measuring stick.

> If the tank is empty, the stick will come up dry.
> The stick does not come up dry.
> _____
> The tank is not empty.

As things developed, however, I never had to make this direct investigation, since the hypothesis that the tank was empty was confuted in a less direct but equally decisive manner. For I heard a sound that I recognized, on the basis of past experience, as the sound of the oil burner.[4]

> If I hear the sound of the burner, then it is operating.
> If the burner is operating, it is getting oil.
> If it is getting oil, then the supply tank isn't empty.
> I do hear the sound of the burner.
> _____
> The supply tank isn't empty.

[3] Recall our discussion of antecedent probability, Section 27.1 above.
[4] Do not overlook the fact that *hearing* the burner is one way of observing it. Most of us are so "visually minded" that we mistakenly think we're observing something only if we're seeing it.

In a similar fashion, my hearing the burner in operation served to confute Hypothesis 2, that an air lock had formed in the supply line.

Confutation of Hypothesis 6: The hypothesis that I might have mistakenly turned the thermostat down too far for the night was readily confuted by observing that it stood at its usual nighttime setting of 63°.

> If the thermostat was turned down too far, observation will
>   show that it is set below the usual 63°.
> Observation does not show that it was set
>   below the usual 63°.
> _____
> The thermostat was not turned down too far.

Has Hypothesis 4 been confuted? The status of Hypothesis 4, that the thermostat contacts were dirty, is less clear. At one point in the investigation, when I had observed the warm air from the kitchen register, I even thought this hypothesis had been confirmed. For, you will remember, I had just shoved the thermostat up from its nighttime setting to its daytime one of 70°. And I reasoned that perhaps this change of setting had improved the contact, so that the furnace had gone on and everything would be all right.

When, however, I later discovered that the bedroom register was still as cold as ever, I took this as evidence that something further was wrong, which the thermostat-contact hypothesis did not account for. Note that no evidence has turned up to show that the thermostat contacts were *not* dirty, and that my resetting the thermostat did *not* restore the circuit, and that the furnace had been off until that time. What rational grounds have I, then, for not taking this hypothesis more seriously in the rest of the investigation? My grounds are these: (1) While I have no evidence to establish that the thermostat contacts may not have been faulty, neither do I have any evidence to establish that they were, except that shortly after resetting the thermostat I heard the burner in operation. But it is perhaps more plausible to explain this in terms of my having been previously too far away from the furnace to hear it.[5] (2) While the thermostat and the blower might both be at fault, it is antecedently somewhat im-

_____

[5] It is not at all clear that this latter explanation is really any *simpler* than the other, so I can scarcely here invoke the so-called PRINCIPLE OF SIMPLICITY. This "principle," which both science and common sense take quite seriously, tells us to reject a more complicated explanation when a simpler one suffices. This is in general good advice, but the "catch" is in the word *suffices*. An apparently sufficient explanation may turn out to be too simple to account for later data.

probable (though not of course impossible) that these two things would both go wrong at the same time. (3) Most important of all, the fact that the bedroom register remained cold after I heard the burner in operation cannot be adequately accounted for by the thermostat-contact hypothesis. This hypothesis would adequately account for the house being cold, but it does not account for the house being cold in just this particular way.

We shall later examine more closely the manner in which the original problem (the cold house) becomes reformulated and made more specific during the course of the inquiry. (See Section 27.8 below.)

27.3. NARROWING THE FIELD BY CONFUTATION OF RIVAL HYPOTHESES

We have thus far confined our attention to the confutation and consequent rejection of various proposed explanations of the cold house. It is by no means always the case that all but one of a group of rival hypotheses will be confuted before positive confirmation turns up for the remaining one. Anything can happen. Sometimes such overwhelming confirmation appears for one hypothesis in the course of an inquiry that, in practice, we feel justified in ignoring the other hypotheses. Sometimes all our hypotheses are confuted, and we have to try again to find an adequate explanation of the difficulty.

Before going on to an analysis of the manner in which the blower-failure hypothesis was confirmed, let us see what indirect effect the confutation of one or more hypotheses has on the probability of the remaining rival hypotheses.

There were six hypotheses that occurred to me fairly early in the investigation. When I discovered that the bedroom lights would go on, this discovery eliminated one of the hypotheses. This narrowing of the field increased the probability of the remaining hypotheses.[6] The evidence that various further hypotheses were also confuted further increased the probability of the remaining ones. If five of the six had been confuted, we should have been tempted to consider the remaining one highly probable, even before we had any independent confirmation of it.

Actually, as the inquiry progressed, no one of these six hypotheses was confirmed. Evidence which turned up in the course of the investigation

[6] The theoretical justification of the increased probability here is a controversial matter into which we shall not enter.

pointed rather to a seventh alternative, that something was wrong with the blower. This fact will remind us that probability is a relation between a conclusion *and a body of evidence.* A conclusion that is highly probable on a given body of evidence may be confuted in the light of other evidence.

In summary, we may agree that: (1) The evidence that certain hypotheses are not correct accounts of a difficulty does increase the probability that one of the surviving hypotheses is a correct account. (2) It is nevertheless crucial to understand that such purely negative evidence does not in general give us grounds for any great confidence in the surviving known hypotheses. The trouble is that we do not usually know how many other relevant hypotheses there may be that we have not even thought of. About all we can say is that it is antecedently quite *improbable* that, in a given difficulty, we shall ever think of all the relevant hypotheses.

All this indicates the need for something more than confutation. Such confutation, by itself, is not wholly adequate, and needs to be accompanied by confirmation of one of the surviving hypotheses, or of some hypothesis that has not yet occurred to us.[7] We shall next consider in more detail this positive process of confirmation.

27.4. CONFIRMATION OF A HYPOTHESIS

Since my analysis of the possible causes of the cold house was by no means exhaustive, it might have been that available evidence would have confuted all seven hypotheses. In this case, I'd have had to try to get some new ideas. As it turned out, evidence appeared which confirmed the hypothesis that something was wrong with the blower. Note that this hypothesis happens to have a somewhat different position in the inquiry from the others. By this I do not mean that it is the one that was finally confirmed, although this is of course a crucial point. I mean rather that this seventh hypothesis, unlike the others, did not occur to me more or less spontaneously at the outset of my inquiry, merely on the basis of previous knowledge and experience. I thought of it only after (1) several of the more obvious hypotheses had been confuted by further observation and reasoning, and (2) I had acquired certain new information.

We must now examine more closely the logical pattern of the con-

---

[7] We speak of an empirical hypothesis being "confirmed" rather than "proved." We reserve the word *proof* for cases of valid deduction from accepted premises.

firmation of Hypothesis 7, which we may call for convenience the "blower hypothesis." This hypothesis was judged to be *relevant* to the inquiry because, as I thought about the purpose of the blower in the heating system, it seemed likely that:

> If there is something wrong with the blower, then the house will be cold.

It is a simple matter to set up a diagnostic argument having as its conclusion the hypothesis in question. The argument will not, of course, be conclusive. If I were mistakenly to regard it as a deduction, all I could say would be that it is invalid. But this would be to misconceive its real nature and to overlook its diagnostic intent:

> If something is wrong with the blower, then the house will be cold.
> The house is cold.
> --
> Something is wrong with the blower.

But as we saw in our discussion of the hypothesis that the electrical supply had failed, this can scarcely be regarded as a *confirmation* of the hypothesis. For consider the premises of this diagnosis. The first merely expresses our judgment, on the basis of previous knowledge, that the hypothesis is *relevant* to the inquiry. The second premise merely states the difficulty which gave rise to the inquiry. The argument as a whole in no way *increases* the probability that the blower is at fault. It is merely an expanded way of expressing our original belief that the blower hypothesis is relevant to the inquiry, that is, that this hypothesis offers a possible explanation of the cold house.

27.5. THE ROLE OF PREDICTION IN CONFIRMING A HYPOTHESIS

Significant confirmation of a hypothesis requires something more than merely showing the hypothesis to be *relevant*. We must be able to use the hypothesis as the basis for *predicting* further data which are verified by further observation or experimentation. The logical pattern here is again diagnostic. The conditional premise states the prediction based upon the hypothesis. In other words, it has the form:

> If (the hypothesis) then (the predicted result).

The second premise of the confirmatory argument is an observation statement, reporting that the predicted result occurs. This premise asserts the consequent in the manner of all diagnoses. The conclusion asserts the hypothesis. Let us also describe the pattern a little less formally. Against the background of our knowledge to date, we ask, "If this hypothesis is correct, what *else* will be the case?" Then we turn to experience to determine whether this "something else" actually is the case. If it is, we may say that the prediction is VERIFIED, and the hypothesis to this extent CONFIRMED. Before proceeding, a word about terminology may be helpful. "Verifying" is a somewhat stronger word than "confirmed." For reasons we have already explored, we speak of *confirming* or *confuting* an empirical hypothesis rather than, say, of *proving* or of *disproving* it. Since the occurrence of a predicted consequent is also an empirical matter, we might also speak of confirming or confuting a prediction based upon a hypothesis. But when the prediction is established or upset by direct observation, as it sometimes is, we may perhaps permit ourselves to use the somewhat stronger words, *verified* or *falsified*. The justification for this stronger wording is the fact that the probability of a direct observation is often so high that it amounts to practical certainty.

To provide significant confirmation of a hypothesis, the predicted consequent must be something more than a mere restatement of the original difficulty. If you have any doubt about this point, or do not understand what it means, reexamine the diagnostic argument given in the preceding section before going further. In that argument, the consequent, "The house will be cold," is not really a *prediction* (literally, a "saying in advance") at all, and the argument as a whole merely shows the hypothesis to be relevant to the difficulty. To confuse relevance and confirmation may seem too crude a mistake to be troublesome, but this confusion is perhaps one of the commonest blunders in common-sense inquiry. We tend mistakenly to think that just because a hypothesis can be shown to account for the difficulty, the hypothesis must be correct. This blunder is unfortunately sometimes also made at more advanced levels of thought than common sense.

In order to avoid possible confusion later on, there is one other point we need to clarify before proceeding. Note carefully that the diagnostic pattern we have been discussing is not that of a *prediction,* but rather of the use of a prediction in *confirming a hypothesis*. The hypothesis here appears as the conclusion of a diagnosis. In a PREDICTIVE ARGUMENT, on the other hand, the *prediction* occurs as the conclusion, and the pattern is deductive. For example, I predict that a given tree will shed its leaves before winter, on the evidence of the established generalization that cherry trees shed their leaves before winter and the observation that this is a cherry tree:

> If anything is a cherry tree, it will shed its leaves before
>   winter. (Generalization)
> This is a cherry tree. (Observation statement)
> _____
> It will shed its leaves before winter. (Prediction)

We shall encounter this deductive pattern of prediction when we discuss generalizations (see for example Section 29.4, Argument 2) and again at a higher level of generality when we examine the role of theories in the discovery of laws (see Section 30.8).

Now to proceed with our investigation, what prediction can we use in a diagnosis with the hope of confirming the blower hypothesis? A very simple but basic prediction is that inspection of the blower will reveal something wrong. In other words, the conditional premise of a possibly confirmatory diagnosis would be:

> If something is wrong with the blower (Hypothesis), then
>   inspection will reveal that there is (Prediction).

In order to check up on this prediction (that is, to verify or falsify it), I go to the furnace, remove the rear panel, turn my flashlight on the blower, and have a good look. I see that the blower is motionless, although the blower motor is spinning. I look more closely and observe that the pulley on the motor shaft is slipping. Yes, inspection reveals that something is wrong with the blower. There is no need to argue that, in the course of my inspection tour, I explicitly reason this matter out. Here I am making a simple observation, and such observations seem to involve, not a process of reasoning, but a learned, nonreflective interpretation of clues. Yet the diagnostic argument helps us see the grounds for my procedure. The logic of the situation is by this time familiar enough:

> If there is something wrong with the blower, inspection will
>   reveal that there is. (Prediction from hypothesis)
> Inspection reveals that there is something wrong with the
>   blower. (Verification, by observation, of the prediction)
> ---
> There is something wrong with the blower. (Diagnostic
>   conclusion)

Of course, once I observe that something is wrong with the blower, I do not need a diagnostic argument to convince me of the fact. But if we reflect on what has happened, the diagnostic argument reveals the logic of our success. The occurrence of the predicted result has confirmed the hypothesis. In many inquiries, this is about as far as we need carry the matter. In the present case, with one exception to be noted later, we have confuted all the main competing hypotheses but one, and this we have confirmed by verifying through observation a prediction based upon it.

27.6. APPROACH TO COMPLETE CERTAINTY IN A FAVORABLE CASE

When we have reached this point, we may feel assured that the practical aspects of the inquiry into the Case of the Cold House are well under control. Our interest in the more general problem of factual inquiry, however, will lead us to explore further the logic of confirmation. The analysis which we have just completed puts us in a position to see why, in favorable cases at least, we may reasonably place great confidence in the conclusion of a diagnosis. But we must note carefully just what it is that makes this a "favorable case."

If you are ready to investigate this matter, take another look at the conditional statement which expresses our hypothesis and the prediction based upon it: "If there is something wrong with the blower, inspection will reveal that there is." This is at least highly probable, although we can perhaps conceive of a case in which our inspection would be unable to find anything wrong, even though something were wrong. But now consider the *converse* of our conditional statement.

> If inspection reveals that there is something wrong with the blower, there is something wrong with the blower.

We know that a given conditional statement does not logically entail its converse, but this is not the point. Let us consider this converse independently. Isn't this converse just about as sure as you could wish? From one point of view, it seems to be not much more than a tautology, and thus to be necessarily true, as when we assert, "If a house has a red roof, then it has a red roof." If you still feel there is some possibility that this converse might be false, it is probably because you detect a possible ambiguity in the statement, "Inspection reveals that there is something wrong with the blower." Thinking perhaps of the possibility of an error in observation, you might urge that inspection might *seem* to "reveal something wrong" even though nothing were wrong. Hence, you would urge, the statement in question is at best only very highly probable. In practice, however, you would be more likely to accept without question the results of a careful inspection, and treat the statement as true without qualification. Let us now use this converse of our original statement as a premise. Let us complete an argument, using the same second premise and conclusion that we had in our diagnosis:

> If inspection reveals that there is something wrong with the
> blower, then there is something wrong with the blower.
> (Converse of original)
> Inspection does reveal that there is something wrong with
> the blower.   (Report of observation)
> _____
> There is something wrong with the blower.

Here we have, not a diagnosis, but a valid deductive argument. What is more, if we are right in thinking that we know the premises to be true without qualification, the conclusion is completely certain.

Now let us, for the moment, suppose that we have overstated the case. Let us accept, for the time being, the view of those who insist that in such matters we can never attain more than a high degree of probability. Let us suppose that our conditional statement is only very highly probable, and that our report of observation is also only very highly probable. We shall then have to qualify our conclusion by the insertion of the phrase, "with very high probability." This conclusion follows, not with probability from the premises (as in a diagnosis), but necessarily, since the argument is a valid deduction. It is a necessary conclusion about a very high probability or, as we may synonymously say, a necessary conclusion about a practical certainty.

27.7. ESTIMATING THE STRENGTH OF A DIAGNOSIS

We are now in a position to examine how the strength of a diagnosis may be estimated. Our earlier argument about the eggs (Section 26.3) seemed somewhat weak; the present argument seems very strong. Let us see if we can get beyond this mere appeal to how an argument "seems" or "feels."

Consider our diagnosis about the object that contained a yolk:

> If any object is a chicken egg, then it contains a yolk.
> Object X contains a yolk.
> --
> Object X is a chicken egg.

Let us admit the fairly high probability of the conditional premise, in spite of the fact that some chicken eggs contain not yolks but baby chickens ready to hatch out. Let us also admit the practical certainty of the observation report. The probability of the conclusion none the less seems rather low, doesn't it? There is a simple way of checking this impression. It is the method we used in estimating the strength of the blower diagnosis.

Convert the conditional premise, and consider independently the probability of this converse:

> If any object contains a yolk, then it is a chicken egg.

By considering the probability of this converse "independently," we do not of course mean independently of available evidence, but rather independently of what we may know about the probability or truth of the statement from which it was derived by conversion. In the light of available knowledge, the probability of this converse is not high. Confining our consideration to bird's eggs alone, it is clear that there are a great many possibilities consistent with an object's containing a yolk other than its being a chicken egg. The probability would be considerably higher if we took into account the fact that most of us seldom encounter yolk-containing objects other than chicken eggs. But to do so would be to change somewhat the nature of the statement we are analyzing. For that converse was intended quite generally for *any* object containing a yolk, and not simply for those yolk-containing objects that we in our provincialism most frequently encounter.

Let us, as in our evaluation of the blower diagnosis, now use this converse along with our original observation report and the conclusion of our original diagnosis. The result will be a valid deduction:

> If any object contains a yolk, then it is (only somewhat probably) a chicken egg.
> Object X contains a yolk.
> --
> Object X is (only somewhat probably) a chicken egg.

We know that the conclusion of a valid deduction can never be more probable (on the evidence provided by the premises) than the premises themselves. Hence our conclusion, though valid, is in this case only somewhat probable. Contrast this result with that of the blower argument.

The probability of a given diagnostic conclusion may be estimated in the following way:
1. Convert the conditional premise of the diagnosis.
2. Consider, on the basis of available knowledge, the probability of this converse.
3. Assuming that our observation report is practically certain, the probability of the diagnostic conclusion will be roughly that of the converse of its conditional premise.

It should be clear that this estimate can be only an approximation for at least two reasons: (1) The probability of the conclusion is also affected by the probability of the second premise (observation report). (2) The probability of the converse conditional itself is estimated on the basis of independently available evidence, and this of course will vary according to how much you happen to know about the matter in question.

27.8. SOME HYPOTHESES CAN BE CONFIRMED ONLY INDIRECTLY

In the Case of the Cold House, I was in the favorable position of being able to confirm one of the hypotheses by direct observation of the slipping pulley. In some cases, the only available confirmation is of an indirect nature.

Suppose, for example, that I had been unable to inspect the blower directly. I would still have had some evidence to go on. Most of this evidence was not available to me at the outset, but turned up in the course of the inquiry. The evidence was of two types:

1. Evidence which confuted some of the rival hypotheses.
2. Evidence which offered indirect confirmation of the blower hypothesis.

We have already discussed the evidence of the first type, and have seen how it narrowed the field by eliminating some hypotheses, thus increasing the probability of the remaining ones. But we also saw the need of something more than this negative approach. We sought some positive confirmation of one of the remaining hypotheses, or of some other hypothesis that had not yet occurred to us.

Even if I had not been able to inspect the blower directly, evidence turned up which offered a degree of indirect confirmation. I observed that, although the burner was on, very little heat was coming out of the kitchen register and none at all out of the bedroom register. Note how much more specific and detailed the situation has become. It is no longer just a matter of what we might call a cold-house-in-general. It has become a matter of a house that is cold in just this specific way. This is a good example of the reformulation of an original problem during the course of an inquiry, in the light of new information revealed by the investigation.

As we have seen, any one of the seven hypotheses was relevant to the general problem of the cold house. Any one of them could account for the house being cold. But of the seven, only the blower hypothesis seems able to account for the house being cold in just this particular way. We may, in fact, use our previously explained method to estimate the strength of the blower hypothesis at this stage of the inquiry:

> If there is something wrong with the blower, then a small amount of heat may rise to the kitchen register, which is near the furnace, but no heat will reach the bedroom register in the far end of the house. (Previous experience and knowledge of the purpose of the blower)
> A small amount of heat does rise to the kitchen register, but no heat reaches the bedroom register. (Report of observation)
> --
> There is something wrong with the blower.

If we convert the conditional premise of this diagnosis, the independent evidence derived from our general knowledge makes this converse highly probable:

> If a small amount of heat rises to the kitchen register, which is near the furnace, but no heat reaches the bedroom register in the far end of the house, then there is something wrong with the blower.

Accepting our observation report as practically certain, we validly conclude that it is quite highly probable that there is something wrong with the blower.

It should be noted that our original conditional premise above did not strictly contain a *prediction,* for the consequent merely set forth data which had turned up in the investigation, and which led me to think of the blower hypothesis in the first place. In practice, we tend to overlook this theoretical weakness if we have available independent evidence which makes the *converse* of this conditional highly probable.

From a stricter point of view, we could regard the above diagnosis as merely establishing the *relevance* of the blower hypothesis to the more specifically formulated difficulty, namely that there was but little warm air at the kitchen register and none at the bedroom register. Compare our earlier consideration of the hypothesis that the electrical supply had failed, where we distinguished between an argument which showed the hypothesis to be *relevant* and the type of argument that would have been needed to *confirm* it (Section 27.2 above).

Even from this stricter point of view, however, the superiority of our present hypothesis to its rivals is evident. For it is difficult to see that any of the other hypotheses is relevant to this more specifically formulated situation. On the basis of our general knowledge, the following statement, for example, is quite improbable:

> If the thermostat contacts are dirty, there will be a little warm air at the kitchen register and none at the bedroom register.

With one possible exception, a similar improbability attaches to corresponding conditional statements having any one of the remaining hypotheses as antecedent.

The possible exception is the hypothesis that the windows were open too wide. On the basis of previous knowledge, I might seek to establish the relevancy of this hypothesis to the more specifically formulated problem somewhat as follows: When people open windows at night during cold winter weather, it is usually bedroom windows that they open, not windows in other parts of the house. If a stiff cold wind blew in through these windows, it is possible that the efforts of the blower would, at this distance from the furnace, have been nullified. It is possible, in other words, that the bedroom register would be cold, even though the blower were operating, provided a strong cold wind had been coming in through the open bedroom windows. But it would seem much more difficult to account, on this hypothesis, for the fact that only a little warm air was coming out of the kitchen register. At the very most we could only urge that the hypothesis was a possible explanation of at least part of the more specifically formulated difficulty.

27.9. AN EXAMPLE OF INDIRECT CONFIRMATION

Granting all this, we see the desirability of pushing further the investigation of our blower hypothesis. It seems clearly relevant to our reformulated problem, but can we base a prediction upon it which will go beyond the data already at hand? Such a prediction, if borne out by further observation or experiment, would provide important indirect confirmation of the hypothesis.

Drawing upon previous general knowledge, we may use this hypothesis as the basis for the following prediction:

> If the blower is not functioning, then although there may be a small amount of heat coming out of other registers *near* the furnace, there will be no heat coming out of other registers *at a distance from* the furnace.

If further investigation revealed, let us say, that the dining-room register was slightly warm, but that the other bedroom registers and the bathroom register were cold, this new evidence would verify the prediction made in the consequent. The hypothesis would thereby be indirectly confirmed. I say "indirectly," because this new confirmatory evidence still falls short of direct observation of the blower itself, such as we made when we discovered that the blower was idle although the blower motor was turning.

In summary, we are sometimes unable to get at further data which *directly* confirm a hypothesis. In such cases, it is often possible to make predictions which, when verified by observation or experimentation, indirectly confirm the hypothesis.

27.10. APPLYING THE RESULTS OF THE INQUIRY

My investigation of the cold house might have been an expression of a THEORETICAL INTEREST, that is, I might have been seeking only to understand why the house was cold in order to expand human knowledge and satisfy my own intellectual curiosity. It is obvious that my actual interest in the problem was of a different order. I had a PRACTICAL INTEREST in the problem. I wanted to find out why the house was cold, in order to do something about it.

If my interest had been purely theoretical, the inquiry might have terminated with my observation that the pulley on the blower motor was slipping. "So that's it!" I might have said, and gone back to bed, pleased with this expansion of my knowledge of the world. In the circumstances, however, my interest in the problem was intensely practical. Once I confirmed the hypothesis that the house was cold because there was something wrong with the blower, I sought to remedy the cold house by applying this newly gained knowledge.

Here again, I was not aware of going through any explicit process of reasoning. I simply got a wrench, tightened up the pulley, and went upstairs, confident that everything was now all right and that the house would soon warm up. To what extent was this confidence logically justified?

For one thing, I had by empirical inquiry established that half a dozen possible causes of a cold house were not operative in the present situation. In terms of this information and the antecedent improbability of two things being wrong at once, I believed that the faulty blower was the only factor keeping the house cold. It might, of course, have been the case that the electricity should go off just after I had fixed the blower, or that an air lock should just then develop in the supply line, and so on. But in spite of the folk adage that "troubles never come singly," the antecedent probability of something else going wrong immediately was not very great.

This knowledge of the detailed circumstances and of the antecedent probabilities gave me grounds, although not conclusive ones, for accepting the following biconditional statement:

> (In these special circumstances) if and only if there is something wrong with the blower, will the house stay cold.

Having tightened the pulley and having observed the blower to spin normally, I was in a position to assert with practical certainty:

> There is (now) not anything wrong with the blower.

Since the first premise is biconditional, we may derive a valid conclusion by asserting:

> The house will not (now) stay cold.

The conclusion, though valid, is of course not completely certain, for I do not really know for sure that the biconditional premise is true.

When, however, I return upstairs and find the house warming up nicely, and when somewhat later I find that the thermometer now reads its normal daytime 70°, I have all the confirmation that it is reasonable to desire for my earlier assumption that the blower was the only thing that was wrong:

> If the house temperature returns to normal after I fix the blower, then almost certainly the blower was the only thing that had gone wrong.
> The house temperature does return to normal after I fix the blower.
> _____
> Almost certainly the blower was the only thing that had gone wrong.

• SOME REMINDERS

1. The antecedent probability of a hypothesis is the probability it has on the basis of previous experience and general knowledge, apart from new evidence that may turn up in the course of the inquiry.
2. The Case of the Cold House helps us to understand the central role of hypotheses in inquiry and the place which deductive reasoning has in empirical investigation.
3. The pattern of the confutation of a hypothesis is typically deductive.
4. The probability of surviving hypotheses is indirectly increased by confutation of rival hypotheses.
5. Elimination of all but one hypothesis does not show that this remaining hypothesis is true. Positive confirmation is also needed.
6. Significant confirmation of a hypothesis requires more than merely showing it to be *relevant*.
7. The strength of a diagnostic argument may sometimes be estimated through the use of converses.
8. Some hypotheses can be confirmed directly; others, only indirectly.
9. In the course of an inquiry, the original problem may be transformed because of new information arising during the inquiry.

APPLICATIONS

1. Analyze each of the following examples in terms of the concepts and principles of empirical inquiry discussed in this and preceding chapters. Show

the extent to which the example reveals the various stages of inquiry described in Section 26.4, and explain the specific form of reasoning involved.

a. "If the Moon had been separated from the Earth at a time when the latter was still completely molten, the liquid would have immediately covered the site of the rupture, and no more trace would have been left on the body of our planet than there is on the surface of a well from which a bucketful of water has been taken. But if at the time of rupture the Earth was already covered with solid crust, the newborn satellite must have carried away a large section of this rocky crust, leaving a clearly visible scar. A glance at the map of the Earth's surface discloses such a scar in the deep basin of the Pacific Ocean, which now covers about one-third of the total surface of the Earth. It would, of course, be rather unwise to draw such a far-reaching conclusion merely from the vast area and roughly circular form of the Pacific, but geologists have discovered an additional fact that lends strong support to the hypothesis that the Pacific basin is really the 'hole' left in the Earth's crust by the separation of its satellite. We have already mentioned that the upper crust of the Earth is a layer of granite from 50 to 100 kilometres thick resting on a much thicker layer of heavier basalt. This is true of all the continents and also of parts of the Earth's crust that are submerged beneath the waters of the Atlantic, Indian, and Arctic Oceans . . . where, however, the granite layer is considerably thinner. But the vast expanse of the Pacific is a striking exception—*not a single piece of granite has ever been found on any of the numerous islands scattered through that ocean.* There is hardly any doubt that *the floor of the Pacific is formed exclusively of basaltic rocks, as if some cosmic hand had removed the entire granite layer from all this vast area.* Besides, in contrast to the other oceans, the basin of the Pacific is surrounded by a ring of high mountain chains (Cordilleras, Kamchatka, the islands of Japan, and New Zealand) of pronounced volcanic activity, known as the 'ring of fire.' This indicates that this roughly circular border line is much more closely connected with the structure of the entire crust than the shore lines of other oceans. It is, therefore, quite likely that the area now occupied by the Pacific is the very place where the huge bulk of matter now forming the Moon was torn away from the Earth." (George Gamow: *Biography of the Earth*, New York, The Viking Press, 1941, pp. 55–57)

b. "During the late war and since, rapidly moving spots of light frequently appeared on the luminous screens of the radars of both Army and Navy installations. A high-flying airplane could cause a spot of light on the scope, but it moved slowly and regularly.

"The so-called angels, however, darted back and forth, defying all the known laws of thermodynamics, with or against the wind, were observed in daylight and at night, but were noticed more in balmy weather than in cold. . . .

"Since then the Bell Laboratories and the Naval Electronics Laboratory have been carrying on a series of tests at Gila Bend, Ariz., to explain the mystery. A variety of atmospheric conditions calculated to produce angels or their equivalents were created by exploding charges of nitro-starch, building bonfires, pouring water on hot rocks, and so on, as observers flew over the turbulent areas in radar-equipped planes. No angels.

"However, while at work one night under the rays of a powerful searchlight, with radar beams trained upward, observers stationed at various heights on a 200-foot tower counted the bugs attracted by the light as other scientists counted the blips on the radar screen, and the mystery was solved.

"It was the bugs, or at least the Bell experts think so, for no other theory or fact seems to fit the case so well, they say. At least it has been established that a darting bug can reflect a radar pulse and cause a blip of light." (*New York Times*, April 4, 1949)

c. Sheriff's deputies in Council Bluffs, Iowa, found a wrecked car which had apparently leaped sixty feet through the air before hitting a power pole and then dropping eight feet into a ditch. They found a pair of shoes in the car, but no other signs of the driver. They believed that he had been thrown from his shoes by the crash, but they failed to locate the body. Later the driver turned up and explained that he had been forced off the road by another car, and had jumped from his own while it tottered on the edge of the ditch after hitting the pole. The shoes found in the car were an extra pair. (Data from *New York Times*, November 13, 1951)

d. One spring one of my white pines showed a sooty deposit on the lower branches which I could not explain. An inquiry to the Forest Service of the U. S. Department of Agriculture brought the following reply:

The white pine specimen you submitted . . . was referred to this office for examination.

The blackened condition of the twig and needles is caused by a sooty-mold which usually follows heavy feeding by sucking insects such as aphids or leaf hoppers. At this time of year both these types of insects are in hibernation so it is impossible to tell whether or not your trees will again be infested and by what insect.

It is suggested that you examine this tree again in late May or early June for evidence of aphids or leaf hoppers. Aphids on pine bark usually form a white cottony mass which is easily observed.

Examination of the tree a few weeks later revealed several white cottony masses.

e. "Dr. George F. Carter, chairman of the Isaiah Bowman School of Geography at Johns Hopkins, now contends that humans inhabited North America 100,000 years ago and perhaps 400,000 years ago. In 1949, he figured they were here only 40,000 years ago.

"Dr. Carter's newer and higher ante is based on what he considers proof of evidence—the authentication of hand-fashioned rock flakes or fragments of crude stone cutting and chopping implements found in gravel terraces or interglacial deposits in California. . . .

"He said the flakes bore unmistakable evidence of crude hand craftsmanship and controlled chipping. Nature could not duplicate them, he said, because man strikes directed blows, creating sharp edges, whereas the random strokes of nature make for rounded forms. Furthermore, he said, source rock reveals that the stones were split to obtain rough flakes and the flakes were chipped in a planned manner to serve a certain need.

"The theory is based also, he said, on a knowledge of soil and land forms, climatology, anthropology, botany and conditions and aftereffects of the glacial periods. The gravel terraces in which the artifacts were found, he said, were deposited by streams between the fourth and last glaciers more than 100,000 years ago.

"Two 'yardsticks' were used to determine the age of the sites. One was a chemical analysis of the soil content, indicating that the soil had been in place during the humid, glacial eras.

"The other was based on a knowledge that ocean levels around the world dropped as much as 300 feet below the present beaches during the four glacial advances and rose somewhat higher than present levels when the ice caps melted." (*New York Times,* January 13, 1953)

f. "Research balloons soaring 110,000 feet (20 miles) in the stratosphere above northern Canada have collected new cosmic ray data that may force scientists to revise their theories about the sun, the National Geographic Society reported today. . . .

"Dr. Martin A. Pomerantz of the Bartal Foundation headed the expedition. He set out to test the widely held theory that the sun has a permanent magnetic field about 100 times as powerful as the earth's. This field, many scientists believed, was too strong to permit any cosmic rays of low energy to escape and 'bombard' the earth.

"But Dr. Pomerantz reported to the society that his balloon-borne instruments picked up cosmic radiations of such small penetrating power that they could not possibly have entered the earth's atmosphere if the sun had the magnetic field scientists have assumed.

"Even if the solar field were only one-twentieth as strong as previously believed, he said, the weak rays recorded by the expedition would have been held back." (*New York Times,* November 15, 1949)

g. "An expedition from the Bronx Zoo in New York, weaving its way through a mass of ancient town records, recollections of old settlers and the carvings on local tombstones, has come up with evidence it believes will help substantiate the 109 years claimed by a box tortoise found here June 14.

"The party of turtle date-hunters searching the countryside yesterday to find the origin of the aged turtle bearing the dates and initials, E.B.K. 1844 and G.V.B., July 22, 1860, found the most rewarding clue in the Wood River Cemetery. There, Dr. James A. Oliver, curator of reptiles of the Bronx Zoo, encountered Sam Reynolds, 86, of Richmond, who pointed out the grave of Edward Barber Kenyon.

"E.B.K., whose tombstone bore the date 1825, was found to have lived one-half a mile from where the turtle was discovered, on the William E. Bidgood farm. Since turtles are notoriously slow walkers, the curator is convinced that even in 109 years it would likely have made little more distance than that. The turtle experts figure that Mr. Kenyon would have been 19 years old at the time—just the age for carving his initials on a turtle in the spring." (*New York Times*, July 30, 1953)

h. "The planet Jupiter, while in its formative stage billions of years ago, may have lost one or more satellites, now observed as asteroids or minor planets traveling in unusual orbits around the sun.

"This proposal was made originally by a University of Chicago astronomer, Dr. G. P. Kuiper, and it has now received support as a result of calculations at the University of Cincinnati Observatory by Dr. Eugene K. Rabe. . . .

"Dr. Rabe . . . assumed that at some time in the past, during its formation, Jupiter had a larger mass than at present. . . . Then he selected a particular satellite orbit with reference to Jupiter, and found that because of Jupiter's large mass the orbit would be unstable and the satellite would not be able to maintain a constant period.

"Beginning at a point when the satellite was on the outside of the orbit, on the side away from the sun, Dr. Rabe proceeded step by step to calculate its course around Jupiter, only to find that the moon would be finally ejected from the planet's gravitational control in a direction away from the sun—that is, toward Saturn's orbit.

"The satellite, however, would still be in the sun's gravitational control, as are all the planets, and it would become one of the minor planets, of which thousands are known today, mostly revolving between the orbits of Mars and Jupiter.

"But this new minor planet would be unusual, for its orbit would stretch all the way out to Saturn. This matches rather well the present observed orbit of Hidalgo [one of the asteroids], for which Dr. Kuiper already had suggested an origin from Jupiter during Jupiter's formation." (Charles A. Federer, Jr., in *New York Times*, December 31, 1953)

CHAPTER 28

ESTABLISHING A GENERAL FACT
BY INDUCTION

PREVIEW

At times in empirical inquiry we are concerned with diagnosing a particular difficulty or establishing a specific fact about an individual case. But sometimes we investigate individual cases, not so much for their own sake, as for the insight they give us into general facts which hold for some or all cases of a kind. In other words, we seek to "generalize from experience." In this and the following chapter we shall consider the nature of the inductive process by which generalizations are established.

28.1. GENERALIZATIONS AND COMMON-SENSE INQUIRY

Much of our empirical inquiry, especially at the common-sense level, is directed toward establishing individual or singular facts. The results of such an inquiry are expressible by means of a singular statement. What is this? It is an apple. Why is the house cold? The blower pulley is slipping. What's wrong with Barbara? She has chickenpox. Will Jack Smith live until his next birthday? Very likely.

When our concern is directed toward the individual, as it is in cases like those above, we are likely to be impatient with more general questions. We are not at the time interested in the general problem of childhood diseases, but rather in what is wrong with Barbara. We want a discussion, not of life expectancy in general, but of Jack's own chances of surviving.

Yet, in spite of the fact that our interest at such times is in the individual, we can seldom answer our questions about the individual case simply in terms of the individual case. In our reasoning about an individual, we continually draw not merely upon singular statements about the individual, but also upon previous generalizations about the classes to which the individual belongs. For example, the pattern of confirming a hypothesis about an individual is diagnostic. One premise of every diagnosis is a conditional statement. These conditional premises are in many cases generalizations based upon previous knowledge and experience. The pattern of confutation, in contrast to the pattern of confirmation, is deductive rather than diagnostic, but here also one of our premises is commonly a generalization from past experience or a general statement accepted on authority or by hearsay.

At other times, common-sense inquiry not only makes use of generalizations in arriving at individual solutions, but is concerned with establishing new generalizations. Parents ask, "What effect is television having on family life?" College administrators wonder, "Can the small liberal arts college survive without new sources of income?" College students inquire, "On the whole, is it a good idea to stay up all night studying before an examination?" The answers to these questions would typically be generalizations.

It is interesting to consider that many of our folk adages must have been arrived at by the rough-and-ready processes of common-sense generalizing.[1] "Too many cooks spoil the broth." "A stitch in time saves nine." "Red sky at night, sailor's delight." "Troubles never come singly." "As the twig is bent, so the tree is inclined." The fact that such adages may often be matched by others having an opposite import ("Too many cooks spoil the broth" vs. "Many hands make light work") suggests that such generalizations are often rash, being based on striking cases of one type with accompanying neglect of other cases. One of the clearest differences between common sense and science lies in the contrast between the amount of evidence and confirmation which each regards as sufficient to establish a generalization. (Compare Section 23.2.)

28.2. GENERALIZATIONS AND SCIENTIFIC INQUIRY

When we pass from common-sense inquiry to scientific inquiry, the importance of generalizations becomes even more obvious. For in scientific

---

[1] Many of our social and racial clichés, although stated in general form ("Greenskins are all liars," "All Lenitians smell bad," "Plutonians are wife-beaters," and so on), are probably not generalizations at all, but disguised persuasive definitions put forth and repeated for their emotive and directive effects.

reasoning, we are not merely continually drawing upon prior generalizations, but our inquiries are themselves for the most part directed toward
the establishing of further generalizations. Whether in a beginning course
in zoology or an advanced piece of research in nuclear physics, your central concern as a theoretical or "pure" scientist is with the general. When
you dissect a pickled cat in the laboratory, you may for fun name her
"Esmeralda." You may even develop a certain attachment to her before
you are through. But all this is quite irrelevant to your scientific interest
in her. This interest is directed toward a *specimen,* that is, toward an instance *of a type.* And your job as a budding scientist is to see what you
can find out about felinity-in-general through a study of this particular
feline. Your laboratory instructor will rightly insist that you "record what
you observe" rather than what the textbook says you will see. But if your
specimen exhibits any important abnormalities, not characteristic of the
general type, it will be part of the instructor's job to help you understand
this fact.

From ancient Aristotle to contemporary Whitehead, this concern of
theoretical or "pure" science with what is general has been recognized.
Aristotle pointed out that "None of the sciences theorize about individual
cases," and illustrated his point by referring to medical theory (in contrast
to its application by the practicing physician). "Medicine," he said, "does
not theorize about what will help to cure Socrates or Callias, but only
about what will help to cure any or all of a given class of patients; this
alone is its business." (*Rhetoric,* 1.2.1356b.28) Similarly Whitehead points
out that the aim of science is to "see what is general in what is particular." [2]

When we pass from theoretical science to applied science, our concern
does indeed shift from the general to the specific and individual case. But
we are still at every point dependent upon the prior generalizations fur-
nished us by theoretical science. In its concern with the solution of individual problems through the use of established general knowledge, applied science is akin to the type of common-sense inquiry we have been
considering. (It differs, of course, in the source of the generalizations upon
which it draws.) The family physician is, in this sense, a medical engineer.
He seeks to apply his knowledge of medical theory, which is general, to
the solution of specific individual problems such as what's wrong with
Barbara. So too, the industrial engineer, undertaking to design an electric

[2] A. N. Whitehead: *An Introduction to Mathematics,* New York, Henry Holt and
Company, 1911, p. 11.

toaster that will pop the completed toast onto the breakfaster's plate, draws upon his general knowledge of ballistics. It is a well-known fact that the speed with which the United States was able to produce an atomic bomb during World War II was possible only because the scientists working on this problem in engineering already had at their disposal a large body of theoretical knowledge relevant to the solution of the specific problem.

28.3. GENERALIZATIONS ARE REACHED BY INDUCTION

In everyday English, we commonly call any broad statement a *generalization*. We shall use the term in a somewhat more technical sense, one which stresses the notion of process or making which is implied by the suffix, *-ize*. We shall, in other words, distinguish between the genus, *general statement*, and the species, *generalization*.[3] A GENERALIZATION, in the specific sense in which we shall use the term, is a statement that has been arrived at in a specific way, that is, by a process of generalizing or *induction*. An inductive argument, you will recall, is one which moves from the known constitution of a part of a class (the "sample"), to the probable constitution of the whole class from which the sample was taken.

We shall want to examine the pattern of inductive arguments more thoroughly. Before we do so, however, let us distinguish two types of generalization, and then contrast generalizations with general statements that have been derived in ways other than induction.

28.4. UNIVERSAL AND PARTICULAR GENERALIZATIONS

Many generalizations are universal statements. If I examine a number of pencils of a certain brand and discover that they are all very brittle, I may conclude by induction that probably all pencils of this brand are very brittle. Such a conclusion may be called a UNIVERSAL GENERALIZATION, since it is a universal statement reached by induction.

Many generalizations, on the other hand, are particular statements. On the basis of the fact that most of my college classmates got married, I

---

[3] Recall that a general statement is either a *universal* statement or a *particular* statement. General statements are contrasted with *singular* statements, which "single out" and refer to one definite individual. A *generalization* is a general statement that has been arrived at in a certain way.

might conclude by induction that probably most college students eventually get married. Such a conclusion may be called a PARTICULAR GENERALIZATION, since it is a particular statement reached by induction. A special type of particular generalization is the STATISTICAL GENERALIZATION. In such a generalization, a numerical quantifier is used, as in the statement, "84% of college students get married eventually." Still another type which, like the statistical generalization, is especially useful in the social sciences, is the TENDENTIAL GENERALIZATION. Such a generalization states, not a proportion, but a tendency, for example, "College students tend to get married eventually." Note that the import of such a generalization is particular, not universal; it is merely a way of saying that many or most college students get married eventually.

It might be thought that, in view of the existence of particular generalizations, we should have to modify our definition of induction. For we have defined induction as a process of inference which moves from the known constitution of a sample to the constitution of the *whole class*. But it is convenient to stick to this definition, noting that even a particular generalization asserts something about the constitution of the whole class, namely that in this whole class, a proportion of members ("some," "most," "84%," etc.) are probably characterized in such-and-such a way.

28.5. GENERALIZATIONS DISTINGUISHED FROM VARIOUS OTHER STATEMENTS

GENERALIZATIONS vs. SPECIFICATIONS

Since generalizations are distinguished by the manner in which they are derived, we shall want to contrast generalizations with general statements that are derived in other ways. A statement may, for example, have been reached by deduction from other statements. If we know that all mammals have four-chambered hearts (and know also that all squirrels are mammals) it follows that all squirrels have four-chambered hearts. When derived in this way, it is clear that "All squirrels have four-chambered hearts" is not a generalization in our sense, but rather a deductive SPECIFICATION of the statement, "All mammals have four-chambered hearts." (It may be noted that the premises from which such a specification is deduced are, most likely, themselves generalizations.)

If, however, we asserted this same statement on the grounds that a sampling of squirrels had revealed that each one examined had a four-chambered heart, then our statement would not be a specification but a generalization.

GENERALIZATIONS vs. DISGUISED DEFINITIONS

To consider another type of case, many universal statements are simply disguised definitions. (Compare Section 6.6.) It is particularly important to distinguish these from generalizations.[4] We can get at the heart of this fundamental distinction by considering a concrete example.

My grandmother was a staunch defender of the contention that no nice girl swears. It is true that she did not move in circles in which she was likely to hear a girl swear, but that is not the point. For her, it was inconceivable that a "nice" girl should swear. If an apparently nice girl swore, this would merely show that she was not really nice after all. Why? Because my grandmother was not really offering an empirical generalization, but a disguised definition. Her definition of "nice girl" included, as an essential attribute, the characteristic of nonswearing. As long as Grandmother stuck to her stipulated definition, no conceivable experience could confute her assertion that no nice girl swears. In terms of her definition, it was not merely the case but *necessarily* the case that no nice girl swears.[5]

Now, I think Grandmother would have been inclined to say that it is *self-evident* that no nice girl swears. This appeal to self-evidence usually turns out, upon analysis, to be an appeal to a definition. As long as we stick to our definition, no amount of empirical evidence can force us to speak in a manner that violates our definition. It is only in this sense that a definition can be said to "legislate the facts." It thus turns out that the *facts* determined by a definition are really facts about our verbal usage, and about the labels we shall apply to nonverbal facts.

It is instructive to consider, by way of contrast, the well-known case of the black swans of Australia. Europeans formerly believed that all swans are white. It would have been possible to take toward this belief the atti-

---

[4] We can of course undertake an empirical study of people's actual verbal usage, and can arrive at generalizations about this usage which function as conventional definitions. This is approximately what dictionary makers do.

[5] This illustrates what people mean by saying that some statements are "true by definition." "Truth" in this special sense is not an empirical but a syntactical matter; "true by definition" means the same as "follows validly from the definition" or "is logically necessitated by the definition" or "cannot (if we accept the definition) be denied without contradicting ourselves."

tude of my grandmother, and to maintain that it was logically impossible that there should be swans that were not white. In other words, the characteristic of being white might have been regarded as an essential part of the signification of "swan." If this type of definitional approach had been taken, the discovery of the black birds in Australia would have had no effect upon the "fact" that all swans are (necessarily) white. It would merely have revealed that there are other birds, similar to "swans" to be sure, but differing from them in an essential respect, namely that of not being white. As it happened, of course, the sentence, "All swans are white," was treated, not as a deduction from a definition, but as an empirical generalization which turned out to be mistaken and to need correction in the light of a more adequate sampling of swans.

GENERALIZATIONS vs. SUMMATIONS

There is still another way to reach a general statement. Unlike the definitional statement we have just considered, the type of statement in question is empirical, yet it is not a generalization. Suppose I ask a new class in logic, "How many of you are freshmen?" And suppose everyone raises his hand. On this evidence, it is reasonable to assert the universal statement, "All of you are freshmen." Such a statement was indeed arrived at by considering individual cases, but it is not in our sense a generalization. Why not? A generalization is the result of a process of induction. Induction, as we pointed out earlier, always involves an inference from the known constitution of a sample which is less than the whole class, to the probable constitution of the class from which the sample is taken. In the present case, no such inference is involved, for our examination of the class has been complete. Our statement does not generalize, it merely *summarizes*. Such a statement may be called a SUMMATION.

There is an important reason for noting this distinction between a generalization and a summation. Under ideal conditions, a summation may be taken as final, whereas a generalization is at best always subject to correction in the light of further sampling. This is as true of the generalizations of science as of the generalizations of common sense. They are at best only highly probable, for they all go beyond the observed sample to say what we may expect to find in the class as a whole. A scientific generalization about falling bodies applies not merely to the relatively few falling bodies that have been observed, but to all falling bodies past, present, and future. A generalization would have no value in prediction unless it referred to future cases as well as present and past ones. And future cases are in principle unobservable at the time the generalization is made.

28.6. THE PROCESS OF INDUCTION

The cartoonist, George Price, once drew for *The New Yorker* a picture of a couple opening their Christmas presents. They had quite a lot of them, but curiously enough the packages, in spite of their varied wrappings, were all of the same shape and size. The couple had already opened several of the packages, and the contents stood exposed on a table. Each of the opened packages had contained an identical monstrosity, an electric lamp shaped like an alligator with a light bulb in its opened mouth. In the picture, the wife has (as I recall) just picked up another of the packages which she is about to open. With a look of anticipation she says, "I wonder what *this* one can be?"

Now of course it ruins a joke to analyze it, but at the moment we are more interested in the analysis than in the joke. So let's go ahead. Here is a good simple case of empirical inquiry: What's in the package? A process of sampling is well under way. The thing that makes the picture funny, if I may now proceed to spoil it, is the disparity between the wife's and the reader's willingness to generalize on the basis of the sample.[6] One might urge that the wife is only using proper scientific caution. After all, they've opened relatively few packages. The sample is still fairly small in relation to the whole class of packages. Perhaps this next one will contain something different. But as you size up the situation, the wife seems a bit slow to get the point. As for yourself, you are ready to take the so-called INDUCTIVE LEAP from the known constitution of the sample to the probable constitution of the whole lot. On the basis of the sample, it seems extremely likely to you that *all* the packages contain alligator lamps.

Before going further, we had better clear up one point. If we are to be able to think clearly about the probability of a generalization, we must distinguish between two related questions. We need to understand that

[6] In this particular case, our willingness is no doubt in part due to our knowledge of the artist's probable intent: he presumably intended that all the packages, without exception, should contain alligator lamps. Also, this case differs from many in that the class is small, so that exhaustive enumeration, leading to a summation, would be possible.

the question, "How probable is it that all the presents are alligator lamps?" is not the same question as "How probable is it that the *next* package we open will also contain an alligator lamp?" The first question concerns a generalization; the second concerns a diagnosis. The difference between these two types of question may be seen most clearly by considering a slightly different case. Suppose, for example, that out of four packages opened, three were found to contain alligator lamps, while one contained something else. On the frequency analysis, the probability on the evidence of the sample that the next package will contain an alligator lamp is $\frac{3}{4}$. Or, more colloquially, the chances are 3 out of 4. But note that it would be absurd to say that on this evidence, the probability of the *generalization,* "All the packages contain alligator lamps" is $\frac{3}{4}$. On the evidence, this generalization has been confuted. The evidence shows this generalization to be false, for the contradictory is true, namely, "Some of the packages do not contain alligator lamps." The evidence does, however, point to another generalization, not *universal* but *particular.* On the evidence, it is probable that "Most of the packages contain alligator lamps" or, numerically expressed as a statistical generalization, it is probable that three-fourths of the packages in the whole collection contain alligator lamps.

Now to return to your willingness to generalize about the contents of all the packages. The evidence upon which your inductive conclusion is based may be expressed by a number of singular statements. The sample shows complete uniformity with respect to contents. On the basis of this evidence, you conclude that *probably* the whole class will exhibit this uniformity:

> This package contains an alligator lamp.
> So does this one.
> And this one.
> And this one.
> --
> All the packages contain alligator lamps.

It is obvious that this argument has a pattern quite different from that of a deduction. The argument is not, like a valid deduction, conclusive. It is quite possible that the conclusion is false even though the premises are all true. Yet the line of reasoning is a good one and gives us, in simplest form, the pattern by which most of man's general knowledge of the world was originally obtained. This pattern is inductive. The example specifically illustrates what is called induction by SIMPLE ENUMERATION; it merely involves noting supporting instances (packages which contain alligator lamps) as they turn up. If no confuting instances (packages which do not contain alligator lamps) are encountered, the hypothesis becomes increasingly probable as additional supporting data accumulate. We shall later consider examples of inductive reasoning in which more complex considerations come into play.

We saw earlier, in discussing a simple case of observation, that the process by which we arrive at a belief and the process by which we justify a belief are not necessarily the same. A similar comment applies to the more complicated type of situation we are now considering. We have just noted the typical process by which we arrive at a generalization. This process consists of reasoning from what we find to be true of a sample to what is probably true of the class from which the sample was taken. But on what grounds can we *justify* such a process of reasoning?

28.7. JUSTIFYING AN INDUCTIVE ARGUMENT

The pattern of justifying an induction, like that of justifying a simple observation, is deductive in nature. You will discover this for yourself if you ponder the question: Why do we think that the constitution of a sample offers a basis for concluding something about the probable constitution of the whole class? Isn't it because we are making the crucial assumption that the characteristics possessed by the individual members of the sample will probably also be possessed by the members of the whole class that are not in the sample? Understanding the CONSTITUTION of a class to mean the characteristics possessed by its members, we may state this assumption more compactly:

> If the sample has such-and-such a constitution, the whole class will probably also have it.

We may for convenience call this assumption the POSTULATE OF INDUCTION.[7] When on the basis of observation we find that a given sample has

[7] In this section, we are concerned not with the general philosophical problem sometimes called "The Justification of Induction," but rather with the manner in which we justify specific inductive arguments. We are saying this can be done on the basis of the Postulate of Induction. The questions of whether this postulate can itself be justified, or whether lacking it there is any other way to justify a specific induction,

such-and-such a constitution, we conclude by a valid deduction from the postulate and this observation statement that the whole class will probably have it too.

28.8. INCREASING THE PROBABILITY OF A GENERALIZATION

Whether we consider the pattern of the inductive process itself, or consider the deductive argument by which we may justify an induction, we find that a generalization can never be more than probable. This does not end the matter, however, but rather shifts our attention to another question: How is the probability of a generalization to be increased? In general, the answer to this question is: By increasing the reliability of our sample. Let us first note why this is so, and then consider the principles which govern reliability of samples.

The probability of a conclusion might conceivably be increased by improving either the form or the content of the argument. The general form of an inductive argument, however, is fixed: the premises are singular statements reporting a sampling process, and the conclusion asserts that the make-up of the whole class is probably similar to that of the sample. Improvements must in general come, therefore, not in the form of the argument but in its content. To speak in this way of the fixity of the *general form* of an inductive argument is not to imply that we cannot improve the form of the individual statements that enter into the argument. In fact, as we shall see in Chapter 29, an important aspect of improving some generalizations consists in substituting for a statement of the form "If A then B" a statement of the form "If A, in circumstances C, then B." It is perhaps somewhat arbitrary whether we think of this refinement as a change in the form of the statement or as merely a greater explicitness of content. For as we shall see, the *circumstances* constitute part of the antecedent of the statement.

At present, however, we want to note that in more general terms we increase the probability of an inductive inference by improving and refin-

or whether it is reasonable to ask for a *general* justification of induction—all these raise controversial philosophical issues of great complexity which we cannot here discuss. As logicians, however, we may be interested in noting that the attempt to treat the Postulate of Induction, not as a postulate, but as itself an inductive generalization from experience, seems to involve circular reasoning if we then go on to use this postulate to justify specific inductions. Our common-sense justification of the postulate seems purely pragmatic: "Well, it works, doesn't it?"

ing the evidence upon which it rests. This evidence (with one exception) consists, as we know, of statements about a sample.[8] In induction, we take the sample as a representative of the whole class. Anything we can do to increase the probability that the sample is genuinely representative of the whole class will increase the probability of our generalization.

A thorough analysis of the means by which the reliability of a sample may be increased would take us beyond the scope and intent of our present study. It would take us into the heart of the technicalities of contemporary statistical theory. Our present purpose is rather to note some general considerations governing the reliability of a sample.

The principle of quantity: [9] Other things being equal, the reliability of the sample increases with an increase in the size of the sample.

Induction at the simplest common-sense level tends to rely on this principle almost exclusively. If our sample of alligator-lamp Christmas presents is only two, we would probably feel that it was too small a sample to be very reliable. As the sample increases to four, we feel somewhat more confident about its reliability. And if we open eight packages and find them all to contain alligator lamps, we may feel that the sample is now large enough to give us quite a good clue to the nature of the whole lot of presents. But a closer look at this principle is called for.

(a) Thus far we have merely noted the way our *confidence* in the reliability of a sample tends to increase as the size of the sample increases. But we emphasized earlier the fact that this subjective feeling is not itself to be identified with the relation of probability. The question is: Are

---

[8] The exception is the evidence indirectly provided by the way in which the generalization fits into the body of previously established knowledge. At times, particularly in a highly systematized field of well established knowledge, this factor is given considerable weight.

[9] This manner of speaking in empirics of "The Principle of So-and-so" is convenient, but perhaps somewhat pompous and grandiloquent. It may even be misleading. Most of the "principles" of empirical inquiry have a rather different status from the principles of, say, syntactics and mathematics. Such formal principles are constitutive. The principles of empirics, on the other hand, are largely heuristic, that is, guides to discovery. Such principles are primarily convenient ways of summarizing and calling attention to procedures or considerations that have been found helpful in our search for the facts. For this reason, they need to be taken into account in intelligent inquiry. With this word of warning, we may permit ourselves the convenience of this mode of speech.

there any logical grounds for this feeling in the present case? Is there any reason for thinking that the increased size of the sample is accompanied by an increase in the probability that the sample is a reliable one? Yes, there is a reason, though it is not conclusive: As we increase the size of the sample, we increase the chances that we shall turn up variations, exceptions, and peculiarities in the class if such exist.

(b) We cannot attach any simple or direct numerical measure to this increase in the probable reliability of our larger sample. For example, it would be incorrect to urge that a sample of eight is probably twice as reliable as a sample of four.

(c) The probable reliability of the sample is affected by the size of the class we are sampling. If the whole class has only eight members, a sample of four would have a greater probable reliability than if the class contained 80 members or 800. If the size of the whole class is known, it is possible to assign a numerical value to the probable reliability of a sample of given size. In practice, however, we often have no way of knowing how large the total class is. This is perhaps even truer of typical scientific inquiry than of common-sense inquiry. At the common-sense level we do have some occasion to deal with fairly small collections, the extent of which may be known (for example, the number of presents we receive on a given Christmas). In scientific inquiry, where we are usually concerned with generalizations of great scope, applying to past, present, and future cases, we know only that the classes involved are very large. In scientific work, however, we depend less upon the mere size of the sample, and are concerned more with other ways of increasing its probable reliability.

(d) The Principle of Quantity is the easiest of all to apply in practice. For anyone can tell whether his sample is getting larger or not. This ease of application is no doubt the main reason that common-sense inquiry depends so extensively upon this single principle. It is important to recognize, however, that the probability of getting a more representative sample *merely* by increasing its size is not particularly high. There is always the danger that some selective factor is operating, so that even though our sample becomes very large, we are failing to get an adequate cross section of the whole class. A simple illustration will emphasize this danger.

Suppose a person is sitting on the bank of a stream. Around the bend

upstream is a farm. As he sits there, he sees a number of small downy yellow ducks paddling around the bend. As he watches, more and more small
yellow ducks swim downstream. If he knows nothing about ducks and
barnyards, and is entirely dependent upon the increasingly large sample
before him, he may become more and more confident that all the ducks
on the stream are small, downy, and yellow. But as the rest of us might
suspect, there are plenty of large and, let us say, pure white ducks upstream just around the bend. They are prevented from swimming downstream and becoming part of the sample by a wire fence, the meshes of
which are too small for a grown duck to swim through.

(c) The importance of a large sample varies with the constitution
of the class being sampled. This is why we introduce our statement of the
Principle of Quantity with the phrase, "other things being equal." We may
distinguish two different types of class with respect to constitution. A
HOMOGENEOUS CLASS is one all the members of which have the same or
basically similar characteristics. A HETEROGENEOUS CLASS is one which is
not homogeneous. A class may, of course, be homogeneous with respect
to certain characteristics and heterogeneous with respect to others. It is
therefore not safe to assume that a class which has been found to be
homogeneous in certain respects will necessarily prove to be homogeneous
in all respects.[10]

The importance of the Principle of Quantity increases with the heterogeneity of the class in question. The more heterogeneous the class is, the
more important it is to get a large sample, so that the likelihood of getting
a representative cross section of the class will be increased. If the class
could be known to be homogeneous, on the other hand, a very small
sample would suffice.

There is, of course, a certain paradox here. For we can in general discover the extent of heterogeneity in a class only by sampling. In practice,
this is the way it works out: (1) When we have little or no background
knowledge of the field being sampled, we lay considerable stress on getting
a large sample. (2) Once we have learned something of the constitution
of the field on the basis of previous sampling, we take this knowledge into
account in deciding how important a large sample will be for further
investigations. If our original sample turns out to be homogeneous, we

[10] This is one of the main weaknesses of arguments from analogy.

may in future work attach less importance to the size of the sample. If, however, our original sample is very heterogeneous, we shall insist on large samples for our further investigations. In all such judgments, we are trying to make the best of available information, but it is clear that we are here dealing with probabilities rather than with certainties.

The principle of randomness: The reliability of a sample increases as the sampling process approaches randomness.

When in everyday English we speak of selecting items "at random," we usually mean selecting them in a hit-or-miss fashion without any preconceived plan or pattern. To explain randomness somewhat more technically, we may say that a RANDOM SAMPLE is one selected in such a way that the probability of selecting any one item in the class is the same as that of selecting any other. While it is thus a simple matter to explain what we mean by a random sample, it is in practice more difficult to judge whether we are actually getting one.[11]

(a) Our attempts to sample at random encounter a paradox somewhat similar to the one we ran into in trying to apply the Principle of Quantity. Random sampling is of greatest importance when we have little or no background knowledge about the constitution of the class being sampled. But without some such knowledge, it is difficult to choose that technique of sampling which is most likely to produce a random sample. Again, a trivial example will make the difficulty clearer.

Let us imagine a person ignorant of the characteristics of popcorn, faced with the problem of securing a random sample of the contents of a particular sackful. He can see the large fluffy white kernels on top. Although he is ignorant of the specific characteristics of popcorn, he has had enough experience with other types of collection to realize that it

[11] One difficulty, for example, is the possibility that an unconscious bias on the part of the sampler is affecting his procedure. A common precaution is the use of independently prepared tables of random digits that tell him which items in a series to take for his sample. A shortcut which is often used as a substitute for random sampling is to select items for the sample by taking every *n*th one. The result will of course not be equivalent to a random sample unless the arrangement in the reference class is itself random. On these points, see E. Bright Wilson, Jr.: *An Introduction to Scientific Research*, McGraw-Hill, 1952, pp. 155f., 163f.

would be unsafe to generalize from the kernels he sees on top. He knows enough, that is, to realize that the class in question may not be a homogeneous one. So he attempts to get a random sample of the whole class. He does this, let us suppose, by shaking the sack so that new kernels come to the top. They too, he finds, are large, white, and fluffy. As he continues this shaking-up process, he finds that all the kernels which come to the top have the basic characteristics of his original surface sample. He concludes that the whole sackful is uniformly constituted. But what we know and he does not is that his *technique* for securing a random sample has been unsuccessful. The very technique introduced for this purpose has resulted in separating out the well-popped kernels from the unpopped "old maids" which have settled to the bottom of the sack.

Here again we simply have to do the best we can, making use of whatever background information we have, trying out various techniques of sampling that occur to us, and hoping that our knowledge of the constitution of the class will increase with further sampling.

(b) As our background knowledge increases, we may be able to select a highly representative sample by introducing considerations other than randomness. Suppose, for example, that we are trying to determine campus opinion on the question of whether freshman women should be permitted to stay out later at night. We already know a good deal about the make-up of the college population. We know, let us say, that we are dealing with a coeducational school. We know that there is faculty, administrative, and parental opinion to consider as well as student opinion. We know that the student body consists not merely of freshman women, but of freshman men, and sophomores, juniors, and seniors of both sexes. What is equally important, we know from past experience that the opinions of these different groups differ on a number of subjects, and it seems likely that there may be important differences among them on the present subject. We know, in other words, that we are dealing with a STRATIFIED CLASS, that is, a class which contains subclasses differing in various respects which may be important for the current inquiry.

We make the best use of this background information we can in order to obtain as representative a sample as possible. Instead of seeking ways of getting a truly random sample, that is, one which is just as likely to contain any one member of the college community as any other, we make sure we obtain a properly stratified sample. We see to it that our sample includes representatives of all the basic subclasses of the campus community. We question not only women but men, not only freshmen but upperclassmen, not only students but faculty, administration, and parents. While such a sample introduces other considerations than that of size and randomness, it is likely to give us an excellent cross section of the class being sampled, for it makes good use of available background information.

In the light of this discussion, we may state a third principle governing the reliability of a sample and hence the probability of a generalization based upon this sample:

The principle of stratification: If the class being sampled is a stratified class, the reliability of a sample increases as it more accurately reproduces the stratification existing in the whole class.

Note carefully that the Principle of Stratification does not altogether replace the Principle of Randomness even when we have considerable background knowledge of the nature of the stratification existing in a class. We seek a sample which will accurately reproduce the stratification known to exist in the class as a whole, but *within* each stratum we should usually seek to obtain a random sample. Here again we try to make the best use of background knowledge. We aim at a random sample of the stratum of faculty members, for example, for we know from experience that they are not a homogeneous class with respect to opinions.

Even though we recognize certain stratifications *within* the stratum of faculty members and realize that they may be correlated with differing opinions on how late freshman women should stay out, we may in practice probably ignore these special subclasses if we are confident that our "random" polling of the faculty stratum as a whole will give a reliable sample in which all these subclasses are proportionately represented. But the possibility must always be borne in mind that our sampling procedure may not be truly random and may not give us a reliable sample. It may omit one stratification or give too much representation to another. Suppose we plan to poll faculty members as they walk across the campus. There may be an important subclass of the faculty which doesn't walk across the campus at all but always uses cars. Excluding these may introduce serious errors in our estimate of the views of the whole faculty.

• SOME REMINDERS

1. To decide whether a statement is a generalization, you have to know how it was derived.
2. Generalizations may be either universal or particular. Statistical and tendential generalizations are special types of particular generalization.
3. Generalizations must be distinguished from deductive specifications, disguised definitions, and summations.
4. The process of induction involves reasoning from a sample.
5. The pattern of justifying an induction is deductive.
6. Principles dealing with such factors as quantity, randomness, and stratification guide us in our attempts to select a sample that will be representative of its class.

APPLICATIONS

1. In each case, decide whether the given sentence is most likely a generalization, a specification, a disguised definition, or a summation. Since context is lacking, a variety of interpretations are possible. Therefore in each case indicate the type of premises needed to support your interpretation.
   a. Everyone should be kind to dumb animals.
   b. It nearly always snows in December.
   c. All men are brothers.
   d. Truthful people do not prevaricate.
   e. Newborn babies do not speak English.
   f. All the coins in my pocket are pennies.
   g. Fur-bearing animals are always warm-blooded.
   h. All chairs should be capable of being sat on.
   i. Whales are the largest mammals.
   j. All my neighbors are very friendly.
2. Criticize or justify the following sampling procedures. If there is something wrong with them, explain what it is, and how they might be improved.
   a. To decide whether the tax levy for schools should be increased, we poll all members of the Parent-Teacher Association.
   b. To judge the effectiveness of an advertisement, we include a coupon on which the reader may apply for a free booklet.
   c. To decide whether a particular road should be paved, we for one week interview all drivers using the road.
   d. To judge the uniform quality of a product, we ask the manufacturer to submit samples for our inspection.
   e. To predict who will win an election, we interview people whose names have been selected at random from the telephone directory.
   f. To determine the desirability of drafting soldiers in alphabetical order, we interview all men of draft age whose next birthday falls on a Wednesday.

CHAPTER 29

CAUSAL GENERALIZATIONS

PREVIEW

We have seen that induction rests upon sampling, and have considered various ways in which the reliability of a sample may be increased. We turn now to a type of case in which a precise generalization is sought through a careful analysis of the circumstances which accompany the individual instances in the sample. Here again, as in the Case of the Cold House, we shall try to get an insight into general principles of inquiry by seeing them actually at work in a concrete situation.

29.1. "CIRCUMSTANCES ALTER CASES"

Induction rests, as we have seen, upon sampling. We generalize about the constitution of a class on the basis of an examination of a sample of the class. The more reliable the sample, the more probable the generalization based upon it. Such considerations as size, randomness, and stratification guide us in our efforts to select a sample which will accurately represent the class from which it is drawn. In some investigations, particularly those in which we are trying to determine what characteristics go along with certain others, such considerations dominate. An example would be an inquiry to determine what proportion of brown-eyed women in the American population are left-handed. Here our concern is with what John Stuart Mill called UNIFORMITIES OF COEXISTENCE,[1] and here the sampling factors discussed in the last chapter are central.

While such considerations are always relevant in inductive inquiry, there are cases in which they play a less dominant part. This does not mean that in such cases they are inconsequential, but rather that they are

[1] *A System of Logic*, p. 407.

overshadowed by a further type of analysis. Such cases are best represented by inquiries which seek to answer the "What will happen if . . . ?"
type of question. The first thing to be said in reply to all such questions
is, "It depends on the circumstances." One reason we do not, at the
common-sense level, always recognize the importance of the accompanying circumstances in such cases is that we *assume* certain "standard" or
familiar circumstances. Thus, to the question, "What will happen if I throw
this switch?", the common-sense answer may be "The light will go on." But
such an answer assumes that the circumstances are those which have
normally been present in the past when experience has shown the light to
go on if the switch was thrown. It is assumed, for example, that the light is
not already on (for then throwing the switch would normally make it go
off), that electrical power is available, that the fuse has not blown, that
the wiring is intact, that the light bulb has not burned out, and so on. If
we grow impatient over the enumeration of such circumstances, it is only
because we have been assuming them in asking our original question, and
regard them as too obvious to mention. Yet the importance of paying attention to the circumstances is recognized even at the common-sense level
in the folk adage, "Circumstances alter cases."

The generalizations which are the outcome of successful inquiry into
the "What will happen if . . . ?" type of question deal with what Mill
refers to as UNIFORMITIES OF SUCCESSION (*ibid.*). Once we recognize the
importance of the circumstances, we can distinguish three different types
of question dealing with such uniformities.

(1) If such-and-such a type of event occurs in such-and-
such circumstances, what (if anything) will regularly
happen? (Inquiry into "effects")
(2) In what specific circumstances (if any) will an event
of such-and-such a type regularly lead to an event of
such-and-such another type? (Inquiry into accompanying circumstances)
(3) What type of event (if any) regularly occurs immediately before such-and-such another type of event
in such-and-such circumstances? (Inquiry into "cause,"
in one sense of the word)

The generalizations which provide empirical answers to these three types
of question are commonly called CAUSAL GENERALIZATIONS. It is important
to recognize, however, that the question initiating such inquiries need not

be a question about a cause (Question 3 above) but may be about effects or circumstances. Note also that the parenthetical "if any" in the above questions reminds us that we cannot conclude, in advance of inquiry, that two types of event *are* regularly connected. Finally note that, as the word "regularly" in the above questions indicates, we are here asking for universal generalizations. Such generalizations, when highly confirmed, are commonly called CAUSAL LAWS, but we should remind ourselves that some regularities are not *causal* regularities. This use of the term "laws" sometimes gives rise to semantical difficulties when people confuse such laws (which are highly probable empirical generalizations) with governmental or statutory laws (which have rather the nature of stipulations, conventions, or rules of the game).[2]

The upshot of all this is that when we are concerned with any but the simplest and roughest of generalizations dealing with successive occurrences, other considerations than those discussed in the last chapter become important. Instances in the sample must be further analyzed to find out which factors are relevant and irrelevant to the generalization, and precise circumstances must be determined. For the rough purposes of primitive common sense, it may be enough to know that "If water gets very cold, it will freeze." [3] But for more advanced purposes, we need empirical generalizations that will specify precisely *how* cold, and in what specific circumstances. Enlightened common sense advances some distance toward greater precision here, and says, "If water gets as cold as 32° Fahrenheit, it will freeze." But even this is, for scientific purposes, an inadequate account of the circumstances. Will water freeze at 32° if it is being rapidly stirred? What effect will certain impurities in the water have upon the point at which it freezes? May differences in atmospheric pressure be ignored, or must the generalization take them into account? We may, even in science, sometimes permit ourselves to speak in a condensed or approximate form. But we need to understand clearly just what circumstances are assumed to be present even when we do not take time to mention them explicitly.

[2] For one analysis of such semantical confusions as they relate to the question of moral responsibility, see Moritz Schlick: *Problems of Ethics*, New York, Prentice-Hall, Inc., 1939, Chapter VII, especially pp. 146–148.

[3] The conditional statements used to set forth causal generalizations are of course general conditionals, not molecular ones (see Section 9.6). While we could use atomic statements for this purpose (for example, "All cases of water getting very cold are cases of water freezing"), the directional relation between cause and effect is perhaps more clearly brought out by the conditional form of expression.

In the following section, we shall begin a detailed examination of the type of case in which such further analysis is important. In most investigations of this type, we already have at hand a great deal of general knowledge which aids us in making judgments of relevance. In a given case only a detailed inquiry will help us understand precisely which circumstances must be taken into account; antecedent knowledge, however, often permits us to disregard, with a high degree of antecedent probability, some particular accompanying factor. We have learned from experience, for example, that the breaking of a window by the impact of a hurled rock is not significantly affected by whether the sun is shining at the time. In order to get some appreciation of the importance of such judgments of relevance, it would be instructive to consider an example chosen from some newly opened area of science, where little antecedent knowledge of the phenomena was available. By following through the efforts of the scientist in his first attempts to establish causal generalizations in this new field, we should learn a great deal about how careful empirical inquiry proceeds. It is obvious, however, that such an example would demand on our part an understanding of advanced techniques in some specialized field. But this, let us admit, is something that few of us will have time to acquire before finishing the present chapter.

A different approach will, however, have some of the same advantages as the study of such a pioneer investigation. Let us select a very simple example from an area where we all understand pretty well what is going on. But let us in imagination follow the efforts of a hypothetical individual who has little or no knowledge of the field. In order to permit him to get somewhere within the limits of a chapter, let us endow him with considerable logical and analytical skill. We shall, however, purposely deprive him of as much factual knowledge as possible, so that his struggles will force us to notice the important role of judgments of relevance and irrelevance.

29.2. LETTING GEORGE DO IT

Let us imagine, then, a very inexperienced but intellectually eager and logically competent fellow named "George" who gets to wondering. "I wonder," George says, "what will happen to objects when I let go of them?" (Note that the concept of letting go of something assumes a prior condition, namely having hold of it in the first place. While we shall not

keep mentioning this, it should of course be remembered throughout
our discussion.) Here, then, is his problem which sets the stage for
empirical inquiry. He is in search of a hypothesis which will have the general form:

> If I [l]et go of an object, then
> [X]. $L \rightarrow X$[4]   **(1.0)**

As we follow his struggles to arrive at an adequate generalization covering
the behavior of released objects, we shall find him considering a number
of related hypotheses all proposing an answer to this original question. We
shall find that all these hypotheses form a series, which we shall for convenience indicate by the number "1." We shall indicate successive hypotheses in this series by an appropriate decimal following the "1."

George begins to explore the field. He picks up a bottle of ink and lets
go of it. It drops to the cement floor and breaks, splashing ink over his
shoes. It would of course be rash to generalize from a sample containing
only one instance, but at least he has a start. The evidence suggests a
hypothesis for further exploration:

> If I let go of an object, it will
> [d]rop, hit the [f]loor, [b]reak,
> and [s]plash ink over my shoes. $L \rightarrow DFBS$ **(Hypo. 1.1)**

Any instance of supporting evidence for a hypothesis is called a SUPPORT-
ING DATUM, and any instance which is inconsistent with a hypothesis is
called a CONFUTING DATUM. When the hypothesis itself is a conditional
statement, such a datum, whether supporting or confuting, is reported by
a singular conjunctive statement. George's sole present evidence (supporting datum) for this hypothesis may be stated:

> I let go of this object and it
> dropped, hit the floor, broke, and
> splashed ink over my shoes.   LDFBS

---

[4] The purpose of the symbols used in this chapter is mainly to clarify the exposition,
rather than to provide (as in syntactics) a basis for further symbolic manipulation.
Although we shall use capital letters to symbolize the factors involved in a causal
generalization, we shall not in this use require that they represent strictly statemental
elements. To avoid confusing these general conditionals with molecular conditionals
(previously symbolized with capital letters and "⊃"), we shall in this chapter adopt
the arbitrary symbol "→" to represent the general "if . . . then" connective. Alternative procedures (both less desirable for our present purposes) would be (a) to
restate these general conditionals as subject-predicate statements, using class-relation
symbols, or (b) to treat them as quantified statement-forms, introducing the more
complex standard symbols for which English versions were given in Section 16.8.

It is sometimes said that the probability of a generalization is increased by making it more explicit. But this notion of increased explicitness needs considerable analysis. In the light of our own broader knowledge (which George does not yet possess) it is obvious that in one sense Hypothesis 1.1 is already too explicit to fit the data which further inquiry will turn up. For the moment, however, merely note where this excessive explicitness occurs: it is in the consequent.

29.3. ELIMINATION OF IRRELEVANT FACTORS IN THE CONSEQUENT

Seeking more evidence, our uninformed friend George next picks up a rubber eraser and lets go of it. It drops to the floor, bounces slightly, and comes to rest. Already George has learned a lot about what happens to objects when he lets go of them. Just what has he learned from these two cases?

For one thing, it has become clear that the consequent of Hypothesis 1.1 is too specific; it says too much. For the eraser, although he let go of it, did not break and splash ink over his shoes. George sees, in other words, that certain factors in the consequent of Hypothesis 1.1 are irrelevant to the *generalization* he is seeking to formulate about what happens to objects when he lets go of them. He therefore corrects his hypothesis by eliminating the factors in the consequent that comparison of the two cases shows to be irrelevant. His revised hypothesis is:

> If I let go of an object, it will
> drop and hit the floor. $L \rightarrow DF$ **(Hypo. 1.2)**

We may state what has happened in another way too. The experiment with the eraser provided a datum which *confuted* Hypothesis 1.1 taken as a whole, since the eraser did not break and spatter ink. In the light of the evidence, therefore, Hypothesis 1.1 had to be rejected. But the combined evidence of the two cases suggested a further hypothesis (1.2) which is consistent with both sets of data. What we need to do is to note the way in which Hypothesis 1.2 is related to the rejected Hypothesis 1.1: factors which occurred in only *some* instances of the sample have been eliminated from the consequent.

What George is here doing is to discard from his hypothesis factors which his evidence shows to be irrelevant. This term "irrelevant" may be misleading if we forget the type of answer that George is looking for. By calling factors "irrelevant" we mean merely that the evidence has shown that they have no place in the universal generalization that George is seeking. On what grounds does he eliminate a factor from the consequent? Simply that he finds cases of the antecedent factor (letting go of an object) occurring without being followed by the occurrence of a case of the given consequent factor (for example, the object breaking or spattering ink).[5] As we shall see, if this procedure were all George had to go on, the results would be devastating, for he would probably soon find that he had no consequent factors left.

George is making some progress, but it would be rash for him to accept Hypothesis 1.2 on the basis of only two sets of supporting data. Without following this phase of his inquiry in detail, we may imagine him seeking to increase the probability of this hypothesis by increasing the size of his sample, in accordance with the Principle of Quantity. His sample will become more representative of released objects in general, as he tries out objects of different kinds: pencils, books, potatoes, saucers, and stones.

Somewhere along the line he makes a further interesting discovery which shows that his generalization is in need of still further correction. He lets go of a pencil, let us say, and finds that it drops, not to the floor, but to the surface of the desk over which he was holding it. Here again, evidence turns up in his sample which enables him, in accordance with the above procedure, to rule out another irrelevant factor in the consequent. His revised hypothesis is:

If I let go of an object, it will
drop. $L \to D$ **(Hypo. 1.3)**

In this form, the statement is a good example of a typical common-sense generalization.[6] In the light of our own broader knowledge, we all recog-

---

[5] It is often convenient to speak as we have above of *factors* in the antecedent and consequent of a causal generalization. These FACTORS are events or states, for example, my letting go of an object. Now, since a generalization is a *statement*, it cannot really contain things like events, but only things like words. Thus the convenient expression, "factors in the antecedent," must be understood as a rough and condensed manner of speaking. It means "the type of event or state referred to in the antecedent." For example, the type of event referred to by "I let go of an object" is my letting go of an object.

[6] Note that the point at which we regard a generalization as no longer a hypothesis but as a statement of established general fact (a "law") is somewhat arbitrary. As we saw in Section 23.2, a much higher degree of confirmation is typically demanded in a science than in common-sense inquiry.

nize that this generalization, like many at the common-sense level, is still subject to improvement. But before going further, let us note four points about the progress of the inquiry thus far: (1) The refinements (in this case eliminations) have all concerned the consequent of the generalization; the antecedent has remained the same throughout. (2) These eliminations have been made in order to take account of new evidence that has turned up in the sample. (3) The process is clearly one of induction; on the evidence provided by a sample, statements about the probable constitution of the whole class are being made. (4) Perhaps most important of all to note is that the increased probability of Hypothesis 1.3 in contrast to the earlier ones results not merely from the larger sample upon which it is based, but even more upon the *greater care with which factors are being analyzed*. The increase of probability from this latter source helps explain why, in scientific inquiry, a relatively few cases, thoroughly analyzed under controlled conditions, may yield a much more reliable sample than a much larger but relatively unanalyzed sample such as we often use in common-sense inquiry.

29.4. NEED FOR FURTHER REFINEMENT OF THE HYPOTHESIS SHOWN BY CONFUTATION OF A PREDICTION BASED UPON IT

From the vantage point of our own superior knowledge, we know that George is in for some further surprises if he keeps sampling long enough. Let us suppose, for example, that he is toying with his watch which lies in front of him on his desk. Seeing the possibility of getting a further supporting instance of his refined Hypothesis 1.3, he takes hold of the watch as it lies flat on the surface of the desk, and then lets go of it. Nothing happens; the watch remains precisely where it was. In the light of his previous sampling, this is so astonishing that he tries it again. Same result. Here is some negative evidence which confutes Hypothesis 1.3. Let us note the exact pattern of this confutation. On the basis of Hypothesis 1.3 and his additional knowledge that the watch is an object, he reasons:

Argument 1

If I let go of an object, it will drop.   (Hypo. 1.3)
The watch is an object. (By observed conformity to definition)

If I let go of the watch, it will drop. (Specification of Hypo. 1.3)

This specification of the hypothesis may be used as the conditional premise of a syntactically valid prediction:

Argument 2

If I let go of the watch, it will drop.
I let go of the watch.
_____
It will drop.   (Prediction)

But the experiment shows this conclusion to be false.[7] It also shows that the conditional premise of Argument 2 (Specification of Hypothesis 1.3) is false, for by observation he discovers that the following conjunctive statement is true:

I let go of the watch, but it does not drop.

This conjunctive statement is, of course, the contradictory of his conditional premise, and that premise must be false if the conjunctive statement is true.

This takes us back to Argument 1, which we know to be valid. We have just shown that it is practically certain that the conclusion of this Argument 1 is false. Since the argument is valid, we know that if the conclusion is actually false, this must be because one or both of the premises is false. But there is no reason to question the truth of the second premise ("The watch is an object") so the difficulty must lie with the first premise, Hypothesis 1.3. George concludes, with practical certainty, that this hypothesis is false. In the light of his earlier evidence, this cannot mean that *no* released objects will drop (the logical *contrary* of Hypothesis 1.3) but only that *some* do not (the logical *contradictory* of Hypothesis 1.3).[8]

29.5. THE NEED FOR A NEW APPROACH

If all George has to go on is the previous procedure of eliminating factors from the consequent, he seems to have reached an impasse. It would appear that in accordance with this approach he has now eliminated everything, and has no consequent left. Just as this principle required him to eliminate breaking and splashing ink as irrelevant factors, so it would require him to eliminate the factor of dropping as irrelevant.

_____

[7] For the sake of brevity, we may here and elsewhere permit ourselves to say that an observation may show a statement to be false or to be true. In the light of our earlier discussion, we should understand this to mean "shows, with practical certainty."

[8] Recall that two statements are logically contrary if they may both be false but cannot both be true; they are logically contradictory, of course, if they can neither both be true nor both be false.

For he has just encountered a case where letting go of an object was not accompanied by its dropping. And he has been discarding from the consequent any factor which is sometimes absent when the antecedent factor is present. It might thus seem that George will have to start all over. Actually, the situation is not this serious.

29.6. HOW THE ACCUMULATED EVIDENCE MAY BE "SAVED"

It is possible for him to frame a new hypothesis making full use of all the evidence he has accumulated. This may be done in either of two ways, although we shall focus our principal attention upon the second.

(1) George may frankly give up the quest for a universal generalization and, in the light of the available evidence, substitute instead a particular generalization, "Most objects will drop if I let go of them." At the common-sense level we are often satisfied with such a solution. Another way of achieving the same result would be to substitute the tendential generalization, "Objects tend to drop when I let go of them." Again, George might seek greater precision by using a statistical generalization which would provide a numerical answer to the question, "What percentage of objects fall when I release them?" But even at the common-sense level, practical needs might require more detailed knowledge of the behavior of released objects than such generalizations afford. Whether to satisfy such a practical need or the theoretical interest of pure science, George might have further questions to ask. For example, just what is it about the objects which *do* fall when released that differentiates them from those which do not fall? This brings us to the second and more important approach.

(2) George may recognize that he must analyze more fully the *circumstances* in which objects will drop if he lets go of them. What he needs is a generalization which is not simply of the form, "If I let go of objects, they will drop," but which has the form, "If I let go of objects in such-and-such circumstances, they will drop." Another way of putting this is that the *antecedent* of his generalization needs further analysis. Hypothesis 1.3 has the form, "$A \rightarrow B$." What is needed is a generalization of the form, "$AC \rightarrow B$," where "C" stands for the circumstances.[9]

---

[9] A clear and convenient notation here is: "$A(C) \rightarrow B$." This notation means the same as "$AC \rightarrow B$," but the parentheses around "C" show that the C-factors are being con-

Note carefully that George might have shifted his attack at an earlier stage of the inquiry. When he found, for example, that some objects hit the floor when they dropped while some did not, he might have contented himself with the weak particular generalization, "Some objects drop and hit the floor when I let go of them." Or, he might at this stage have taken the other approach and asked, "In just what specific circumstances will objects drop *and hit the floor* when I let go of them?" We have, however, let him go along to the point where the need for such a shift in approach was forced upon him by the data which turned up in his sampling. We shall next turn with George to an analysis of the *circumstances*.

• SOME REMINDERS

1. Some generalizations deal with coexisting characteristics; others seek to determine uniformities of successive occurrences.
2. Adequate generalizations of the latter type require many judgments of relevance and irrelevance, and an analysis of circumstances.
3. A factor in the consequent of a hypothesis dealing with uniformity of successive occurrences is eliminated if the basic antecedent factor is found to occur without the specific consequent factor.
4. This procedure of elimination from the consequent must be supplemented by further analysis of factors in the antecedent.

APPLICATIONS

1. In each case, using available knowledge, indicate as explicitly as possible the circumstances that must be assumed if the generalization is to hold.
   a. If you put your hand into the fire, it will get burned.
   b. It is colder in December than in July.
   c. If the cost of wheat goes up, the price of bread will rise.
   d. If milk is churned, it will turn into butter.
   e. If a person is a senior, he knows more than a freshman.
   f. A man can travel faster than a turtle.
   g. Two heads are better than one.
   h. If you want to be healthy, you should drink plenty of milk.
   i. Many hands make light work.
   j. If there are no clouds, you can always see the sun during the daytime.

sidered as accompanying circumstances rather than as what we may call the BASIC FACTORS ("A" and "B") in the generalization. The decision as to which antecedent factor we shall treat as basic, and which factors we shall consider as accompanying circumstances is in some cases quite arbitrary and in others is dictated by our particular interests.

29.7. THE IMPORTANCE OF JUDGMENTS OF RELEVANCE AND THEIR DIFFICULTY WHEN BACKGROUND KNOWLEDGE IS MEAGER

The immediate problem which George now faces is to account for the difference between all the earlier cases, in which the object dropped when he let go of it, and the case in which the watch did not drop when he let go of it. If he had more background knowledge, it would be of use to him in judging which factors in the circumstances *might* be relevant, and which might safely be ignored as irrelevant. In his relative ignorance, however, he has very little to go on.

From the vantage point of our accumulated knowledge, it is easy to overlook the vast number of judgments of relevance and irrelevance that are required in even the simplest inquiry. If George is really as uninformed as we have been picturing him, he may have to spend a great deal of time following out various possibilities on a trial-and-error basis. This is inevitable where background knowledge is lacking. For example, is it safe for him to ignore the fact that, let us say, he has always been holding the objects in his right hand rather than his left before dropping them? Can he assume that it is irrelevant that the lights have been on whenever an object dropped when he let go of it? Does the fact that his watch is made of metal perhaps have something to do with its not dropping when he let go of it? Such questions seem silly to us, but only because we believe that "everyone" knows their answers on the basis of past experience. In new and unfamiliar fields of inquiry, a great many such questions of relevance or irrelevance may require separate investigation.

We have tried to stress the nature of the situation George faces, for it is the type we encounter whenever background knowledge of antecedent probabilities is lacking. If we appreciate his position clearly, we shall have a better understanding of the role which "insight," "horse sense," and just plain "luck" have in empirical inquiry. We shall gain a deeper appreciation of those phases of scientific inquiry which are not a matter of applying established rules, but are rather cases of using whatever ingenuity one can muster in order to uncover a hopeful lead.

29.8. NECESSARY CONDITIONS AND SUFFICIENT CONDITIONS

George thinks about the previous cases in which objects have dropped when he let go of them, and of the case in which his watch did not drop when he let go of it. His problem is not merely to determine what is different in the two types of case (for there are no doubt many differences, some of which are quite irrelevant). His specific problem is rather to determine what differences really "make a difference" in the result. In other words, he must try to find out which differences in the circumstances are relevant to or "responsible for" the observed difference in results. Suppose it occurs to him that the fact that the watch is made of metal, while none of the other objects were, may have had something to do with its *not* dropping when he let go of it.

"Perhaps," George is thinking, "if something is to drop when I let go of it, it is necessary that the object be *nonmetallic*." What does he mean by raising this question of whether a particular circumstance is *necessary* for some result? His question is just a special case of the more general question, "What is meant by asking whether a particular *condition* is necessary for some result?" A CONDITION, in this sense, is any factor in the antecedent, whether that factor be what we have previously called the *basic factor* (in this case, George's letting go of an object) or one of the factors which make up the *circumstances* (for example, the object's being nonmetallic). We have already noted that whether a particular antecedent factor (or *condition*, as we may now say) is regarded as basic or as part of the circumstances is somewhat arbitrary, being usually decided in the light of our particular interests at the time. This point may be most readily understood by contrasting two such questions for inquiry as: "If I let go of an object (basic antecedent factor), then what will happen (consequent) in case the object is nonmetallic (circumstantial antecedent factor)?" and "If an object is nonmetallic (basic antecedent factor), then what will happen (consequent) in case I let go of it (circumstances)?" Instead, then, of asking, "What is meant by saying that a given *circumstance* is necessary for some result?", it will be useful to ask the question more generally about a given *condition*, whether at the time it is being regarded as the basic antecedent factor or as a supporting circumstance.

To say that a condition is NECESSARY for a given result means that if the result occurs, the given condition must also have occurred. Expressed compactly in symbols, "A is a necessary condition for B" means "B → A."

What would be required to show that a given condition A is *not* necessary for B? We can show that a condition is not necessary by pointing to an instance which has the form of the contradictory of "B → A," namely "BA'." To discover a case of B even when A is absent, shows that A is not a necessary condition for B. A statement of the form "BA'" reports a confuting datum for the hypothesis that A is necessary for B. And this hypothesis, as we have seen, may be compactly symbolized by "B → A."

To avoid confusion later, note that *being necessary* and *being sufficient* are two quite different things. To say that a given condition is SUFFICIENT for some result means that this factor is all you need in order to get the result. Symbolically, "A is sufficient for B" means simply "A → B." This latter expression (as we saw above) also means that B is a necessary condition for A. In other words, if A is *sufficient* for B, then B is *necessary* for A.

29.9. DISCOVERING THAT A GIVEN CIRCUMSTANCE IS NOT NECESSARY

George is wondering whether an object has to be nonmetallic in order for it to drop. He wants to know whether being nonmetallic is a necessary condition for an object's dropping. In the light of our formal definition of "necessary condition," this is equivalent to inquiring about the following hypothesis. (Be sure you understand this equivalence before going further.) The hypothesis is:

> If an object drops, then it is
> non[m]etallic. $D \rightarrow M'$ **(Hypo. 2.1)**

You will need to think about how this hypothesis is related to the central hypothesis (Series 1) in which George is interested. Hypothesis 2.1 (and others in Series 2) are subsidiary to his main inquiry and are investigated because of the light their confirmation or confutation will throw on the central hypothesis. Let us now see more specifically the contribution which an investigation of Hypothesis 2.1 can make to the inquiry.

Recalling the logical import of "if . . . then," we know that a *confuting* datum for this hypothesis will be an instance in which an object that drops is metallic. Such a confuting datum can be reported by a conjunctive statement of the form "DM," the contradictory of the hypothesis, "D → M'."

We may be quite confident that if George keeps investigating, he will encounter plenty of cases of this kind, that is, cases in which he will let go of a metallic object and it will drop. For we happen to know that being nonmetallic is irrelevant, and that George has thus far overlooked an important circumstance, that the watch, unlike the nonmetallic objects that fell when he let go of them, was already resting on a level surface. If you are inclined to be impatient with George, on the ground that "Any fool knows that this has something to do with it," remember that the only reason the fool knows this is that he has led a less sheltered life than George. The fool, like the rest of us, has considerable previous experience upon which to draw. Furthermore, we must not underestimate the progress George is making. In his present inquiry, as in the most advanced scientific research, much of the progress in empirical knowledge consists in finding out what *isn't* so.

Discovery of confuting data for Hypothesis 2.1 will lead George to reject it, and hence to conclude that being nonmetallic is not a necessary circumstance for an object's dropping when he lets go of it. In his discovery of such a confuting datum, it is not clear that George is even yet going at the job in a sufficiently critical and controlled manner to be approaching what is strictly called an *experiment*. (See Section 23.2.) But whether George encounters his confuting datum by experiment or by luck, his investigation will then have "eliminated" the factor of being nonmetallic from the circumstances to be specified in his generalization about what happens to objects when he lets go of them. It is important to understand clearly what this elimination amounts to. To eliminate a factor from the circumstances does not of course mean that this factor may not be present in an instance to which the generalization applies. When George succeeds in getting an adequate generalization about what happens to objects when he lets go of them, it will apply to nonmetallic objects too. In what sense, then, can he be said to have "eliminated" the factor of being nonmetallic? This question is answered by noting the *grounds* on which he eliminated this factor; he found it to be *not* a necessary factor in the circumstances.[10] Thus he will not want to include it among the cir-

[10] It is customary to refer to such eliminated circumstance-factors as "irrelevant." Notice that irrelevancy here consists precisely in being not necessary for the result.

cumstances in a generalization of the form "L(C) → D." Why not? Simply because his generalization, a general conditional, is *universal* in intent. He wants, if possible, to determine precisely which circumstances must *always* be present if an object is to drop when he lets go of it. Other factors may *happen* to be present, but these need not concern him as long as the result occurs anyway.

We can now understand precisely what type of factor he would like to include in the circumstances of his generalization, and what type he would like to leave out. He would like to discover a set consisting of the *fewest* factors which are *together sufficient* and *individually necessary* in order for objects to drop when he lets go of them.[11]

29.10. ESTABLISHING THE PROBABLE RELEVANCE OF A CIRCUMSTANCE

Now that we have explored the logic of eliminating a factor from the circumstances as irrelevant to a given generalization, we need not pursue George's inquiries further along this line. We may hopefully anticipate that, given time and reasonably good luck, he will encounter data which enable him to eliminate many other circumstances as not necessary, for example, the color, shape, and size of the objects, the time of day, the temperature of the room, conditions of illumination, and so on. We may also be thankful that in most inquiries which we ourselves undertake, we already have enough background information to indicate that many specific factors are probably irrelevant, without our having to investigate each possible circumstance in turn.

So much for eliminating irrelevant factors in the circumstances. But how are we to establish that certain factors are relevant, that is, that they are necessary? How can it be shown, for example, that if objects are to fall when we let go of them, it is necessary that they be heavier than air, and that they be otherwise unsupported? Our confidence in the necessity of these two circumstances is actually based, of course, not merely on our own empirical inquiries, but is derived in large part from accepted authority and indirectly by deduction from general principles of physics. But

[11] Note that George has not yet specifically raised or investigated the question of whether the basic antecedent factor in his generalization (his letting go of an object) is itself a *necessary* condition for the result, dropping. You will have a chance to think about this further in Application 1 below. See also the comments at the end of Section 29.11.

here again we must for the time being try to ignore these latter sources of knowledge, and confine our attention to the empirical methods by which such knowledge was itself presumably obtained in the first place. For this purpose, we can do no better than to continue to watch the struggles of George, the hypothetical inquirer whom we have endowed with logical competence and intellectual curiosity, but with virtually no knowledge of antecedent probabilities.

We may safely assume that in the course of his investigations, George will encounter a number of instances in which objects do not drop when he lets go of them. George may be fortunate enough to notice that a number of these cases have a possibly significant circumstance in common: they are supported in some further way than by his holding them. The watch which troubled him earlier, he now remembers, was resting on his desk when he let go of it. Certain other objects which failed to drop when he released them were, let us say, hanging on hooks from the wall or suspended by a wire from the ceiling, and so on. We must not underestimate the difficulty an uninformed person would have in noting such a circumstance which the cases have in common, and in suspecting that it may be a significant one. For lying on a desk, being hooked to the wall, and hanging from the ceiling are after all quite different. To classify these apparently diverse conditions under a single head, that of "being supported in some further way than by being held by me" is an important intellectual achievement. We may attribute it to "insight" or "good luck," but all that this means is that we don't know how it happens. On the basis of these observations and this insight, George formulates the hypothesis:

> If an object drops, then it is
> otherwise [12] un[s]upported. $D \to S'$ **(Hypo. 2.2)**

You will notice that this hypothesis has a familiar form, that of the confuted Hypothesis 2.1, that if an object drops, then it is nonmetallic. In the present case, a statement reporting a confuting datum would have the form "DS," that is, the datum would be a case in which an otherwise supported object dropped. But we may feel quite confident that George will never encounter such a confuting datum. We must remember, however, that our confidence is itself reasonable only because of highly probable antecedent knowledge in our possession, knowledge which is at present denied to George.

[12] That is, otherwise than being held.

As George accumulates further supporting data (which may be reported by statements having the form "DS' "[13]) without encountering any confuting data, the probability of Hypothesis 2.2 will increase. We know from previous analysis (of Hypothesis 2.1) that the present Hypothesis 2.2 is equivalent to the statement that being otherwise unsupported is a *necessary* condition for an object's dropping. Hence George's accumulating evidence makes it increasingly probable that being otherwise unsupported is a necessary circumstance in the generalization he is seeking.

The available data point to the hypothesis that if he lets go of otherwise unsupported objects, they will drop: [14]

$$L(S') \rightarrow D \qquad \text{(Hypo. 1.4)}$$

29.11. INQUIRY REVEALS NEED FOR FURTHER ANALYSIS OF CIRCUMSTANCES

George may continue almost indefinitely to accumulate supporting data for Hypothesis 1.4 without encountering any confuting data. The probability of this hypothesis may become so high that George is willing to treat it as practically certain. In so doing, he will be proceeding in a reasonable and logically defensible manner. We happen to know, however, that George's rationally grounded expectations may be upset by certain experiences. Suppose, for example, that he lets go of an otherwise unsupported helium-filled balloon. Contrary to all his accumulated experience, the released object fails to drop, but instead rises to the ceiling. What has happened? George has now encountered a confuting datum for Hypothesis 1.4.

[13] Certain other data, for example, "D'S" and "D'S' " are also logically *consistent* with the hypothesis, "D → S'," but I am inclined to think we would not regard a datum as actually *supporting* this hypothesis unless it had the form "DS'." This is perhaps largely a semantical matter.

[14] How does the confirmation of Hypo. 2.2 "point to" Hypo. 1.4? In other words, how is "D → S' " related to "L(S') → D"? Let us begin by noting the contrapositive of Hypo. 2.2: "S → D'." This contrapositive is of course equivalent to the hypothesis, and means that S is *sufficient* for D' (that is, if an object is otherwise supported, it will *not* drop). Hence, if an instance of dropping (D) is to occur, the sufficient condition (S) of *not* dropping (D') must be *absent*; in other words, the condition of being otherwise unsupported (S') must be present. Thus it follows that S' is at least one required factor in the set of conditions which are together sufficient for D. We therefore include it as a minimum circumstance in our formula, with Hypo. 1.4 as the result: "L(S') → D." Whether L(S') actually gives us a set which is together sufficient for D, or whether the antecedent must be further expanded is a matter which remains to be confirmed or confuted by further experience.

Does this mean that he must toss out Hypothesis 1.4 and start all over again? No, he is here confronting a type of situation that he has been in before, and he knows what to do. (See Section 29.6 above.) He may either shift to a *particular* generalization of the form, "In nearly all cases, otherwise unsupported objects drop when I let go of them," or he may undertake a further analysis of the circumstances. For this new confuting datum has shown him that although being otherwise unsupported may be a *necessary* circumstance for an object's dropping when he lets go of it, this is not by itself *sufficient*.

Since George's further explorations of the circumstances do not involve any new features of empirical inquiry, we may here leave him to his own devices, trusting that in time he will succeed in formulating the hypothesis that it is also necessary that the object be [h]eavier than air. His generalization will then have the form:

$$L(S'H) \to D \qquad \text{(Hypo. 1.5)}$$

As we leave George, let us take a few moments to look back and notice how far he has come, and to indicate briefly certain extensions and refinements of his knowledge which may come with further thought and experience.

George started his scientific career by looking for what always happens when he lets go of things, that is, the necessary condition or conditions that are implied by the letting go. One by one, all the various possibilities are eliminated, except that dropping seems to be the most prevalent result. At this point, his inquiry (which has been rather opportunistic anyway) shifts to looking for the combination of circumstances which would represent a *sufficient condition for something dropping*. He is no longer simply preoccupied with finding various things for which letting go alone is a sufficient condition.

We have already noted that George has not actually faced the question of whether his basic antecedent factor, his letting go of the object, is itself a necessary condition of the object's dropping. Is it? That is, if something drops, did he let go of it? Yes, if we are limiting our discussion to the things he has been holding, but in general, no. Either before or later, he must have seen, or be about to see, other things dropping without his ever having touched them.

This might start him thinking as follows: since being unsupported is *in general* a necessary condition for something dropping, perhaps letting go of something is just one respect in which it is unsupported. The more this seemed convincing, the more he would consider his earlier formula, "L(S') → D," to be redundant. He would be led to reinterpret the "S'," so that it no longer meant "otherwise (than being held by him) unsupported," but simply "unsupported." He would then be in possession of the compact generalization, "S' → D," in which "S'" would have the role of both necessary and sufficient condition of "D."

Later, when he tackles the condition of something being heavier than air as a necessary condition of its dropping, he may be tempted to infer by analogy that the air may be *supporting* an object lighter than air. At this point, his hypothesis is proving to have real heuristic value as it has led him to an interesting and possibly fruitful idea about the nature of air. If he has supposed that being heavier than air is universally a necessary condition of something dropping, his eventual experiments with falling bodies in evacuated containers will reveal its limited application.

Thus, following the pattern of Charles Lamb's "A Dissertation upon Roast Pig," George will have come a long way towards a valuable scientific generalization through analysis of his experience. In so far as he is looking for more and more general laws, he will eventually find his first laws interred as special instances of a more general formulation. As Einstein puts it, this is "the most beautiful fate" that can befall a scientific theory.

29.12. MILL'S "METHODS" OF CAUSAL INQUIRY

Sometimes our interest in causes is diagnostic; we want to know what caused some specific event. At other times our interest is inductive; we want to establish (as did George) a causal generalization covering all cases of a given type. Certain aspects of inquiry into causes are conveniently summarized by MILL'S METHODS, so called because they were given a classical formulation by the nineteenth-century logician John Stuart Mill.[15] We shall state the three central "methods" in somewhat revised form, and illustrate and comment briefly upon each. These principles are by no means foolproof, and too much must not be claimed for them. You will probably find that they are much easier to apply with some confidence in *analyzing* cases in which you already know the answer than in *discovering* new causal facts.

[15] *A System of Logic,* pp. 278–292.

The PRINCIPLE OF AGREEMENT states that if a given result occurs under a variety of sets of conditions which have only one condition-factor in common, that condition-factor is probably the cause of the given result. *Example:* A town's water supply is blamed for a typhoid epidemic, because use of this water was the "only" factor found to be common to all cases of persons having the disease. *Comment:* Note the crucial role of judgments of relevance here. These cases no doubt had many other factors in common too, including the fact that the people involved were all human beings, were all more than twelve inches tall, and all wore clothes in public.

The PRINCIPLE OF DIFFERENCE states that if two sets of conditions are exactly alike except that a certain factor is present in one set and absent from the other, and the set containing that factor is followed by the result while the other set is not, then that factor is the cause of the result. *Example:* If two "identical" geraniums are treated alike in all respects except that one is watered and the other is not, the death of the latter is attributed to lack of water. *Comment:* Were the geraniums really alike to begin with? Was presence or absence of water the only difference? Note that if we have *already* established the generalization that geraniums require water, we can then use the generalization in diagnosing the difficulty in the specific case. Note also the role of judgments of relevance here: Since the two plants can't really be *identical,* just how similar must they be?

The PRINCIPLE OF CONCOMITANT VARIATION states that if variations of a certain factor in otherwise constant conditions are accompanied by corresponding variations in the result, then the varying condition-factor is the cause of the result. *Example:* Changes in the temperature of the surrounding air account for the rise and fall of mercury in the thermometer tube. *Comment:* This principle is a special case of the Principle of Difference and somewhat similar comments apply. The varying factor identified as the "cause" may actually, like the given result, be an effect of some unknown variable which is causing both.

29.13. THREE SENSES OF "CAUSE"

We have purposely left until the end a consideration of the word "cause." We pointed out at the beginning of the chapter that generalizations which deal with uniformities of successive occurrences are commonly called "causal," but we did not go further than that. The word "cause" has been used in so many different senses, not only at the common-sense level but also in the sciences and in philosophy, that we can sometimes think more clearly by not using it. If we are to use it in any more precise manner than that of common sense, it is imperative to do two things: (1) to introduce limiting adjectives or some other device to distinguish various senses of the word, and (2) to define clearly what we mean in each case.

With the background of the present chapter, it is a relatively simple matter to distinguish three fairly basic and useful senses of "cause." At the end of Section 29.9 above we spoke of a set of circumstances which were individually *necessary* for a given result and which, *along with* the basic antecedent factor, were *together sufficient* for that result. Such a complete set of individually necessary and together sufficient conditions may be called the TOTAL CAUSE of the result in question. In a successful and fully explicit generalization of the type we have been discussing in this chapter, the whole antecedent expresses this total cause.

By contrast, the basic antecedent factor itself may be called the SPECIFIC CAUSE of the effect *in the given circumstances*. The notion of a specific cause makes consistent sense only when circumstances are given, for to speak of a *specific cause in general* is self-inconsistent.

Some antecedent factors are events, while others are more the kind of thing we call "states." Thus "letting go of an object" names a kind of event, but "being heavier than air" names a state. Sometimes for convenience or for more abstruse philosophical reasons, we call all the factors mentioned in a generalization "events." This problem need not detain us, but it is mentioned to prepare the way for a third sense of "cause." Sometimes it is useful to stress the time-aspect in the antecedent, and to single out the event which occurs last and thus completes the set of individually necessary and together sufficient conditions. This last event may be called the IMMEDIATE CAUSE of the effect which then follows. This immediate cause is often the same event as the specific cause, but it is easy to see that this is not necessarily the case. The reason is this: The *specific cause* is by definition the basic antecedent factor of a generalization, but as we have seen, it is somewhat arbitrary just which factor we shall use for this purpose. The *immediate cause*, on the other hand, is determined not by how we happen to state our generalization, but by the temporal order in which the antecedent factors, basic and circumstantial, occur in a given case. Note a further consequence. Once an established generalization has been stated, we can tell just by looking at the generalization (a statement) which of the factors is being regarded as the *specific* cause. (How?) The *immediate* cause, however, may differ from case to case falling under this generalization. (Why?)

• SOME REMINDERS

5. In a "causal" generalization, the *conditions* of a given consequent include the basic antecedent factor and the circumstances.
6. Necessary conditions must be distinguished from sufficient conditions, and from factors that happen to be present but are neither necessary nor sufficient.
7. A given circumstance is shown to be not necessary to the result by finding cases in which the result occurs in the absence of the given circumstance.
8. The antecedent of a successful causal generalization will mention all the conditions which are individually necessary and together sufficient for the occurrence of the result mentioned in the consequent.
9. The probability that a given circumstance is relevant to a generalization is increased indirectly by the confirmation of a related hypothesis. The nature of this relation is explained in Section 29.10.
10. Mill's "methods" are principles dealing with certain aspects of causal inquiry.
11. The word "cause" is used in so many different senses that it is perhaps easier to think clearly about "causal" generalizations if we use other language.
12. In the light of the analysis in the present chapter, three senses of "cause" may be clearly distinguished.

APPLICATIONS

1. George has always stated his basic antecedent factor as "I let go of an object." Further analysis would help him see that this factor really contains two subfactors, the letting-go and the person doing the letting-go.
   a. How might George investigate the question of whether *his* being the person is a *necessary* condition?
   b. When he discovers that it is not, how will this affect the "final" statement of his generalization?
2. Answer the questions "How?" and "Why?" at the end of Section 29.13.
3. Consider the generalization: "If a person has graduated from high school, he can enter this college as a freshman."

    a. Drawing on available knowledge, improve this generalization to the point where you believe it to take account of all relevant factors.

    b. In terms of this improved generalization, distinguish between the total cause, the specific cause, and the immediate cause of *your own* entrance to this college as a freshman. (If you didn't enter as a freshman, pick someone who did!)

4. From the practical point of view, knowledge of "causal" generalizations may help us get the results we want and prevent those we do not want.

    a. If you want to bring about a particular result, which type of condition will you want to control, a necessary condition or a sufficient condition? Why?

    b. If you want to prevent a particular result, which type of condition will you want to control? Why?

This matter is discussed by Max Black: *op. cit.,* pp. 323–325, but try to think this through for yourself.

5. Make a list of the "principles" for investigating a causal hypothesis which have emerged during the analysis of George's inquiry. As a preliminary, reread note 9 of Section 28.8.

6. Relate the following definitions of "cause" to the distinctions made in Section 29.13:

    a. "The cause, then, philosophically speaking, is the sum total of the conditions, positive and negative taken together; the whole of the contingencies of every description, which being realized, the consequent invariably follows." (John Stuart Mill)

    b. "The cause of the particular change K was such particular change C as alone occurred in the immediate environment of K, immediately before." (C. J. Ducasse)

    c. "We may define a cause to be an object, followed by another, and . . . where, if the first object had not been, the second never had existed." (David Hume)

7. Analyze the following in the light of the distinction made in Section 29.8 between two types of condition.

"The International Court of Justice, handing down its first decision, ruled in effect today that the Soviet Union's string of vetoes against five states applying for United Nations membership was illegal. . . .

"The majority opinion of the court said that conditions for membership were these:

    (1) That the applicant be a state.

    (2) That it be peace-loving.

    (3) That it accept the Charter's obligations.

    (4) That it be able to carry out the obligations.

    (5) That it be willing to carry out the obligations.

"Those were the conditions and the only conditions, said the majority report, and it added:

" 'These conditions are exhaustive and not merely stated by way of information or example.' " (A. M. Rosenthal in *New York Times,* May 29, 1948)

8. Analyze each of the following examples in terms of the concepts and principles of empirical inquiry discussed in this and preceding chapters. Explain the type of reasoning involved. Show the extent to which the example reveals the various stages of inquiry described in Section 26.4. Comment on any significant features such as instances of Mill's methods, use of deduction, indirect confirmation, and so on.

a. "Now I have discovered a formula regarding the comparative comfort of furniture. This formula may be stated in very simple terms: the lower a chair is, the more comfortable it becomes. Many people have sat down on a certain chair in a friend's home and wondered why it is so cozy. Before the discovery of this formula, I used to think that students of interior decoration probably had a mathematical formula for the proportion between height and width and angle of inclination of chairs which conduced to the maximum comfort of sitters. Since the discovery of this formula, I have found that it is simpler than that. Take any Chinese redwood furniture and saw off its legs a few inches, and it immediately becomes more comfortable; and if you saw off another few inches, then it becomes still more comfortable. The logical conclusion of this is, of course, that one is most comfortable when one is lying perfectly flat on a bed. The matter is as simple as that." (Lin Yutang: *The Importance of Living*, New York, The John Day Company, Inc., 1937, pp. 209–210)

b. "High blood pressure can be relieved in rats just as it can in humans by a salt-free diet, Victor J. Rosen, Jr., 16-year-old Beverly Hills (Calif.) High School senior, has just demonstrated.

"Patterning his experiment on ideas he got from reading technical literature on the subject, Mr. Rosen produced high blood pressure, or hypertension, by removing one kidney from each of six rats. After they had been six weeks on standard rat diet, he divided them into two groups of three each.

"One group got a salt-free diet and the other got rice with salt added. Autopsy showed that each of the salt-free rats had a normal heart and kidney while the other rats showed definite signs of hypertension." (*Science News Letter*, March 4, 1950, p. 134)

c. "A couple of years ago, Hugh S. Robinson, a mild and reclusive civil servant of Alton, in Hampshire, became interested in the visual power of insects.

"He worked out a theory that moths and other night-flying insects were actually repelled, not attracted, by light, but when they tried to escape, the almost invisible light at the lower end of the spectrum disturbed their motor apparatus and forced them to fly 'in conic curves with the light as a focus.'

"Mr. Robinson rigged up some lamps and displayed them to a gathering of scientists at the Royal Society in London. His audience was dazzled but unconvinced, and the disappointed moth trapper went back to Hampshire to devise bigger and better lamps.

"This year he discovered that mercury vapor threw out a band of light at the lower or ultra violet end of the spectrum that seemed to be highly perceptible to insects and when he got down to the 3,000 angstrom mark the moths found his apparatus irresistible.

"An angstrom is a unit of measure for light waves, being one hundred-millionth of a centimeter.

"The first time he tried out his trap at night with a sixty-watt generator Mr. Robinson netted about 6,000 insects. With 125 watts his record bag was 26,000, and when he stepped up the power to three kilowatts Mr. Robinson cautiously kept the score to himself but acknowledged that it was 'quite fantastic.' The total catch was believed to be between 30,000 and 40,000 insects in one night." (*New York Times,* December 24, 1951)

d. "There has been a good deal of question about the mode of spread of histoplasmosis, a lung disease widely prevalent in the Middle West. Now Carroll K. Palmer of the U. S. Public Health Service thinks he knows at least part of the answer: the fungus that causes the disease may be borne by tornadoes.

"*Histoplasma capsulatum* normally lives a sheltered life in the soil or in old wooden buildings. Palmer reasoned that a windstorm which lifts large quantities of dirt into the air and which can pull apart wooden buildings should stir up the fungus spores. He checked the records of 160,000 persons tested for histoplasmosis against the Weather Bureau's records of tornadoes during the past decade. Areas in the path of these storms proved to have a much higher incidence of the disease afterward than before. After a tornado that hit Tulsa in 1950 the histoplasmosis rate rose from almost nothing to 40 per cent among lifetime residents of the city. There was no such increase in nearby counties.

"Palmer plans to test his theory by on-the-spot examinations after the next tornado." (*Scientific American,* January 1955, p. 44)

e. A high level of antibodies in the bloodstream is thought to indicate immunity to the disease in question, since it is found that people who have acquired immunity by having the disease, also have a high level of antibodies in the bloodstream. Thus, it is argued, the effectiveness of a vaccine may be determined by examining the level of antibodies induced by it in persons who have been vaccinated.

f. "Our American habit of eating intensely cold and piping hot foods at the same meal may be the chief cause of tooth decay.

"Such thermal shocks, or rapid temperature changes from boiling water to ice water, cause otherwise healthy human teeth to be more vulnerable to cracking, Douglas G. and Herbert A. Pohl of this city found. Dr. Herbert Pohl is a research chemist with the du Pont Company.

"Of a group of teeth given seventy-two thermal shock cycles, twenty-one of fifty broke under the strain. Of a group of control teeth not subjected to the temperature change shock, eleven out of fifty broke in the test." (*New York Times,* December 28, 1954)

g. "A commercial forestry expert said today there would be plenty of Christmas trees this year—because the fishing is good off the Atlantic Coast of Northern Canada.

"The good news came from Harry Cooke, who buys large quantities of Christmas trees for a Philadelphia chain of supermarkets. He explained there was a definite relationship between the lumber and fishing industries of Northeastern Canada.

"About 95 per cent of the Christmas trees going annually to the Philadelphia market, he said, are balsams from the Gaspé Peninsula, Nova Scotia and New Brunswick. Most of the men who cut the trees make their regular living by fishing, Mr. Cooke said. When the fish are scarce and the prices high, the fishermen are loath to leave their boats to head for the forests.

"This year, Mr. Cooke added, there are plenty of fish—thus plenty of Christmas trees." (*New York Times,* December 15, 1952)

h. The Salk polio vaccine administered on a national scale in the spring of 1955 was produced by several different laboratories. At a certain stage of the program, 294,000 children had received injections of vaccine produced by one of the laboratories. During the next to the last week in April, five of these children came down with polio, and in the following week, thirty more. Data from years before the vaccine was available indicated that, in a group of this size, and taking into account the season and area, the normal weekly expectancy would be one new case. Among the more than five million children who received vaccine produced by the other laboratories, the number of cases was below the normal expectancy. It was concluded that something must be wrong with the vaccine produced by the first laboratory. (Data from *Time,* May 23, 1955)

i. "A timeworn theory holds that correspondents who have to file their stories only once a week really show the world they're describing better than correspondents who file every day. Why that should be so is never fully explained, since it would logically lead to the corollary that if they had to file a story only once a year it would truly be bursting with the richest essences of truth." (Charles Poore in *New York Times,* January 12, 1952)

j. Professor Gerard Baerends, zoologist of Groningen State University, Holland, has been studying the nesting habits of herring gulls on Terschelling Island in the North Sea. Making wooden "eggs" of various shapes, sizes, and colors, he placed them near a gull nest to see which the nesting gull would accept. He found that a herring gull pays little attention to plain "eggs," but will try to hatch even square ones if they are speckled. (Data from *Life,* July 18, 1955, p. 73)

k. "Dr. Alexander G. Gilliam of the National Cancer Institute told military surgeons today that the link between cigarette smoking and lung cancer had been established.

"The only 'controversy,' he added, was whether cigarettes were a direct or an indirect cause of cancer.

"At the sixty-first annual convention of the Association of Military Surgeons at the Hotel Statler he traced scientific findings in the field back to German experiments in 1939.

"Since that time, he said, there has been 'abundant further evidence of a similar nature, chiefly from the United States and England.' The 'cigarette hypothesis,' first arrived at by limited case history research, is now being borne out by broad population studies, he added.

" 'It may now be regarded as an established fact,' he asserted, 'that white male cigarette smokers in England and the United States suffer a substantially greater risk to cancer of the lungs than nonsmokers. Controversy revolves around the conclusions which may be drawn from the facts.

" 'The readiest and most plausible position to be taken is that cigarette smoke is carcinogenic [cancer-producing] or cocarcinogenic to the human lung and, as a result, the widespread increase in recorded mortality is in large part due to the great increase in cigarette consumption.

" 'This, in general, is the hypothesis which has been proposed and by many already considered as proven.'

"Dr. Gilliam took up the various arguments against the 'cigarette hypothesis.'

"To the contention that a lung cancer death increase was not real, but resulted from better diagnosis, he replied that the real increase had become apparent to the point where some doctors considered the disease pandemic, like influenza, and that, regardless of theories, it was 'today of sufficiently frequent occurrence to be regarded as a community problem.'

"On the argument that if the 'cigarette hypothesis' were true women should get lung cancer faster than men because they had taken up smoking more rapidly than men in recent years, he commented that 'there is no quantitative data on when and to what extent women have adopted the habit.' He asserted also that there were 'unknown factors' in the sex distribution of cancer. He added that it was much more prevalent among males than among females.

"He declared that a higher urban than rural lung cancer rate tended to support 'the hypothesis,' since cigarette smoking was more prevalent in the city than in the country. He noted that the trend might be heightened by industrial atmosphere pollutants 'which might of themselves induce the disease or might act with cigarette smoke as cocarcinogens.'

"He added, however, that New Orleans had a higher lung cancer death rate than either Pittsburgh or Detroit.

"To the argument that England had more lung cancer than this country, although it did less cigarette smoking, he replied that it apparently was common practice in England to smoke each cigarette more completely.

"Proof of a medical hypothesis in the mathematical sense is unattainable, Dr. Gilliam asserted, but it is 'perfectly clear' that the cigarette theory in lung cancer 'cannot now be rejected without some alternative explanation for present evidence' that white male cigarette smokers 'experience an excessive liability for this cancer.'

"Thus far data on other races, and on females of any race, are lacking, he said." (Bess Furman in *New York Times,* November 30, 1954)

CHAPTER 30

FURTHER ASPECTS OF EMPIRICAL INQUIRY

PREVIEW

In this chapter, we shall round out our account of empirical inquiry by first considering analogy as a form of inference by which we seek to establish facts. We shall then ask what it means to explain something, and shall explore some basic types and patterns of explanation. We shall conclude by examining the role played in empirical inquiry by theories, not merely as explanatory devices but also as instruments of discovery and as systematizers of our knowledge.

30.1. THE USE OF ANALOGY IN FACT-FINDING

Early in our study of empirics we noted that there are four patterns of reasoning by which we undertake to determine what is probably the case. Among these was analogy. (See Section 26.3.) We have deferred the discussion of analogical argument until this point so that we may consider it against the background of our knowledge of other forms of probable inference, particularly induction.

In everyday English, we use the name "analogy" for almost any case in which similarities between two things are being pointed out. Often the comparison is intended only figuratively, or for the purpose of some literary or esthetic effect. We are here however concerned with analogy, not in these senses, but as a form of argument. What form? Every argument moves, as we know, from given statements (premises or evidence statements) to another statement (the conclusion). In an analogical argument, the evidence presented by the premises is of two sorts. (1) The things being compared (called ANALOGUES) are known to have something in common; they are known to resemble each other in one or more re-

spects. These respects in which the analogues are known to be comparable make up the KNOWN PARITY. In a *simple analogy,* there are just two
analogues, but the known parity may of course include any number of
characteristics in which the analogues are known to be similar. (2) One
of the analogues in a simple analogy (the BASIC ANALOGUE) is known to
have some further characteristic. This combined evidence provides
grounds for the conclusion that probably the second thing (the DE-
RIVATIVE ANALOGUE) also has this further characteristic (the IMPUTED
PARITY). When I reason that, since I enjoyed a given author's last book,
I'll probably enjoy the next one, I am arguing by simple analogy.

The logical pattern of a simple analogy is set forth in the following
diagram.[1]

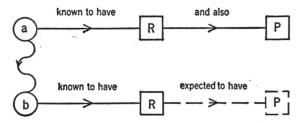

In this diagram, *a* represents the basic analogue, and *b* the derivative
analogue. *R* stands for the known parity, and *P* for the imputed parity.
The solid straight arrows indicate information set forth in the premises,
while the broken arrow represents the probable inference from these
premises to the conclusion.

Arguments from analogy are notoriously precarious, but we all use
them continually, and some are stronger than others. In our earlier brief
look at analogies, we noticed that one way in which the strength of an
analogy may be increased is by increasing the number of basic analogues.
Analogies having more than one basic analogue are, as you will remember, called *compound analogies.* If I have read a lot of books by a particular author and have enjoyed them all, the probability is greater that I
shall enjoy his next one than if my sole evidence was that I enjoyed his
last one. We had better add that the probability is greater *other things
being equal,* for it may be that having read so many, I am beginning to
tire of his style, or perhaps he is beginning to repeat himself. One im-

---

[1] Max Black: *Critical Thinking,* Second Edition, (Copyright 1946, 1952 by Prentice-
Hall, Inc., New York), p. 321. Reproduced by permission of the publisher.

portant factor in brand-name advertising and labeling is the fact that people reason by analogy. If you have tried one or more products with a given brand-name and have found them to be superior, you are likely to try that brand again when you select a new product. This may be no more than the unreflective conditioned response the advertiser would like to establish in you. In so far as it involves deliberation, however, the pattern of your thinking is analogical.

There is a second factor which determines the strength of an analogy, and that is the number of characteristics the basic and derivative analogues are known to have in common. Starfish and whales are both adapted for living in water, but they do not otherwise have a great deal in common. The argument that since the whale suckles its young, starfish must too, is a weak one because the known resemblances between the analogues are somewhat limited.

But as this last example also shows, there is a third important factor to consider, namely the known *disresemblances* or DISPARITY between the analogues. Democracy and totalitarian dictatorship are both forms of government, but it is dangerous to reason from one to another because of the many basic differences known to exist between them.

We have many times in the course of our discussion of empirical inquiry seen the importance of judgments of relevance. We are therefore not surprised to find them playing an important role in analogy too. (This lack of surprise on our part is itself a product of our analogical expectations.) If we try hard enough, we can find resemblances between the most unlikely things. But merely to increase the known resemblances between two things does not increase the strength of the analogy based upon them unless the resemblances are relevant. This is easy to say and to understand, but quite difficult to apply, because only experience can determine which resemblances are relevant and important for a given purpose and which are not. An orange and an orange billiard ball have a good deal in common. They are both material objects. They are about the same size and weight. They are both round. They will both roll along the floor. They can both be carried in a pocket, placed in a drawer, or wrapped up in a package and mailed to Chicago. They are both treacherous things to stumble over in the dark, and they both can be used for breaking windows. They both—but need I go further? Only to point out that an orange is good to eat. In the light of all these known resemblances, and many more that I could mention, how probable is the analogical conclusion that a billiard ball is also good to eat? Not very. Why not? Because the enumerated resemblances, except the fact that both objects are material, are quite irrelevant to the question of edibility. How do we know this? By experience.

We have now considered the nature of an analogical argument and several factors which affect its strength. One additional factor can be better discussed at the end of the following section.

30.2. ANALOGY, INDUCTION, AND THE JUSTIFICATION OF AN ANALOGICAL ARGUMENT

How is analogy related to induction? A simple analogy, having only one basic analogue, seems to have very little in common with induction other than being a form of probable inference. But when we consider the manner in which a simple analogy may sometimes be strengthened by discovering more basic analogues, the resemblance between analogy and induction increases. Premises of the form "Object C is an egg and contains a yolk" or "Object D is a package and contains an alligator lamp" provide the basis for either an analogical or an inductive conclusion. What is the difference between a compound analogy and an induction by simple enumeration? The differences are two: (1) The compound analogy contains a premise of a further type, pointing out that the derivative analogue shares certain characteristics with the basic analogues. ("Object E is also a chicken egg" or "Object F is also a Christmas package of such-and-such a shape and size.") This type of premise is absent from an inductive argument. (2) The conclusion of an analogy is typically a singular statement, while the conclusion of an induction is always a general statement.

We may now ask, how are we to justify reasoning from analogical premises to the analogical conclusion? That is, in terms of our egg example, how can we justify the inference from "Objects A, B, C, and D are eggs and contain yolks" and "Object E is also an egg" to the probable conclusion, "Object E contains a yolk"? Perhaps the most widely held view is that analogical arguments involve an appeal to an implicit or concealed generalization. A number of recent writers on analogy adopt this analysis. In discussing a particular example of analogical reasoning, Arthur Pap, for example, speaks of the "suppressed (tacitly entertained)" premise, the "generalization that whatever has properties *a, b, c* also has property *d,* that the inferred property, in other words, is 'connected' with the properties that constitute the basis of the analogy." [2] Lionel Ruby likewise remarks, "Note also the enthymeme which is present in such reasoning, for we assume the major premise: 'Anything which has the characteristics r, b, a, m, and g will also have the characteristic 1.' " [3] And Max Black, having cited the analogical conclusion that this egg like the last will have a yolk, speaks of "the generalization that sustains this analogy, viz., that all eggs have yolks." [4]

On this view, the justification of a specific analogical argument may be seen to involve a combination of inductive generalization and deductive general conditional argument.

Induction
Object A is a chicken egg and it contains a yolk.
Object B is a chicken egg and it contains a yolk.
Object C is a chicken egg and it contains a yolk.
Object D is a chicken egg and it contains a yolk.

If anything is a chicken egg, then it contains a yolk.

Deduction
If anything is a chicken egg, then it contains a yolk.
Object E is a chicken egg.
_____
Object E contains a yolk.

This reasoning does provide a justification of the analogy. J. O. Wisdom, however, has recently urged that the strength of a given conclusion by compound analogy is usually greater than it could be on this pattern of justification. We shall not attempt to settle the issue here, but a few comments will help us to see what the problem is. We know, don't we, that if the grounds for a premise are weak, the conclusion of a deduction from this premise will also be derivatively weak. Thus, if the analogical conclusion, "Object E contains a yolk" is justified in the above manner, it cannot be stronger than the generalization, "If anything is a chicken egg, then it contains a yolk." Now, to simplify matters, let us assume that the *only* inductive evidence we have for this generalization is that Objects

[2] Arthur Pap: *Elements of Analytical Philosophy,* New York, The Macmillan Company, 1949, pp. 200–201.
[3] Lionel Ruby: *Logic, An Introduction,* Chicago, Philadelphia, New York, J. B. Lippincott Co., 1950, p. 427.
[4] Max Black: *op. cit.,* p. 321.

A, B, C, and D (mentioned in the premises of our compound analogy) are chicken eggs and contain yolks. It should be clear that on this evidence we do not have rational grounds for much confidence in the generalization. (See Section 28.8, point "c".) The generalization on this evidence is quite weak, and the weakness clearly affects the conclusion of the deductive argument which is based on it. J. O. Wisdom urges, however, that such a conclusion as "Object E contains a yolk" has a higher "degree of credibility" when drawn directly from the premises of the compound analogy than when drawn by way of the weak inductive generalization. In more general terms, he states his objection to the pattern of justification above discussed by urging that if we think of the matter in that way, then

> the degree of credibility attaching to the compound analogy would be no more than that attaching to the generalisation, whereas in general a compound analogy has a higher degree of credibility than a corresponding generalisation from which it could be deduced.[5]

Whatever may be the outcome of this particular controversy, we may note one further point about the inductive generalization and the analogical conclusion. To simplify the example, we earlier assumed that the premises of the given compound analogy set forth *all* the information we had on the subject at the time. Suppose, however, that we happened to have *further* evidence, not mentioned in the premises of the analogy, which supported the inductive generalization. In such a case, the probability of this generalization might (even if we accept Wisdom's thesis) be considerably *higher* than the analogical conclusion which was drawn from the more limited evidence. When this is the case, the analogically derived conclusion may of course be strengthened by deducing it directly from the generalization. This suggests a further factor which it is useful to consider in evaluating an analogical conclusion. Would this conclusion be strengthened by drawing upon an available generalization which takes into account further evidence than that set forth in the premises of the analogy? Do we know, for example, that not merely Eggs A, B, C, and D, but nearly all chicken eggs that have been opened have contained yolks? If so, we will have a stronger conclusion by deduction from the generali-

[5] John Oulton Wisdom: *Foundations of Inference in Natural Science,* London, Methuen & Co., Ltd., 1952, p. 107n. A similar point was made by Bertrand Russell a number of years ago in his *The Problems of Philosophy* (first published in 1912), London, New York, Toronto, Oxford University Press, 1948, p. 80.

zation than by analogy from our limited premises. If Wisdom is right, however, we should be in an even stronger position if we simply incorporated this evidence about nearly all eggs into the analogical premises themselves, and drew the analogical conclusion directly from these augmented premises.

• SOME REMINDERS

1. On the basis of known resemblances between two or more things, an argument by analogy imputes some characteristic to one of the things.
2. Analogies vary in strength; an estimate of their strength requires the consideration of several different factors.
3. An analogy may be justified by a combination of induction and deduction.
4. It has, however, been argued that the strength of a given compound analogy may be greater than this pattern of justification would indicate.

APPLICATIONS

1. Analyze and evaluate each of the following arguments, drawing upon the considerations set forth in the text.

   a. Several years ago, when the question of resuming diplomatic relations with Spain was under discussion, Senator Tom Connally argued for their restoration. In a speech reported by the *New York Times* for May 11, 1949, he made the following points: (1) He did not "see the logic of" refusing to have diplomatic relations with Spain on the grounds that we did not approve her form of government, so long as we had such relations with countries like Soviet Russia, whose form of government we also disapproved. (2) Traditionally, the United States has not made agreement with our political concepts a condition of a foreign country's having diplomatic relations with us. Specifically, we maintained relations with totalitarian Japan and with Czarist Russia, in spite of our opposition to their social and political ideas.

   b. The Federal "Rent Control" Act of 1949 contained "local option" provisions which permitted a community to set aside the rent control requirements of the act. In ruling the act unconstitutional, Judge Elwyn R. Shaw said that he could "see no difference" between this situation and two others. (1) A case in which a national selective service law would provide that any state that didn't wish to become involved could pass a law to that effect and be excused from sending soldiers. (2) An interstate commerce act which provided that any state that did not wish to be governed by its provisions could refrain from adhering to them. (Data from the *New York Times*, July 26, 1949)

c. An advertisement of Bergdorf Goodman of Fifth Avenue, New York, offered for sale a "famous aid to younger looking skin." It pointed out that this was "more than a cosmetic" for it was "skin sustenance." The preparation contained "vividerm (Trade Mark Registered), an extract taken from the young skin glands of tortoises which renew their skin throughout extremely long lives."

d. When the butter industry was opposing legislation to liberalize restrictions on the coloring of margarine, a reader of *Life* magazine wrote to the editors, urging the following points: (1) The margarine industry has as much right to use yellow as a color for its product as the butter industry has. (2) The butter industry didn't invent yellow as the color of butter; the color was placed there by nature. (3) If butter looks too pale, the butter industry has no hesitation in adding yellow color artificially.

e. The French writer, Simone de Beauvoir, examines and rejects the following considerations when used to support the conclusion that it is in accordance with nature that "woman's place is in the home," not out in active public life: (1) The human sperm is slender, agile, motile. (2) The human egg is passive, motionless, rounded with nutrient material. (Simone de Beauvoir: *The Second Sex*, New York, Alfred A. Knopf, 1953)

f. "In order . . . to understand the nature of communism, we must rid our minds of all preconceptions drawn from our experiences of the traditional parliamentary parties. If we do not, it will be like trying to infer the nature of chess from an acquaintance exclusively with checkers, merely because they happen to use a similarly constructed board. Our success in dealing with communists will be comparable to that of a checkers player, so instructed, in a chess tournament." (James Burnham: *The Struggle for the World*, New York, The John Day Company, Inc., 1947, p. 59)

g. "Dr. Leonell C. Strong, research associate in anatomy at Yale's School of Medicine, finds that the age of the mother at pregnancy may endow the offspring with many characteristics, including either a susceptibility or a resistance to cancer. He has worked with inbred strains of mice but believes that his findings hold good for man and for higher animals in general.

"Dr. Strong has observed that mice born to older mothers are less susceptible to cancer than mice of early litters from the same mother. Like other scientists he has found that the mother's age influences three distinctly different kinds of malignancy: induced cancer of connective tissue, virus-caused cancer of the breast and leukemia. The first two types increase with the mother's age, whereas leukemia decreases." (Waldemar Kaempffert in *New York Times*, August 16, 1953)

h. An advertisement for the Hillman Minx ("light car performance with heavy car safety") raised the question, "Ever hear of a two-ton race horse?", and pointed out that neither Man o' War nor Seabiscuit nor

Demon Hanover weighed more than 1,100 pounds. It added that the style, fleetness, and take-off of these horses is what you expect in a car, and what you will get from the car in question.

i. "It seems unfortunate that Frits W. Went chose to step outside the field of ecology in order to draw a moral from his desert plants. Though I cannot dispute his conclusion that mankind would be better off with more birth control . . . nevertheless his desire to reach this conclusion seems to have led him into making some rather curious statements. . . .

"The analogy drawn by Went between birth control in human beings and germination control in certain plants through adaptation to factors of the environment is an imperfect one. These adaptations and other adaptations are largely the result of natural selection. They are thus the *result* of the 'struggle for existence'; they are not means of circumventing it through altruistic motives. Birth control, on the other hand, *is* a means of reducing competition (though not of eliminating it) and thus of alleviating human suffering due to excess population. This is a unique property of human culture and not an imitation of nature. . . ." (Paul A. Fryxell in *Scientific American,* June 1955, p. 4)

30.3. TYPES AND PATTERNS OF EXPLANATION

"Explanation" is another one of those terms that people use in a number of different ways. Its most general, functional sense is, I believe, well stated by Abraham Wolf when he says that "anything is explained when it is shown in its relation to some other thing or things, so that it does not appear, so to say, to hang in the air, detached and isolated." [6] Some writers on empirics use the word in a much narrower sense, confining its application for example to cases of *causal* explanation. This procedure is justified for certain purposes, but it is quite arbitrary, and it achieves nothing that cannot be accomplished by inserting the adjective "causal" when that is the specific type of explanation we have in mind. Here again we do not want to become involved in a purely verbal dispute, but rather to focus our attention on the nonverbal aspects of the problem. If we use "explanation" in the broad functional way suggested by Wolf, what more specific types of explanation may be distinguished? We shall note four basic ones: definition, classification, causal explanation, and explanation of laws by means of a theory. We shall also explore the logical patterns of such explanations.

[6] A. Wolf: *Essentials of Scientific Method,* Second Edition, New York, The Macmillan Company, 1937, p. 114.

30.4. DEFINITION AS SEMANTICAL EXPLANATION

Sometimes the kind of "thing" we are trying to explain is the *meaning* of some word. This type of explanation was discussed at length in Chapter 6, and is of course the type we call *definition*. It is this type of explanation with which we have been concerned in the first sentences of Section 30.3, for we were there trying to explain the meaning of the word "explanation." When we wish to consider definition along with other types of explanation, we may conveniently distinguish it by the name SEMANTICAL EXPLANATION. In most contexts, however, the commoner name, "definition," is adequate and preferable.

30.5. EXPLANATION BY CLASSIFYING

A second type of explanation in our general functional sense is explanation by indicating the class to which something belongs.[7] If I am puzzled by a strange animal encountered along a country road at night, I will be helped by your explanation that it is an albino raccoon. Here you are not telling me what a word *means*, but are rather explaining what a thing *is* by referring it to an appropriate class. You have, to be sure, done this by uttering the name "albino raccoon," but our present interest is in the nonsemantical aspects of the situation. We should note, however, that naming, defining, and classifying are closely related activities, although the first two are basically semantical while the third is basically empirical. Often an explanation by classification merges into a *description* of the thing being classified. In fact, it is sometimes convenient to consider description as a separate type of explanation.

How an item is to be classified is determined by two quite different factors: (1) the characteristics which the item possesses and (2) the purposes or interests of the classifier. The characteristics which anything possesses are determined by empirical inquiry, which may in some cases

[7] Sometimes the "something" is itself a class, which we classify by indicating a more general class of which it is a species (for example, by indicating that frogs are amphibians). Note carefully that we are here speaking of the *classes* and not their *names*. To explain that the name "frog" means such-and-such a type of amphibian is a definition, not a classification. To *classify* the name "frog," we should have to refer it to some class of words (for example nouns, or words containing four letters, or words beginning with "f"), or to some broader class of semantical entities (for example, artificial signs).

involve not much more than simple observation and in others require lengthy and intricate diagnostic investigations. Against the background of antecedent knowledge, I am able to classify a particular tree as a sugar maple on the basis of fairly simple observations. In only slightly more complex fashion, a musician will classify a particular composition as a sonata because of its observed characteristics, and a geologist will classify a particular specimen of rock as schist. The element of inference is less apparent in simple cases of classification than in more complex ones, but the basic logical pattern lying behind all classification of items is deductive. For example:

> If anything looks like this, it is probably an albino raccoon.
> This animal looks like this.
> _____
> This animal is probably an albino raccoon.

It is easy to overlook the second factor that determines how an item is to be classified, namely the purposes or interests of the classifier. A simple illustration will help us see how important this factor is. A particular purpose may lead you to group together items which I would consider quite unrelated if I were unaware of your purpose. For example, a stone, a book, a hammer, a quart jar, and a ruler might seem to have not much more in common than that they are all material objects, until I discover that you are looking for something to keep a window from sliding shut. The way in which we classify items depends not merely on their characteristics, but also upon how those characteristics fit in with our purposes.

This second factor seems to many people to be absent from scientific classifications. We are inclined to feel that the classifications of natural science are not influenced by such factors as purpose, but are based simply on "what things really are." But, to put the matter a little too simply, the scientist's purpose is precisely to find out what things really are, and this purpose is just as indispensable a factor in his classifications as your desire to keep a window open was in yours. To put the matter more precisely, avoiding the loaded word "really," we may say that the natural scientist is concerned with discovering those aspects of nature which are publicly observable and confirmable (that is, open to scrutiny and confirmation by other competent investigators) and which are most dependable as a basis for further inferences and most fruitful in revealing further relationships. For such reasons, biology rejects the primitive classification of bats with the birds, and classifies them instead with the mammals. To be told that a particular stone is a window-prop does indeed classify it, but it tells you less about its relations to other aspects of nature and provides a scantier basis for further inferences than the knowledge that it is a piece of dolomitic limestone. The natural scientist's purpose of discovering confirmable structures and interrelations in nature leads him to select certain aspects as the basis of his classifications, just as your more limited purpose of keeping the window open led you to select certain others.

30.6. CAUSAL EXPLANATION

When we are concerned with throwing light on an *event*, we most commonly appeal to a causal explanation. We typically reply to the question, "Why did this happen?", with an answer which has the form, "Because such-and-such else happened." We explain an event by calling attention to its cause, most often to its *immediate cause*. (See Section 29.13.) Thus, if I ask George why a particular piece of chalk dropped, he will probably reply, "Because I let go of it." On many occasions, this explanation will satisfy me, provided I already have adequate background knowledge. But it is clear that George's having let go of it is only part of the story. When he tells me that the chalk dropped because he let go of it, this will not adequately explain the event to me if my own knowledge is meager. I may properly ask him a further question, "What does that have to do with it?" In order to satisfy me, George will have to do some more explaining; he will need to mention an established *causal generalization* or "law" such as, "If you let go of things, they drop." In many cases, this too would satisfy me, but we know enough to recognize that the law has been sketchily stated. If I accept it in this form, it will either be because I know so little about the matter that this is as far as I care to press it at the moment, or because I know so much that I myself supply the *circumstances* which George is assuming but failed to mention. I may be satisfied anywhere along the line: with the mere mention of the immediate cause, with the addition of an incompletely stated generalization which applies to the case, or not until the generalization has been fully stated with reference to the circumstances, so that I am informed of the *total cause*.

It should be clear that the pattern of such causal explanation is de-ductive. This is true even when only the immediate cause is mentioned, although in this case the deductive argument is an enthymeme. Let us first summarize the pattern of *questioning* and then note the completed pat-tern of *explanation.*

> "George, why did that piece of chalk drop just now?"
> "Because I let go of it."
> "What did that have to do with it?"
> "Why, stupid, whenever you let go of things they drop."
> "Really? How about that watch? Remember?"
> "Well, yes. I meant to say that whenever you let go of some-
>   thing that is heavier than air and is otherwise unsupported
>   it will drop."

The pattern of explanation is a general conditional argument which pro-ceeds validly by asserting a substitution instance of the antecedent. We shall modify the tenses to fit the time when the explanation was given:

> If a person lets go of an otherwise unsupported object that
>   is heavier than air, it will drop.
> George let go of this piece of chalk, which was otherwise
>   unsupported and heavier than air.
> _____
> It dropped.

It is interesting to note than when we are speaking colloquial English, we will sometimes ask the question "Why?" in such a sense that the answer will not be a causal explanation, but simply an explanation by classification.

> "Why does a bat have hair, even though most flying verte-
>   brates have feathers?"
> "Because the bat is a mammal, not a bird."
> "What does that have to do with it?"
> "Mammals typically have hair; even a whale shows traces
>   of it."

The complete pattern of explanation here, as well as in causal explana-tion, may be presented in deductive form:

> If anything is a mammal, it has some hair.
> A bat is a mammal.
> _____
> A bat has some hair.

The sense of "Why?" which is satisfied by classifying seems well estab-lished in everyday English. For certain technical purposes we may wish to avoid this usage, but we should not overlook its prevalence in ordinary English.

30.7. THEORETICAL EXPLANATION

Thus far we have been considering the explanation of specific items such as a given event or a singular fact. We have seen the role played by empirically established general "laws" in such explanations. But sometimes, particularly as our knowledge moves toward a higher level of generality as in the sciences, we ask for explanations of the generalizations or laws themselves. Why, we ask, do otherwise unsupported objects heavier than air drop when people let go of them? Just as we appeal to a generalization in explaining a specific event, so we appeal to a broader generalization or *theory* in explaining a specific generalization.

The word "theory" is used in a number of different ways, both by common sense and by science. The common-sense individual sometimes uses the word "theory" and its adjectival form "theoretical" simply as a Bad Name. In this usage, which is of course not our present one, it signifies an impractical, hare-brained, or highly speculative idea with little or no evidence to support it. A more respectable sense of the word is that in which it is simply a synonym for "hypothesis." In this sense, a theory is a suggested solution of a problem, a tentative suggestion made to guide inquiry. In this usage, a theory need not be a general statement at all, but, as in many cases, may be simply a statement about a single individual. Throughout this book, we have refrained from using the word "theory" in this sense, not because it isn't good or normal usage, but because we have had a less ambiguous term available, namely *hypothesis*. The third sense of "theory," which is the only one immediately relevant to the purposes of this section, is the sense in which a THEORY is simply a high-level inclusive generalization from which more specific generalizations are deducible.[8] In this sense, we may speak of the Theory of Gravitation, and may explain George's rather limited generalization about released objects by showing that it follows by deductive specification from the more general theory.

Unless one happens to be pretty well acquainted with the science

[8] When the adjective "theoretical" is used to describe a type of *knowledge* (for example, theoretical physics) it often combines the notion of generality and the idea of knowledge as sought "for its own sake," apart from its possible practical applications. Compare the distinction between "theoretical" and "practical" interests in Section 27.10.

under discussion, reference to such-and-such a theory and the more specific laws which it explains is not likely to be very illuminating. The logic of this situation, however, is fairly simple and may be illustrated by slipping down the ladder of generality a few rungs until we encounter familiar material. Or better yet, let us begin at the bottom and work up just far enough to see the relation between a specific generalization and a more inclusive theory.

> "Why does this animal have hair?"
> "Because it is a bat, and all bats have hair."

Here we have offered a low-level generalization to explain an individual case. But now suppose we are asked to explain this generalization itself. We shall do it by appealing to the Theory of Mammalian Hirsuteness:

> "But why do bats have hair?"
> "Because bats are mammals, and all mammals have hair."

Here we have explained a specific low-level generalization ("All bats have hair") by showing that it is a deductive specification of a more comprehensive generalization ("All mammals have hair"). It can only be in fun that we call this latter generalization a "theory," for it is itself at a relatively low level of generality. For more lofty examples, you will want to look into such matters as the way in which Newton's theory of gravitation explains both Galileo's laws of falling bodies and Kepler's laws of planetary motion. Or for one of the most interesting examples of all, investigate the way in which the Kinetic Theory of Gases explains a whole group of more specific laws which had been first formulated as hypotheses and then empirically confirmed before a satisfactory general theory was attained. Among these specific laws are those named for their discoverers, Gay-Lussac, Avogadro, Boyle, Charles, and Graham.[9] On the very frontiers of contemporary theoretical science we may mention the late Albert Einstein's attempts to work toward a Unified Field Theory which, if successful, would explain the whole range of physical laws.

30.8. THE CONFIRMATION OF THEORIES, AND THEIR ROLE IN DISCOVERY OF LAWS

In their first formulation, theories like any generalizations are merely hypotheses. If they are to be accepted, and to become a part of the body

---

[9] A good reference on such matters for the general reader is Sir William Dampier: *A History of Science and Its Relations with Philosophy and Religion*, Third Edition, rev. and enl., New York, The Macmillan Company, 1943.

of knowledge, they must be confirmed. In our earlier discussion we noted that adequate confirmation involves more than showing merely that the hypothesis is relevant, that is, that it will account for the difficulty. We saw that, in spite of our common-sense laxness at this point, a good hypothesis must have predictive power. The hypothesis, along with already confirmed knowledge and available empirical data, should be able to predict some as-yet-unknown fact. The verification of this prediction provides confirmation of the hypothesis. We here want to note that these remarks apply to theories quite as much as to more specific generalizations.

Let us illustrate these remarks both at the level of our simple Theory of Mammalian Hirsuteness and at a more advanced level. Let us suppose that our own theory was in the first instance suggested by empirical generalizations dealing with the hairiness of monkeys, bats, and mice. On the basis of empirical investigations of a large number of these animals, we confirmed three generalizations with practical certainty:

1. If anything is a monkey, it has hair.
2. If anything is a bat, it has hair.
3. If anything is a mouse, it has hair.

These generalizations, together with our knowledge that monkeys, bats, and mice are all mammals, suggested to us a more general hypothesis, the Theory of Mammalian Hirsuteness. (Note that we call it a "hypothesis" because of the stage of its development, that is, because it is not yet adequately confirmed; we call it a "theory" because of its level of generality.) At this stage, the theory does indeed explain the three generalizations which are known to fall under it. In other words, it is relevant. But it has not yet revealed its predictive power, and hence cannot in any stringent sense be said to have been confirmed. Suppose we have never investigated tapirs, and know nothing about them except that they are mammals. Our hypothesis provides the basis for the general prediction that if anything is a tapir, then it has hair. The pattern of prediction is deductive (see Section 27.5):

> If anything is a mammal, then it has hair. (Theory)
> If anything is a tapir, then it is a mammal. (Previous
>   Knowledge)
> ———————————————————————————
> If anything is a tapir, then it has hair. (Predicted Law)

This predicted conclusion now itself functions as a hypothesis calling for inductive investigation. Is it really the case that tapirs have hair? Empirical inquiry establishes this generalization with practical certainty. What is the effect of the confirmation of this predicted law upon the theory from which it was deduced? The establishing of this prediction by inductive inquiry constitutes an important confirmation of our Theory of Mammalian Hirsuteness. The confirming datum in this case is not a singular fact (as in previous cases we have studied) but a general one, expressed by our statement that if anything is a tapir, then it has hair. This general fact itself, of course, was confirmed by singular data; examination of the inductive sample of tapirs showed that this, that, and the other one each possessed hair.

Our discussion of this relatively simple example not only helps us see how a theory is confirmed by confirming general predictions deduced from it, but also shows us the manner in which deduction may lead to important extensions of our knowledge by helping us know what to look for.

The need for the confirmation of theories through verified predictions is pointed up at a more advanced level by an anecdote about Einstein. At the time of his announcement of his latest theory, a newspaper reporter is said to have asked him whether he had any reason to believe the theory was true. Einstein, according to the story, told the reporter to come back in twenty years. The point of the story is that the theory cannot be confirmed until it is possible to verify predictions based upon it. At the time of its announcement, Einstein had not as yet been able to deduce any consequences of his highly abstract mathematical formulas that were susceptible of empirical investigation. Einstein himself described his work as "gropings in the dark," but during the summer of 1953, Professor Vaclav Hlavaty, an eminent Czech refugee mathematician, announced solutions of Einstein's equations which may be interpreted in physical terms, and thus may open the way to deducing specific predictions that can be empirically tested.[10]

30.9. THEORIES AND THE SYSTEMATIZATION OF KNOWLEDGE

When, at the outset of our study of empirics, we called attention to noninductive aspects of empirical inquiry, we said something that perhaps didn't mean very much to you at the time. We noted that "as our em-

---

[10] Professor Hlavaty's achievement was reported by William L. Laurence in the *New York Times* for July 30, 1953.

pirical knowledge in a given field becomes more and more comprehensive and adequate, our reasoning approaches more and more the pattern of deduction" (Section 23.1). We are now in a much better position to appreciate this statement. We have seen the important role which deduction plays, not only in prediction, but in explanation. At the present stage of physical knowledge, a physicist no longer needs to spend his time as George did and as Galileo did, collecting instances of falling objects and attempting to derive a satisfactory generalization from them by induction. In this specific area of inquiry, the inductive stage is pretty well in the past, and the physicist handles specific problems by applying to his empirical data highly confirmed generalizations or laws. He does this by using his data as substitution instances in deductions from established generalizations. At the more abstract and general levels of his science, he similarly draws upon *theories* to understand and explain the more specific generalizations or laws which fall under them.

In this manner, theories not merely explain specific laws, but show the interrelations between various originally separate lines of empirical investigation and discovery. Theories unify and systematize our knowledge.

• SOME REMINDERS

1. We explain something by showing how it is related to other things.
2. Depending on what we are explaining and how we go about it, an explanation may involve defining, classifying or describing, indicating a cause or causal law, or referring to a theory.
3. The pattern of nonsemantical explanation is deductive.
4. Although people often use "hypothesis" and "theory" as synonyms, we distinguish an important sense of "theory" which differs from this usage.
5. Theories are important in human knowledge because of their explanatory, predictive, and systematizing power.

APPLICATIONS

1. In each of the following cases, name the type of explanation called for, then give it in such a way that its logical pattern is clear.
   a. Why are icy sidewalks slippery?
   b. Why can't we see the stars in the daytime?

  c. Why is Tabby purring?

  d. What does "hirsute" mean?

  e. Why do most three o'clock classes seem longer than ten o'clock classes?

  f. What kind of thing is a jerkin?

2. What other types of explanation, not mentioned in the text, seem to you to be important? In so far as possible, set forth their pattern.

3. It has sometimes been urged that science does not explain, but merely describes. What do you think? Distinguish between semantical and nonsemantical issues here.

4. Auguste Comte held that science never answers the question "Why?" but only the question "How?" What do you think he meant by this? Is there anything to be said for this point of view? Distinguish as carefully as possible the semantical from the nonsemantical issues involved.

5. In general, scientists carefully avoid giving TELEOLOGICAL EXPLANATIONS, that is, explanations in terms of purpose. (For example, the mother bird builds a nest so that she will have a place to lay her eggs, or the sun shines in order to make life possible on the earth.)

  a. Why do you think scientists avoid explanations of this kind?

  b. Is it inconsistent for a scientist *purposely* to avoid purposive explanations? How will he explain why *he* is doing this?

  c. Are there cases in which you believe purposive explanations to be permissible?

CHAPTER 31

COMMON PITFALLS IN THINKING

PREVIEW

In this final chapter we turn again to consider, as we did in the first chapter, all three areas of logic. But now we have at our disposal a reflective and critical awareness of some of the basic principles of thinking things through. In the light of this understanding of logical principles, it will be useful to consider some of the common pitfalls in thinking into which we stumble through neglect of these principles.

31.1. FALLACIES AND OTHER PITFALLS

The study of logic helps us to understand what is involved in thinking clearly and critically. In becoming aware of logical principles, in learning "what to do," we are at the same time implicitly learning what not to do. A convenient way to review much of what we have been studying in preceding chapters is to consider the difficulties and obstacles which arise through violation of logical maxims or principles.

When we violate a logical maxim or principle, we COMMIT A FALLACY. What are some of the commoner and more persistent fallacies against which we need to be on our guard? In exploring this question, we may at the same time pick up some convenient labels for identifying the various violations. Some such labels we have already learned, principally in the area of syntactics. Can you name some examples of syntactical fallacies?

A FALLACY is a violation of a logical maxim or principle. Since these are of three main types, semantical, syntactical, and empirical, it will be convenient to consider fallacies under this three-fold classification. A word of warning, however, is in order. Since we can often look at a given difficulty from several points of view or with differing emphases, we must not be surprised to find some overlapping in the traditionally distinguished fallacies. Suppose, for example, you have an atomic argument in which a class-name is being used in two different senses. Superficially, the name appears to apply to the same class in both its occurrences. But actually, because of the shift of meaning, two classes rather than one are involved. It is easy to see that an invalid argument might appear valid if we failed to detect this shift of meaning, and supposed that the same class was being referred to throughout. Now, such a difficulty may be considered either semantically or syntactically. From the semantical point of view, we may call attention to the SHIFT OF MEANING. From the syntactical point of view, we may point to the resulting defective form of the argument. When such a defect occurs in an apparent syllogism, it is traditionally called the FOUR-TERM FALLACY. Such an argument may also be called a PSEUDO-SYLLOGISM; it looks like a syllogism, but it isn't really, because it violates one of the defining maxims of a syllogism. (See Section 19.1.)

In connection with our exploration of fallacies, we shall also have occasion to notice certain common obstacles to thinking which, although not "fallacies" in our strictly defined sense, are dangers and difficulties of which we need to keep aware. We may include such dangers along with fallacies under the general term, PITFALLS IN THINKING.

Before turning to a more detailed consideration of special semantical, formal, and empirical difficulties, let us note a common pitfall which arises from the very fact that there are these three different types of problem for thinking. As long as you overlook these differences, you are bound to think in a confused manner. For, as we have seen, the types of solution appropriate to a semantical, a syntactical, and a factual problem are quite different. One type requires an analysis and clarification of meaning, the second requires a consideration of logical form, while the third demands inquiry into the facts of experience. In our study of semantics, we saw how easy it is to mistake a disagreement about the meaning of a word for a disagreement about nonverbal facts. Such confusions can be solved only by an awareness of the differences in types of problem involved in thinking, and a knowledge of the solutions appropriate to the different types. For convenience, this pitfall may be labeled CONFUSION OF TYPES.

31.2. SEMANTICAL PITFALLS

Many of the problems we encounter in the use of signs arise from the very nature of signs themselves. A sign has a representative function; it calls attention to something other than itself, which we loosely call the sign's *meaning*. Let us remind ourselves of some of the problems involved.

(1) While it is difficult to believe that people would ever confuse a word with what the word means, there are numerous evidences that they do so. It is not difficult to recognize that the *word* "cat" is one thing, and the animal cat another. We are not likely to argue that horses must be bigger than cats, because "horse" contains five letters, and "cat" only three. But there are other subtler types of confusion. For example, the emotional reaction we have toward something may rather easily carry over to the word we use in naming the thing. The title of a recent magazine article, "Abortion is an Ugly Word," indicates such a confusion between what may perhaps properly be regarded as an "ugly" practice, and the word by which the practice is named. As far as the *word* "abortion" goes, it is presumably no uglier than the words "absorption" or "proportion."

(2) We also run the risk of supposing that because we have a word, there must be some actual thing to which the word applies. (a) The most extreme case of this kind involves MISTAKING A MEANINGLESS SOUND FOR A SIGN, as we were tempted to do in using the words "morthroplat," "tryphoglyptera," and "grandopore." These look like nouns, but actually they are not signs at all, and they have neither signification nor application. Other examples would include the nonsense syllables occurring in many folk songs. The point here is, of course, not that we should never use nonsense syllables, but rather that we must recognize them for what they are if we are to think clearly. If I ask, "But what does 'fa-la-la' really mean?", the appropriate answer is, "It doesn't mean a thing." (b) Another pitfall of this same general type is SIGNIFICATION-APPLICATION CONFUSION. As we saw in Chapter 4, we cannot reliably argue that since a word has a definite meaning, it actually applies to anything. The cognitive meaning of some words lies entirely in the dimension of signification. We must not, for example, assume that because we can clearly explain what is meant by a "complete vacuum" that there are any actual cases.

(3) The use of emotively toned language may also, as we saw in

Chapter 3, make clear thinking difficult. There is of course nothing wrong in using toned language as such. But in the presence of such language, we run the risk of mistaking a loud noise or a rich voice for a coercive argument or adequate evidence. In the present critical international situation, merely to label a person a "Communist" is in many circles enough to damn him, whether or not he is actually Communistic in outlook or allegiance. Similarly, to label a particular program or procedure "the American way" is sometimes enough to rally uncritical support for it, regardless of its actual content or relation to American ideals and traditions. Thus BAD NAMES and VIRTUE WORDS, when we react to them uncritically, constitute important pitfalls in thinking. The same may of course be said for the persuasive techniques in general, in so far as we fail to recognize them for what they are, and mistake them for evidence or logical argument.[1]

(4) Other semantic difficulties arise from a characteristic of signs which we have called their AMBIVALENCE: a given sign may have more than one meaning. We have already seen how problems of AMBIGUITY, both personal and interpersonal, stem from this characteristic of signs. But there are related difficulties which are not strictly speaking matters of ambiguity in either of the senses which we have distinguished. These difficulties arise because we tend to overlook the possibility of a shift in meaning. We may note three forms of this ONE-WORD, ONE-MEANING FALLACY: (a) to suppose that because a word has a given meaning in one occurrence, it necessarily has the same meaning in another occurrence; (b) to suppose that because a given thing is called a given name on one occasion, it must have this same name on another occasion; (c) to suppose that because *you* are using a word in a certain sense, others are necessarily using it in this sense. This last supposition not only makes us easy victims of interpersonal ambiguity but also blinds us to the nature of the solution required.

We need not repeat here what was said in Chapter 5 about personal

---

[1] Our earlier discussion of persuasive techniques was within a semantic context, for we were considering various ways in which language functions. In classifying pitfalls in thinking, however, we need to note the extent to which these persuasive devices also involve empirical and even formal problems. For example, CARD-STACKING involves a lopsided or unrepresentative selection of empirical evidence. SIDE-TRACKING and TRANSFER are, from the formal point of view, cases of the fallacy of NON SEQUITUR. BAND WAGON and PLAIN FOLKS are varieties of the device traditionally called ARGUMENTUM AD POPULUM, or Appeal to the Masses. They have both empirical and formal aspects.

ambiguity. But we may note a special case which arises through careless-
ness in expression. An AMPHIBOLOUS SENTENCE is one which causes a personal ambiguity because of the way in which the sentence is put together.
AMPHIBOLY is personal ambiguity which arises, not because you are in
doubt about the meaning of a given word or phrase in the sentence, but
because the structure of the sentence leaves its meaning open to more
than one interpretation. Often an amphibolous sentence is merely amusing, and not really ambiguous, because we are quite clear about which
meaning is intended. Thus when someone tells us that he is making a
traveling cage for his dog with an aluminum bottom, we may chuckle, but
we know what he means. But what does it mean to say, "Children who
lie more often than not come from unhappy homes"? Does it mean that,
more often than not, children who lie come from unhappy homes? Or
does it mean that children who lie more often than they don't lie, come
from unhappy homes? Probably the first was intended, but the amphibolous sentence leaves us in some doubt. And how are we to understand
the assertion, "If you sell five subscriptions on Wednesday you will receive a bonus"?

(5) Various obstacles to thinking arise through the use of inadequate
definitions. The function of a definition is to clarify or explain to someone
the meaning of a word. We cannot judge the effectiveness of a definition
by any formal set of rules, for what is needed will depend upon the situation. (See Chapter 6.) We may note, however, three general types of
inadequacy. (a) A MEANINGLESS DEFINITION results when we talk over
the head of the person for whom the definition is intended. *We* may know
what we are talking about, but if we define a term in such a way that our
hearer cannot understand the definition, it is meaningless to him and thus
fails to fulfill its function. Milder forms of this difficulty are of course possible. Our hearer may dimly grasp our meaning, but still have no clear
idea of it. (b) An INCOMPLETE DEFINITION is one that does not go far
enough to pin down the meaning precisely. An obvious case would be a
class-difference definition which stops with mentioning the genus, and
fails to mention the differentiating characteristic. (See Section 6.5.) If
you tell me that "wallaby" means a kind of animal, I am still ignorant of
just what kind of animal is meant. Note, however, that the completeness
or incompleteness of a definition is a relative matter. Here again we must
recall that the effectiveness of a definition depends, not upon its formal

pattern, but upon whether it succeeds in doing what it is trying to do. For some purposes, it is quite enough to be told that "wallaby" means a kind of animal. The definition would be quite adequate if the question at issue was whether "wallaby" is the name of a geographical feature, a disease, a mournful lullaby, or an animal. (c) When defining at the significative level, we should avoid giving a CIRCULAR DEFINITION. Thus, to define "sedative" as a drug with sedative properties is open to objection. For if a person does not understand the noun "sedative," he is likely to have the same difficulty with the adjective. Note that the kind of circularity we are here criticizing keeps the definition from fulfilling its function. If in defining a word we make use of that same word in explaining what it means, we are defeating our purpose. But there is no objection to defining "slender" in terms of thin, and then in some other situation, defining "thin" in terms of slender. Here again we need to judge a given definition in terms of whether it fulfills its function in the specific context in which it is offered.

31.3. SYNTACTICAL PITFALLS

Any violation of a rule of syntactical procedure constitutes a FORMAL FALLACY. Since we have analyzed and named many of these fallacies in Part II of our work, we may here be relatively brief. When a formal fallacy is committed in the course of an argument, the argument is made invalid. A convenient general term for such a fallacy is the old label, NON SEQUITUR, "it doesn't follow." This term has the advantage of indicating a difficulty without having to specify it in detail. But the term is of course less informative than one which indicates the exact type of fallacy committed in a given case, for example, the fallacy of ASSERTING THE CONSEQUENT in a simple conditional argument. In analyzing fallacies, it is in general advisable to indicate the source of the difficulty as precisely as possible by picking the most specific label available.

Some difficulties we encounter in formal reasoning have both semantical and empirical aspects as well. A simple example is that of the problem raised by a MISSING QUANTIFIER. If someone says, "Pumpkins are vegetables," I shall understand him to be making a universal statement, rather than a particular one. But if he says, "College students are more interested in dates than in studies," I am in doubt about whether he intends to make a sweeping universal statement or a more moderate particular statement. Viewed from the semantical side, this is a simple case of ambiguity. There is of course an empirical question involved too. Do the facts warrant the universal quantifier, or not? The formal problem arises when such an unquantified statement is introduced into a line of reasoning, or when we want to consider its relations to other statements. For a universal statement and a particular statement have differing formal properties. To consider a simple illustration, if my friend means that all college students prefer dates to studies, it should be relatively easy for me to show him that he is wrong. To refute his universal statement, all I need to do is to establish that at least one student is not more interested in dates than in his studies. But if only a particular statement was intended, I shall have a much harder job. To refute his particular I-statement, I should have to establish its contradictory, the corresponding universal E-statement.

We have seen that a missing quantifier makes it difficult to determine the logical form of the statement. There are of course many instances in which the looseness of everyday conversational English raises a similar problem. When, for example, people use the "either . . . or" connective in colloquial speech, it is often unclear whether they intend to assert a simple alternative or the stronger disjunctive-alternative. (See Section 9.6.) Most of our difficulties in "either . . . or" reasoning arise from a failure to distinguish clearly between these two types of "either . . . or." Similarly, we are often very unprecise in our use of "only if." At times we mean just what we actually say, but at others we mean "if and only if." This particular problem is further complicated in that some people don't even take the trouble to notice that "only if" has a directional force precisely opposite to that of a simple "if." (See Section 9.6.)

There also is the problem of PSEUDO-CONTRADICTION, that is, thinking we have contradicted a statement when we have not. The commonest form of this fallacy is that of asserting the contrary instead of the contradictory. (See Sections 10.1 and 18.4.)

The fallacy of ILLICIT CONVERSION arises when we mistakenly suppose that two nonequivalent converses are logically equivalent, or that the assertion of the one entitles us to assert the other also. A special case of this fallacy consists in converting an A-statement simply, rather than by limitation, and mistakenly supposing that the simple converse follows logically from the original statement. (See Section 18.1.) It would be useful to remind yourself of just which types of statement have logically equivalent converses and which do not.

Similar difficulties arise in connection with contrapositives, and give rise to the fallacy of ILLICIT CONTRAPOSITION. What types of statement have equivalent contrapositives, and what types do not?

We may also remind ourselves that each special form of argument is subject to fallacy through violation of the validity maxims which describe valid procedure for that type. Thus a simple alternative argument may go astray through the fallacy of ASSERTING AN ALTERNANT, a syllogism is invalid if it commits the fallacy of UNDISTRIBUTED MIDDLE, and so on.

The invalidity of arguments may, of course, also be analyzed in terms of violations of the three contraform principles. Violations of Principle 1 lead either to the fallacy of NO INEQUATION or the fallacy of MULTIPLE INEQUATIONS. When we violate Principle 2, we are guilty of the fallacy of INCOMPLETE PAIRING. Failure of a test form to satisfy Principle 3 constitutes the fallacy of FAULTY INEQUATION.

In rounding out your study of syntactical fallacies, you should review the validity maxims developed in Part II and the fallacies which result from their violation.

31.4. EMPIRICAL PITFALLS

Some of our difficulties in determining what the facts are arise, as we know, from semantical and formal aspects of the problem. But what special pitfalls confront us in factual inquiry? In analyzing the alternatives open to us in a given factual situation, our thinking naturally takes the form of a dilemma. (See Section 15.7.) The dilemma itself, of course, is a syntactical structure, but we here want to note an empirical difficulty. It lies in our tendency to overlook possible alternatives which would widen the choice before us. This pitfall of inquiry consists in INADEQUATE AWARENESS OR ANALYSIS OF AVAILABLE ALTERNATIVES. Sometimes the problem is simply one of inadequate information on hand at the time. But there are often psychological factors involved too. One of the most important of these is our tendency to think in terms of opposites, and to overlook other possibilities that lie between. We are prone to think in terms of black and white, and to forget about all the intervening shades of gray. This tendency has been called BLACK-AND-WHITE THINKING.

We know that, from a formal point of view, we can always set up a strict open-or-shut case by alternating a statement with its contradictory: "Either this is a white pine or it is not a white pine." Whenever we really succeed in stating alternants that are contradictory, the alternative statement is necessarily true. But we must not overlook the fact that such a statement as "This is not a white pine" covers a great many possibilities. There are lots of ways of not being a white pine.

Another way in which we blind ourselves to possible alternatives is this: we sometimes treat possibilities that are not strictly contradictory as if they were. Considered in isolation, this is simply a formal blunder. But it can clearly have practical consequences for our handling of factual possibilities. Suppose a student gets to thinking, "I must either get a scholarship next year or drop out of school." If he thinks of these two possibilities as contradictories, he is incorrectly limiting the choices before him. It is quite possible, for example, that he could stay in school even without a scholarship, perhaps by getting a job next summer, by borrowing money, by getting a board job next year, and so on.

Sometimes alternatives shade into one another and form a continuous series, as in our above example of black, various shades of gray, and white.[2] If we overlook the nature of the series we are dealing with, we may get into further difficulties. For we may mistakenly suppose that, because the items form a series in which one fades by imperceptible degrees into the other, there is "really no difference" between the extremes of the series. Let us first consider a trivial example where nobody will be fooled. When does a man become bald? Seldom all at once. At one stage he has a good head of hair, but then one by one the hairs fall out until eventually he is undeniably bald. We can all see that the question, "At just what point does he become bald?" is misleading if it suggests that we ought to be able to give a precise answer. Yet how silly it would be to argue that, since we can't draw the line at any precise point, there really is no difference between being bald and having a good head of hair. In such a case we are not likely to fall into the trap of IDENTIFICATION OF EXTREMES. But there are less obvious cases in which we all run this risk. For example, take the much more complex case of the use of

---

[2] All contemporary writers on this problem are indebted to the clear analysis made by Robert H. Thouless in Chapter 9 of his lively and rewarding book, *How to Think Straight,* New York, Simon and Schuster, 1939.

force in human relationships. It is sometimes erroneously argued that a person cannot "logically" oppose the use of weapons of mass extermination if he upholds, let us say, the desirability of spanking children on occasion, or if he defends the use of restraining measures on a violently disturbed mental patient. Yet here again we are dealing with a phenomenon (the use of force) which forms a continuous series from one extreme to the other. To deny that the extremes are really different (on the grounds that they form part of a continuous series), or to deny that a person may reasonably and responsibly condemn the one and advocate the other, is just as fundamental a blunder in thinking as to say that being bald and having a good head of hair are really the same thing.

In all factual inquiry we run the risk of JUMPING TO A CONCLUSION. Let us examine how this tendency appears in induction, in analogical reasoning, and in diagnosis. In induction, the specific form that this fault takes is that of hurrying on to a generalization on the basis of an inadequate sample. A generalization arrived at in this way is a RASH GENERALIZATION.

A parallel temptation confronts us in reasoning by analogy. We grasp some one resemblance, possibly a striking but quite superficial one, and rush on to an analogical conclusion without adequate analysis of the things being compared. Such an argument is a FORCED ANALOGY. Even when the two analogues have a much broader range of characteristics in common, our analogy may still be a weak one because we have not bothered to notice or to give adequate weight to the fundamental ways in which the analogues *differ*. This fault may be called NEGLECT OF ANALOGICAL DISPARITY. At this point you may wish to review our earlier discussion of analogies and the factors that determine their relative strength or weakness. (See Sections 30.1 and 30.2.)

In diagnostic arguments, probably the chief danger that we run is that of basing the diagnosis upon an UNRELIABLE SYMPTOM. The more frequently a symptom is found associated with the *absence* of the phenomenon being reasoned about, the less reliable it is. Thus, as we have seen, possession of a yolk is a fairly unreliable symptom of being a chicken egg. A yolk is present in a great many cases that are not chicken eggs. Similarly, the mere presence of a rash is not a very reliable symptom of measles, since rashes occur in numerous other situations in which measles is absent. If, however, we can discover something distinctive or peculiar about the type of rash present in measles, this more specific symptom may have a high degree of reliability, while the symptom, rash-in-general, does not.

We considered above the difficulty that arises in induction when we base a generalization on too small or hasty a sampling. This pitfall may be considered a special case of a more general difficulty, that of basing our generalization upon a sample which is, for any reason whatever, an UNREPRESENTATIVE SAMPLE. In Chapter 28 we noted various elementary principles which help to determine the reliability of a sampling process. (See Section 28.8.) When an unrepresentative sample is used as the basis for a generalization, we err in supposing that what we have found to be true of the members of the sample will also be true of all members in the class as a whole. The traditional name given to this error is FALLACY OF CONVERSE ACCIDENT.

An opposite kind of difficulty may arise when we attempt to apply a generalization to a specific case which superficially appears to fall under the generalization. We may overlook the special features of the specific case which prevent the generalization from applying to it. Traditionally called the FALLACY OF ACCIDENT, this is the blunder of supposing that something which holds in general also holds in a special case in which the circumstances make a difference. Thus to argue that since "Everyone enjoys a good joke," a person will therefore enjoy a joke on himself, is to commit the Fallacy of Accident. We are perhaps sometimes led into this pitfall through an ambiguity in the phrase, "in general." Sometimes this is intended to mean "in all cases"; at other times it means only "by and large" or "in most cases" or "in usual circumstances." Thus I may agree that, in general, it is unwise to swim in cold water immediately after eating a heavy meal. But this need not imply that I should think it unwise to swim under these conditions in order to rescue someone from drowning. This example suggests a second reason why we are led into committing the Fallacy of Accident: generalizations are often stated loosely, without adequate analysis or specification of the circumstances in which they hold. This would seem to be the source of the difficulty in an example like the following: "Poison will kill a man. The doctor admits that the pill he gave me contained strychnine, a poison, as one of its ingredients. Call the undertaker." We may therefore note that a LOOSE GENERALIZATION may in itself constitute a pitfall in thinking.

There are two traditionally recognized pitfalls which run somewhat parallel to the Fallacy of Converse Accident and the Fallacy of Accident. Beginners sometimes have difficulty in distinguishing between the two pairs. It will help to notice that the fallacies of Accident and Converse Accident deal with relations between a generalization and instances which are thought to fall under it. The fallacies which we shall now discuss, however, deal with relations between a whole and its parts. The FALLACY OF COMPOSITION consists in supposing that a property which characterizes a part of the whole will also necessarily characterize the whole. The following argument commits this fallacy in a crude but clear form: "This piece of pie is wedge-shaped, therefore the whole pie from which it was cut must be wedge-shaped." Another case would be to suppose that since the chemical elements of which an organism is composed are not alive, therefore the organism itself cannot be alive. The opposite whole-part fallacy is traditionally called the FALLACY OF DIVISION. It consists in supposing that a property which characterizes a whole will also necessarily characterize a part of the whole. Consider the following two examples and relate them to the examples just given. "This pie is circular, therefore a piece of this pie will also be circular." "Since this body is alive, the chemical elements of which it is composed must be alive."

In rounding out our discussion of pitfalls which involve some type of confusion between the part and the whole, we should note what may be called the NOTHING-BUT FALLACY. This consists in supposing mistakenly that, because something has a certain characteristic, that's all there is to it. For example, "Love is nothing but a matter of glandular secretions." As this example suggests, the Nothing-But Fallacy is often rooted in MISTAKING A NECESSARY CONDITION FOR A SUFFICIENT CONDITION. (See Section 29.8.)

There are certain difficulties which arise particularly in connection with inquiry about causes. In our earlier study of the manner in which the probability of a causal generalization may be increased, we saw that the consequent of such a generalization may contain irrelevant factors that need to be eliminated by further experimentation and analysis. The failure to carry through along this line may be labeled INADEQUATE ANALYSIS OF CONSEQUENT FACTORS. (See Section 29.3.) The corresponding difficulty with respect to antecedent factors may be called INADEQUATE ANALYSIS OF CIRCUMSTANCES. (See Sections 29.5–29.10.) This latter pitfall, of course, is by no means confined to situations in which the goal of inquiry is a causal generalization.

One of the commonest pitfalls in connection with inquiry about causes is the POST HOC FALLACY. (See Section 23.2.) As we have seen, it consists in supposing that since a given thing happened *after* something else, it necessarily happened *because of* this something else. When, for example, three devastating hurricanes hit the East Coast in the fall of 1954, a fairly widespread popular opinion was that they had somehow resulted from recent hydrogen bomb explosions in Siberia and the Pacific. As a concluding but less somber example of this fallacy, we may consider an opinion which my father held when he was a very small boy. In his town,

• SOME REMINDERS

I. **GENERAL PITFALLS IN THINKING**
   A. Confusion of Types
   B. Neglect of Circumstances

II. **SEMANTICAL PITFALLS**
   A. Shift of Meaning
   B. Word-Meaning Confusion
   C. Meaningless Sound-Sign Confusion
   D. Signification-Application Confusion
   E. Difficulties from Emotively Toned Language
     1. Bad Names
     2. Virtue Words
   F. Persuading-Convincing Confusion
   G. Difficulties from Ambivalence of Signs
     1. Ambiguity
       a. Personal
         Special case: Amphiboly
       b. Interpersonal (Verbal Disputes)
     2. One-Word, One-Meaning Fallacy
   H. Inadequate Definitions
     1. Meaningless Definition
     2. Incomplete Definition
     3. Circular Definition

III. **SYNTACTICAL PITFALLS**
   A. Non Sequitur
     1. Side-Tracking
     2. Argumentum ad Populum
       a. Band Wagon
       b. Plain Folks
     3. Transfer

band concerts were held on the town square every Saturday evening during the summer. My father and his family attended these functions with some regularity. With apparently equal regularity, Grandfather treated the family to ice cream after the concert. So consistent was the pattern that my father came to suspect that a fundamental causal relationship was involved. After considerable reflection he concluded that the ice cream was being manufactured every Saturday evening by the bass drummer as he beat upon the drum and clashed his cymbals.

APPLICATIONS

Examine the following examples for fallacies and other pitfalls in thinking. Label (if you can) or explain the type of difficulty involved, if any, and be prepared to defend your analysis.

1. Each of these floor lamps is on sale at 50% off. If I buy two of them, that will be 100% off, so I'll really be getting them for nothing.

2. Primitive people often conceal their "real names" for fear such knowledge would give an enemy power over them.

3. Chanticleer, the rooster in an old folk tale, gets to thinking he is a very important individual because early every morning he crows and lo! the sun comes up.

4. Why won't anyone tell me what the song really means when it says that Jenny Jenkins is going to buy herself a tildy-toldy, fildy-foldy, seeka double-use-a causa roldy binding?

5. We know that no reptiles have fur, so of course no animals without fur are nonreptilian.

6. A visitor at a large observatory is said to have expressed admiration for the astronomers' great achievement in having been able to discover the names of so many stars.

7. "The aborigines believe that *wond'ina*—the strong, gentle spirits of rain and fertility—made the pictures originally, by casting their shadows on the rocks.

   "Before each rainy season, naked aborigines reverently approached the painted shadows, and touched them. Sure enough, the rains came." (*Time*, January 27, 1947, p. 63)

8. All men are rational animals, so of course all rational animals are men.

9. [The King told Alice that he had sent the two messengers to town, and asked her to look down the road to see whether they were returning.]

   "I see nobody on the road," said Alice.

   "I only wish *I* had such eyes," the King remarked in a fretful tone. "To be able to see Nobody! And at that distance too! Why, it's as much as I can do to see real people, by this light." (Lewis Carroll)

10. "Analogue: that which is analogous to some other thing." (Webster's Collegiate Dictionary)

11. We must assume that he is a Communist, because he says that he is not, and we know that Communists are taught always to deny party membership.

12. A report from a meeting of the Executive Committee of the Thirty-eighth World Conference of Esperantists stated that "Esperanto . . . is based on Latin and contains few words and grammatical rules to which there are no exceptions."

13. Some fish are halibuts, so of course all halibuts are fish.

14. An advertisement of the L. A. Young Golf Co. for the Hagen Coreless Golf Ball states: "The entire ball except the cover is formed of Para thread. And if, as you've always been told, it's winding that makes a golf ball,

what can be better than a ball of all winding? That's exactly what you get in the Hagen Coreless."

15. If I get a haircut, I am sure to catch cold. Therefore, either I shall get a haircut or I shall catch cold, maybe both.

16. A number of years ago the manufacturer of a machine-made cigar put on an advertising campaign with the slogan: "Spit is a horrid word—but it's worse on the end of your cigar."

17. It cannot both be that this is a piece of pure gold and that it is not ductile. Experimentation shows that it is ductile, so I conclude that it must be gold.

18. My daughter can't be very bright. She asked me what a skunk is, and even after I had carefully explained that a skunk is a fetid, musteline animal of the genus Mephistus, she didn't understand. She apparently doesn't know a precise definition when she hears one.

19. "*The Teacher.* Time—let me see. While we are talking, time flies. Consequently time is something that flies while we talk.
"*A Boy.* Now you are talking, teacher, and while you are talking, I fly: consequently I am time.
"*The Teacher.* That accords completely with the laws of logic." ("The Dream Play" in *Plays by August Strindberg*, First Series, translated by Edwin Björkman, New York, Charles Scribner's Sons, 1912, p. 70)

20. The Dean was showing a visitor around the campus. The visitor asked, "About how many students do you have here?" After a moment of reflection the Dean replied, "Oh, I'd guess about one in a hundred."

21. If God meant man to smoke, he would have put a smokestack on him.

22. In *Fellowship* for July 1949, Milton Mayer writes: "When John Foster Dulles says in March that adoption of the North Atlantic Pact means war, and when he says in May that rejection of the North Atlantic Pact means war, I want to contend with him. I want to prove to him that of two contradictory statements, both may be wrong and one must be."

23. *The New Yorker* reports a sign in the El Paso National Bank: "Forging Ahead with El Paso."

24. In his book, *Inuk*, Father Roger Buliard tells how he sought to overcome Eskimo superstitions by opposing them with something better. Once he defied the Eskimo belief that killing a crow will bring about bad weather. He killed the crow. A few hours later a violent windstorm blew down every tent in the neighborhood.

25. A woman wrote to the college president about getting a speaker from the college to address her club. "Don't," she requested, "send us anything lower than a dean." The president is said to have written back, "There isn't anything lower than a dean."

26. A House Armed Services subcommittee found that, to order a box of colored pencils from the Army Quartermaster, you had to ask for: "Pencil, wood-cased, colored lead, drawing, thin diameter, assorted, twenty-four to box."

27. In 1951 a live box turtle was found in Killbuck, Ohio, with "D. Boone,

1763" carved on its back. Daniel Boone might have done the carving, for he was in the Ohio, Kentucky, and Tennessee area about that time. But it is known that box turtles usually live only sixty or eighty years.

28. A few years ago, crops in a certain region of India were being badly damaged by large wild animals of the antelope family, called "nehil gae." The farmers refused to harm the animals, however, because "nehil gae" means "blue cow," and cows are considered sacred. So the Indian government changed the name to "nehil goa" or "blue horse" and the problem was solved.

29. "A lady on the way to her hairdresser's passed a building that was being sandblasted. When, a few minutes later, the hairdresser ran his fingers over her scalp, he said, 'Ah, it is good to see Madame back from Florida!' " (*The New Yorker*, January 27, 1951, p. 21)

30. As you travel west across the country, you gain an hour each time you enter a new time zone. In flying around the world in a westerly direction, you gain a total of 24 hours. Thus, when jet planes or rockets get fast enough so that they can complete the whole round-the-world trip in 24 hours, the trip will actually consume no time at all.

31. *The New Yorker* for January 4, 1947, tells about two young girls overheard on the Lackawanna ferry. They noticed a freighter passing by. It was carrying no cargo at the time, so it rode high on the water, with its propeller churning up spray. The girls were very puzzled about this, and tried to figure out an adequate explanation. Finally, one of them brightened up and announced confidently, "Now I know what it is. Low tide."

32. A geologist friend of mine tells of his struggles to get the size of shaving cream he wanted. Since he was on a field trip, he wanted a small tube for convenience in traveling. He located the shelf with shaving cream in the drug store, spotted the small-sized tube he wanted, and noticed that it was marked "Large Size." When the clerk asked what he wanted, he pointed and asked for a "Large Size" tube of shaving cream. The clerk reached, not for the small "Large Size" tube, but for a large tube marked "Economy Size." Actually, there were three sizes in this line; the small one was labeled "Large," the middle-sized one was labeled "Giant," and the large one was labeled "Economy" size.

33. Nothing is better than perfection. Our work is better than nothing. Therefore, our work is better than perfection.

34. In a letter to *Time*, June 26, 1950, Mahalah Deviney tells about two men who saw a windmill near a canal in a windy meadow. Asked by his companion the principle on which the mill operated, one man replied that water from the house nearby was pumped through pipes to the top of the mill. This water, flowing down to the canal, turned the mill arms, and the revolving arms created the delightful breeze.

35. In a dissenting opinion on the Rosenberg spy case in 1953, Justice Black said, "I am not unaware of the Government's argument that this court can and should give full effect to both these statutes, one of which deprives the district court of unconditional power to impose the death sentence, and one which grants such unconditional power. This would be a strange argu-

ment in any case, but it is still stranger in a case which involves matters of life and death."

36. *The New Yorker* for July 9, 1955, reports that a sign on a Florida motel reads:

A BETTER PLACE TO STAY COSTS
NO MORE

37. So I was right. Or perhaps it would be more accurate to say that I wasn't wrong.

38. On August 2, 1949, the *New York Times* carried a story about a woman whose pet monkey was trained to wash and stack dishes. The woman remarked, "I don't doubt that we are all descended from monkeys when I see him wash dishes."

39. Ruth Montgomery, in a column syndicated by the *Chicago Tribune* and the *New York News*, told of a conversation at a Washington dinner party. A recent order of the Postmaster General, reducing home mail deliveries to one a day, was being discussed. From there talk drifted to the possibility of Senator Margaret Chase Smith capturing the GOP presidential nomination in 1952. When her dinner partner asked her what her platform would be, she replied, "I'm for two mails a day." A woman who had only half-heard the previous conversation gasped, "Margaret!" Senator Smith hastened to explain, "I meant to say I would favor two deliveries a day." Everyone roared.

40. "When Detroit newsmen asked the police to issue new 1949 press cards— usually a routine procedure—they got a surprise. Last week, Harry S. Toy, the squat, eagle-beaked police commissioner who has talked darkly about a 'Red revolution in Michigan,' said that, to get a press card, every reporter would have to (1) fill out a form listing his press experience, and (2) swear he was not a member of 'any organization affiliated with the Communist Party or Communism.' . . .

"By week's end, Toy seemed ready to retire from his beachhead. 'I haven't said,' he pussyfooted, 'that I would not give out press cards if they do not sign.' " (*Time*, January 31, 1949, p. 50)

41. ". . . The judge disputed the conclusions of many psychiatrists who blame comic books for crime. . . .

" 'Many psychiatrists attribute the commission of crime to the fact that a person has been reading comic books,' said Judge Streit. 'After they ask the patient if he reads comic books and the patient replies "Yes," they come to the conclusion that comics are the reason for crime.

" 'They do not take into consideration the fact that hundreds of thousands of persons who read comic books never are charged with a crime.' " (*New York Times*, May 6, 1949)

INDEX

INDEX OF SYMBOLS

GENERAL INDEX

Where more than one reference is given for a term, the defining entry is preceded by an asterisk. The letter "n" following a page number refers to a footnote on that page.

Abbreviation symbol, *104, 114
Absurdity, logical, 52, *54-55
Accident, fallacy of, 434
Accompanying factors in causal generalization, 386n-387n; see also *Circumstances.*
Addition rule, 174n
Advertising, 43-44
"A few," 223
Agreement, principle of, 397
"All," 217
"All are not," 219-220
Alternant, 112
Alternative statement, *112, 123-124
    consistency table for, 136
    how to symbolize, 123-124
    logical import of, 135-136
    maxim for contradicting, 136
    zeroform for, 142
Ambiguity, *62-66, 427; see Chapter 5.
    interpersonal, 64-66
    personal, 62-64
    resolving by MacKaye's Method, 66-68
Ambivalence, *61, 427
Amphiboly, 428
Analogue, basic vs. derivative, 406
Analogy, 323-324, *405-408
    and induction, 408-411
    compound, 323-324, *406
    diagram of, 406
    forced, 433
    justification of, 408-411
    simple, 323-324, *406
    weakness of, 372n
Analysis:
    at common-sense level, 107-108, 154
    of appeals, pattern for, 42-43
    of persuasive definition, 87
    three levels of, 107-109
Antecedent, 112
Antecedent probability, 335-336 *336n
Antilogism test, 249-250
Appeal, 29
    analysis of, see Chapter 3.
    effectiveness of, 30
    pattern of analysis for, 42-43

responding intelligently to, 44-45
two types of, 31-32
Appeal techniques, 33-42
    labels for, see Index of Symbols, preceding General Index.
Appeal to the masses, 427n
Appearance statement, 313n
Applicate, 51
Application, 51
    actual vs. total, 51n
    of a statement, 58
Applicative definition, 73-74
Appropriateness of language response, 27
Argument, 94
    analogical, 323-324, *405-408
    analogical, diagram of, 406
    atomic, see *Syllogism* and *Argument, nonsyllogistic atomic.*
    deductive, 93; see also Part II.
    deductive, of probability, 326-327
    diagnostic, 325-326
    dilemma, 191-192
    "drift" of, 105-106
    extended syllogistic, 268-269
    indirect, 192-194
    inductive, 324-325; see also Chapters 28 and 29
    invalid, 98-99
    involving probability, types of, 322-327
    molecular vs. atomic, 159, 159n
    nonsyllogistic atomic, 259n, *271-272
    nonvalid, 99-100
    penevalid, 260
    predictive, *344-345, 385, 420-421
    prevalid, *97-98, 260
    pure conditional, 189-191
    simple alternative, 180; see also Chapter 18.
    simple biconditional, 185-187
    simple conditional, 148; see also Chapter 12.
    simple disjunctive, 184-185
    simple disjunctive-alternative, 188
    sound, 321
    valid, 94-95
Argument-form, 103

Psychological certainty, 296, *301
Pure conditional argument, 189-191
  validity maxim for, 189

Quality, *203, 217-218
Quantifier, *203, 217
  missing, 429-431
  supplying missing, 222
Quantity, *203, 217
Quantity, principle of in induction, *370-373, 383

Random sample, 373
Randomness, principle of, *373-374, 375
Rash generalization, *325, 433
Reasoning, questions about, 4; see also Part II.
Reference class, 306
Reference table, class analysis, 226
Relationships, logical, between statements; see also *Argument, Conclusion, Premise, Valid.*
  consistency, 130, 132, *133
  contradiction, 128n, 133, *137, 234, 235
  contraposition, *144-145, *231-232
  contrariety, *133, 234
  conversion, *131, *227-230
  conversion, limited, 228
  equivalence, 127-128, *133, 143
  inconsistency, 133
  opposition, 234-235
  subalternation, *175, 235
  subcontrariety, 234-235
Relevance, judgment of, 380, 388
Redefining, 82
Renaming, 82
Reply, 25n
Response, appropriateness of, 27
ROBINSON, RICHARD, 71n
"Round-square," as logically absurd name, 55
RUBY, LIONEL, 409
RUSSELL, BERTRAND, 410n

Sample, 325n
  random, 373
  unrepresentative, 434
SCHLICK, MORITZ, 379n
"Science," ambiguities of, 64-65, 278-280
Science, see also *Scientific Method* and Part III.
  and generalization, 360-362
  vs. common-sense inquiry, 282-289
Scientific experiment, 284-287
  ideal of, 285

Scientific method, 278-281, 329; see also Part III.
  vs. scientific techniques, 280
Second-order molecular statement, 123
Semantics, 7; see also Part I.
Shift of meaning, 425
Side-Tracking, *35, 427n
Sign, 14
  ambivalence of, *61, 427
  artificial, 17
  linguistic, 18
  natural, 17
Signification, 51
  of a statement, 57
Signification-application confusion, 426
Sign-meaning relationship, confused with cause-effect, 26n
Sign-situation, elements in, 15-16
Simple analogy, 406
Simple alternative argument, 180-184
  fallacy of, 181
  validity maxim for, 183
Simple biconditional argument, 185-187
Simple conditional argument, 148; see also Chapter 12.
  fallacies of, 152
  validity maxim for, 152
Simple disjunctive argument, 184-185
  fallacy of, 185
  validity maxim for, 185
Simple disjunctive-alternative argument, 188
Simple existence statement, 204
Simple enumeration, induction by, 368
Simple molecular arguments, reference table of valid procedures, 185
Simple nonexistence statement, 204
Simple zeroform, 159
Simplification rule, 166n
  special form of, 164n
Singular statement, 116
  traditional treatment of, 218
Snob Appeal, 41
"Some," 217
"So probably" line, 323n
Sorites, 268-269
  Aristotelian, 269n
  Goclenian, 269n
Sound argument, valid argument not only type of, 321-322
"So what?" as key question of syntactics, 4
Species, 75-76
  co-ordinate, 76n
Specific cause, 398-399
Specification, 363

Square of opposition:
  revised (cross of contradiction), 235-236
  traditional, 234-235
Standard form, 112
  of alternative statement, 112
  of biconditional statement, 122
  of conditional statement, *112, 121
  of conjunctive statement, 113
  of disjunctive statement, 113
  of disjunctive-alternative statement, 125
  of subject-predicate statements, 216-218
  restating in, 121-122, 223-225
Statement, 18, *56-57
  A, E, I, O forms, 203
  alternative, *112, 123-124
  and declarative sentence, 56-57
  appearance, 313n
  atomic, analyzed, see Chapter 16.
  atomic, unanalyzed, 116
  atomic vs. molecular, 113
  biconditional, 122
  basic types of, see Chapter 9.
  bi-negative, 126-127
  conditional, 112
  conjunctive, 113
  disjunctive, *113, 125
  disjunctive-alternative, 125
  general, 116
  logical relationships with other statements, see Relationships.
  negative, *114, 203, 218
  observation, *292, 313n
  particular, *203, 217
  positive, *114, 203, 218
  simple existence, 203
  simple nonexistence, 204
  singular, *116, 218
  subject-predicate, see Chapter 17.
  universal, *203, 217
  vs. proposition, 57
Statemental connectives, 112
Statemental elements, 112
Statement-form, 103
  quantified, 213-214
Statistical certainty, *299, 301
Statistical generalization, 363, 386
STEBBING, L. S., 32n, 85n
STEVENSON, C. L., 85n, 86
Stipulated definition, 80-81
Stratification, principle of, 375
Stratified class, 374-375
Strict vs. richer interpretation, 122, 210-213
Stroke symbol, 125
Subaltern, *175, 235

Subalternation, 175, *235
Subcontrary, 234-235
Subject-predicate analysis, see Chapter 17.
Subject-predicate contrapositives, 231-232
Subject-predicate statement, see Chapter 17.
  how to symbolize, 219-221
  restating in standard form, 221-225
Subject term, 217
Substitution instance, *246, 326
Succession, uniformities of, 378
Sufficient vs. necessary condition, 389-390
Summation, 365-366
Superaltern, *175, 235
Supplementary existential premise, 258-260
Supporting datum, *381, 394n
Suspense of judgment, 287-288
Syllogism, 238; see also Chapters 19-21.
  alternative, 238n; see also Simple alternative argument.
  categorical, 238n
  contemporary analysis of, see Chapters 20-21.
  figure of, 239n
  hypothetical, 238n; see also Simple conditional argument.
  mood of, 239n
  particular, 257
  particularized, 257; see also Chapter 21.
  traditional analysis of, see Chapter 19.
  universal, 257
Symbol, 14
  abbreviation, 114
  abbreviation vs. variable, 103-104
  name as type of, 49
  narrower sense of, 15n; see also Symbols.
  variable, *103, 114
Symbols, see also Index of Symbols preceding General Index.
  used in Part II, 118-119
  usefulness of, 117-119
Symmetrical connective, 112
Symptom, *15, 325
  unreliable, 433
Synonymous definition, 72-73
Syntactical certainty, 300-301
Syntactics, *7, 91; see also Part II.
  logical vs. linguistic, 91n
  vs. empirics, 92-94

Techniques of a science vs. scientific method, 280
Teleological explanation, 423